The Injustice

Never

Leaves You

T0385672

The Injustice
Never
Leaves You

Anti-Mexican Violence in Texas

Monica Muñoz Martinez

Harvard University Press

Cambridge, Massachusetts, and London, England

First Harvard University Press paperback edition, 2020
First printing

Library of Congress Cataloging-in-Publication Data
Names: Martinez, Monica Muñoz, 1984– author.
Title: The injustice never leaves you : anti-Mexican violence in Texas /
    Monica Muñoz Martinez.
Description: Cambridge, Massachusetts : Harvard University Press, 2018. |
    Includes bibliographical references and index.
Identifiers: LCCN 2018002094 | ISBN 9780674976436 (cloth : alk. paper) |
    ISBN 9780674244825 (pbk.)
Subjects: LCSH: Mexicans—Violence against—Texas—History—20th century. |
    Mexicans—Civil rights—Texas—History—20th century. | Mexican-American
    Border Region—History—20th century. | State-sponsored terrorism—Texas—
    History—20th century. | Justice—History—20th century.

For my parents and my sister

In loving memory of my grandparents

Contents

The Injustice

Never

Leaves You

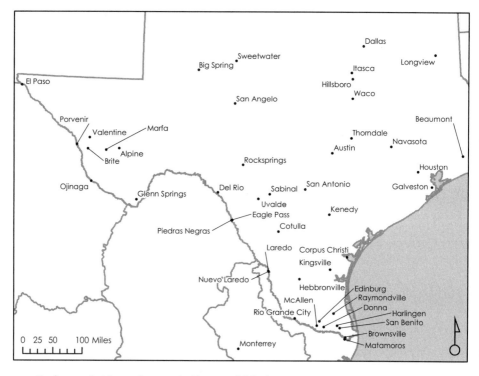

Referenced cities and towns in Texas and Mexico.

Introduction

IT WAS AN OTHERWISE ordinary day in early April 1918, but Miguel García, a Mexican national living in Texas, was growing concerned. His son Florencio, twenty-five years old, had not yet returned home from his job as a cattle herder in Cameron County. García started walking through town, asking relatives, friends, neighbors, and eventually even the county attorney and local law enforcement officers if they had seen Florencio. Days passed without news. Then someone told García that Texas Rangers had arrested Florencio over a week earlier, on April 5, just south of Brownsville. García knew that when ethnic Mexicans disappeared after being arrested, the prisoners' remains were often found hidden in the groves of mesquite trees in the rural Texas landscape. This grim news prompted García to start searching the brush in the countryside for his son's remains.[1]

Miguel García repeatedly asked for help from local authorities. Oscar C. Dancy, the Cameron County attorney, remembered García's persistence: "the old man, the father of the boy, was at my office. He was at my office two or three times and my residence once."[2] Weeks later, local residents found human remains outside of Brownsville. "We found the bones of a human being," Dancy would later testify. "We found a pair of pants and a jumper and as I recollect it, a shirt, black hair and a hat . . . a light Texas cowboy Stetson hat," he remembered, adding that there were bullet holes through the jacket, "Two, perhaps three."[3] The clothing matched the description Miguel García had previously provided, and the investigation suggested that the body had been shot in the back three times. The remains consisted only of clothes, a skull with a tuft of hair, and bones scattered as far as 300 yards, likely by coyotes or buzzards. García arrived at the scene and identified the shoes, hat, and clothing as belonging to Florencio. The father pulled a monogrammed handkerchief out of the jacket they had discovered and verified that it was his son's.[4]

According to witnesses who last saw Florencio, he had been in the custody of three Texas Rangers (the state police) in the Brownsville jail just before his disappearance. An investigation by Mexican consuls in Brownsville revealed that the Rangers, accompanied by two civilians and a US soldier, arrested Florencio at Las Tranquilas Ranch. The Rangers asked a local rancher, Chas Champion, if they could borrow a lock and chain to secure their prisoner to a tree while they slept. Considering this unnecessarily rough treatment, the rancher instead found a judge, who gave the officers permission to place Florencio in jail overnight in the custody of local police.[5]

Pressure from Mexican consuls mounted. On May 24, 1918, Mexican Inspector General Andres G. García in El Paso wrote to Texas governor William P. Hobby asking for an investigation. According to the state police, the remains could not belong to Florencio because the bones had been bleached white by the sun. These bones, they suggested, belonged to someone killed months earlier. They also denied that the father had positively identified his son's clothing. In addition, the Rangers testified that they had in fact arrested Florencio on April 5 but had released him that same evening and did not place him in jail. They refuted witnesses who saw him behind bars. Their prisoner, they suggested, had not suffered any harm. The Rangers furthermore insisted that the truth was quite different: local residents had spotted Florencio across the border in Mexico.[6] Nevertheless, García remained convinced that Texas Rangers had murdered his son.

In light of such discrepancies, how do we go about unearthing the history of violence on the US–Mexico border? If we relied on the Ranger investigation, we would not learn much more. But Florencio, born in Tamaulipas, Mexico, was a Mexican national living and working in Texas.

Without immigration quotas or limits on migration from Mexico, Mexican nationals and American citizens moved easily back and forth across the border. The death of a Mexican national in Texas prompted the local Mexican consuls to investigate his death. Their investigation found that Florencio's arrest had been based on unfounded suspicions. Letters from businessmen in the region defended Florencio's reputation as a diligent laborer. According to Oscar Dancy, locals remembered him as an "absolutely straight, square Mexican boy, above the average laborer or peon."[7] Was Florencio García a threat and a thief or a dutiful laborer?

To these officials, Mexican and American alike, Florencio García was not a friend, relative, or a neighbor. His death was a diplomatic inconvenience. As one diplomat said, the death threatened both relations between the United States and Mexico and the potential for even more farming in the region. In April in south Texas, lots of crops needed tending. If word spread that Mexican laborers were being continually mistreated, workers might flee for other opportunities in the South or the West. Without field hands, the farming economy would be devastated. For Mexican officials, and some Americans, García's story was the latest in a long series of abusive policing by the Texas Rangers. These state police officers had a habit of disturbing the delicate equilibrium of labor and race relations. That equilibrium needed to be reestablished by diplomats and political leaders, who worried about potential economic losses. The records show that officials recognized the systemic impact of Florencio García's death but reveal no sense that they mourned it.

For the relatives and friends of Florencio, on the other hand, his loss was something else entirely. His loss was personal. Furthermore, it signaled the unjust death of yet another ethnic Mexican without recourse from the judicial system, the state administration, or the Mexican consul. Florencio's death was just one short chapter in a long history of racial violence in the borderlands.

On May 27, 1918, the Cameron County acting coroner, Henry J. Kirk, confirmed the family's claims when he filed a death certificate for Florencio García. Since the recovered body revealed little, the coroner had to modify the certificate. Its generic language reads: "I hereby certify that I attended deceased from _____ 191_, to_____191_, that I last saw h__ alive on _____191_, and that the death occurred on the date stated above at ___m." Kirk drew a line through most of this section, and instead followed the statement "I hereby certify that I" with handwritten words. The modified form continued, "found the identified remains and that death occurred on unknown date." Where the certificate asked for the cause of death, Kirk wrote "unknown."[8] The certificate also included important information about Florencio García and his family. Florencio was born on April 30, 1885 and he was married, although there was no space on the form to include his spouse's name. The record identified him as the son of Miguel García and Teburcia Velásquez, both of Tamaulipas. It noted that his remains were buried on May 26, 1918, in Brownsville. Miguel García had identified the remains and helped ensure that accurate information would be on file in the official death registry for the state of Texas.

The García family must have been unsettled by Kirk's decision not to list a cause of death on the certificate, despite investigators who described what appeared to be three bullet holes in the back of Florencio's jacket. Kirk's decision, however, did not prevent the family from filing civil charges. Now with a certificate to prove Florencio was indeed dead, and not alive and well in Mexico as the state police suggested, Texas Rangers George W. Sadler, John Sittre, and Alfred P. Locke were arrested just days after the García family buried their son. The officers filed a bond of $3,000 each and were remanded to the custody of the captain of their company, Charles F. Stevens.[9] The charges were brought before the same Henry J. Kirk who acted as both county coroner and justice of the peace. Kirk convened a grand jury that consisted entirely of Anglo residents with the exception of one local ethnic Mexican. After reviewing the evidence, the grand jury decided not to indict the Texas Rangers. Oscar Dancy later remembered that by 1918 grand juries in the region were "almost solidly Americans, mostly newcomers." The newcomers were Anglo Americans who had migrated from southern states. Their arrival expanded Jim Crow laws, the systemic segregation laws targeting African Americans, to the US–Mexico border. Targeted by "Juan Crow" laws, as historians now popularly refer to them, ethnic Mexicans found themselves increasingly segregated from Anglos in schools, churches, and restaurants and discouraged from voting or serving on juries.[10]

The grand jury's decision gave the state police continued license to characterize the life of Florencio García as they saw fit. In 1919, when Captain Stevens testified to the incident before a committee investigating abuses by the state police, he ignored the certificate of death and again asserted

Death certificates for victims of anti-Mexican violence at the hands of police are hard to find. In the case of the murder of Florencio García in 1918, the acting coroner for Cameron County had to modify the certificate to indicate that the date of his death was "unknown." Later investigations showed that he died in the custody of Texas Rangers. Florencio García, May 1918, certificate number 19810, Bureau of Vital Statistics, State Registrar Office, Austin.

that García never met harm at Ranger hands. He testified under oath that García had last been seen living in Mexico.[11] Stevens's testimony attempted to erase the murder as well as the pain suffered by the surviving García relatives. It also threatened to erase their efforts to seek justice in the aftermath of García's murder. Stevens swiftly disavowed the murder and preserved the reputation of the state police.

García's family pushed the Texas courts and police in multiple ways, imploring them to act on behalf of their son, to find his remains, to record his death, and to prosecute the assailants involved in his murder. His parents, his brother, and his unnamed spouse, as well as Oscar Dancy, Chas Champion, Antonio Valiente, and Leopoldo Espinosa, were impacted by his arrest and his disappearance. They relayed to investigators the details of the last time they saw him alive and provided an opportunity for the judicial system to prosecute those involved in his murder. They left traces from 1918 in the historical record. But with the conclusion of the abuse investigation in 1919, Florencio and his surviving family disappear from the record. And yet this trace, however incomplete, is essential. The small, incomplete traces revealing the collective concern for his life helped ensure that today there are documents that challenge the police accounts. They provide an alternative story to the one where Florencio is a criminal and his family's grief is unfounded.

The larger tragedy of Florencio García's death, and the attempts by the state police to disavow his murder, lies in its utter ordinariness. Searching the Texas landscape for the remains of a loved one was an awful—and awfully familiar—ritual, repeated countless times before. By 1918, the murder of ethnic Mexicans had become commonplace on the Texas–Mexico border, a violence systematically justified by vigilantes and state authorities alike. Historians estimate that between 1848 and 1928 in Texas alone, 232 ethnic Mexicans were lynched by vigilante groups of three or more people. These tabulations only tell part of the story.[12]

Despite popular assumptions that vigilantism in the nineteenth century occurred primarily in regions where law enforcement institutions lacked structure and social influence, vigilantism was in fact practiced in places where criminal justice systems were well established. Violence that superseded judicial procedures regularly articulated popular distrust of the justice system or local frustration with the bureaucracy of criminal prosecution. Lynch mobs commonly took prisoners from jail even though courts would likely have sentenced them to execution. These vigilante actions, however, were tacitly sanctioned by the judicial system whenever local grand juries failed to indict or prosecute assailants who participated in mob violence.[13] Moreover, law enforcement officers facilitated the conditions for making prisoners vulnerable to mob violence and even participated in lynchings. Vigilante violence on the border had a state-building function. It both directed the public to act with force to sustain hierarchies of race and class and complemented the brutal methods of law enforcement in this period.[14]

In addition to these acts by mobs, state and local police committed extralegal acts of violence that are often overlooked in lynching statistics. When including acts of extralegal violence at the hands of Texas Rangers and local police, the numbers of victims of racial violence in Texas soars.

Extralegal violence at the hands of law enforcement has for too long been shielded in a cloak of legal authority. The decade between 1910 and 1920 was a particularly brutal period, when ethnic Mexicans were criminalized and harshly policed by an intersecting regime of vigilantes, state police, local police, and army soldiers. During these years of vitriol and aggression, law enforcement officers, soldiers, and vigilantes claimed the lives of hundreds more ethnic Mexicans, citizens of the United States and Mexico alike. Estimates of the number of dead range from as few as 300 to as many as several thousand.

State racial terror and vigilantism were linked. In particular, police abuse and collusion with vigilante mobs, followed by state cover-ups, set a pattern for sanctioned abuse. The frequency, and normalcy, of anti-Mexican violence seeped far beyond Texas and encouraged a public passivity toward violent policing that has had long-standing consequences for people living near the border.

The violence on the Texas–Mexico border took many forms. Ethnic Mexicans were intimidated, tortured, and killed by hanging, shooting, burning, and beating. Nearly all the known victims were adult men, though a few women and children suffered the same vicious wrath. What this violence nearly always shared was location: death often occurred in the isolation of the rural Texas landscape. The thick mesquite brush and the dark of night frequently cloaked these acts from public view.[15] These events were also linked in a broadly felt injustice. Assailants rarely faced arrest and grand juries regularly failed to indict the accused for wrongdoing. For members of law enforcement, a culture of impunity prevailed.

Terror and intimidation permeated the region. For each victim that died, there were others who witnessed the violence. People organized their daily routines to avoid conflict with law enforcement officers or known agitators of vigilante violence. Children witnessed parents being beaten, or worse, and cousins saw their kin being shot. Many of the dead would not be recovered or given a proper burial. Assailants threatened witnesses and prevented them from tending to the bodies of loved ones. Still, relatives and friends searched, and protested the ongoing murders, for months and years and decades. Some would store the sites in their memories, to share them years later.

Journalists described the violent scenes as they were unveiled in the daylight or exposed in unexpected encounters with corpses hanging from telephone poles or the limbs of mesquite trees. People spotted decapitated bodies floating down the Rio Grande.[16] Such encounters with the dead surely provoked a range of reactions, from horror to anger to a righteous sense of justice served. But for friends, neighbors, or family of the dead, and for allies in the struggle against injustice, finding the remains was also part of a much longer process of grieving and of remembrance.

This book is about the long legacies of violence. It returns to a period of terror acknowledged by historians of the border but forgotten in public memory. Politicians, historians, the media, and historical commissions of the early twentieth century all inscribed a celebratory version of events in newspapers, books, lesson plans, museums, and monuments. This version of history was a key ingredient in their nation building. It hid state crimes and disavowed the loss and trauma experienced by residents. Historical institutions neglected to keep accurate records of racially motivated killings and in this way bolstered efforts to erase this period of terror from state history. Records that do exist often labeled the dead as criminals. *The Injustice Never Leaves You* reveals how the keepers of history convinced the broader United States that this period should be remembered instead as a time of progress.

The architects of official history, however, did not account for the other ways history is made. They did not consider the witnesses and survivors of violence who would pass memories from one generation to another.[17] They underestimated residents who had their own claim in the border region and refused to be intimidated, residents who would share their stories with their children, residents who would leave personal records documenting the terror that shaped daily life. *The Injustice Never Leaves You* is their story. In addition to the recovery of a history of state violence in the borderlands, it reveals valiant acts of preservation and remembrance conducted by people who lived in a world shaped by violence but who refused to be consumed by it.

The efforts of such people, of course, exist outside of official history, just like the murdered human beings they sought to remember. There are no indexes that name all the dead and catalog the circumstances of their murders; all such efforts to remember are partial and unofficial, existing in the margins. There are, however, signal cases that provide insight into the conditions that allowed this vast violence against Mexicans to flourish. In the pages that follow, we will examine a public lynching of a Mexican national by an Anglo mob in central Texas in 1910; a double murder of two Texas landowners by a Texas Ranger and a local posse in south Texas in 1915; and a massacre organized by Texas Rangers, local ranchers, and US soldiers in west Texas in 1918. Separated by time, location, and outcome, these cases give a glimpse into the far-reaching practices of anti-Mexican violence. They show that neither class, citizenship, nor social influence protected ethnic Mexicans in this decade. Studied together, these cases expose the linked practices of racial violence that created a long-lasting, pervasive atmosphere of terror. Mobs lynched ethnic Mexicans with impunity, state and local police colluded with vigilantes, and the militarization of the border fed anti-Mexican sentiment, making racial violence all the more lethal.

This book documents both a ferocious period of terror and also the various techniques grieving relatives and their communities employed to hold vigilantes, police, and governments accountable. Living amidst terror, communities utilized multiple strategies for survival. People still challenged the criminalization of ethnic Mexicans and sought justice for the dead. Residents took up arms and engaged in public protest, witnesses faced assailants in court, journalists documented and criticized violent events in editorials, local politicians petitioned for change, and Mexican diplomats pressed for investigations and arrests. Recounting these myriad acts disrupts the typical narrative: that violence is followed by reconciliation, that the dead were likely criminals anyway, that the mere passage of time can heal wounds.[18]

This book also highlights the long efforts to reckon with loss and shows that mourning can be a practice of resistance, passed from generation to generation, continuing even a century later. Recovering the names of the dead and the names of those who brought them harm is a crucial and ongoing effort in the struggle against state violence. Such enduring efforts, often in direct opposition to popular memory, testify to the value of connecting truthfully with the past. The families who have reckoned with this violence harbor a lesson we all should heed. We must reckon with the fact that the southern border of our country was created—and policed—violently, and not valiantly, and that we have continually suppressed this truer, more accurate past. It is a past that bleeds into the present, a suppression that continues to shape our future.

FORGING BORDERS WITH VIOLENCE

This history of violence takes shape around the contested creation of the US–Mexico border and efforts for economic control by new Anglo settlers. In 1821, Mexico gained its independence from Spain. But within forty years of independence, a tangled series of conflicts—the Texas Revolution (1836) and the US–Mexico War (1846–1848)—resulted in the United States acquiring half of Mexico's territory. As a result, the political border of the region now known as Texas was continually shifting. Native American nations, especially the Comanche, continued to contest outside governance—Spanish, Mexican, Texan, and ultimately American—in the region. Anglo migration into the region ensured that settlers had to contend with Native Americans and Mexicans, two groups that struggled throughout the nineteenth century to maintain their place in the region as the colonial powers shifted.

These constructed and changing boundaries required constant enforcement across the century. In 1823 Stephen F. Austin, an early Anglo settler who lived in the region soon to be Texas, organized a small group of men, called rangers, to protect settlers and their property. After Texas claimed independence from Mexico in 1836, the men worked to ensure that Anglo settlers flourished in the new Republic of Texas. That flourishing, however, came at the expense of groups identified as enemies of the new settlement as well as those groups wanted for labor. The Texas Rangers were described as a "fighting force" created by Anglo settlers to fight in the ongoing war for racial supremacy, battling Mexican landowners and indigenous nations, including the Tonkawas, Lipan Apache, Waco, Karankawa, Kiowa, and Comanche. The Texas Rangers targeted both the "Indian warrior" and the Mexican *vaquero* as enemies of white supremacy.[19]

The Rangers also did their part to help preserve a slave-based agriculture by violently policing enslaved African men and women. During the state's long history of chattel slavery, the Rangers tracked and punished enslaved people trying to cross the Rio Grande into Mexico to freedom. Once across the border, the men, women, and children were out of reach of those attempting to claim them as property, who were not allowed to follow them into Mexico. Of course, Rangers frequently broke the neutrality laws that forbade their trips across the border. They also terrorized ethnic Mexicans accused of harboring runaway slaves. One Texas Ranger described them as "black as niggers . . . and ten times as treacherous."[20]

In the early nineteenth century, Texas Rangers blurred the lines between enforcing state laws, practicing vigilantism, and inciting racial terror. Historians now view the Texas Rangers as the first prominent Western vigilantes to be endowed with legal authority.[21] The most frequent complaints of Texas Rangers abusing their power came through what some referred to as *la ley de fuga,* or the law of flight or escape. Under this morbid legal regime, Rangers released prisoners and ordered them to run. Officers then proceeded to shoot the prisoner while in flight, later filing reports that they killed the prisoner to prevent escape or because the prisoner resisted arrest.[22] As early as 1870, a newspaper editor from west Texas reported disgust at the frequency with which Texas Rangers used the expressions "killed while attempting to escape" and "killed while resisting arrest." The editorial alleged that these expressions had dire resonances "that are fast coming to have a melancholy and terrible significance to the people of Western Texas. They furnish the brief epitaph to the scores who have fallen and are falling victims to the ignorance, the arrogance, or the brutality of those charged with the execution of the law."[23]

The US military also actively policed ethnic Mexicans. They collaborated with Rangers to suppress uprisings that challenged American rule in the region. Ethnic Mexican landowners identified as people of the region and not of Mexico or the United States. They embraced nineteenth-century liberal ideologies that held individual freedom and liberty as core principles. As historian Elliot Young explains, "For border people, freedom specifically meant preventing central-government interference in a region that had been relatively isolated and semiautonomous for its entire history. The centralist versus federalist struggles in Mexico that ultimately resulted in

Texas independence in 1836 were part of this long history of fighting for autonomy."[24]

Some Mexicans resisted federal encroachment by merely continuing to live as they had before the region shifted hands. Others, prompted by threats to their land ownership and economic influence, resorted to armed resistance. A decade after the United States claimed half of Mexico's territory through the Treaty of Guadalupe Hidalgo in 1848, Juan Nepomuceno Cortina took up arms and rebelled against the new nation and new Anglo settlers recruited to south Texas after the state was annexed into the United States. In the summer of 1859 Cortina defended a Mexican *ranchero* from a public beating by shooting Brownsville city marshal Robert Shears. In November 1859, Cortina delivered a proclamation accusing judges and attorneys of expropriating land from Mexican landowners and practicing anti-Mexican violence. The son of a wealthy landowning family, Cortina led an estimated 600 men in a battle against the Texas Rangers and the US Army. He described Anglo settlers as "vampire guises of men" who robbed property and hunted and murdered Mexican men "like wild beasts."[25] Despite being defeated, Cortina would inspire a genre of border ballads sung by ethnic Mexicans to honor those who stood up to discrimination, colonization, and violence.[26]

Ten years after Cortina's revolt, ethnic Mexican landowners suffered losses as Anglo colonization was fortified with technological advances. In 1874, Illinois farmer J. F. Glidden patented his invention of barbed wire, which became a favored tool for defining private property and guaranteed the successful colonization of the western United States.[27] By fencing in the rural landscape in the 1870s, Anglo ranchers created barriers to rivers and streams, blocked previously unfettered grazing patterns for cows and goats, and summarily stifled ideals of open land use and communal access practiced by rancheros for numerous generations. The changes in property ownership and ranching paved the way for Texas land to be subdivided and sold for commercial farming. It took little more than a decade for ranch lands in Texas to be fenced in entirely. Ethnic Mexicans in the Southwest found themselves assigned as manual agricultural labor in this new economy, giving rise to the popular Mexican saying *"con el alambre vino el hambre"*— with the barbed wire came hunger.[28]

Alongside technological innovations, new American property laws and taxation ignored ranchero property rights under the 1848 Treaty of Guadalupe Hidalgo. This culminated in a sweeping reorganization of Anglo–Mexican relations in Texas.[29] Taxation, court-ordered surveys of land boundaries, and challenges to the validity of Spanish land grants kept Mexican landowners depleting their cash to pay legal fees. When landowners came up short on paying taxes or private debts, county sheriffs and county courts would coordinate auctions at which thousands of acres could be purchased for less than a penny an acre. In 1877 the Hidalgo County sheriff sold 3,000 acres for $15.00 and the following year sold another 4,000 acres for $17.15. Texas laws targeted Mexican property owners in the state.[30]

The shifts in economic influence led to increased racial tensions and to resistance. In September 1891, Catarino Erasmo Garza led a group of hundreds of border residents back and forth across the Rio Grande in a revolt against both Mexico and the United States encroaching on a population that had enjoyed living, mostly unimpeded, on the margins of national power. Riding into battle with the motto *libres fronterizos* (free border people) stitched on their hatbands, the Garzistas were a multiclass movement that included wealthy merchants and landowners, lower-middle-class professionals, poor farmers, and landless ranchers. Mexican nationals and Texas-Mexicans, as well as a few Anglos, Italians, and residents from interracial marriages between Anglos and Mexicans, filled out the ranks of the rebellion.[31]

The geographical distance from the central governments made apprehending revolutionaries on the far reaches of US and Mexican soil tactically and strategically difficult.[32] Efforts by the Mexican and US governments to incorporate the borderlands required infrastructure that would connect the regions to markets, transportation, and communication systems. In 1891 two rail lines finally connected Laredo, Texas, to northern tracks. The Texas–Mexico track ran from the port city of Corpus Christi to Laredo. The International and Great Northern Railroad linked Corpus Christi to San Antonio, which then connected to tracks that led north, east, and west. These railroads opened Laredo to the markets in centrally located San Antonio and allowed goods to be transported across the country. It would be another decade before a rail line from Mexico City to the northern Mexican border would open up international commerce, but even so, in the late nineteenth century, the railways and telegraph lines that crossed the US–Mexico border were becoming crucial elements in government attempts to enforce control over the people living in the border regions. These advances in infrastructure were coupled with violent policing.

Military strategies for defeating Catarino Garza's rebellion were brutal and set a precedent for later practices by the US Army and state police alike. US Army captain John Gregory Bourke, leading the suppression, was one of many who embraced cutthroat strategies on the border. He made his approach clear when he wrote, "The cheapest thing to do is to shoot them down wherever [they are] found skulking about with arms in their hands, and to burn down some of the ranchos which gave them shelter." According to the captain, killing rebels was not enough. He wanted the complete devastation of any community thought to support the Garza revolt. Having refined these lethal methods during a fifteen-year effort waging war on the Apache nation in Arizona, the captain brought them to the border region in Texas.[33]

Spanish-language journalists expressed outrage at the devastation. The Rio Grande City newspaper *El Bien Público* published accounts in the 1890s that documented atrocities committed by US soldiers. The editor, Jesús T. Récio, published petitions sent to the governor of Texas and letters substantiating grievances against Bourke and his attempts to terrorize civilian communities. Récio charged the army with burning ranches of suspected Garza allies, threatening residents with lynching, searching houses without warrants, and stealing guns, horses, and private family papers. Complaints were filed with the army, the district attorney, the attorney general, the governor of Texas, Mexican officials, and President Benjamin Harrison. The charges of abuse by the US military would fall on deaf ears, and Captain Bourke would continue to lead a brutal repression of revolutionary activities and spread fear throughout the region.[34]

The Garza revolt was defeated and by 1892 Garza was living in exile. Putting down the revolutions allowed the US state to militarize the Rio Grande and transform the borderlands from a region where people united by culture, tradition, and proximity moved freely across borders into an increasingly political and social boundary.[35]

The US effort to forcibly end the rebellion became a measure of its growing imperial drive for conquest. In these same decades, the United States was also increasing its territory to include Puerto Rico, the Philippines, Guam, and Hawai'i and to exert control in Cuba, the Dominican Republic, and Panama. Military officers like Captain Bourke invoked discourses and strategies employed by the United States in other imperial endeavors that relied on notions of race and Anglo superiority. The military officers inflicted racial terror on ethnic Mexicans in an effort to end challenges to Anglo social, political, and economic control. They enabled a culture of US imperialism that justified Anglo domination in south Texas and in the US West more broadly.[36]

Handily suppressing the revolt showed that the federal government was capable of bringing stability to the border region that encouraged Anglo economic investment.[37] The military campaigns were coupled with media coverage that portrayed south Texas as having infinite economic potential that was wasted in the hands of inferior ethnic Mexicans incapable of developing the land.[38] The remaining ethnic Mexican landowners struggled to maintain their land through the first decades of the twentieth century. With the completion of the railroad in 1904, produce grown in south Texas could be shipped from Brownsville to Corpus Christi and on to national markets via the Missouri-Pacific railroad system. By 1907 the railway hauled approximately 500 carloads of farm products daily. A new wave of Anglo migration came to the Texas–Mexico border region.

The agricultural revolution witnessed skyrocketing land values and inspired outside land developers and commercial farmers to migrate to south Texas in droves. According to David Montejano, land promoters worked to "convert pastures into plow fields" by marketing ranch lands that could grow profitable cash crops and helped replace ranching with farming. By the 1920s, the number of farms increased dramatically while their size decreased. Land developers recruited Anglo buyers from the Mississippi Valley to settle in the region and take part in the "farm revolution." These events meant a drastic reorganization of land and space in south Texas. In Hidalgo County, for example, the 1910 census records showed 677 farms averaging 969.5 acres, but by 1930 the numbers jumped to 4,327 farms averaging 126.9 acres. Successful recruitment efforts resulted in rapid population growth in the region as well. In the early 1900s the population in deep south Texas counties totaled 79,934, but by 1920 the population rose to 159,842, and in 1930 the number doubled to 322,845. Montejano describes this as "one of the most phenomenal land movements in the history of the United States."[39]

Witnessing this social transformation firsthand, Jovita González described this farm colonization as an "American invasion . . . hordes of

money-making Americans poured into the region."[40] A team of land developers encouraged commercial farming practices that literally required a
transformation of the landscape itself. Employers relied on Mexican wage
labor to cultivate the land for the coming agricultural revolution. Teams
of men cleared dense countryside of mesquite trees and cacti covered in
barbs and thorns, which choked the landscape and made farming difficult.
Rows of crops soon replaced brush country.

Anglo farm settlers transformed the social and political landscape as
well as the physical one. They ushered in Juan Crow laws of segregation
and prohibited interracial marriages, formerly a part of the social fabric in
mixed Anglo and Mexican communities. They insisted on the new code
of social relations, which in turn initiated a new racial hierarchy. Political
battles took shape over local governments. The newcomers moved to dis-
enfranchise Mexican residents and minimize their social or economic
influence. They charged Mexican ranchers with using political machines
to fill voting booths with droves of Mexicans seen as ignorant and unfit
for participation in elections. According to Anglo settlers, ethnic Mexican
residents did not merit the rights and privileges of Americans, despite
their status as legal citizens and their long history in the region. One newspaper demeaned local Mexican residents as a "class of foreigners who claim
American citizenship but who are as ignorant of things American as the
mule."[41]

In contrast, several articles published in the Spanish-language newspaper
La Crónica challenged the racism sweeping across south Texas. Texas-
Mexican journalists, writing in the midst of the social upheaval, criticized
Anglo politicians and landowners for denying civil rights to ethnic Mexican
residents in Texas and for relegating them to cheap labor. One article in
1910 described their exclusion from schools as a grave attempt to create
an ignorant class. Moreover, journalists condemned the frequent use of
vigilante violence to create a docile labor force. The article charged that
through violence Anglos attempted to "condemn the Mexicans to a condition of beasts of burden."[42]

Although the farm colonization in the region was well under way, the
new settlers still felt their control was tenuous. Economic dominance of the
region did not remove the threat of revolt in the minds of the Anglo residents
in south Texas. Proximity to Mexico left many feeling vulnerable. Politicians, military leaders, and local residents increasingly portrayed residents

in the Mexican nation as a threat to American capitalist interests in the Southwest. Their fears were soaked in racist perceptions of their south Texas neighbors, and yet Anglo perceptions were, on a numeric level, correct. Even as they altered the land, they remained a minority population.

The ethnic Mexican population was growing, too. Mexican nationals migrated north to escape an economic depression in 1880 and a recession in 1906. Between 1910 and 1920 even more Mexicans crossed over into the United States to escape the Mexican Revolution. During the civil war in Mexico as many as one million Mexicans sought refuge in the United States. Most of them came via the Texas–Mexico border. Although many refugees soon returned to Mexico, the number of ethnic Mexicans in the United States tripled during the decade of the 1910s.[43]

Beyond proximity and population growth, the turbulence of the Mexican Revolution in Mexican towns on the international border caused fear in neighboring American cities. Residents worried that the revolutionary plots to overthrow the Díaz administration and redistribute land in Mexico could spill across the border and threaten Anglo property ownership and US control. Texas governors and residents alike made requests for US troops to guard the Texas–Mexico border. Rumors circulated of the threat to Mexican border towns like Matamoros and neighboring US towns like Brownsville.

State violence was the response. In 1913 Texas governor Oscar Colquitt dispatched over 1,000 state militiamen and the Texas National Guard to appease residents of Brownsville and El Paso.[44] As US soldiers stationed on the Texas–Mexico border trained before deployment in World War I, they transformed the border into a militarized zone. The newest advances in military technology, including barbed wire, spotlights, tanks, machine guns, and airplanes were used to surveil Mexican residents.

Refugees fleeing the Mexican Revolution were met with growing nativist sentiment. Denied humanitarian aid, refugees were portrayed as a threat to Anglo Americans. In 1914, for example, defeated Mexican federal soldiers and panicked civilians crossed into west Texas to escape the devastations of civil war. They were met with hostility and imprisoned at a camp in Fort Bliss, just outside of El Paso. West Texas towns called for arriving refugees and federal soldiers alike to be segregated from US residents. Mexican soldiers and Mexican women and children walked on foot across the unforgiving desert from the border town of Presidio seventy miles

Refugees wrapped in blankets stand with their possessions, guarded by US soldiers. In 1914 approximately 4,500 Mexican refugees fleeing the violence of the Mexican Revolution were imprisoned at a camp in Fort Bliss just outside of El Paso. The camp held Mexican men, women, and children, as well as Mexican federal soldiers. Yale Collection of Western Americana, Beinecke Rare Book and Manuscript Library.

to Marfa, where a train transported them to Fort Bliss. While detained, Mexican soldiers were forced to build a prison camp that stretched across forty-eight acres of land. An intimidating barbed wire fence, stacked ten strands high and secured to the ground by hog-wire fence, surrounded the camp. Some reported that electricity charged the barbed wire fence with a lethal current.[45]

While Mexican federal soldiers and civilian refugees were treated as national threats and placed in prison camps, civilians in Texas accused of being revolutionaries or bandits could expect far worse treatment. During this era, the figure of the menacing Mexican revolutionary and bandit was cemented in popular imaginary. In 1915, for example, the *New York Evening Telegram* published a cartoon by Nelson Green depicting a grinning Uncle Sam using a shovel to toss piles of dead Mexican revolutionaries wearing sombreros into an "international rubbish can."[46]

In the 1910s the figure of the menacing Mexican revolutionary and bandit was cemented in the popular imagination. In 1915 the *New York Evening Telegram* published a dehumanizing cartoon by Nelson Green depicting a grinning Uncle Sam using a shovel to toss piles of dead Mexican revolutionaries wearing sombreros into an "international rubbish can." Cartoon Drawings Collection, LC-DIG-acd-2a08860, Library of Congress Prints and Photographs Division, Washington, D.C.

Depicting Mexicans as waste did no favors for ethnic Mexicans living in the United States. Between 1914 and 1919, state administrations responded to the calls to guard the Texas–Mexico border, creating the conditions for a dramatic increase in violent policing. By 1916 the Wilson administration had deployed approximately 100,000 National Guard troops between Yuma, Arizona, and Brownsville, Texas.[47] Unfamiliar with the border region in Texas, US troops struggled to police the Rio Grande. As calls to militarize the border continued, residents frequently claimed they needed more Texas Rangers, not more outsiders. The state police, they argued, were local and more effective than soldiers from northern states like New York or Rhode Island. In 1915 the state police included only twenty-six men, so the Texas legislature increased the state budget and the governor expedited the hiring process. In 1916 hundreds of new Texas Rangers patrolled the region, and by 1918 the force swelled to approximately 1,350 Rangers. By decade's end, the intersecting regimes of vigilante, state, and military policing took hold of the broader social landscape, declaring all Mexicans enemies of the state.[48]

In particular, the expansion of the Texas Rangers was a response to calls for more police in 1915. In the summer, authorities reported that local residents were planning to subvert US control of the borderlands. *El Plan de San Diego,* a manifesto attributed to Mexican seditionists, called for a revolt to overthrow US rule in south Texas and an end to Anglo economic and political power through a "Liberating Army of race and people" including ethnic Mexicans, African Americans, and Japanese living in Texas, New Mexico, Arizona, California, and Colorado. The plan went so far as to call for the expulsion of Anglos by murdering all Anglo men sixteen years and older.[49]

Resisting the expansion of farm colonization in the region reflected broader pubic sentiment that objected to the economic exploitation of Mexican wage laborers, the institutionalization of racism through Juan Crow laws in Texas, and the increasing military presence. *El Plan de San Diego* called for burning bridges and derailing trains, among other acts of rebellion to interrupt federal, state, and local infrastructure. Raiders also targeted prominent ranches that had become a symbol of Anglo farm colonization. The King Ranch, for example, was known in this period as the greatest symbol of Anglo domination on the frontier. As the first ranch to be fenced with barbed wire in the nineteenth century and the first to develop a new breed of cattle in the United States, the ranching empire maintained a staggering two million acres of land at its peak and maintained property across several counties.[50]

As a method for transitioning from ranching to farming during the agricultural revolution in the early twentieth century, prominent families directed farm towns as bankers, merchants, and political officials. The south Texas town of Kingsville in Kleberg County, for example, located in the middle of the King Ranch, became entirely serviced by the King-Kleberg family companies. The families owned or primarily financed the Kingsville Company, the Kleberg Bank, the King's Inn, the Kingsville Ice and Milling Company, the Kingsville Publishing Company, the Kingsville Power Company, as well as irrigation and cotton ginning companies. This financial monopoly gave the family the power and influence to have a Texas Ranger headquarters. Such intimate relationships with the Rangers led residents of south Texas to commonly refer to them as the King Ranch's private security. The ranch was known as the most well-guarded piece of private property.[51]

On August 8, 1915, some sixty men raided the flag station at the Las Norias section of the King Ranch where the Texas Rangers maintained their headquarters. The response to the raid was swift and brutal, with Texas Rangers leading the charge. One soldier later reflected in his memoir that among the Rangers there was a "savage radical element." He described "glaring abuses in retribution and threatening to clear the Valley of Mexicans."[52] In an indiscriminate manhunt, Rangers killed ethnic Mexican men in revenge for the raid. Locals later lamented that any Mexican man in close proximity to the ranch faced the wrath of state and local law enforcement posses, soldiers, and vigilantes. Local resident Frank C. Pierce tallied at least 102 left dead in the wake of this killing spree, almost double the number of men alleged to have raided the King Ranch.[53] Historians estimate that between August 4, 1915, and June 17, 1916, Texas Rangers and deputy sheriffs killed more than 100 Mexican residents without conducting proper investigations. Some described the violent period as an "orgy of bloodshed"; others estimate that the number of deaths in this short period was closer to 300. Texas judge James Wells estimated that in Hidalgo and Cameron Counties alone Texas officers and vigilantes executed between 250 and 300 Mexican men in less than a year.[54]

Some Anglo investors profited from the period of fear and wartime anxiety. They utilized local and state police to protect their claims to property and to help dismantle the remaining economic control by a class of ethnic Mexicans in south Texas through intimidation and violence. Writer and theorist Américo Paredes wrote that in this era, the Texas Rangers in particular "furnish[ed] the fortune-making adventurer with services not rendered by the United States Army or local sheriffs. And that is why from the point of view of the makers of fortune the Rangers were so important to the 'pacification' of the Border." He continued, "The Rangers and those who imitated their methods undoubtedly exacerbated the cultural conflict on the Border rather than allayed it . . . the Rangers stirred up more trouble than they put down."[55]

The manifesto and ongoing raids gave state authorities ammunition to profile ethnic Mexicans as enemies of the state. The raids also amplified calls by Anglo residents for more policing of ethnic Mexicans. David Montejano wrote of *El Plan de San Diego,* "The losers in these conflicts were usually the uninvolved civilian population, who bore the brunt of escalating and indiscriminate retaliation and counterretaliation."[56]

The dramatic changes of this period turned ethnic Mexican residents into permanent enemies of the state. Any local resident that looked Mexican, regardless of citizenship, social status, or evidence of guilt, could be profiled as a "bandit" or "bandit sympathizer" between 1910 and 1920. State and local police ignored legal procedures and regularly denied residents the right to trial by jury and to presumed innocence. This pattern of violence continued for years. In 1919 the brutality of the Texas Rangers had become so brazen that the state legislature agreed to form a senate committee to investigate abuses by the state police. Anglo residents, civilians, businessmen, and politicians alike lined up to defend the Rangers. They suggested that the violence at the hands of the state police only matched, but did not exceed, the violence against Americans by Mexicans in Texas and across the border. In other words, Rangers responded with violence to quell violence on the US–Mexico border. They described the border region as an area of social crisis. C. L. Jessup, a ten-year resident of Brownsville, went so far as to admit that state police and local residents waged an all-out war against Mexicans. Jessup described local residents as living in "simply a state of war; every home almost was an arsenal."[57] The attorney questioning Jessup reiterated, "The war is on the Mexican banditti."[58]

RESEARCHING HISTORIES OF VIOLENCE

In the early twentieth century, Texas politicians, the state police, the mainstream press, and historians had intersecting interests that resulted in portraying this period of anti-Mexican violence as rightfully done, all in the name of protecting the private property of US citizens and securing the

US–Mexico border. Recovering an alternative account requires returning to the landscape of the Texas–Mexico borderlands and looking for the remains of the departed. But our process of exhumation must be done with great caution; photographs, testimonies, and reports that describe the dead must be handled with great sensitivity, in order to avoid reinforcing their erasure and further normalizing the violence. Our efforts require us to search, first and foremost, for lost humanity.[59]

Across the first half of the twentieth century, both the actions of the state police and the victims of state violence caught the attention of a number of scholars.[60] These accounts typically focused on periodic moments of armed conflict between Anglo and Mexican men; rebellion and repression take center stage. This research offered two competing narratives: the first valorized the actions of the Texas Rangers; the second valorized the actions of residents who challenged the state police with armed rebellion. The two opposing strains of scholarship helped develop two different groups of celebrated heroes who would be fixtures of popular culture for decades.

Walter Prescott Webb, a prolific historian known for his foundational work on the American West, grew up in the rural community of Ranger, Texas, where he attended Ranger High School. In 1935 he published *The Texas Rangers: A Century of Frontier Defense,* which for decades remained the definitive account of the heroic Rangers narrative, a celebration of the Rangers for their dogged efforts to dispel the dangers of the frontier for Anglo settlers.[61] He credited the state police with ushering Texas into a modern era. His account showed little concern for the brutally repressive methods employed by Rangers and US soldiers. Instead, Webb's narrative is full of racist descriptions of Anglo superiority over savage Native Americans and inferior Mexicans cursed with mixed blood. For a quarter of a century, Webb's celebratory interpretation of the state police stood as the official account of this period.

Américo Paredes's publications in the mid-twentieth century helped cast an alternative light on the history of the Texas Rangers. He reinterpreted the Texas Rangers as outlaws who abused their authority to displace Mexican landowners and intimidate residents, and he celebrated Mexican residents who resisted state violence. His first book, *"With His Pistol in His Hand": A Border Ballad and Its Hero* (1958), studied the Mexican ballad tradition, the *corrido,* and the local heroes who featured prominently in the songs. Paredes wrote about figures like Gregorio Cortéz, popularly known by residents on both sides of the Rio Grande for killing an Anglo official in self-defense and undergoing an epic attempt to escape the wrath of the Texas Rangers. Paredes preserved the efforts to memorialize men like Cortéz; he simultaneously embraced the romantic accounts of masculine bravery and resistance through violence. Dismantling their reputation as avatars of civilization, Paredes condemned the Texas Rangers as arbiters of pure, unadulterated racial terror; the only solution to the unjust landscape they had created, he suggested, was to fight back with a virulent Mexican masculinity.[62]

These two competing narratives—those of Webb and Paredes—diverged in their selected heroes, but they were equally patriarchal and celebratory of armed masculinity. Tales of the Rangers, building on Webb's celebratory interpretation, were popularized in fiction as well as television and film. These men were memorialized in the Texas Centennial celebrations of the Texas Revolution.[63] The Texas Ranger took on mythical heroic form in radio, film, and eventually television. *The Lone Ranger* and *Walker, Texas Ranger* are perhaps the most well known of these fictions.

In the face of these celebratory portrayals, people with contrasting memories maintained their own, very different histories of state violence. In the alternative vernacular cultures of the border region, expressed in everything from poetry to music to oral storytelling, residents kept alive a very different vision of the past that refuted the celebration of agents of violence. By the early twentieth century violent conflict was a primary theme in the *corridos* sung on the Texas–Mexican border.[64] These songs celebrated men who fought for their rights armed with pistols in their hands and rarely depicted women as active contributors to the borderlands. The hero-centered narratives of the *corridos* bolstered pride, yet eclipsed the actual day-to-day struggles of local residents to survive in a racially hostile climate. The residents who lived in fear, not to mention the unending consequences of colonization, were not part of those story lines.

This book is the first to focus specifically on the communities left in the wake of violence on the Texas–Mexico border. It documents the stories of those murdered through extralegal executions, but just as important, it lingers in the aftermath of violence to document what happened next—the parts of life rarely recorded in mainstream histories or border *corridos*. It reveals the families, neighbors, and communities connected to and shaped by the violence, communities that, in turn, had to figure out how to respond to the injustice.[65] Historian Kidada Williams encourages us to consider the families forever altered by the murder of a loved one, those men and women and children who experience "the force of their killings and the aftershocks." Doing this requires "pulling from historical limbo the uncounted women, men, and children who lived through this violence, but whose stories have been unheard or underexamined."[66] In both collective memory and historical accounts, perpetrators of violence and the most prominent resisters of violence have taken center stage, while the actual victims and witnesses of violence have receded to the background. Williams argues, "Victims' and witnesses' testimonies of lives transformed by violence and the aspects of violence that mattered the most to them rarely get the scholarly attention they deserve."[67]

Lingering in the aftermath to search for lives shaped by violence can offer an understanding of the ramifications of lynchings, police violence, and a broader culture of impunity. This book thus brings to light the histories of men, women, and children who became targets of intimidation, mob violence, and police violence, who were nearly erased from written history and rarely remembered in conventional accounts. But it also recovers the histories of those who created unconventional and unofficial archives, often outside of state control, and who ensured that a book like this could someday be written.[68]

The legacies of violence can be challenging to recover. Violence becomes embedded in the landscape and in the memories of the residents who live there. Michel-Rolph Trouillot eloquently outlined how past events leave their mark: "What happened leaves traces, some of which are quite concrete—buildings, dead bodies, censuses, monuments, diaries, political boundaries—that limit the range and significance of historical processes." The many vestiges of violence, despite efforts to erase them, do leave traces. The archives of the state of Texas or old issues of local papers offer invaluable understanding, but an understanding that is always partial. To grapple with the layers of emotional devastation, we must also reckon with the people themselves, which is why oral histories are so valuable. Michel-Rolph Trouillot explains, "in the case of oral transmission, the moment of fact creation is continually carried over in the very bodies of the individuals who partake in the transmission. The *source* is alive."[69] To recover the identities of the victims who suffered violence during this period, then, requires an examination of historical documents, the landscape, and community memory. Learning from previously ignored or overshadowed vernacular histories offers new opportunities to grapple with the long legacy of violence on the border. Oral histories offer important information that fill gaps in institutional archives and clue historians into records long overlooked.[70]

POSSIBILITIES OF ORAL HISTORY

With the rise of social history in the 1960s and 1970s, scholars interested in writing history from below began to collect oral histories as a means of recording community knowledge. This shift recognized the limits of institutional archives to record the historical contributions of underrepresented voices and also inspired initiatives to preserve community memories before the passing of older generations. Reflecting on the rise of this method, oral historian Donald A. Ritchie writes, "historians have examined how people have constructed the past to make it useful to them in the present. As they gradually recognized how collective memories can preserve or distort a community's past, scholars grew more appreciative of oral history. How, what, and why people remember and narrate the past is, after all, the primary business of the oral historian."[71]

Oral histories also provide a unique opportunity for studying the relationship between history, memory, and social relations of power. Editors T. Fujitani, Geoffrey White, and Lisa Yoneyama explain in their book *Perilous Memories* that nationality, class, gender, sexuality, religion, and race all shape how a person remembers or forgets. In the case of war, the authors explain that localized memories become submerged within dominant narratives that emphasize national unity across ethnic lines. Critical remembering, as they describe it, refuses the impulse of official state history to create one monolithic interpretation of the past. Studying the memories that challenge mainstream accounts shows how people maintain alternative interpretations of the past to "unsettle historical common sense."[72]

Survivors of state terror pass critical memories that challenge mainstream histories along to the next generation. Critical black memory in the United States is a mode of historical interpretation, a tool responding to histories of exploitation, dehumanization, and violent policing. In the US–Mexico borderlands, critical memories help to undermine national narratives that define the border as a space in need of violent policing.[73]

Storytelling in this form acts as a source of knowledge exchange, as a process that refuses forgetting, and as a resource that allows residents to find some resolve by keeping these histories alive. In studying critical memories, tensions between official and vernacular histories are made visible, and the machinations of power to proclaim the former and deny the latter are revealed.

When I started researching histories of anti-Mexican violence in 2007, I met residents engaged in what I call vernacular history-making, an effort to participate in shaping popular understandings of the past by making histories of racial violence, preserved in community memory, available to the public. Through blogs, poetry, historical essays, websites, digitized archives, and documentaries, residents are contending with the power of mainstream histories.

In 2009 I traveled to the homes of Norma Longoria Rodriguez in San Antonio and Benita and Evaristo "Buddy" Albarado in Uvalde to record oral histories. I listened to their life histories and the tragedies their relatives experienced nearly 100 years earlier. As the interviews continued, I realized that Mrs. Rodriguez and the Albarados were sharing their histories of state violence from memory and from years of research. Both families had file folders and books laid out on their table, ready for my arrival. As they spoke about their family histories, they referred to documents, photographs, and maps. Mr. Albarado frequently interrupted the recording to leave the room and return with a folder, or a box, or a book. In their spare time, they had become historians in their own right. Traveling to institutional archives, preserving family records, recording interviews, and reading histories of the period, they had created their own private archives. In my conversations with descendants over the years, I realized that the legacies of violence in the early twentieth century stretched well into the twenty-first century. To write about the histories of violence required writing about the continued effort to challenge mainstream accounts that criminalize or erase the dead.

Vernacular histories that lament anti-Mexican violence open new opportunities to recover marginalized histories. The families that circulated accounts of dispossession and loss thus passed their narrative of injustice from one generation to the next. They refused the erasure of this violent past. The efforts to condemn vigilantism and state violence offer histories that expose state terror and memorialize both the casualties and the survivors of violence. They linger in the aftermath.[74]

Norma Longoria Rodriguez is one Texas resident leading these efforts. During an interview, she reflected on how learning of the double murder of her grandfather and great grandfather by a Texas Ranger and local posse in September 1915 interrupted her life. It set her on a path to spend decades researching this history. This tragedy filled her with a deep sense of grief and left her with unanswered questions. She dedicated weekends and vacations to searching state archives and public records for information, to no avail. Instead, she took to preserving her own family history, conducting oral interviews with living relatives, and caring for family records. The sentiments of loss have remained with Rodriguez. She explained, "It's an injustice. It never leaves you. It's inherited loss."[75]

Many people who witnessed acts of racial violence carried sentiments of loss and injustice along with their memories. Descendants of those who witnessed violence, learned the histories, and then went on to build archives that unveil emotions alongside dates, names, and locations. While historians tend to shy away from grappling with emotions, residents working to preserve familial or local histories of violence confront pain and suffering. They are preserving histories of loss. In recording interviews with their loved ones, they help transform ephemeral memories, packed with facts and tangled sentiments of loss and indignation, into a material record for future generations.[76]

Cultural theorist Saidiya Hartman suggests that writing and circulating history is how the secular world attempts to attend to the dead. Hartman encourages us to reflect upon the purposes of histories of racial violence: "to what end does one open the casket and look into the face of death. . . . Why subject the dead to new dangers and to a second order of violence?"[77] Attending to histories of violence requires more than attempts at recovery. The urgency with which descendants of racial violence take on their practice of vernacular history-making calls attention to the ongoing need for redress. In the past sixty years an international consensus has developed that recognizes the importance of confronting traumatic histories of slavery, genocide, ethnic cleansing, police violence, and war crimes. Some crimes are so cruel that the damage extends beyond the immediate victims "to encompass entire societies."[78]

The critical memories analyzed in this book call out for continued efforts to recover histories of racial violence and for a public reckoning with violence. This is a call understood by Margaret Burnham, human rights lawyer and founder of the Civil Rights and Restorative Justice Project. She explains, "It's a human right to have your case prosecuted if you've been the victim of a crime. Just because prosecution is no longer possible it doesn't mean that that obligation disappears. It's the obligation then of government to tell us why the cases weren't prosecuted, why justice was never achieved."[79] Residents in Texas insist that the state and cultural institutions stop disavowing this history and instead participate in the long process of reckoning.

The first three chapters of this book uncover incidents of anti-Mexican violence in 1910, 1915, and 1918 by Anglo mobs, Texas Rangers, and the US military. They provide insight into the wide-ranging nature of violence, showing the shifting regimes of violence and collaboration between state police, local police, vigilantes, and the US military to incite terror in the Texas–Mexico borderlands and to cover up state crimes. But as important as the crimes themselves are the wide-ranging methods that victims, survivors, and those that witnessed violence utilized to resist these dehumanizing processes of terror. These chapters also highlight witnesses, sometimes generations removed, who preserved these histories and made them available to the public nearly a century later.

After recounting the individual cases, the book switches its focus to the role of state administrations, state institutions, and historians alike in allowing cultures of violence to be celebrated throughout the twentieth century. Politicians, civil rights advocates, and descendants of victims have worked to challenge interpretations of state violence in Texas and complicate our typical understanding of the past. Tensions continue today between the celebratory tales of the Texas Rangers and Anglo vigilantes and the vernacular histories that address state-sanctioned denial of civil rights to ethnic Mexicans. Alongside those tensions are attempts to memorialize histories of violence as a means for reckoning with the past and its painful legacy. As they play out in the public arena, it is easy to forget that all these battles, at some point, began with individuals, with a father or sister or neighbor who was killed, and with the community that attempted to remember that life and called for justice.[80]

CHAPTER ONE

Divine Retribution

ROCKSPRINGS is the seat of Edwards County, located on the southwestern edge of what is known as the hill country, a region spanning twenty-five counties in central and south Texas.[1] The town is named after the natural spring waters that bubble up through the porous limestone rock that cloaks the area. It is known as the Angora goat capital of the world, and for most of the twentieth century the wool and mohair industry motored the economy for miles around the town. The rural population is currently just over 1,000 people and is isolated from other larger rural hubs by miles of meandering asphalt. If you come to Rocksprings from the south, you wind up Texas Highway 55. The two-lane highway scales the hills so close to the edge that the speed limit drops to twenty miles per hour for long, windy stretches. During large portions of this trip, you are without radio signal or cell phone reception. Those who dare to pull over onto the sliver of a shoulder can stand on cliffs that overlook deep and narrow limestone valleys. These white rocky ravines are spotted with cedar and mesquite trees and cacti that grow above short grasses. In the twentieth century, ranchers primarily used the rough terrain for grazing livestock, making this treacherous landscape home to cattle, goats, and barbed-wire fences. Twisting roads and a large population of white-tailed deer make traveling at dusk or dawn hazardous, but during these times, the rising and setting sun reveal some of the most breathtaking views in Texas.

The harsh and unrelenting beauty of Edwards County was the backdrop for the most well-known and widely documented lynching of a Mexican national in the United States. On November 2, 1910, forty-year-old Effie Greer Henderson lay dead on her porch, shot once in the back and once in the head. After discovering his wife's body, Lemuel Henderson reportedly rode two miles on horseback to the nearest ranch with a phone to call the police.[2] A posse of family members, neighbors, and local officers set out to look for answers. The next day they apprehended and arrested Mexican national Antonio Rodríguez. The local sheriff placed Rodríguez in the Edwards County Jail, located in the Rocksprings town square. That afternoon, a mob grabbed the accused from his prison cell and marched him toward the edge of town. They bound him to a barbed mesquite tree and encircled him with limbs of dry cedar. They saturated the heap with kerosene, set it on fire, and burned Rodríguez alive.[3]

Despite the geographic isolation of Rocksprings, news of the murdered woman and the impending lynching spread like wildfire. Newspapers later reported that thousands of local residents attended the lynching. The crowd that gathered to marvel at the sight of a live man burning to death went to great lengths to be there. Over the next days, weeks, and months, reporters, diplomats, and state police would descend on Rocksprings to investigate the lynching of Antonio Rodríguez.

The Rocksprings lynching has captivated historians and local residents alike for over a century. The size of the viewing party alone stands in contrast to most other lynchings of ethnic Mexicans in the United States, which typically took place at night and outside of public view. Likewise, the decision to burn Antonio Rodríguez alive, in a slow, deliberate, and ritualized death, was more like the lynchings suffered by African American victims, which took place in public squares in broad daylight. In addition, the lynching prompted international protests and calls for mob participants to be prosecuted. Finally, the lynching itself has endured as the most well-documented incident of anti-Mexican mob violence in the twentieth century. Newspapers foreign and domestic, consulate records, and state records preserve the details of this act of vigilante brutality. Historians' accounts

Reminders of the lynching of Antonio Rodríguez in 1910 are inscribed on the landscape in Rocksprings. This marker rests under a live oak tree in Edwards County cemetery. Local residents who spoke with the author did not know who paid for the granite headstone. Author photo, August 17, 2009.

further entrenched this story along the borderlands.[4] The written archive provides access to journalists, students, elected officials, diplomats, and historians that interpreted the lynching for various constituencies. But there is a larger story to tell that is not preserved in the written record.

Tensions in the town of Rocksprings continued to smolder long after the embers of the pyre of 1910 went cold. Memories of the event lingered in the rural community. Residents circulated stories among themselves and passed the history on to the next generation. After the reporters, diplomats, state police, and visitors left the isolated rural community, the Anglos and Mexicans in Rocksprings would be left with the remains of the brutal lynching and all it entailed.

It would be difficult for those in Rocksprings to forget the tragic events that took place. After all, there are reminders all over town. The county jail where the mob removed Rodríguez from police custody still stands in the town square, adjacent to the courthouse, still in use over a century later.

These matching buildings of white limestone sit on manicured lawns that are the site of town gatherings and are draped with decorations during holidays. At the Edwards County cemetery, a granite tombstone reads "Antonio Rodriques [sic] Died November 3, 1910 Burned at Stake." Not more than fifty yards away stands the tombstone for Effie Greer Henderson, which reads, "Mother: Born July 20, 1869 Died November 2, 1910."[5]

In the century after Rodríguez's death, competing histories of mob violence would be inscribed in local memory and the landscape.[6] Depending on how a resident interprets the history of the lynching, reminders are imbued with different meanings. Whether these sites conjure sentiments of loss, injustice, or anger depends on the perspective of the viewer and which victim they mourn. Over a century later, the community of Rocksprings remains divided. Some continue to believe the lynching was an act of justice. Some argue that the lynching was an example of racism in action. Others would rather the history remain in the past. Just as the limestone county jail and the granite tombstones endured, so do frictions in the town. The lynching of Antonio Rodríguez, in other words, offers an opportunity to see the politics of memory on a local level.

Although hundreds of documented lynchings took place across the state, not all communities are branded as the site of a lynching in quite the same way. Conflicting accounts of the lynching circulated regionally and led to Rocksprings holding a reputation as one of the most racially hostile towns in Texas. Even the Texas State Historical Association's online encyclopedia, *Handbook of Texas Online,* includes a reference to the lynching in its entry for Rocksprings. The description notes that the town is the county seat of Edwards County, that it is one of the top producers of mohair in the world, and that it is located 100 miles west of San Antonio. The reference to the lynching itself is flanked by two mundane sentences: "The name of the town was originally written as two words, but it was changed after the first courthouse burned in 1897. The town drew attention from across the state and Mexico after the lynching of Antonio Rodríguez, who was accused of murder, on November 3, 1910. By 1914 Rocksprings had a population of 500 and a bank."

In this encyclopedia entry, the lynching is stated as fact and a crucial point of significance for the community history. The year 1910 became a signpost, like a major fire or significant population growth.[7] What did it mean for residents to live in a town defined and understood in relation to an act of mob violence? How did the community interpret and make sense of the past? Residents are still looking for answers.

On November 4, 2010, approximately fifty people gathered at the county cemetery in Rocksprings to recognize the 100-year anniversary of the murder of Effie Henderson and the lynching of Antonio Rodríguez. The group of Anglo and Mexican Americans, representing all ages, met at the Sacred Heart of Mary Catholic Church for a memorial service for the lynching victim. Later residents moved to the cemetery for a candlelight vigil where the group prayed, sang, and surrounded the local priest as he blessed the graves of the departed. During the mass, the priest led the residents in a prayer for the souls of Rodríguez and Henderson, for both families, and for the persons who brought them harm. The priest also prayed for residents to release any lingering grief or tension. He ended his sermon by asking God to give the residents of Rocksprings the strength to forgive and heal.

On November 3, 1910, a mob removed Antonio Rodríguez from the Edwards County jail in Rockspring and burned him alive at the stake. The same county jail is still in use today. Author photo, August 17, 2009.

The memorial service was a reminder of the histories of anti-Mexican violence that are embedded in the landscape and that reemerge in public memory. In Rocksprings the passage of time has not brought comfort or closure. Violence between neighbors magnifies the trouble with forgetting or remembering.

INTERNATIONAL NEWS

The Rocksprings lynching became the subject of newspapers in the United States and abroad. The widespread media coverage provides a record of international efforts by journalists to interpret the lynching for the public and to shape US—Mexico foreign relations. By the early twentieth century, newspapers had become popular vehicles for circulating ideas about race and nationalism. The press publicized racial violence through the re-telling of mob acts. Newspapers provided a site for debates that either con-demned or justified vigilantism. In the 1910s, English-language newspapers popularly justified the murders of men described as Mexican bandits as a necessary defense of Anglo livestock, property, and finances. In 1915 one article explained, "Lynch law is never a pleasant thing to contemplate, but it is not to be denied that it is sometimes the only means of adminis-tering justice."[8]

Newspapers represented the lynching of Rodríguez in 1910 as a means of protecting "property." To rationalize racial violence in Texas, residents and newspapers alike turned to familiar tropes frequently used in the Amer-ican South. During the Reconstruction era, Southern white men chal-lenged black men's rights by constructing the trope of the menacing black rapist who threatened Southern women. White Southerners regularly de-fended segregation and vigilante lynchings of African American men as necessary for protecting white women.[9] These defenses correlated with the typical public response to the Rocksprings mob. An editorial in the *New York Times* noted that "the action of the mob was justified as the lives of the ranchers' wives had been unsafe because of the attempted ravages of Mexican settlers along the Rio Grande."[10] The piece represented Antonio Rodríguez, and other "settlers" like him, as new arrivals to the US—Mexico border region, a group apparently prone to ravage and plunder. This re-porting borrowed from familiar justifications for mob violence, describing Rodríguez as a threat to Anglo women, and cast ethnic Mexicans like him as a dangerous foreign element in southwest Texas. The majority of the US press endorsed this use of vigilante violence and stoked national fears of Mexican nationals crossing the border. The murder of Effie Henderson, almost immediately overlaid with racial overtones, became sensational news.

Critics, both community members who fought against local racism and a wider group of reporters and organizations that protested US empire, challenged the use of violence in state-building efforts and protested the grotesque representations of Rodríguez as a danger to white women. For these journalists, the lynching became a symbol of US repression and injustice and an opportunity to denounce the brutality inflicted upon Mexican nationals and ethnic Mexicans in the United States. Accounts of the Rodríguez lynching in the Spanish-language press triggered immediate reaction in Mexico and across the American Southwest. Mexican journalists portrayed Rodríguez as a compatriot and vehemently condemned the act as an embodiment of American racism. The newspaper *El Debate* raged, "The iron hoof of the Texas 'Yankee' in his barbarous and savage sentiments of race hatred, is now trampling upon the Negro; but the rottenness of his core has spread out so as to wound and even kill a Mexican, by the iniquitous method of lynching."[11] The article suggested that without intervention, the brutality practiced on African Americans could continue to spread to all vulnerable groups in the United States.

The Spanish-language press gathered momentum from their coverage of the lynching and expanded their scope to protest American expansion more broadly. An editorial published in the Mexican newspaper *El Diario Del Hogar* criticized representations of the United States as a civilized nation. Instead, the editorial characterized the United States as "rabble from beyond the Rio Grande" and "the hungry condor of the North" that practiced "blood barbarism."[12] The US–Mexico War, which resulted in Mexico ceding half its territory to the United States in 1848, remained on the minds of Mexican nationals. "Not even today," the editorialists wrote, "are obliterated the traces left by your putrefying claws which in 1847, like hungry buzzards, you feasted upon Upper California, Texas, New Mexico . . ."[13] Anti-Mexican violence, in this case, was interpreted as a part of US colonization. Articles coupled violence with greed. One journalist labeled Americans "Giants of the dollar" and "barbarous whites of the north." The newspaper asked, "Where is the boasted Yankee civilization?"[14]

The lynching of Antonio Rodríguez helped Mexican journalists make the contradictions of American democracy and racism transparent.

These critiques reverberated throughout countries that had felt the wrath of US empire. Journalists as far away as Cuba criticized the lynching. One article drew parallels between the incident and violence on the island by exclaiming, "exactly the same thing happened in Cuba when barbarian US soldiers murdered two poor Cuban seamen in their boat in Coloma."[15] With ongoing American expansion into Latin America, the Caribbean, the Philippines, Hawaii, and Guam in the late nineteenth and early twentieth centuries, the lynching of Rodríguez felt all too familiar—in its essence if not its specifics—as part of a long and broad pattern of American aggression in numerous parts of the world.

Students in Mexico City circulated a pamphlet highlighting the irony of American politicians and newspapers that persistently portrayed Mexico as a backward nation. The lynching provided an opportunity to expose the brutality hiding in plain sight in American democracy. "Barbarous Mexico they call our country," the pamphlet declared, "they who applied the torch to the clothes of Rodríguez; barbarous Mexico, they, who defied and outraged the law, snatching from it a man whose life ought to have been sacred because it was under society's protection; barbarous Mexico, they, those organized assassins of defenseless strangers and oppressed Negros; barbarous Mexico, they, those idolizers of the dethroned king of the prize ring, Jim Jeffries!"[16] The students described Mexico as a nation where tribunals retained the power to punish alleged offenders and where "sentiments of humanity exist." They viewed the United States as united in white supremacy, rather than ordered behind ideals of democracy and civilization. Moreover, they criticized Anglo claims to racial superiority. They reminded Americans that when African American boxer Jack Johnson defeated Jim Jeffries, known to American boxing fans as "the great white hope," it shattered their imagined superiority of the white race to racial minorities.

Through their reports, the Mexican press seized on an opportunity to highlight the racism embedded in the American public and its institutions. They were acutely attuned to the long history of anti-Mexican and anti-black violence in the United States. In the newspaper *El Regeneración,* journalist Práxedis G. Guerrero wrote about Rodríguez's lynching as occurring "on the same piece of land that still has not escaped the shadow cast by the hanging of John Brown."[17] Guerrero thus tied the US history of lynching to its history of slavery by recalling the execution of the prominent abolitionist in Virginia in 1859. Guerrero sarcastically clarified that the mob was not made up of "hordes of cannibals, nor equatorial Africans, nor wild men from Malaysia, nor Spanish inquisitors." To the contrary, the white vigilantes were "descendants of Washington, of Lincoln, of Franklin," and the men were "well dressed, educated, proud of their virtues."[18] These articles exposed the deep roots of slavery and colonial violence in American democracy.

Interpretations of the lynching were also informed by a long history of American capital in Mexico. Antagonistic relations between the United States and Mexico turned to war in 1846, but American expansion continued well after the signing of the Treaty of Guadalupe Hidalgo in 1848.[19] Given the long history of US–Mexican tensions, American capitalist expansion in Mexico in the late nineteenth and early twentieth century carried particular weight. When Porfirio Díaz took the presidency in Mexico in 1876, he initiated a national modernization project that relied heavily on foreign investment. By 1911, foreigners controlled an astounding 80 percent of Mexican industries; the United States, not surprisingly, was at the top of this list, controlling 38 percent of this foreign investment. American companies controlled 75 percent of all Mexican mines, 72 percent of the metallurgical industry, 68 percent of the rubber business, and 58 percent of the nation's petroleum production. With over $1 billion invested in Mexico, American capital became a highly visible and dominating force in the early twentieth century. As Anglo ranchers rapidly accumulated property in the southwestern United States, the Díaz government welcomed ranchers to amass property south of the Rio Grande border. In 1902 Americans owned approximately $30 million in property in Mexico, but by 1921 American ownership had swelled to $125 million in property. By this time foreigners owned nearly half of the agricultural colonies in the northern states of Mexico.[20]

The lynching of Antonio Rodríguez, amid this broader feeling of American encroachment, inspired a rapid string of protests across Mexico. As news of the lynching spread, students and laborers took to the streets in Ciudad Porfirio Díaz, Guadalajara, Morelia, San Luis Potosí, Parras, Chihuahua City, Oaxaca, San Juan Batista, and Mexico City to express their

anger. Protesters targeted American stores, companies, and consulate buildings; threw stones at the homes of Anglo miners living in the border town
of Ciudad Porfirio Díaz; and reportedly burned American flags.[21] In Mexico
City, students argued that this history would forever leave a stain on American civilization "that can never be effaced and which provokes the loathing
of mankind."[22]

Student protests sometimes came at a high cost. The Díaz administration ordered law enforcement agents to arrest student demonstrators. As
many as three Mexican protesters died in Mexico City during a protest
when local police charged into the crowd with drawn swords. Police intervention led to the creation of El Pais, an organization that sought the
immediate release of imprisoned compatriots and demanded a full investigation into the lynching in Texas.[23]

Protests in Mexico stirred emotions across the northern border, where
some English-language journalists divorced the protests from the lynching
and instead highlighted the dangers to American civilians in Mexico. In
Mexico City, protesters broke windows at the home of US consul Luther T.
Ellsworth. During a protest in Guadalajara, while "defending his home
against a riotous attack" by protestors, Carlos B. Carothers—an American
citizen selling real estate in Mexico—claimed he shot and killed Jesús Loza,
a fourteen-year-old Mexican student, and wounded Prudencio Chávez.
The English press widely reported that Americans in Mexico lived under
imminent threat.[24]

Anti-American protests, as described by English-language newspapers, stirred fears of Mexicans seeking vengeance on US soil for Rodríguez's lynching. On November 14 the El Paso Times published an article
titled "Armed Mexicans Marching on Town of Rock Springs" that
claimed a Mexican mob had been sighted marching toward Rocksprings
to seek revenge.[25] Although a march through rough and unforgiving
terrain was unlikely, the rumors caught national attention. The New
York Times reported that more than 2,000 "Texas cowboys" descended
on Rocksprings to defend the rural community from the oncoming
Mexican demonstrators. While American readers prepared for news of a
battle in Rocksprings, only two days later the El Paso Times confessed
that the claims of encroaching Mexican demonstrators proved to be
mere rumor.[26]

DIPLOMATIC INTERESTS

Stirring newspaper reports on both sides of the border helped elevate the lynching of Antonio Rodríguez into a diplomatic dilemma for the United States and Mexico. As early as October 21, 1910, the American ambassador to Mexico, Henry Lane Wilson, filed a confidential report alerting Secretary of State Philander C. Knox to rising anti-American sentiment in Mexico. Wilson concluded that on the horizon he could see an international affairs crisis that "must be of vital importance to the American Government, to American commerce, and to American capital invested here."[27] In response to the report, President William Howard Taft telegraphed Secretary Knox, articulating full confidence in Díaz's ability to suppress protests and calm disturbances between the two nations.[28]

With little faith that local courts would hold mob participants accountable, Mexican consuls requested permission to conduct their own investigation in Rocksprings, which Taft approved. Knox, fearing that local residents might meet the diplomats with violence, telegrammed Texas governor Thomas Campbell and requested he provide protection for the Mexican consuls. Texas Rangers traveled to Edwards County and joined the county sheriff, taking on the responsibility of protecting the consuls from Texas residents. For a brief and unprecedented moment, the Texas Rangers, often the source of anti-Mexican violence, chaperoned Mexican officials investigating mob violence.[29]

While some Mexican officials were conducting an investigation in Rocksprings, others were searching for Rodríguez's surviving relatives in Mexico. On November 11 Mexican ambassador Francisco León de la Barra presented a claim for reparations to the US State Department in response to the Rocksprings lynching. The demand anticipated that the Texas judicial system would fail to convict residents who participated in mob violence. On November 18 the *El Paso Times* reported that any punishment of the Rocksprings vigilantes seemed unlikely. It alleged that even the Mexican community in Rocksprings did not show signs of protest over the lynching. The article noted a lack of remorse because "the entire town took part in the lynching," which made any convictions unrealistic. Nearly a month after the lynching, on December 15, Judge Burney convened the Edwards County district court and directed the jury to investigate the burning of Antonio Rodríguez at the stake.[30]

Despite being under scrutiny by Mexican officials, the grand jury would not indict mob participants. The vigilantes and local police who failed to protect Rodríguez would not be held accountable for one of the most brutal lynchings on record. The grand jury verdict came as no surprise. The citizens of Edwards County serving on the grand jury were not unlike other grand juries in Texas that consistently failed to indict mob participants. However, the absence of judicial and diplomatic resolutions signaled that violent racism would continue unchecked. This conveyed to residents that Mexican life remained vulnerable to violence.

Foreign investigations did little to change the failure of the state judicial system to prosecute assailants who participated in the lynching. Instead, the political responses by the US and Mexican governments helped manage the disturbance of international relations without directly engaging the ongoing racial tensions on the US–Mexico border. US district attorney W. H. Atwell was one notable exception; he used the lynching to reflect on the consequences of the lynch law in the United States. Atwell critiqued the US judicial system and its repeated failure to convict vigilantes. He found it indefensible that the US government did not offer a solution for state courts' systemic sanctioning of mob violence. The federal government, Atwell argued, needed to pass legislation giving federal courts jurisdiction to try American citizens charged with assaulting a foreign citizen. The speedy punishment of mobs, he believed, would remove imminent sources of war or trouble with foreign nations. He warned, "We understand that an assault on the Japanese on our Pacific Coast would instantly put an invading army in our Philippines . . . in the eyes of the foreign Nation the General Government is held responsible and the responsibility exists in the face of the fact that there is no National remedy."[31]

Atwell worried that assaulting foreign citizens in the United States could trigger war with foreign nations and make US territories and American-owned businesses abroad vulnerable to attack. In the case of Antonio Rodríguez, the lynching also brought about international tensions that impeded American commerce and citizens in Mexico. "Every American who is in Mexico is held liable for the assault because a Texas mob burned a Mexican," he continued, "The wrath cannot be limited to Texas. . . . National responsibility should have National remedy and National power to punish."[32] Atwell prodded the US government to take justice into federal hands, alleviating state governments of the burden of meting out justice to their residents. He argued that, for the good of the nation, assailants needed to be tried before a federal jury.[33]

Diplomatic calls for the US federal government to ensure prosecution of mob participants and to reduce lynchings in the United States echoed calls by Ida B. Wells-Barnett and other anti-lynching activists in the nineteenth and early twentieth century.[34] While activists described the inherent immorality and denial of humanity that resulted from lynchings, Atwell did not describe the victims of lynchings, the survivors, or the tormented witnesses as his primary concern. In his eyes, the abuse of foreigners in the United States threatened American citizens abroad but also American colonial and commercial holdings. In short, when local judiciaries failed to convict assailants who murdered foreign citizens, American racism became a threat to diplomatic relations. His plea, recognizing that lynchings threatened the security of America's empire, provided one avenue for mobilizing federal anti-lynching legislation. If the federal government was not interested in passing legislation to protect individual people, perhaps it would intervene to maintain control of its new territories.

Atwell's requests for federal prosecution of mob violence went unheeded. State governments continued to take the sole role of prosecuting, or failing to prosecute, vigilantes in the early twentieth century. With little faith in the Texas judicial system, Mexican diplomats began to look for justice in the form of US reparations for the murder of Mexican nationals in the United States.

For diplomats to succeed in their quest for financial reparations, they needed to find Antonio Rodríguez's next of kin. English- and Spanish-language newspapers were gripped by the search for his surviving relatives. Spanish-language newspapers introduced a nameless Mexican national in Guadalajara who claimed to be the wife of Antonio Rodríguez. Reports described a woman whose husband, with the same name as the lynching victim, worked as a stonemason in northern Mexico before he traveled to find work in Texas. After some time the wife never heard from her husband. When she believed her husband was the man lynched in Rocksprings, residents in Guadalajara began collecting funds for the widow. On November 19 *La Crónica,* a Spanish-language newspaper in Laredo, reported that Rodríguez's mother, Francisca Estrada, lived on San Felipe Street in Guadalajara, Mexico. His wife, identified by the paper as Genoveva Rangel, and his daughter Francisca Rodríguez, allegedly lived on Mungia y Angulo Street in the same town. The article reported that Rodríguez left the town just a few months earlier, on August 29, looking for work, and kept in communication with his family in Guadalajara by writing home. He made his way north, mailing letters home from several stops along the way to Texas. His wife, according to *La Crónica,* was "deeply affected by the death of her husband," and readers were encouraged to give donations for the family, who "remained in a precarious situation."[35]

English-language newspapers offered a competing account of the relatives of Antonio Rodríguez. On November 19, the *Advocate* of Victoria reported that Mexican consul F. de P. Villasana located Antonio Rodríguez's mother in the US border town of Eagle Pass. The article alleged that Rodríguez grew up and went to school in Ciudad Porfirio Díaz, where his grandmother lived, and that his mother lived in Eagle Pass at the time of the tragedy.[36] This article signaled a shift in how the English-language press would describe Rodríguez. Previous accounts described him as an isolated and menacing foreigner. This rhetorical move portrayed him as lacking local allies, as a dangerous man undomesticated by marriage or fatherhood. When Mexican consuls increased pressure on the US government for reparations for the murder of a Mexican national, describing Rodríguez as a foreigner became less lucrative. To the contrary, it put the US government at risk of paying an indemnity. Not long after Mexican investigations into the lynching began, the mainstream media shifted its portrayal in order to prove he maintained American, not Mexican, citizenship. As an American citizen, Rodríguez's relatives would effectively be denied the support of Mexican diplomats.[37]

On November 13 the *Dallas Morning News* broke a story that Rodríguez might have been born somewhere in New Mexico. While no source could be quoted, the newspaper reported, "If this should prove to be the case of course the Mexican government would be obligated to withdraw its protest and demand no reparation."[38] In this light, the Mexican government would no longer have grounds to lead an investigation and charge the United States for the murder of its citizen. The lynching of Antonio Rodríguez would remain a domestic issue free of intervention from Mexico.[39]

Here we see, once again, how the people killed were quickly subsumed by larger stories. As the diplomatic power struggles between Mexico and the United States took precedent over seeking justice for the victims of vigilante crimes, neither Henderson nor Rodríguez was at the center of media concern. Instead, losing sight of the lynching of Antonio Rodríguez, as well as the murder of Effie Henderson, international diplomacy and the US press saw either the United States or Mexico as the "aggrieved party" in the crimes in Rocksprings and the protests in Mexico.

Journalistic accounts and government documents proved limited in reckoning with the violent murders of Henderson and Rodríguez. After all, newspaper readers knew little more about Effie Henderson than they did about Antonio Rodríguez. Journalists and historians alike have given little attention to the lives of those in the Henderson family. Most focused on the lynching without considering those impacted by violence.

US census and family records provide a few insights into the Henderson family. Lemuel Kenneth Henderson, known as L. K., was born on October 25, 1849, to Sam Henderson and his wife, Emily Winkler, who lived with their four children on a plantation in Mississippi. On his twentieth birthday, Lemuel struck out on his own for Texas. Riding a mule and with only "one thin dime in his pocket," the young Henderson lived for a time in Gatesville, in east Texas, where he met and married Virginia Dodson. Soon he and his brother-in-law Will Dodson partnered to start a cattle business.[40] Family histories report that in the spring of 1880 Henderson moved his herd to Edwards County, where he and his wife raised their daughters, Mary Eunice, Laura Alline, and Nancy Holland. Four years later, on July 9, 1884, his wife died.[41] On July 2, 1885, L. K. Henderson joined Texas Ranger Company F of the Frontier Battalion under William Scott. When state authorities reduced the force, Henderson returned to raising livestock. During this time he met Effie Greer, who came to Texas from Arkansas to teach school in Green Lake. Henderson married her in February 1893.[42] This second marriage generated five children: Brownie, Gus, Thomas, Hadie, and Lemuel Kenneth Jr., the youngest born in 1910.[43] That year would be a watershed in the Henderson family.

Just months after census officials visited the Henderson home, the murder of Effie Greer Henderson forever changed the household. She was survived by her husband and five children. In 1912 Mollie Green, who came to the Henderson ranch to teach the children, married the twice-widowed Henderson, nearly forty years her senior. Together they had two daughters, Ouida and Onie.[44] Hadie Henderson Seale wrote in a short biography of her father, "Thus lived and died a man, honest to the nth degree, with a tender heart as a woman's, a true friend and a wonderful father."[45] Effie Henderson, then, was a former teacher, a mother, and the wife of a prominent Anglo rancher and former Texas Ranger. The murder of a well-known Anglo woman with this social status, allegedly killed by a Mexican national laborer, transgressed race and class.

In the press, more details about her life or her family were omitted. Instead, across the country the lynching of Antonio Rodríguez, the Mexican protests that quickly followed, and questions about his origins provided gripping headlines. The English-language media soon even stopped including the name of the Henderson family in their accounts. The sensational reporting on the Rocksprings lynching exposed a tendency for newspapers to capitalize on the murder of an Anglo rancher's wife to stimulate an emotional rise in their readers, while simultaneously omitting insight into Henderson. Paradoxically, journalists who justified the lynching gave little attention to the tragedy of Henderson's murder.

In the United States, most of the English-language press expressed moral outrage about both the murder of Effie Henderson and the responding anti-American protests in Mexico. They excused the lynching culture in the United States and called for vigilance against the ever-present danger of retaliation at the US–Mexico border. In sharp contrast, the Spanish-language press expressed moral outrage about the lynching of a Mexican compatriot. The event became symbolic of a longer history of American colonial violence and racism practiced against its own citizens. For these two competing press circuits, the race, gender, and nationality of Henderson and Rodríguez mattered more than the individual identities of the two victims. In the media, the lynching of Antonio Rodríguez became a platform for journalists to claim a moral authority to criticize the neighbor across the border.

The widespread media coverage across the United States and Mexico would ensure that anti-Mexican violence in the United States influenced international power negotiations and shaped anti-American sentiment in Mexico. These reports offered little insight into the lives of Henderson, Rodríguez, or their surviving relatives. Instead, they stoked the flames of tensions between citizens of the United States and Mexico.

Rocksprings would eventually fall from the headlines of the national news and diplomatic agendas. On November 19, 1910, Francisco Madero crossed into Cuidad Porfirio Díaz and delivered a plan that called for a revolution to overthrow the Porfirio Díaz regime in Mexico. The start of the Mexican Revolution soon replaced the name Antonio Rodríguez with Francisco Madero in the media. One local historian wrote that just as quickly as Rodríguez escaped from obscurity, he would "disappear from the international scene and rapidly become a forgotten man."[46] However, measuring the significance of a lynching merely by tallying newspaper headlines misses the lasting effects on local politics and on communities that lived in the wake of mob violence.

BORDER JOURNALISTS, CIVIL RIGHTS, AND THE ROCKSPRINGS LYNCHING

International news coverage brought attention to the small town of Rocksprings, but presses in south Texas continued to circulate stories of the lynching long after 1910.[47] In some border towns, English-language journalists were sensitive to the ongoing social influence of ethnic Mexicans and the new Anglo settlers in the region. They covered the lynching with caution to avoid antagonizing readers. Spanish-language newspapers in the region, on the other hand, powerfully condemned the news of the lynching to inspire civil rights campaigns. Spanish-language presses, circulated widely on both sides of the international border, protested systemic discrimination against ethnic Mexicans in schools, labor, and the judicial system. Aside from the diplomats, who represented national interests and all of whom were male, a small group of journalists writing in Spanish as well as a larger group of women living in the borderlands would play an important role in providing accounts of the lynching that lamented the death of Antonio Rodríguez.

In the early twentieth century, ethnic Mexicans maintained social and political clout in border towns like Brownsville and Laredo. The local English-language press thus attempted to strike a delicate balance when reporting on the Rocksprings lynching. For example, an editorial in the *Brownsville Herald* outlined Henderson's murder as a tragedy but made it clear that Texans should deplore vigilante violence no matter the cause. The article condemned Rodríguez as guilty of a "most atrocious deed" that understandably could possess men to act so violently. Trying to comprehend the events leading up to the lynching, the author explained, "one can realize the terrible heat of passion which possessed those men as they stood before the lifeless form of that young mother, violated and then ruthlessly shot to death, and how they must have sworn to execute a fearful vengeance upon the fiend that committed this awful crime."[48] With this description of Rodríguez as a "fiend" who violated Effie Henderson, the murder of the young mother was presented as understandably driving a mob to lynch him.

The *Brownsville Herald* also warned that, despite Henderson's gruesome death, seeking vengeance took on the work of the devil. The article continued, "It is not for human beings to assume the offices of Satan. The punishment of the diabolical deeds should be left to that potentate of the lower regions to those whose keeping the souls of such wretches as Rodríguez must be consigned." Further, the newspaper saw it as the duty of the Texas press to employ its power to allay any further "evil" that could result from the murder and the lynching in Rocksprings. The press, the editorial argued, had the potential to misconstrue public perceptions of Texans, of race relations in the state, and, perhaps more important, of ethnic Mexican men. Just as the Rocksprings residents did not represent all of Texas, so the press also needed to stress that Rodríguez did not represent his race. "The 100,000 Mexicans living in Texas constitute as a rule a peaceable, law abiding body, whose men have the highest regard for women," the article declared.[49]

The *Brownsville Herald* editorial openly condemned the mob violence in Rocksprings and the prevalence of the lynch law in Texas. It even went so far as to defend the reputation of ethnic Mexicans and described the events in Rocksprings as a "double outrage." While this piece articulated the murder of the young Effie Henderson as the catalyst for mob violence, it argued that no crime could justify vigilantism. The *Laredo Times,* the major English-language newspaper in the city, likewise openly condemned the mob violence in Rocksprings and the lynch law in Texas. The press in Laredo covered anti-Mexican violence as well as the efforts of local residents to protest the ongoing discrimination, segregation, and violence.

The Spanish-language press in Texas gives insight into a dynamic border community that moved fluidly back and forth across the Rio Grande both for business and for pleasure and also to organize against racism and discrimination. In San Antonio, *El Regidor* echoed Mexican journalists' critiques of the contradictions of American "civilization." One article described tensions in the Southwest as "tremendous" and declared that the same Americans who committed such crimes and diminished Mexico "will never deserve the label civilized."[50]

Anti-Mexican violence remained a topic for the newspapers because lynchings continued. In June 1911 *La Crónica,* a Spanish-language newspaper owned by the Idar family of Laredo, profiled a Mexican boy slain at the hands of a Texan mob. In June the local authorities in Thorndale arrested fourteen-year-old Antonio Gómez for murder. Accused of stabbing a local store owner, the mob removed Gómez from jail and hanged him from a telephone pole. The Thorndale mob, they reported, capped their murder with a terrifying display, tying Gómez's corpse to a buggy and dragging it through town. Some English-language newspapers in Dallas and Beaumont condemned the lynching and expressed lost confidence that local authorities would promptly prosecute mob participants. Their concerns proved correct. In November 1911 a grand jury failed to indict one such participant, Z. T. Gore, for his involvement. On February 27, 1912, a grand jury in a new venue took only twenty minutes to acquit Garrett F. Novack, Ezra W. Stephens, and Henry Wuensche.[51] The journalists at *La Crónica* reported outrage at the newest terror of lynch mobs targeting children. In a series of articles, one titled "Cobarde Infame e Inhumano Lynchamiento de Un Jovencito Mexicano en Thorndale" and another "Lo Mismo de Siempre," the newspaper chronicled the Gómez lynching, as well as another attempted lynching, of León Cárdenas Martínez in Pecos.[52] In May 1911 fifteen-year-old Martínez stood accused of murdering an Anglo teacher, Emma Brown. Texas courts sentenced him to death by hanging and called in the Texas Rangers to prevent a mob from lynching the teenager. In a report by the Mexican ambassador, the boy's father explained that after being arrested, authorities placed a double-barreled shotgun to his son's head and coerced him into confessing to the murder. The efforts by diplomats and journalists failed to save the teenager. Martínez was hanged on May 11, 1914.[53]

In stark contrast to the English-language national news coverage that prematurely convicted lynched residents or justified mob brutality, presses in south Texas, like *La Crónica,* offered a narrative lament of the brutality of anti-Mexican violence.[54] *La Crónica* published editorials calling for the unification of ethnic Mexicans for protection against officially tolerated racial violence along the border.[55] In June 1911 activists heeded these calls and in San Antonio organized La Agrupación Protectora Mexicana (Mexican Protective Society) to provide legal protection for ethnic Mexicans from vigilante practices.[56]

Anti-Mexican violence proved to be a catalyst for rallying residents on both sides of the border. The Idar family helped organize El Primer Congreso Mexicanista (First Mexican Congress) on September 16, 1911, which brought together Mexicans from across the state of Texas and the northern region in Mexico. The conference addressed rapidly growing economic disparities between Anglos and ethnic Mexicans, racial violence, labor exploitation, inadequate educational opportunities for Mexican students, women's rights, and the growing number of laws and policies that legalized segregation in south Texas.[57] Situated on the US–Mexico border, Laredo functioned as a central meeting place for ethnic Mexicans in south Texas and in the Mexican border state of Coahuila. The city's self-described Texas-Mexicans had significant influence in the area's political, educational, and cultural life.[58] The congress's delegates used their social clout to critique anti-Mexican violence and institutional racism in Texas. Several speakers at the conference referenced the lynchings as a motivating factor for organizing the Congreso. At the conference La Agrupación Protectora of San Antonio congratulated the many women who had spoken out publicly on the violence against ethnic Mexicans.[59]

The same weekend, women had their own conference. Jovita Idar, writer for *La Crónica,* became the first president of La Liga Femenil Mexicanista (League of Mexican Women). The league included a cross-class, transnational group of women in Laredo and Nuevo Laredo, Tamaulipas, Mexico. Delegates to the conference included professional and working-class women from across the state, and organizers encouraged the women to see beyond patriarchal social hierarchies within their own communities. They encouraged women to pursue educational opportunities and work beyond their domestic spheres. In their speeches, women also addressed the need to provide educational opportunities for Mexican children and echoed efforts to end racial violence. They promoted children's bilingual education, organized aid for immigrant families, protested the working conditions of laboring women (particularly the *lavanderas,* women who washed clothes, and agricultural workers), and advocated for women's suffrage.[60]

Participants in both conferences hoped to develop long-range solutions to the various problems facing ethnic Mexicans in Texas by creating an organization with chapters located across the state. Men and women with American and Mexican citizenship formed La Gran Mexicanista de Beneficencia y Proteción. Participants, like the Idar family, would continue their efforts to fight discrimination and exploitation. *La Crónica* and other Spanish-language newspapers, such as *El Clamor Publico* and *El Fronterizo,* continued to publish anti-lynching editorials.[61] The lynching of Antonio Rodríguez lit a fuse that mobilized civil rights efforts.

Jovita Idar, in particular, is well known for being a bold journalist and civil rights pioneer who took risks in challenging both the local political conditions in Texas and Mexico and US government efforts to militarize the border. After the passing of her father, Nicasio Idar, the press closed and Jovita continued writing for the Laredo newspaper *El Progreso.* In 1914, the newspaper caught the attention of Texas governor Oscar Branch Colquitt, who ordered the Texas Rangers to shut it down. In defiance, Idar stood in front of the printing operation and refused the agents entry into the building. In 1916 she wrote vehemently opposing Woodrow Wilson's decision to send more US troops to the Rio Grande.[62]

The Spanish-language press on the border provided an important alternative account, one that challenged mainstream celebrations of mob violence, criticized the failures of the judicial system, and mourned the lynching victims. Like anti-lynching activists writing for the National Association for the Advancement of Colored People (NAACP), they publicly denounced the immorality of lynchings and humanized those condemned by the mainstream press.[63] The Rodríguez lynching was exceptional in the widespread coverage it received. In other cases of racial violence, publications in south Texas offer some of the only written accounts of anti-Mexican violence. They were also important for journalistic accounts untainted by racist assumptions of the victims' guilt.

LIVING WITH MEMORIES OF RACIAL VIOLENCE

Media coverage of the Rocksprings lynching in the international press and local newspapers created a written record. Despite this, most residents who over the following century circulated the memory of the lynching have not relied on historical archives to support their stories. Instead, they continued the tradition of sharing oral histories with the next generation. This method also privileged local knowledge of the past that challenged sensa-

tionalized reports or newspapers justifying vigilante violence against racial minorities. Examining surviving memories offers an opportunity to
gain insight into the social significance of the lynching in the late twentieth and early twenty-first century.[64] Locally, by the twenty-first century
the diplomatic crisis between the two nations had largely been forgotten.
After all, the intervention of diplomats did little to change the course in the
region. Instead, local accounts kept the memories of Effie Henderson and
Antonio Rodríguez central in their histories.

People remembered and retold these accounts in an episodic fashion.[65]
For this reason especially, it is difficult to study how memories of the Rocksprings lynching evolved or changed over the course of the twentieth
century. We know that the lynching, and anti-Mexican violence more
broadly, shaped civil rights efforts for residents like the Idar family in Laredo
and contributed to the founding of the League of United Latin American
Citizens. And yet, until more documents or memories are uncovered, we
do not know how the lynching was remembered, passed along, and revis-
ited in the first half of the twentieth century. During the civil rights era,
as we will see, scholars made great efforts to collect the history of ethnic
Mexicans in the United States. The history of the lynching of Antonio
Rodríguez resurged in private conversations, in public conversations, and
eventually in academic writing.

During the 1960s and 1970s, Mexican American political activism dis-
rupted Juan Crow laws of racial segregation that disenfranchised and segregated ethnic Mexicans. Participating in what has been described as *El
Movimiento,* the movement—also known as the Chicano Movement—
activists linked the US war in Vietnam to a long history of racial violence
on US soil. As the political climate of the 1960s challenged injustices across
the country, news of Mexican American laborers joining the United Farm
Workers in California labor strikes spread throughout the region and mobilized youth activists in the Southwest. A series of labor protests in south
Texas, known as the Valley strikes, succeeded in mobilizing protests for
civil rights. From struggles for political rights, labor justice, educational eq-
uity, and desegregation, to protests against the Vietnam War, demonstrations
spread across Texas in both urban and rural areas, linking this area to national civil rights efforts. Historian David Montejano described the significance of these efforts in Texas: "By the late 1960s, this movement was
seriously challenging the dual structure of rural society. While the protest

of the 1950s had focused on the cities, that of the 1960s was centered in the countryside."[66] By 1963, organizing for Mexican American voting rights in Crystal City, a rural community in south Texas, had resulted in the election of its first ever completely Mexican American city council. This effort overturned the town's long-standing Anglo political structure and longtime patterns of voter disenfranchisement.[67]

For movement organizers, especially college students, teaching the history of conquest, colonization, racial violence, and inequality in local communities helped them develop a critical consciousness. Students circulated reading lists of history, poetry, and literature to inspire pride in a young generation. Aside from reading books, organizers honored the histories preserved in community memory that challenged mainstream narratives. Understanding experiences of discrimination and racism over time helped a younger generation understand their struggles as a part of a longer pattern. In particular, some young activists tried to understand the disproportionate number of Mexican Americans fighting and dying on the front lines in Vietnam in the context of ongoing brutality at the hands of police in their communities at home. This called for histories that reflected on the long-standing vulnerabilities of minority bodies. Violence, indeed, was a consistent factor shaping the lives of ethnic Mexicans in the borderlands. Remembering the histories of violence became critical for educating a new generation.

The lynching of Antonio Rodríguez was the basis for another powerful critical memory of racial violence. I first learned about the Rocksprings lynching in August 2005, while conducting oral histories with residents who had been involved in student protests in the 1960s and 1970s. I interviewed my uncle, Rogelio Muñoz, who migrated to the United States with his family in 1953 at the age of five. He grew up in Uvalde and attended segregated public schools. As a teenager, Muñoz and others participated in the Uvalde chapter of the Mexican American Youth Organization, a civil rights group with chapters in rural communities across the state. Later, as a college student at the University of Texas at Austin, Muñoz enrolled in Chicano Studies courses and continued his efforts as a civil rights organizer.

When I asked what prompted his involvement in El Movimiento, he described his experiences as a Mexican immigrant growing up in Uvalde and his work as a field laborer and sheep shearer. While laboring in the Texas hill country, he learned the story of Rodríguez's lynching. Sitting around a campfire, exhausted from wrestling 200-pound animals, engulfed by the scent of burning cedar, Mexican laborers shared the story of a mob of Anglo vigilantes who lynched a Mexican man in Rocksprings for having had intimate relations with a white woman.[68] The often-quoted dedication in Américo Paredes's first book, *"With His Pistol in His Hand,"* thanks old men who sat around summer nights "in the days when there was a chaparral, smoking their cornhusk cigarettes and talking in low, gentle voices about violent things; while I listened."[69] These oral traditions of sharing community memories took place within masculine spaces such as a laborers' campfire. The literary scholar Sonia Salívar-Hull reminds us of the histories also preserved "in the lacunae of family stories" shared by grandmothers and great-grandmothers in "late-night kitchen-table talks."[70] These memories provided history lessons to guide a new generation on how to navigate the racism and gendered expectations they would encounter in daily life.

Muñoz carried this memory with him. As a volunteer for Volunteers in Service to America (VISTA), a youth service organization established by Lyndon B. Johnson, Muñoz trained a new volunteer, Joaquín Rodríguez, a student from Corpus Christi whose grandmother lived in Rocksprings. Remembering the story of the lynching he learned when he was younger, Muñoz asked Rodríguez to inquire whether his grandmother was familiar with the event. The two decided to travel to the small town and interview her for a class project. In the interview, Rodríguez's grandmother recalled that her uncle worked chopping and selling wood. In 1910, she lamented, some of the wood he cut was used in the lynching. The students submitted that interview for an assignment for their professor, Américo Paredes.[71]

Paredes, who had been key in preserving the *corrido* tradition—the oral tradition of storytelling through song—had encouraged his students to participate in efforts to document Mexican American history as they learned about it in his course. He shared with them the need to conduct oral histories, preserve records, and build archives for future research. The history of anti-Mexican violence thus gripped another generation. As a final assignment for a later course with George I. Sánchez, an emerging leader in the relatively new field of Chicano studies, Muñoz submitted an essay that studied the long history of anti-Mexican violence.[72] His college coursework helped confirm the vernacular histories he had learned while growing up in segregated south Texas.

The work of Muñoz and Rodríguez, as guided by Américo Paredes, to preserve the memory of the lynching of Antonio Rodríguez offers evidence of the efforts to document long circulated anti-lynching narratives. But this was far more than just the idle telling of campfire stories. Rather, these memories and their retelling were the flames that stoked a new generation's demand for civil rights. When asked what motivated his participation in the movement as a young adult, Muñoz responded by describing this long history of racial tensions between Anglos and Mexicans in Texas that he learned from his community and at college. After describing the lynching, he explained, "That's the kind of conflict that existed and where the guys wanted to come back and organize."[73] Just as moral outrage at the lynching of Antonio Rodríguez had mobilized ethnic Mexicans to political action in the early twentieth century, the continued circulation of the story in the 1960s helped mobilize young activists like Rogelio Muñoz to protest contemporary segregation and violence at the hands of local and state police. He and his fellow students found the motivation to return to Uvalde and other small towns to make social change.[74]

Memories of this lynching and the documentation of these accounts by scholars provide a unique opportunity to study one moment when informal circuits of alternative histories and academic attention converged. As a graduate student at the University of Texas at Austin in the 1970s, José Limón studied under the guidance of Américo Paredes and George I. Sánchez. In 1974 he published an article analyzing the significance of El Primer Congreso Mexicanista and telling the story of the Rocksprings lynching. He described the parallels between the plight of Texas-Mexicans in the early twentieth century and struggles in the contemporary Chicano movement. He noted that the pervasive problem of discrimination in schools, ongoing struggles for the restoration of land (particularly in New Mexico), protests against police brutality, commitment to women's rights and advancement, and dedication to cultural pride were all reverberations of earlier calls to action by Texas-Mexicans.[75]

Limón's early writing on El Primer Congreso Mexicanista and La Liga Femenil Mexicanista offered an important scholarly contribution to the history of political organizations and resistance by ethnic Mexicans in the United States. He offered a historical precedent for the struggles and strategies of the ongoing civil rights efforts. Equally important was his work to position the lynching of Antonio Rodríguez as an early example of discrimination and violence faced by ethnic Mexicans in Texas. This allowed activists in the 1970s to make sense of their continued struggles against police brutality by connecting their efforts to previous eras.

College coursework with pioneering Chicano scholars, however, could not answer all of Muñoz's questions regarding the lynching. Like the newspaper archives and government records that had documented the lynching a half-century earlier, academic publications analyzing the lynching did little to change the lived reality for local residents. Muñoz remained unsettled by the failure of judicial procedures to prosecute the mob participants. In part, this informed his decision to become a defense attorney and, eventually, a district attorney for Uvalde County.

Remembering and telling stories of racial violence functioned as a political act of resisting dominant historical narratives and provided solace to those left with the sting of injustice. This circulation of information among workers, family members, activists, students, and scholars across multiple generations demonstrates how narratives of violence have shaped memory and scholarship, its politics and practices.

CONFLICTING MEMORIES

Histories critical of racial violence had to contend with long-standing descriptions of the Rocksprings lynching that justified brutal vigilantism. Conflicting accounts coexisted in the same rural community. In Rocksprings there are two opposing accounts that describe how and why a mob burned Antonio Rodríguez at the stake on November 3, 1910. When I interviewed Nicholas Gallegos, then the Edwards County judge, he described two different versions of the Rocksprings lynching that continued to be shared in town. Just as with any story that has been told and retold for more than a century, the details have changed over time, and the emphasis varies widely depending on who is doing the telling and when, but in essence the story exists in two opposing versions. Each tends to make either Effie Henderson or Antonio Rodríguez the central victim.

One version describes the lynching of Antonio Rodríguez as an act of justice. He is portrayed as an isolated Mexican laborer who crossed the border in search of work and who, after encountering Henderson alone in her home, murdered her. Variants of this version describe Rodríguez as a disgruntled laborer on the family ranch, while others claim that the family had no prior connection to Rodríguez. In these accounts, the moral outrage is directed at Rodríguez, the inhumane murderer of a young (and, we are invariably reminded, white) mother. In Edwards County, Effie Henderson was a relative, friend, and neighbor to some who circulated the story. For those connected to the Henderson family, her murder remains central to the retelling of the history. In this telling, the Rocksprings lynching was a punishment fully deserved.

Local accounts that focus on the Henderson family's loss highlight what most historical accounts overlook. They do not usually record Effie Greer Henderson's name or list the surviving family members. In most publications, Effie Henderson is referenced merely as a murdered Anglo rancher's wife, or as Mrs. Lem Henderson.[76] The lynching of Antonio Rodríguez and its prominence in written accounts tends to overshadow a crucial detail: in November 1910 not one but two tragic events occurred.

The second version of the Rocksprings lynching is quite different. In Rocksprings, Rodríguez was not related to residents of the small community. His death did not signal a personal sense of loss similar to the death of Henderson. Despite this presumed distance, some residents interpreted the lynching as a brutal act of mob violence that denied a man his right to a trial. They retold the story as an example of the era's widespread racial prejudice against ethnic Mexicans. From this perspective, an Anglo mob took Rodríguez from his jail cell and burned him at the stake without a proper investigation or evidence that he murdered Henderson. The narrators express moral outrage at the mob and at the county judicial system for failing both to protect the prisoner and to convict the mob participants. These accounts insist that an innocent man was murdered and that, as a result, ethnic Mexicans lived in fear after the lynching.

Some of the accounts include suspicions about the true identity of the murderer. L. K. Henderson's name continues to be circulated as someone who could have killed his wife and framed an innocent Mexican laborer. Other residents insist we will never know the true identity of the murderer of Effie Henderson because the lynch mob took Rodríguez as a handy proxy. According to Judge Gallegos, the town generally divides along racial lines: Anglo residents believe Rodríguez murdered Effie Henderson while ethnic Mexicans believe the mob lynched an innocent man.[77]

Both accounts continue to be circulated. In the latter part of the twentieth century, siblings Hadie Henderson Seale and Tom Henderson, children of L. K. and Effie Henderson, publicly shared their account of the murder and the lynching. In 1984 the Rocksprings Women's Club Historical Committee published the book *Edwards County History* and dedicated it to the "beloved pioneers and to all who have contributed to making Edwards County what it is today." The book aimed to preserve a history of the founding of the county as told by individual families whose ancestors settled the area.[78] Hadie Seale contributed a short family history for the book. She depicted her father as an honest family man with a tender heart and included a brief account of her mother's tragic death. "On the afternoon of November 2, 1910," she wrote, "a Mexican national shot and killed Mrs. Henderson. No one knew why. He said she was mean to him—an impossibility, since she had never seen him before."[79] In this brief reference to the murder, Seale maintains that Rodríguez, an unnamed stranger to the family, confessed to murdering Henderson because she mistreated him. Seale made no mention of the lynching that followed. Instead, the narrative moved on to document the lives of the Henderson family after 1910.[80]

While many residents agree with Hadie Seale and Tom Henderson that Antonio Rodríguez shot and killed their mother, others, who believe in Rodríguez's innocence, suspect that the murderer was actually L. K. Henderson. Amid these competing narratives, some of which blame L. K. Henderson for the lynching of an innocent man, Seale's account publicly defended her father's character and declared him innocent of any involvement in his wife's death.

By writing a family history for *Edwards County History,* Seale inscribed this version of events into a published local history sanctioned by a local history committee. In small towns like Rocksprings, local libraries and historical organizations collect, preserve, and shape community histories. A library, after all, may be the only cultural institution in the town. Historical organizations, in particular, fill a void. The histories they publish or promote claim authority to represent the region. Whether or not Seale wanted to set a historical record with her entry, publishing her family history in the committee's collection gave credence to her account.

This was not the first time Hadie Seale's memories were preserved in a written record. In 1977 Herbert E. Oehler published an article on the lynching of Antonio Rodríguez in a local periodical, *Real West,* using newspaper articles and Hadie Seale's account. In Oehler's article, on the day of her mother's murder, Seale stayed home. At some point in the afternoon, "the serenity of the day was interrupted by the appearance of a roughly dressed Mexican who rode up to the house and dismounted from his jaded-looking horse." As she described it, the man wore a large black hat and carried a rifle in his hand as he dismounted his horse. The man asked Mrs. Henderson if he could speak with Mr. Henderson. After Seale's mother replied that her husband was tending to stock, she turned to walk into the house. Next, Seale recalled seeing the man raise his rifle without warning and shoot Effie Henderson in the back. After Henderson fell forward onto the floor, Oehler reported, "without pity the murderer placed the rifle to the back of her head and sent a bullet crashing through her brain."[81] The unnamed man then rode away toward Rocksprings without harming the two children.

Oehler's report continued by saying that Seale ran for help to Dora Castañuella, the wife of Manuel Castañuella, a laborer on the Henderson ranch. The family lived in a tent nearby, and Dora Castañuella reportedly heard the gunshots and hid in the bushes as a "very dark Mexican" rode passed them.[82] She then took her two children and the two Henderson children to hide until her husband and Mr. Henderson returned. Seale remembered that "Dora nursed her youngest child and mothered her and Lem, Jr. as if they were her own during the time that they waited on the hilltop." Oehler quoted a letter that Mr. Henderson wrote to his sister-in-law describing what he found when he returned home that day. Henderson wrote that Lemuel Jr. crawled over his mother after she was shot, and he was "bloody as beef when they handed him to me."[83]

Tom Henderson also relayed a version of his mother's death to friends and colleagues. When Henderson grew up, he became the sheriff of Rocksprings and worked for years with Vincent Vega, his deputy sheriff. I interviewed Vega in the gas station he owned in town. He told me that Henderson relayed bits and pieces of the story over the course of their time working together. According to Vega, Henderson recalled that on the day of his mother's murder, he, his father, and other laborers were working out in the pastures while his mother stayed home with her daughter Hadie and L. K. Jr., her infant son. On their return home after a full day's work, Henderson remembered hearing a baby crying. He entered the house and saw his baby brother trying to nurse from his dead mother. Both his mother and brother were covered in blood. Tom was nine years old. According to this version, the family and Mexican ranch laborers immediately knew that it was Antonio Rodríguez who had shot Effie Henderson because he was a disgruntled ex-employee. According to Vega, Henderson described the lynching as follows: "They caught [Rodríguez] getting water from a water trough, they brought him into town. Here there was a family by the name of Sandovales living near the north end of town. And [the mob] went and told that family what they were going to do with him. They said, 'We're going to do justice. We're going to kill him. Is it all right with y'all?' And [Mr. Sandovales] said, 'I guess so, can't do anything about it.'"[84] The account, passed along by Vega, accused Rodríguez of murdering Effie Henderson and represented the lynching as an act of vigilante justice.

The accounts by Effie Seale, Tom Henderson, and their father, L. K. Henderson, include some contradictory information about Rodríguez's relation to the family, but my interest in their accounts is in what they decided to include. Both orally and in print, the surviving family members condemned Rodríguez as the murderer and lamented the loss of their mother. They do not describe the lynching or the residents who participated in the mob. Instead, they emphasize the graphic memory of a bloodied L. K. Jr., crawling atop his mother and crying. This detail provides a tragic image of the loss of a young mother and recenters Effie Henderson as the victim of the tragedy in Rocksprings in 1910.

In contrast, accounts that have circulated through ethnic Mexican communities dispute Rodríguez's guilt. These accounts suggest that L. K. Henderson, or another, unknown resident, murdered Effie Henderson and that Rodríguez became a convenient proxy—an innocent victim of a murderer's attempt to cover his crime. The accounts are varied, and the accusations made about Henderson's involvement range in severity. Some speculate that he had a hand in her death because he had been previously widowed and remarried multiple times. The death of a previous wife and the murder of Effie Henderson mark him, in some local memories, as a reasonable suspect. In other accounts, Rodríguez is portrayed as an unfortunate laborer who—in an awful case of bad timing—happened to visit the ranch looking for work in the hours after Henderson shot and killed his wife. In still another version, Henderson shot his wife and later gave the rifle to Rodríguez, a laborer on the family ranch, and ordered him to hunt rabbits on the property, so he would be caught in possession of the rifle. Ideas about Henderson's motive range from a pattern of behavior in which Henderson violently moved from one wife to another, to punishing his wife for illicit relations with Rodríguez. In the end, residents who share this history are consistent in explaining that because of the lynching the town will never know who committed the brutal murder on November 2, 1910.

If, for various Anglo residents, the lynching of Antonio Rodríguez was remembered as a necessary evil and an example of expedient justice, for ethnic Mexicans there were multiple lessons to take away from the act of mob violence. One popular account depicts the burning of Antonio Rodríguez alive as important for understanding social relations in Edwards County nearly 100 years later. Vincent Vega, who worked with Tom Henderson, remembers the stories he heard from older Mexican residents who frequented the bar he owned in the 1960s and 1970s: "They took [Rodríguez] down the road five, six miles, according to older people, tied him to an oak tree, live. Put a bunch of wood, kerosene, and threw a match. And the Hispanic people who used to live here, at the time were young, I remember one guy, Luis Jimenez Sr., his parents told him that when [Rodríguez] was burning he cursed the county and town and said, 'Y'all gonna be cursed from now on.'"[85]

As a deputy sheriff under Tom Henderson for nearly twenty years, Vega witnessed a high number of violent deaths in Edwards County: sexual violence, including the rape and murder of multiple women; two cases of pedophilia in a local church; a number of suicides; and various unsolved murders. He continued, "One time we counted over one hundred murders for Edwards County. Doesn't have over three thousand people in the whole county."[86] The number of violent events left Vega convinced that Rodríguez had cursed the town. In addition to the violent crimes, the persistence of racial hostility between Anglos and ethnic Mexicans came up in oral histories relating to the lynching of Antonio Rodríguez. "It's always been like this," Vega explained, "It's not going to change. . . . In this town, like I said, I guess, Antonio when he cursed this town, everybody hates each other."[87]

Aside from the notion of the lynching as a curse that has plagued residents with hate and devastation, the story has carried particular messages

about pervasive racial boundaries in the twentieth century. Harkening back
to newspaper articles that justified the lynching as a means of protecting
ranch wives from the "ravages of Mexican settlers," accounts of the fate of
Antonio Rodríguez ultimately functioned as a warning about violent repression of interracial relationships in the region. As we have seen, Rogelio Muñoz first learned about the lynching from the laborers in the hill
country who shared stories during their evening meals. *Tacinques* (Mexican sheep and goat shearers) shared the story of a mob of Anglo vigilantes
who had lynched a Mexican man in Rocksprings for having had intimate
relations with a white woman.[88] In this account, Rodríguez met his fate
because he had an affair with an Anglo rancher's wife. For an agricultural
laborer to cross a boundary and have intimate relations with his employ-
er's wife remained uniquely charged because it transgressed social norms
that deterred racial mixing as well as class boundaries. The lesson was clear:
laborers in southwest Texas who transgress racial and class norms face the
threat of violence from Anglo vigilantes. To expound on the violent consequences, this version highlighted that in Rodríguez's case, as in most,
mob violence escaped legal prosecution.

These lessons might have been particularly important for laborers in the
sheep-shearing industry, whose profession necessitated frequent migration
within and outside of Texas. In 1883 William Landrum brought a herd of
150 Angora goats from California to Uvalde County and settled on the
Nueces River. As the goat and mohair industry became more lucrative,
other ranchers joined the endeavor, increasing the demand for *tacinques*.[89]
Mexican muscle made the profitability of sheep and goat shearing in the
hill country possible. Following the shearing season also required the
agricultural laborers to spend months separated from their families.
Jose Canales and his crew from Uvalde frequently started their season in
February, shearing angora goats in Texas, and then traveled through New
Mexico, Colorado, Wyoming, Montana, and Utah until finally returning
to Texas in October.[90]

While migrating to different ranches, laborers created a congenial community. They ate, slept, and worked at a campsite near the animal pen. After
a day of working, the men cleaned up and settled around the campsite to
eat dinner and entertain each other before sleeping under the open sky.
Isolated from their families back in Texas, the campfire became a site where
veteran shearers shared collective wisdom about the trade and life in general.

Jose Canales Jr. worked for his father's shearing company as a young boy and remembered that when the men sheared near Rocksprings they would tell a story of the lynching of Antonio Rodríguez. He remembered that the story was widely known and that the popular Mexican saying went, "Mucho cuidado con rocke'spring [sic]. Son muy desgraciados." (Be very careful in Rocksprings. They are disgraceful and miserable people.)[91] While Uvalde had its own history of racial violence, for residents in the region, the racial tensions in Rocksprings had a widespread reputation that encouraged ethnic Mexican residents to avoid the area or to travel through with particular caution.

The long periods of time spent migrating to northern states provided space for older generations to share community histories with younger laborers, but the travel also offered laborers exposure to race relations outside of Texas. For young sheep shearers without families in Texas or Mexico, this travel opened up prospects to start new families with women living in northern states. Presumably shearers experienced racial hostilities during their trips, but for those traveling, the lynching of Antonio Rodríguez proved an important reminder that crossing racial boundaries could have deadly consequences. In the twentieth century, the message from the violent act against Antonio Rodríguez rang loud and clear: Mexican men should not interact with Anglo women.

The practice of circulating histories of racial violence also extended beyond the campfire. Variations of the history circulated locally consider what occurred to the remains of Antonio Rodríguez. The story Judge Gallegos retells is one he learned at home from family. At the time of the burial, the cemetery was still segregated by race. A fence divided the "white" side of the cemetery from the nonwhite. He described a controversy over burying Rodríguez at the Edwards County Cemetery. According to the stories he heard, neither Mexican nor Anglo residents wanted the remains buried on their side of the cemetery. According to this account, to appease the residents, the grave was placed next to the fence marking the racial divide in the cemetery.[92]

Discussing this detail the judge described a longer history of racial segregation in Rocksprings that divided ethnic Mexicans from Anglos in residence, schools, and employment. Like nearly all the accounts of this area, the history of the Edwards County cemetery sheds light on the history of racial segregation in Rocksprings more broadly. As Judge Gallegos walked

me around the cemetery to point out the Rodríguez tombstone, he also
showed me a nearby grave with the inscription "Negro Woman." According to a story told to the judge by an older Anglo resident, an Anglo
rancher impregnated an African American woman in Rocksprings years
earlier. The rancher allegedly murdered the woman to prevent the birth
that would reveal he had engaged in an interracial relationship. The older
resident claimed that the judge could find a tombstone marking her death
at the cemetery. Although Gallegos could not know for certain, he believed
this grave marked another victim of racial violence in Edwards County.[93]
Looking back to one history of racial violence, as future chapters will show,
often reveal more histories of racial violence.[94]

MEMORIALS AND LYNCHING MEMORIES

Cemeteries hold within them community traumas and local histories.[95] In
Texas a history of racial violence, although discussed widely among residents, is not often officially acknowledged in public memorials. So it is all
the more remarkable that the remnants of this history in Rocksprings are
visible. In 1921 a local resident named Mr. Barnes sold part of his property
to Juan Vela to develop a section of the cemetery, divided by a fence line
reinforced with a row of trees, for ethnic Mexican residents not allowed to
bury their kin in the white cemetery. In both life and death, residents would
remain segregated.[96]

At the turn of the twenty-first century, the Rocksprings Cemetery
Association organized funds to publish a history of the cemetery that would
list the names of residents buried and map their graves.[97] Local resident
Romana Rendon Bienek became interested in helping to preserve the
names and locations of residents in the segregated portion of the cemetery.
Bienek started using the association's book, only to realize that residents
with Spanish surnames buried in the cemetery had not been included.
When she questioned the organization about the omissions, Helen Fred,
the head of the association, explained that the book was intended to preserve the history of the Edwards County Cemetery, which did not include
the area known as the "Mexican cemetery."[98]

Bienek's father's family, the Rendons, had deep roots in Rocksprings.
They moved to Rocksprings in 1923 and owned one of the earliest sheep
shearing companies. In the off-season the men in the family helped build

fences, and the men and women migrated around Texas to harvest crops in the fields. As a longtime resident, she recognized the racism and discrimination her family experienced as well as the ongoing tensions. She attended segregated schools and remembered that in the sixth grade her principal did not allow Mexican and Anglo children to interact. The Mexican school, a building still standing but now used for storage, is physically isolated from other school buildings, which helped ensure that Mexican and Anglo students were kept apart.

Bienek also noted that racism continued in the small town. She recalled that a few years before our interview, in 2010, her teenage daughter came home from school crying. Her boyfriend, an Anglo classmate, had ended their relationship because his parents did not allow interracial dating in their home. Bienek shook her head remembering the devastating timing of the breakup. The young couple had planned to go to prom, but by the time of the party her daughter's boyfriend was refusing to speak to her.[99] The racist refusal would be difficult enough for any teenager, but in the context of a tiny rural town, where classmates see each other every day, rejection because of one's race felt especially hostile. In the schoolyards, racial lines of segregation continued to be enforced by parents and their children.

Bienek took great offense at the Rocksprings Cemetery Association's book. She believed the book was tantamount to intentionally keeping the cemetery segregated. The exclusion of ethnic Mexicans from the historical preservation effort inspired her to take on the tedious project of piecing together a list of plots in the Mexican cemetery, one grave at a time. Although she worked full-time at the Rocksprings Insurance Company, Bienek searched through county death certificates before work and during her lunch break to compile a list of every death certificate with a Spanish surname. Bienek patiently walked the cemetery grounds with her list of names, mapping each section of the Mexican cemetery. The work was painstaking. The graves were not systematically organized, and many plots had tombstones with names too faded to read. Some graves were unmarked entirely. "I guess there was no order to it," Bienek speculated, "you found a spot and that's where you put them."[100]

To aid her efforts Bienek received recognition from the city council for her new organization, the Southside Cemetery Association. The organization solicited volunteers and eventually she received help from some high school students. Soon, elderly residents joined the effort and started to point out where friends and relatives had been laid to rest. On the nearly two acres of land, Bienek mapped 800 graves. By November 2010 only 100 plots remained unidentified. She decided her research would culminate in a book of her own, to document and preserve the history of the segregated cemetery.

The fence dividing the cemetery has since been removed, but the physical and emotional divisions in Rocksprings persist. As Bienek sees it, "You can see the line where it's been divided. It's, like, [literally] a line of trees. If you stand on one end and look towards your left you can see where there is a line of trees. That's where the fence line was and it used to have a small little gate."[101]

In addition to this trace of racial segregation, the tombstones in the cemetery reveal more about the region's violent past. While collecting names for the Southside Cemetery Association, Bienek looked at the county court house for Antonio Rodríguez's death certificate. She wanted to know whether they listed his death as a result of the lynching. Did it include information about his family? Who signed the death certificate? Although there was no document preserved in Edwards County, a reminder of his death is at the local cemetery. Walking past the grave that describes Rodríguez's violent death, shaded by a large tree, reminded Bienek of the local stories.[102]

Like Judge Gallegos, Bienek also heard that controversy had followed the burial of Rodríguez's remains and that residents had fought over whether the body would rest on the Mexican or Anglo side of the cemetery fence. There is a pink granite tombstone on the Mexican side of the cemetery that reads "Antonio Rodriques Burned at Stake November 3, 1910." Some residents claim that the marked grave is not the true resting place for the Mexican laborer. Augustine González, longtime Rocksprings resident and owner of a prominent shearing company, for example, grew up hearing about the lynching. In an oral history he described an unmarked tombstone that stands about thirty yards away from the "Rodriques" tombstone. The unmarked tombstone, also resting on the Mexican side of the cemetery, is a round stone with a hole for a single candle and a cement cross standing behind the stone. González, Bienek, and others believe that this is the actual resting place of Rodríguez.[103] These two graves do not stand in tension with one another. Instead, they help serve as a reminder that while the true location of Rodríguez's remains may continue to be unknown, local residents tell the story that someone took the time to treat the lynching victim with dignity and laid him to rest.

Some residents in Rocksprings believe that this unmarked grave is the final resting place of Antonio Rodríguez. At a memorial to mark the centennial anniversary of the 1910 lynching, residents gathered for a candlelight vigil at this grave in Edwards County. Author photo, September 10, 2010.

I could not find information about who paid for the tombstone to mark the lynching of Antonio Rodríguez. The etched letters on the rectangular block look relatively new, resting about six inches above an older unmarked concrete slab. Some suggest that the different spelling may be because a relative who traveled to Rocksprings decades later paid for the tombstone with the accurate spelling of the victim's name. Without more information, the only motivations we can assume about the anonymous effort is that someone, or some group, wanted the historical event to be etched into local memory on a tombstone. There is no poetic lament inscribed in stone, only the name, date, and method used to kill Antonio Rodríguez. The tombstone stands in the absence of a historical marker for the lynching or even a death certificate for Antonio Rodríguez.

Most Edwards County residents I spoke with knew the location of the headstone that has Antonio Rodríguez's name on it; a few people also knew about the unmarked grave. However, of all the individuals I interviewed, none knew, or had even thought much about, the final resting place of Effie Henderson. Judge Nicholas Gallegos believed she might have been buried in a family cemetery on their ranch; when I asked Romana Bienek, she responded that she had never thought about where Henderson might be laid. Neither of them believed that they had overlooked Henderson's grave, so prominently displayed in the Anglo section of the Edwards County Cemetery, right next to her husband Lem Henderson. I described the location of the graves I found when walking through the cemetery; Bienek was eager to visit the site and took careful notes. The two graves, like the competing histories, remained in close proximity to one another.

Although knowledge of the grave of Effie Henderson escaped most who critically remembered the lynching of Antonio Rodríguez, they were especially aware of reminders like the marked grave and the county jail. These became touchstones of their accounts and of the tours they gave me of the town. These reminders stood in tension with other, seemingly unrelated, public history markers. In their retelling of the past, for example, local residents returned to a historical event preserved by a historical plaque, which they saw as a reckoning that superseded the judicial system.

In the stories Rogelio Muñoz told me, he remembered an act of vengeance from God as a result of the lynching. The oral history the sheep shearers had passed on to Muñoz explained that a natural disaster, which had leveled the town, was "punishment from God" and retribution for the local failure to apprehend mob participants.[104] For some ethnic Mexicans who grew up in a climate of sanctioned extralegal violence, the only hope of redress may have been faith in a higher being as the executor of justice.

On April 12, 1927, a tornado tore through the town of Rocksprings, killing seventy-two residents, seriously injuring over 150 more, and leaving nearly 900 people without homes.[105] For a population of just over 1,000, the tornado was devastating. The American Red Cross and Mexican Blue Cross came to assist survivors at makeshift hospitals set up in the few remaining buildings. Mrs. J. W. Patton, designated head nurse at the makeshift rescue sites, described the devastation: "Twisted houses, smashed awry by side-winds, chairs lodged in church steeples, pieces of flesh and blood splattered everywhere, timbers piled in criss-cross over moaning and broken creatures."[106] Justice, as local residents remembered, had taken another form in Rocksprings.

It seemed that no one escaped the wrath of the tornado. To some it felt appropriate that the entire town, ethnic Mexicans included, felt the repercussions. Even those who did not participate in the mob, they believed, were implicated by the lynching. Vincent Vega's mother escaped death during the infamous storm but suffered a wooden two-by-four piercing her leg. She described the tornado as retribution from a higher power. According to Vega's mother, Perry Mase, identified by some residents as the man who threw the first match to ignite the flames at the lynching, died a particularly brutal—and symbolic—death during the tornado. Vega described high winds that launched a wooden post through Mase's heart, killing him instantly.[107] For some residents who lived in terror after the lynching and remained frightened by mob participants who walked freely in town, the devastation of Rocksprings, and the deaths of certain residents signified a greater act of justice.

This interpretation of the tornado is one strategy that helped some explain how God could let such violence take place. Similar accounts of divine retribution circulated throughout the twentieth century in Waco, over 250 miles northeast of Rocksprings, a town where as many as 15,000 gathered in May 1916 to witness the beating and burning of eighteen-year-old Jesse Washington. In May 1953 a tornado tore through Waco, killing 114 and destroying $51 million worth of property. Members of the African American community interpreted the tornado as divine retribution. The tornado, they recalled, tore through the same path the mob participants walked when they dragged Washington's remains through town nearly forty years earlier. Of this enduring interpretation, historian William Carrigan wrote, "Why has the folktale survived? At its deepest level, the narrative of the tornado was a survival mechanism designed to help black Wacoans cope with the lynching of Jesse Washington."[108] This interpretation challenged media depictions that justified anti-black violence, highlighted the injustice of mob violence, and gave some solace to those who remained plagued by the town's violent history.

The symbolic force attributed to the Rocksprings tornado, however, was overlooked by the local newspaper and public history efforts that reflected on the significance of the storm. Fifty years after the tornado, on April 8, 1977, the Edwards County newspaper, the *Texas Mohair Weekly,* published a cover story acknowledging the storm's anniversary and celebrating the town's perseverance. The *San Antonio Express News* dubbed Rocksprings "The Town That Wouldn't Die."[109] The theme of surviving adverse conditions in response to the tornado is preserved in public monuments throughout Edwards County as well.[110] A historical plaque commemorates the reconstruction of the county courthouse following the tornado.

People who recall an alternative interpretation of the storm imbue these public markers with different meaning. As former district attorney of neighboring Uvalde County, Rogelio Muñoz frequently traveled to the courthouse in Rocksprings. The narrative of supreme vengeance lingered with Muñoz throughout his adult life. For him the history of the tornado and the history of the lynching were intertwined. Viewing the courthouse plaque triggered memories of the story of the 1910 lynching, which became embedded—for Muñoz, Bienek, and Gallegos—in the physical buildings of the courthouse and the county jail, both of which survived the storm. Muñoz reflected, "Well, every time I go to Rocksprings there's a plaque at the court house and the plaque talks about the storm that occurred in the 1920s that came to the town. And the Mexicans believe that it was punishment from God for burning this guy."[111] The lessons of the lynching infused how Muñoz interpreted the histories of Rocksprings and historical markers in Edwards County. When reading seemingly unrelated historical markers, he recalled the sordid past of the town passed on to him by local members of the community. Without a historical marker for the lynching itself, this act of critical remembering gives insight into how residents with memories of racial violence engage with public monuments, historical markers, and the absence of public memorials to racial violence.

The omission of the history of the lynching from public memorials in Edwards County prompted some residents to take memorializing the event into their own hands. While conducting her research for the Southside Cemetery Association, Romana Bienek continued to be unsettled by the story of the lynching of Antonio Rodríguez. Coincidentally, her research in the cemetery overlapped with the 100-year anniversary of the event. Despite the passage of a century, she recognized ongoing racial tensions between residents who thought of Rodríguez as either a victim or as a villain. This continuing conflict encouraged her to organize a memorial service to help bring the community together to recognize the lynching as an injustice. She remained disturbed by the thought of Rodríguez's excruciating death and that he never received his last rites. Inspired to do something about it, she petitioned the Catholic Church's local priest to conduct a service in his name and to bless the unmarked grave.

To advertise the service, Bienek wrote a press release and circulated it to the local newspaper and newspapers in San Antonio. She worried that some, unfamiliar with the lynching, might doubt that it occurred. She decided to reprint an article from the *Philadelphia Public Ledger* published on November 13, 1910, that gave an account of the lynching. She described hopes to ease long-standing resentments: "It is time to close up old wounds and fix our future as each one of us can see."[112] The press release described the lynching of Antonio Rodríguez as an open wound dividing the community in Rocksprings and explained that organizers for the event hoped for an amicable gathering. Despite these encouraging sentiments, Bienek worried that some who disagreed with holding a memorial for an alleged murderer would misunderstand or misrepresent the efforts. Scheduled on the same day of the memorial was a high school football game against a neighboring rival. With so many from Rocksprings traveling to support their hometown team, she wondered whether anyone would come to the service.

On November 4, 2010, approximately fifty Anglo and Mexican American residents gathered at the Sacred Heart of Mary Catholic Church for a memorial for Antonio Rodríguez. When mass began, the priest asked how many at the service came for the memorial. All in attendance raised their hands. The gospel readings for the mass included "The Commemoration of All the Faithful Departed." When the time came for the priest to give his sermon, he asked whether any family members of Antonio Rodríguez sat in the congregation. No one present raised a hand. The priest then asked whether anyone who knew Rodríguez wished to say anything on his behalf. No one raised a hand. No one spoke until Romana Bienek, sitting in the back pew, filled the church with her bold voice. She described Rodríguez, as she had been told, as a Mexican laborer passing through the area in search of work. No living residents knew Rodríguez personally. Vincent Vega, sitting in a pew near the center of the church, followed her account by explaining the history he learned. Rodríguez was accused of murdering Effie Henderson and met his death in Rocksprings at the hands of a lynch mob. The priest seemed a bit baffled that no one in the church knew Antonio Rodríguez or his family. New to the area, he knew little about the history of the lynching itself. Indeed, it seems self-evident that memorial services are organized for family, friends, and neighbors. It quickly became clear to the priest that this was no ordinary service.

As these public testimonies lingered in the air, the priest continued his sermon and encouraged the community to pray for the souls of Antonio Rodríguez and Effie Henderson, for both of their families, for the persons who brought them harm. He asked for residents to release any anger or misgivings about past events. He asked them to pray for the strength to forgive and heal past indiscretions.

Despite the absence of living relatives, residents of Rocksprings felt the need to pray for the soul of Antonio Rodríguez for being the victim of an act of vigilante violence. The judicial system had failed to prosecute mob participants. A century later the organizers of the service looked for redress by recognizing an often-disavowed history of racial violence in Texas and mourning the dead.

On another level, it appeared that residents hoped the service would put to rest the history of the lynching as well as ongoing racial tensions in the community. Residents had grown weary, it seemed, of bearing the burden of the violent history. They prayed for a higher power to bring healing for both the victim of the lynching and for those who acted as witnesses. It is not surprising, then, that during the service, while some described the events of the lynching and while the priest led prayers for Antonio Rodríguez, some sitting in the pews cried in both sadness and perhaps relief.

After the closing prayers, the interracial group solemnly left the mass and moved to the cemetery for a candlelight vigil. The priest led the group in reciting the Lord's Prayer, and everyone sang "Amazing Grace." Following these offerings, the group of adults and children surrounded the priest with candlelight as he blessed the unmarked grave of Antonio Rodríguez with holy water. After several minutes of silent prayer, the group followed the priest as he blessed the graves of some family members of those present and the grave of Effie Henderson. The vigil started as the sun began setting, and by the time the priest finally blessed Henderson's grave the sky was dark and only candles lit the vigil.[113]

The memorial continued with participants gathering at a local community center across the street from the cemetery to drink coffee and eat *pan dulce* (Mexican sweet bread). Romana Bienek had printed copies of about ten different newspaper accounts of the lynching for participants to read and take home with them. As the residents mingled, the conversation sounded like what happens at most wakes: small talk about the weather and the local football team's record, interspersed with small references to the deceased and hopes that Rodríguez and Henderson would be able to rest in peace.

Lingering over the memorial was the fact that, in the midterm elections days prior, Republicans had regained control of the House of Representatives. It appeared to most that following the election of the first African American as president of the United States, a conservative backlash continued to bring racial tensions in Rocksprings to the forefront. During one trip to a local restaurant in 2010, the anger targeted at the US president was palpable. As customers ate the famed enchiladas from the Mexican American–owned King Burger, I overheard patrons cussing and hissing at Barack Obama's image on the television screen. The volume was too low to hear the president speaking, but the mere sight of Obama enraged some Anglo patrons in the restaurant.

In local county elections, racist rhetoric had again reared its head. Around Rocksprings some residents started a campaign to remove "those Brown people" from elected office. Romana Bienek explained that the campaigns for city council reignited racial tensions. Although she had felt racism in town previously, after the presidential election hatred and discrimination became more pronounced: "It brought up old wounds. . . . Oh my gosh we're going back!"[114] Just two days before the memorial service, County Judge Nicholas Gallegos lost to Republican candidate Souli Shanklin in the general election, and Romana Bienek lost to Republican candidate Joe Baker for the position of County Justice-of-the-Peace. A few years earlier the Rocksprings City Council had acquired a majority Mexican American council, but in the 2010 elections all the Mexican American members lost their seats. The newly elected city council was made up exclusively of Anglo residents.

These tensions permeated Rocksprings during the memorial. Vincent Vega reminded me during the service of what he had told me during our initial interview. He was the first Mexican American to graduate from the local high school in the 1950s; he lived through the era when residents were segregated residentially, in schools, and at the rodeo; and he remembered when Mexicans were banned from local restaurants. He seemed weary and doubted the possibility of change: "It's always been like this in this town.

It's not going to change. To me, it's not going to change. . . . It's just the way we're brought up. Hispanics are the same way here in town. In this little town, like I said, I guess Antonio, when he cursed this town everybody hates each other. We'll speak to each other, but that's about it. That's how things are. There's just too much hate."[115]

The Rodriguez memorial raises pressing questions about the lasting legacy of racial violence in Texas and concerns for how this history should or can be represented historically. In her book *Temporal Geographies,* literary critic Mary Pat Brady argues that categories of gender, race, and sexuality are created, and then enacted, both in words and in space. The colonization of the Southwest was executed, in part, through the organization of space and belonging. She argues that history is instrumental in this process. Histories written in books and taught in schools also use space to tell history. Monuments, historical markers, and named streets and parks help organize space according to the lessons of history. In Rocksprings, physical artifacts, like the marked grave of Antonio Rodríguez, inscribe the history of mob violence onto the landscape. The Edwards County Jail, from whence the mob forcibly removed Rodríguez before burning him to death, is another reminder of this history. Located in the center of town, the jail serves as lasting symbol of racial violence. If space is colonized, then it makes sense that, like Rogelio Muñoz and Nicholas Gallegos, residents informed by community histories of racial violence read public space through an alternative lens that laments the violent past.

Although vigilante violence forms an important part of history in southwest Texas, public memorials—officiated by the Texas Historical Commission in Edwards County—overlook these uncomfortable moments. Instead, most historical markers indicate a building, cemetery, military campsite, or an association the commission deems significant to the region's past. Markers in Edwards County recognize the prominent ranches in the region, the first Baptist and Methodist churches in local towns, old buildings such as the Edwards County Courthouse and jail built in 1891, and the headquarters of the American Angora Goat Breeder Association. No markers in Edwards County make reference to the lynching of Antonio Rodríguez. Instead, markers like the one memorializing the Coalson family as pioneers in the community, which stands outside the town of Barksdale, create a public memory of Native violence suffered by Anglo settlers. The marker installed in 1972 describes the murder of the Coalson family during a series of "Indian raids" on their goat ranch in 1877 and 1878. The plaque does not name the tribe or consider the long histories of the Kickapoo, Lipan Apache, or Comanche nations in the region. Rather, it recalls that US Army captains and scouts were called to collaborate with Texas Rangers in capturing the raiders. The posse failed to make any arrests. The inscription ends by listing the location of the victims' graves and describing the Coalsons as heroes in Texas history.[116]

This plaque, and others describing violent conflicts between Native Americans and both Anglo and Mexican settlers in the region, fail to give a complex understanding of these encounters. Instead, they serve to portray anonymous indigenous nations as hostile while congratulating Anglo heroics and survival on the frontier. At the same time, these memorials create a limited depiction of violence in Texas history by excluding mob violence in the state.

In part, the historical markers are certainly a reflection of the politics of the Texas Historical Commission, but they also give insight into local county politics. The state commission largely approved or rejected markers suggested by county historical commissions. Included in county applications for state-approved markers is a requirement that county commissions agree to pay for the costs of casting, installing, and preserving the marker. The histories represented in Edwards County are thus selected and funded by local committees. In the midst of civil rights movements in Texas, the county insisted on marking the landscape with simplistic and outdated tales of brave Anglos and savage Indians.

In 2006 the Texas Historical Commission publicly recognized the considerable power that county historical commissions maintained in curating histories officially recognized by the state. The commission instituted an application process for "Undertold Markers" that "address historical gaps, promote diversity of topics, and proactively document significant underrepresented subjects or untold stories." To establish a funding incentive for counties, the state agreed to pay the costs for creating the markers. To ensure that "untold" applications were submitted, the commission decided to open the application to any resident, rather than requiring that local county commissions submit the applications. This process, however, did not remove the influence of county historical commissions. After reviewing the proposals, if the state commission deemed an application for a historical event, place, or person worthy of a state historical marker, the county commission had to approve the marker before it could be installed. The county commission also had to approve the narrative inscribed on the marker.[117]

During the memorial service in 2010, Rocksprings residents asked that I submit an application for a historical marker for the lynching of Antonio Rodríguez. Although the centennial anniversary had passed, residents saw a need for official state acknowledgment of the history of racial violence and condemnation of mob brutality. I drafted an application that spoke to the significance of the lynching as the most well-known and widely documented lynching of an ethnic Mexican. The Texas State Historical Association rejected three applications for a state historical marker to designate the history of the Rocksprings lynching, in 2014, 2015, and 2016.

The Texas Historical Commission agreed to the historical significance of the event but rejected the application. County historical commissions are responsible in part for coordinating unveiling ceremonies and maintaining historical markers. With little support from the local county commission for a marker in Edwards County, the THC decided not to approve the application. My efforts to e-mail and call committee members in Edwards County resulted in little information regarding the application. The state committee instead decided to memorialize the lynching in a historical marker that would be placed in Webb County to honor El Primer Congreso Mexicanista in 1911, the early civil rights conference. The plaque makes mention of the broader lynching culture in Texas as causing concern: "Delegates frequently referred to the recent lynchings of Antonio Rodríguez in Rockpsrings and Antonio Gómez in Thorndale as examples of the dire threats they faced." Residents in Rocksprings who want to see the state historical marker acknowledging the significance of their local history have to drive approximately 200 miles south to Laredo for a visit.

CHAPTER TWO

From Silence

IN SEPTEMBER 1915 Jesus Bazán and his son-in-law, Antonio Longoria, faced a difficult decision. A group of armed men rode onto their ranch and stole horses and other supplies, though they did not harm anyone. Bazán and Longoria now faced a predicament. They had to decide whether to report the robbery to local police. On the one hand, they knew that if they reported the robbery to authorities, they could face the wrath of the group that raided the ranch and become targets for ongoing robberies, or worse. On the other hand, if Bazán and Longoria did not inform local authorities and the assailants were later arrested in possession of the stolen horses, the family could be accused of supporting what the government described as bandit activities.

That reporting a robbery to authorities might place someone in danger was unquestioned. The costs of being involved in bandit activity were high, as most accused of banditry were denied judicial protections and were routinely shot on sight. With the recent violence, Mexican residents, regardless of their nationality, class, or social status, remained exposed to the risk of violent arrest or extralegal violence. That summer a group of Mexican raiders coordinated attacks on new Anglo infrastructure. A group burned a railroad trestle and cut telephone wires near Harlingen in July. In early

August another band crossed paths with US soldiers just north of Brownsville, and in an ensuing firefight one soldier died and two more were injured. Another group burned a railroad bridge and cut more telegraph wires
near Sebastian. On August 6 about fifteen men described as "armed Mexicans" robbed stores. As they looted, the group also searched for newcomer
farmers Alfred L. Austin and his son Charles. Alfred Austin had a reputation for abusing his Mexican laborers, calling for strict segregation, and
headed the local Law and Order League. The group located the Austins at
home, confiscated their weapons, marched them into a nearby field, and
shot them both. According to Nellie Austin, Charles's wife, who witnessed
the executions, both men died from shots to the back and the head. On
September 24 an American soldier, Henry Stubblefield, died from a gunshot after trying to stop a raid near Progreso.[1]

Bazán and Longoria were living in the midst of what residents in south
Texas described as a race war. In a response to calls to secure the border,
politicians flooded the region with US soldiers and Texas Rangers. This
increase in soldiers and state officers, targeting ethnic Mexicans in the region, led to a devastating period of violence. Some recall this period as the
"bandit wars," a conflict between law enforcement, Texas Rangers, US
soldiers, and vigilantes against armed rebellion by Mexican seditionists.
Other residents remembered this period as *la matanza,* the massacre, a period
of indiscriminate murder of ethnic Mexicans without fear of prosecution.
Historians estimate that anywhere from 100 to 300 ethnic Mexicans were
murdered between August 1915 and June 1916.[2] Living in terror, many
remember an "exodus" of ethnic Mexicans—families who fled to Mexico
to escape state terror in Texas.[3] Lon C. Hill, appointed to the Texas Rangers
as a special Ranger in August 1915, noted that the exodus became so
widespread that farmers raised concerns because their field laborers were
fleeing to Mexico. The workforce, according to Hill, seemingly "evapo-
rated." Hill noted that even landowners fled to Mexico, some leaving thousands of head of cattle behind.[4]

That entire communities would abandon their homes, jobs, land, and
livestock to flee to a country in the throes of a civil war reveals the danger
of being Mexican in Texas. Ethnic Mexicans made difficult decisions on a
daily basis. They had to evaluate when to travel, how to interact with law
enforcement agents, and how to avoid being caught in the cross fire of the
violent period.

Weighing the risks, on September 27 Bazán and Longoria decided to report the robbery to Texas Rangers camping on the Sam Lane Ranch while they patrolled the region. Laborers witnessed what looked like an uneventful conversation between the two men and Texas Ranger captain Henry Ransom. Bazán and Longoria left and made their way home on horseback. Witnesses recalled that when Bazán and Longoria were about 300 yards away, Captain Ransom and two civilians, William Sterling and Paul West, climbed into a Model T Ford and followed the men. As the vehicle approached, one of the men reached outside the passenger-side window and shot both men in the back. Bazán and Longoria fell from their horses and died on the side of the road.

Captain Ransom, in charge of Texas Ranger Company D, had a reputation for violence and for abusing his power. When he returned to the camp, he warned witnesses not to bury or move the bodies. He intended for the corpses to be left to decay in the hot summer air, to intimidate all who encountered them. Ransom forced the victims' neighbors and friends to endure an extreme act of disrespect by denying Bazán and Longoria a proper burial.[5] As the appalling news swirled through the ranch, witnesses reported that Captain Ransom, seemingly unfazed, returned to his campsite to take a nap.[6]

Some witnesses reported that Bazán and Longoria were left on the dirt road for days. Some remembered that wagons had to maneuver around the bodies. While some felt sympathy, most were too fearful to tend to the remains. Two of the Longorias' friends, Martiriano and Timotea Cantú, lived on a ranch nearby. They were tormented by the order not to tend to their friends. Sometime in October, they took the risk and buried the remains of Bazán and Longoria with the help of other witnesses, including Roland Warnock.

In the immediate aftermath of the double murder, there were no police investigations into the shooting. Captain Ransom made no mention of his actions in his monthly report to the adjutant general, nor did he contact local officials to file a police report.[7] A. Y. Baker, the sheriff of Edinburg, the closest town, did not interview witnesses or write a report. Not surprisingly, the sheriff did not arrest Captain Ransom or the civilian passengers in the car. The local justice of the peace did not visit the bodies and did not issue death certificates. Although news of the event undoubtedly traveled throughout the region, there were no protests or public demands for justice. What, then, accounted for the event being remembered 100 years later?

Quantifying the number of violent deaths in the borderlands during the early twentieth century is a slippery task. Numerical estimates of violence that resulted in death are varied; invariably, there are competing approximations. This is further complicated when trying to record death at the hands of law enforcement agents. To be sure, institutional negligence by state police, local law enforcement agents, and county judicial systems have erased countless deaths from historical records. When police shootings were recorded in the 1910s, the dead were generally not named; instead they were categorized—as bandit, thief, or other labels that criminalize the deceased. The common practice of leaving dead bodies to decompose beyond recognition and failing to write death certificates also makes naming the dead a difficult task. My goal here is to disrupt those long-held patterns of erasure by naming the known victims.

Naming is essential because names have the potential to place an individual within broader social connections (including families, churches, and place of residence) and provide insight into their lives. Murder had tremendous consequences on the communities left in the wake of violence. Some witnesses were moved by the injustices they observed. Some went on to preserve the names, provide access to the lives of those who died, and collect evidence. By turning to local memories and local responses to state regimes of terror, historians can help with the process of recuperating these disavowed or erased histories. Documenting the double murder of Jesus Bazán and Antonio Longoria was a difficult process. It required learning from the private collections and vernacular history-making efforts of local residents. I met Norma Longoria Rodriguez, for example, in her home in San Antonio after she answered my request for an interview. I had stumbled upon her essays on the double murder of Bazán and Longoria, her great-grandfather and grandfather, on the website *Los Tejanos,* created by her cousin, Hernán Contreras. Sitting at her dining room table and drinking iced tea, I listened for hours as she shared her family history and the story of the double murder. When I turned the recorder off, she brought out a piece of apple pie for me to eat while she showed me the photographs and artifacts that documented the lives of her great-grandfather and grandfather.

I learned that Jesus Bazán and Antonio Longoria were pillars of the community, both from prominent Tejano landowning families, and one an elected official. Jesus Bazán and his wife, Epigmenia, were both American citizens and longtime property owners. To navigate the shifting economies, and the arrival of Anglo farmers to the region, Jesus Bazán made his own dictionary. He translated phrases and words related to business, agriculture, and ranching from Spanish into English. Antonio Longoria and his wife, Antonia, maintained property secured by an eighteenth-century land grant from the Spanish crown. Despite the turbulence of the Texas Revolution, the US–Mexico War, and the Mexican Revolution, the Longorias held onto the property in Hidalgo County. As a young adult, Antonio gained local distinction as a public servant, an educator, and a political official in Texas.[8] At the time of his murder, he was the Hidalgo County commissioner. These were well-respected families. The absence of public outrage, or even, it seems, public concern, is puzzling and yet speaks volumes to the era's climate of fear. The double murders were a particularly brutal manifestation of the troubling era. Citizenship, political positions, and social prominence did not offer ethnic Mexicans protection from violence.

Grappling with racial violence requires broadening the focus from documenting a singular historical act of violence to exploring how people lived in and navigated a violent world. Violence also included intimidation and sexual threats against men, women, and children alike. These histories are especially difficult to trace when survivors did not engage in public protest or revolution or lawsuits; there was no visible form of resistance to challenge the state. Political scientist and anthropologist James Scott reminds us that people subordinate to the state, power, and violence are not often afforded the luxury of "open, organized, political activity." These acts often are met with brutal repression. He writes, "Everyday forms of resistance make no headlines."[9] Following Scott, I want to shift the focus, call our attention to the everyday forms of resistance to state violence, all those seemingly insignificant acts that stopped short of collective defiance.

To explore these strategies requires returning to the violence in order to gain a glimpse into the decisions residents made on a daily basis. In some

On September 27, 1915, Jesus Bazán *(pictured)* and his son-in-law, Antonio Longoria, were murdered by a posse. Jesus and his wife, Epigmenia, were both American citizens from prominent Tejano landowning families. Courtesy Norma L. Rodriguez. Photo provided by the Bullock Texas State History Museum.

cases everyday acts involved tending to the dead, burying the remains of a friend, neighbor, or stranger, or leaving a wooden cross below a tree to mark the absence of a loved one. This behavior resisted blatant attempts to disrespect the dead and intimidate the living. Searching for the remains of a loved one constituted an act that defied those who meant for a person to be forgotten. Remembering, even whispering the names of the departed, resisted efforts to erase their death and existence.[10] Studying the aftermath of conflict in a local context highlights residents' varied efforts to rebuild their communities and reclaim a place to live. In the case of the double murder of Jesus Bazán and Antonio Longoria in 1915, their relatives rejected

Portrait of Antonio and Antonia Longoria dated June 6, 1898, a year after their marriage, taken by traveling photographer E. C. Olivares. Courtesy Norma L. Rodriguez and Heriberto F. Longoria Jr. Photo provided by the Bullock Texas State History Museum.

efforts to intimidate the family and other ethnic Mexicans, even those with economic, political, or social clout. Instead, the family remained on their property and quietly preserved for future generations the history of the violent injustice they suffered.[11]

The Bazán and Longoria case allows for an examination of how witnesses and survivors navigated the violent reality of daily life. Beyond the event itself is the history of how the double murder was shared with the next generation as a practice of mourning their loss. It reveals sentiments of loss and injustice that continued in the telling of the history. Members of the next generation engaged in what theorist Jean Franco calls the struggle for interpretive power to challenge mainstream narratives that disavowed histories of racial violence. These mainstream historical accounts, circulated by historians and Texas Rangers themselves, asserted both cultural and social control over ethnic Mexican residents in Texas.[12] Here we will focus on Norma Longoria Rodriguez and Kirby Warnock, two residents who have labored for over forty years to memorialize the double murder of Bazán and Longoria and to challenge the celebratory histories of the Texas Rangers.

Both Rodriguez and Warnock learned of the event from family members as young adults. They each independently dedicated years to researching the double murder.[13] Through a practice of vernacular history-making, they brought into the public sphere alternative histories previously shared only in private settings among trusted friends and family. They attempted to provide residents with both real and virtual forums to reckon with the long legacy of the violence. Examining their memorialization efforts shows that ethnic Mexicans—American citizens and Mexican nationals alike— as well as Anglos suffered from and resisted violent policing regimes on the border. These efforts take us beyond simplistic racial binaries and gendered narratives to uncover previously understudied struggles for power between residents and the state.

POLICING STRANGE MEXICANS

Between 1915 and 1916 calls for an increased military presence on the Texas–Mexico border transformed the region. As residents worried about the turbulence of the Mexican Revolution, the state administration answered their calls for an increased police presence. To some extent the residents were right to be worried. There was a relatively small military presence there. In November 1913 a mere 300 soldiers patrolled the entire south Texas border region. Texas governor Oscar Colquitt ordered over 1,000 men from the Texas National Guard, as well as five cavalry troops, to reinforce the border. The majority of the state militia took up stations in Brownsville, and the remaining troops spread out to maintain stations at seven other towns near the border.

The governor's orders were clear: the presence of the troops was meant to warn Mexican officials that any violence against Texas residents by a rebel or a Mexican federal soldier would not be tolerated. He directed officers to "notify the Mexican commander at Matamoros that if he harms a single Texan, his life will be demanded as forfeit."[14] In response to the governor's actions, Secretary of War Lindley Garrison proposed to replace the state troops with regular army personnel.[15] Soldiers from across the country descended on the US–Mexico border.

The soldier population on the Texas–Mexico border swelled, altering both the rural landscape and city centers. By 1916 over 100,000 US troops patrolled the border. This militarization was inseparable from the country's larger military strategy. Sending troops from northern and midwestern states, such as New York and Indiana, provided an opportunity for soldiers to perform military drills in preparation for US involvement in World War I. In particular, the foreign landscape of dense mesquite brush in south Texas and the hills of the Chihuahuan desert in west Texas allowed troops to master the latest military technologies in unfamiliar terrain. Armed with machine guns and searchlights, soldiers patrolled both private and national borders.

Residents of south Texas saw displays of military might in town centers as well. In Brownsville, residents were just getting used to the sounds and sights of the industrial railroad that ran through town. They now had to become accustomed to the footsteps of soldiers marching and the hooves of cavalry horses packing down the dirt roads. Soldiers showcased military-grade automobiles and tanks that rumbled over the dirt streets. The parades signaled the arrival of new wartime technologies in the border region.

In an effort to exert control in the region, soldiers and state agents made policing private property an important task. US soldiers filled military forts along the border, but they also erected camps on prominent ranches in south Texas. The King Ranch and the Montecristo Ranch in south Texas, for example, became models for securing ranch property lines with new technologies. Both ranches hosted soldiers and Texas Rangers. R. L. Cooper lived in south Texas on the Magnolia Ranch. She remembers that as a child she watched the large searchlight placed on the roof of the mansion on the neighboring King Ranch. The light cut through the dark, swinging around in every direction, searching all night for any thieves hiding in the thick

US soldiers and local children excitedly circle a tank that arrived in Brownsville by train. The tanks were part of military parades in border towns. Robert Runyon photographed soldiers performing drills with the latest in military technology and sold the images as postcards. Robert Runyon Photograph Collection, RUN00894, The Dolph Briscoe Center for American History, University of Texas at Austin.

brush. The searchlight became such a symbol of security for local residents that photographers captured it to sell as a postcard.[16]

The national press covered the increasing military presence on the border. Photographers snapped soldiers performing drills and traversing the landscape. Newspapers published these photographs of soldiers on the border and celebrated the policing of local ethnic Mexicans. The press helped consolidate a US common identity in opposition to both the foreigners of neighboring Mexico and ethnic Mexicans in the United States. In April 1916 an English-language newspaper, the *Laredo Times,* published a photograph of a US cavalryman walking in front of three men identified as Mexican. The three men stood in a line, holding their hats in front of their chests with both hands, their gaze turned down to the ground. The angle of the photograph and the shadows in the image protect the investigator's face

and identity and shield his gun from the viewer's sight. The three unidentified men dressed as laborers stand unarmed. The caption reads, "The
photograph shows strange Mexicans being questioned by military authorities of the United States on the border. The men were liberated. Two of
them later were found shot."[17] Their deaths by unidentified assailants, it
seems, did not inspire a formal investigation. The newspaper never printed
their names and made no further reference to the incident.

Instead of concern for the murdered men, the title of the photograph,
"Keep Eye on Border Mexicans," positions the viewer on the side of the
government agents who monitored the Texas–Mexico border. The image
does not encourage readers to feel sympathy for the victims, to question
the officers' role in the murders, or to consider whether the death of the
men constituted a justifiable act. The racialized label "Mexican" suggested
a foreign or "strange" quality. The death of the two men was not the newspaper's concern. The caption aimed to comfort readers by showing law
enforcement agents actively patrolling both social and national borders.
However, when reading the title of the photograph, the role of who should
perform this practice becomes unclear. The title could be read as a call

In April 1916 the English-language newspaper the *Laredo Times* published a
photograph of a US cavalryman walking in front of three men identified as
Mexican. Taken together, the title, photograph, and caption underscore the
common practice of state violence and regular denial of judicial rights to ethnic
Mexicans in Texas in the early twentieth century. "Keep Eye on Border Mexicans,"
Laredo Times, April 23, 1916.

to readers to join officials in monitoring the movement of "Border Mexicans."

On the ground, however, military attempts at bringing stability were slow to appease residents. Soldiers unfamiliar with the border region struggled to navigate the terrain. Although their physical presence reassured some residents, others noticed that the troops did little to slow raids on ranches near the border. San Benito resident William G. B. Morrison observed that 20,000 US soldiers stationed in Hidalgo County were ill equipped to patrol the county's approximately sixty-mile stretch of border. In fact, military tactics were all wrong for suppressing banditry; the sheer volume of soldiers, Morrison reported, actually hampered their ability to patrol the area. Large troop patrols made too much noise and small bands of assailants easily avoided capture. To add insult to injury, Morrison continued, the soldiers were so inept at preventing raids, the soldier themselves became victims, their own outposts raided a time or two.[18]

In spite of the increased military presence on the border, local residents petitioned the state to increase Texas Rangers and to station some officers on private ranches. For Anglo ranchers, state police remained the preferred form of protection. To meet local requests, the number of Texas Rangers spiked under the administration of Governor James Edward Ferguson from January 1915 until August 1917. In September 1913 only thirteen Texas Rangers patrolled the entire state. The state police consisted of two companies of six rangers, including one captain, one sergeant, and four privates. A third company consisted of a solo Ranger. By April 1915 the number of officers had doubled to twenty-six Rangers, but the number was still deemed insufficient.[19] To meet popular demand, the Texas legislature increased the state budget to cover the salaries for more state police. Ferguson accordingly expedited the hiring process. He expanded the number of Texas companies, appointed captains, and enabled them to select Rangers to fill their ranks.[20] With the state legislature and Texas governor providing resources, the number of Texas Rangers dramatically increased.

The state police consisted of regular Rangers, officers who received monthly salaries. Special Rangers, in contrast, worked without pay but maintained all the legal authority of a regular Ranger. Increasing the number of officers with unpaid Texas Rangers swelled the force beyond administrative control.[21] During World War I, the addition of another category of volunteers, called loyalty Rangers, who acted as a secret service for the state, also increased the number of state police officers. By the end of the war, the Texas Rangers included well over the state allotment of 1,000 agents. It consisted of eleven Ranger captains, 150 regular Rangers, 400 special Rangers, and approximately 800 loyalty Rangers—a total of approximately 1,350 Texas Rangers.[22]

The dramatic increase in the number of Texas Rangers was reflected in the growth of untrained officers. These new state police officers wielded state authority to carry firearms and make arrests. Men who received special Ranger appointments did not need prior experience in the military or in law enforcement. Instead, residents with local knowledge of the terrain were recruited as special Rangers.

These qualities, however, were preferred by Anglo property owners who feverishly petitioned for Texas Rangers to be stationed on their ranches and in local towns. Cattle stockmen's association inspectors, ranchers, and railroad conductors—all isolated from local law enforcement agents in towns and county centers—frequently made cases for Texas Rangers to be stationed nearby. The Texas Cattle Raisers Association (CRA), for example, employed fifty-nine inspectors and "hunt men" to investigate cattle theft and monitor cattle brands. When the inspectors found men believed to be guilty of cattle theft, they called on the Texas Rangers to make the arrest. The Texas CRA argued that increased raids made swift arrests crucial to protecting private property. The adjutant general responded by giving special Ranger status to many of the association's brand inspectors.[23] This led to a class of men who were both on the payroll of local ranchers and wholly unqualified to act as law enforcement officers. Without a formal process for screening these new agents or training them, the Texas Rangers took to selectively enforcing self-interested laws for their employers. As one historian reflected, "they caused the Ranger force more trouble than they were worth and sometimes acute embarrassment." Even historian Walter Prescott Webb, who celebrated the state police in his writings, frankly described some of these men as "incompetent."[24]

Despite growing abuses, Texas Rangers received wide support from the governor's office to use any means necessary to exert control over the border region. Successive Texas governors, first Oscar Colquitt and then James Ferguson, gave the state officers clear instructions to use their authority without hesitation. During his administration, Colquitt wrote

to Captain John R. Hughes, "I instruct you and your men to keep them
[Mexican raiders] off of Texas territory if possible, and if they invade the
State let them understand they do so at the risk of their lives."[25] When
Governor Ferguson took office in 1914, he offered similar instructions to
his captains and even assured the men he would protect them from future
prosecutions. One Anglo rancher from Monte Cristo, near San Guadalupe del Torero Ranch, later explained that the governor assured him that
he "had given [Captain Henry] Ransom instructions to go down there
and clean it up if he had to kill every damned man connected with it."
According to the rancher, the governor explained: "I firmly told Ransom
that if he didn't do it—if he didn't clean that nest up down there that
I would put a man down there that would. . . . I have the pardoning
power and we will stand by those men, and I want that bunch—that
gang cleaned up."[26]

In 1917, local attorney Frank C. Pierce reflected in his writings that state
administrations most likely considered it "cheaper and speedier to entrust
to them [Texas Rangers] the capture, trial, and infliction of the penalty
upon those who might be suspected." In his history of the region, Pierce
diligently developed a list of violent conflicts from the nineteenth through
the early twentieth century. The resulting chronology of violence details
the collaboration of federal soldiers, state and local agents, and Anglo vigilantes, all following orders to clear the Texas border region of "Mexican
bandits." He concluded, "The author cannot let pass this opportunity to
say that during the bandit raids of 1915 many evil influences were brought
to bear to clear the country of the Mexicans."[27] Stocking the border with
poorly trained and overly eager citizens offered the manpower to repress
raids attributed to *El Plan de San Diego* and led to increasingly violent and
lethal conflicts. A rebirth of earlier brutal policing tactics, accompanied by
new lethal technologies, emerged in the border region.

As a result, the late summer months of 1915 proved to be exceptionally
violent. Rangers initiated a revenge-by-proxy technique, killing ethnic
Mexicans, regardless of evidence of guilt, merely for being in the approxi-
mate location of a crime. They profiled any ethnic Mexican as a Mexican
bandit and made arrests and then left prisoners vulnerable to mob violence.
Historian Benjamin Johnson describes the Rangers' methods as ethnic
cleansing: an attempt to remove Mexicans, whether citizens of Mexico or
the United States, from Texas.[28]

To cloak these brutal practices, both state and local agents frequently referred to those executed as "bandits"—a generic and overused label that justified violence as a necessary part of securing the border. On July 23, 1915, Hidalgo County sheriff Stokes Chaddick and US Customs inspector John Dudley White shot brothers Lorenzo and Gregorio Manríquez near the small town of Progreso, forty-four miles west of Brownsville on the Río Grande. The officers alleged that the Manríquez brothers participated in a robbery and were shot for resisting arrest.[29] The *Brownsville Herald* reported that the death of the brothers reflected a commitment of people in the region to organize and "administer swift punishment to any thief caught."[30]

One day later Chaddick and White, in the company of Texas Ranger Robert L. Brennan, surrounded a Mexican restaurant in nearby Mercedes. The officers alleged that an unnamed Mexican in the restaurant stole horses, wagons, cows, and other property. The *Brownsville Daily Herald* reported that the unnamed man fired at White. The article continued, "Like a flash, White whipped out his revolver and this would-be assassin bit the dust. The man died from three shots, all well directed."[31] Claiming self-defense, the inspector, who formerly served in the Spanish-American War, received praise for his speed and agility. In contrast, the local press reported the incident without including the victim's name and instead expressed relief that the agent eliminated the public threat of a "would-be assassin."[32] The newspaper repeated the officer's efforts to describe the dead man as a public threat and stripped the victim of any presumed innocence. Associating the man with banditry proved sufficient for the newspaper.

Harlingen resident B. F. Johnson noted that during the peak of anti-Mexican violence in 1915–1916, it was common knowledge that Texas Rangers used *la ley de fuga,* law of flight, to kill prisoners with great frequency. Shooting men in the back became a regular occurrence. Johnson insisted that residents regularly found the corpses of men lying in the countryside who had recently been arrested by Texas Rangers. In particular, he remembered an unidentified Mexican man killed by Texas Ranger captain Walker W. Andrews at Passe Real, alleged to have been a "bandit." Johnson explained, "nearly every day you could hear about people being killed by Rangers." He pointed out that he did not personally see bodies, but there were rumors of killings on a regular basis in the region between the towns of Harlingen, Brownsville, San Benito, and Passe Real. The landscape regularly became littered with a great number of Mexicans who had been "killed in the brush" by Rangers, under the authority of Captain Henry Ransom.[33]

Ransom's techniques did raise concern for some local law enforcement. In 1915 W. T. Vann, sheriff of Cameron County, expressed his concern directly to Governor Ferguson. He explained that Ransom's policing would bring more trouble and asked that the captain be relocated. Ferguson replied, "Ransom will make you a good man if you warm up to him."[34] In 1915 Sheriff Emilio Forto, like Sheriff Vann, attributed violence in the border region to "the reckless manner in which undisciplined 'pistol toters' Rangers and other civil officers, have been permitted to act as trial judge, jury, and executioners."[35] The systematic killing of ethnic Mexicans without criminal trials signaled the collapse of the Texas judiciary into the "reckless" collaboration of civilians and state officers, who executed subjects at will. The sheriff remained troubled by the brutality he witnessed.

On October 19 Mexican raiders successfully derailed a train. In response a posse of Rangers and civilians arrested ten ethnic Mexicans. Railroad developer J. L. Allhands explained that the ten men paid immediately with their lives. He recalled, "four of them were corralled and executed by hanging on trees; the others were shot down by their captors."[36] The local police and Texas Rangers arrested four additional men. Sheriff Vann remembered Ransom's invitation to join him in executing the men. In later testimony Vann recalled the exchange: Ransom said, "'I'm going to kill these fellows, are you going with me?' I says 'No, and I don't believe you are going.' He says, 'If you haven't got guts enough to do it, I will go myself.' I says, 'That takes a whole lot of guts, four fellows with their hands tied behind them, it takes a whole lot of guts to do that.'"[37] Vann kept two prisoners in his custody and went to town to investigate their involvement. He found that the two prisoners had no involvement in the raid and released the innocent men. By the time he returned, Ransom had killed the four prisoners in his custody. If Vann had embraced Ransom's revenge-by-proxy technique, the innocent men would have been killed without hesitation. Vann's insistence on using due process of law to assess the innocence or guilt of a prisoner proved to be increasingly rare among law enforcement officers at the time. Historian Benjamin Johnson wrote, "The Rangers and local vigilantes exerted little effort to distinguish between loyal and rebellious Tejanos. Anybody who looked 'Mexican' was vulnerable."[38]

With the pardoning power of the governor, Ransom continued his notoriously ruthless approach to securing south Texas. As a captain of a Texas Ranger company patrolling the border region, Ransom set a violent example for the state police officers he commanded. If Governor Ferguson wanted a captain who could deliver control through brute violence, he certainly chose one with experience "cleaning up" contested territories. Ransom had developed his brutal methods, and a reputation for bragging about them, as a soldier in the US–Philippines War. He imported those military tactics into south Texas.[39]

His methods became so well known that they took on a reputation of their own. In south Texas to "Ransomize" a prisoner or resident meant to take someone out into the brush and kill him before conducting an official investigation into his guilt.[40] Ransom also developed a reputation for patrolling the countryside and driving ethnic Mexicans from their homes. In one of his monthly scouting reports, written in 1915, he bragged, "I drove all the Mexicans from three ranches. Rancho Leona, Rancho Nueva, and Rancho Viejo."[41] The exodus of residents who fled to safety south of the Rio Grande left properties that could be bought at cheap prices. Rangers like Ransom, with widespread reputations for extralegal violence, enjoyed the endorsement of the state administration.

One San Benito resident, Alba Haywood, resented abusive Texas Rangers, especially when they practiced brutality on his property. Haywood reported finding the bodies of two men, dead from gunshot wounds. He also remembered seeing the bodies of other men brought back from the countryside. After being arrested, the Rangers interrogated them with physical force. Haywood later saw the men badly beaten and suffering wounds from the interrogation.[42]

Prisoners were exceptionally vulnerable to unlawful executions on the long trips from the site of their arrest to the closest county jail. Being placed in a jail cell did not end physical threat. To the contrary, some local and state authorities utilized arrests to create opportunities for local mobs to enact their versions of "swift justice." On July 29, 1915, for example, Cameron County deputy sheriffs Daniel Hinojosa and Frank Carr removed prisoner Adolfo Muñoz from the jail in the small town of San Benito at ten o'clock at night. Local agents had earlier arrested Muñoz on suspicion of robbing and murdering a local merchant. The deputies later alleged that they meant to transport the prisoner to the Brownsville County Jail. Muñoz never arrived in Brownsville. Deputy sheriffs Hinojosa and Carr reported that two miles south of San Benito, a posse of unidentified men ordered the officers to release the prisoner into their custody and leave the scene. The *Brownsville Daily Herald* reported that the next morning residents found the tortured prisoner, riddled with bullets, "dangling at the end of a rope tied to the limb of a mesquite tree. . . . Life was extinct."[43] Local reports also noted that the residents were enraged by rumors that Muñoz had attempted to rape a young girl.[44]

Despite the common understanding that Hinojosa and Carr had created the conditions for Muñoz's lynching, local authorities did not prosecute the assailants or bring charges against the deputy sheriffs, who had the legal responsibility to protect their prisoner. On the contrary, Hinojosa received a promotion in status and prestige when he rejoined the state police as a regular Ranger in 1918. He resigned on February 3, 1919, coincidentally, when the Texas Rangers were being investigated for brutal policing tactics and abuse of power.[45] The role of the state police put on display the vulnerability of racial and ethnic minorities who lived without police protection. The abuses at the hands of Texas Rangers and vigilantes fueled fear and mistrust.

In many cases, agents collaborated with local vigilantes to intimidate and murder prisoners. Lon C. Hill received an appointment as a special Ranger the last week of August 1915. According to him, in 1915 Rangers and local agents failed to distinguish between innocent bystanders of raids and legitimate suspects. Rangers arrested "everybody on suspicion" but sometimes stopped short of committing crimes. Hill explained that Rangers did not always intimidate prisoners themselves because "there are other people that do that."[46] Local residents formed vigilante groups to respond to fears about Mexican raids and did not hesitate to use brutal methods of interrogation. These small posses, for example, incited terror in local communities by interviewing anyone suspected of having relationships or contact with alleged bandits.

In the search for information, some citizens strung residents up by the neck during interrogations. Hill recognized that state laws prohibited state agents from participating in these brutal investigations, but he also admitted their frequent collaboration with vigilantes. "Yes," he continued, "they [the Rangers] are not better than anybody else," and they, too, removed prisoners from jail at night to give them the "third degree."[47] Lon Hill himself encouraged brute force. While serving as a special Ranger, he personally organized vigilante groups to do the work outside the regulations for officers. He later stated that in his opinion "every Mexican in the country" took the side of the Mexican raiders. Hill developed a career by trying to prove this point.[48]

Judge James B. Wells, a resident of Brownsville and a known boss of machine politics in south Texas, years later remembered the gruesome scenes that had become common in south Texas. He described one trip through the rural landscape when he came across eleven dead bodies lying near the side of the road near Edinburg. The judge noticed a bad smell and buzzards circling in the air. The signs of death led the judge to eleven ethnic Mexican men lying in the brush. Buzzards had picked over the corpses, consuming the men's eyes, faces, and scalps. The men's identities could not be determined. "It was a very gruesome sight," Wells explained, "they were too far decomposed."[49] The harsh south Texas elements, however, could not conceal the cause of death. Judge Wells continued, "You could see bullet holes right above the eyes, great big holes you could stick your finger in, the only thing to indicate the wounds or how they had been killed."[50]

Wells's social position as a judge also meant he was familiar with the denial of due process for ethnic Mexicans and had power to rule in such matters. He considered himself a "Ranger man" since childhood, but as a man of the court he cautioned, "I don't think anyone should be given power of life and death."[51] Nevertheless, Wells paradoxically acknowledged that he, as a justice of the court, would defend agents without hesitation. He explained, "I am a Ranger man. . . . You asked me about defending them. I don't know of a man since I have lived in Brownsville, forty-one years . . . that I have not defended voluntarily. . . . I thought it was my duty and I never took a cent of compensation. Defended several for murder . . . I think all our reputable bar would stand by them."[52] In this transcript, Wells reveals himself as simultaneously moved by his encounter with victims of state violence and resolute in his position to defend state agents.

Residents of south Texas remember the brutal tactics Texas Rangers used to murder ethnic Mexicans. Some important witnesses were those who celebrated violence, were engrossed by it, or were seemingly unfazed by their encounters. Several oral histories describe in graphic detail the brutality. For example, Jesse Sterling Campbell, born on June 2, 1888, and sister to William Sterling (present during the murders of Bazán and Longoria and eventually adjutant general of the Texas Rangers), grew up on a family ranch near McAllen, Texas.[53] At the ranch, Texas Rangers and US soldiers maintained a station to organize patrols of the border region.[54] Campbell lauded the Rangers: "We had all this protection you see. Two Rangers was all you needed. . . . Two Rangers are worth two dozen other soldiers."[55] Although the Ranger and military presence provided security for the family, it also brought the violence closer to home. Campbell witnessed the execution of an unidentified Mexican man brought to the ranch. As she recalls, Rangers brought him back to the ranch, bound him, and rendered him motionless during an interrogation. When the officers finished, they released the prisoner in a manner Campbell described as common practice. "The way [the Rangers] do them is they turn them loose and [the prisoners] run. Then the Rangers shoot them. . . . I wish I didn't see that but of course he deserved what he got."

As a witness, Campbell was simultaneously mesmerized and revolted by the violent practices. She provided an account of the events and expressed regret for seeing the murder. However, she justified the violent act by repeating the phrase "he got what he deserved" twice during her account. What evidence, if any, the Rangers found for detaining, binding, and shooting the prisoner in the back is not preserved in the record. Instead, Campbell insinuates that the man committed a crime that warranted inhumane conduct, disregard for his rights, and a summary execution. Testimonies like Campbell's criminalized Mexican residents and defined Ranger brutality as a necessary element for securing Anglo settlement.

Although most of the killings took place on ranches and in isolated areas, others occurred more publicly near rural towns. For Reynolds Rossington, who grew up in the nearby town of Hebbronville, watching agents clear the landscape of Mexican bodies became a grotesque pastime. Every morning, as a young boy, Rossington walked over to the Rangers campsite to watch officers who brought in the corpses of those he described as "desperados." As he remembered in a 1973 oral history, "Dead ones and the ones part dead, [the Rangers] had a clearing and they would burn them up behind this lumber company. Best thing I remember I was there one day, I was sitting there on a bench, and the Texas Rangers were talking about shooting one of these Mexicans and that he bleated like a goat, and I started to laugh."[56] The young spectator laughed so hard he swallowed an iron washer he held in his mouth and almost choked. Rossington's recounting of this sadistic event as a humorous episode underlines popular insensitivity to the systematic killing of ethnic Mexicans, the enjoyment by some at witnessing these acts, and the regular boasting by Rangers about dehumanizing their victims. Campbell and Rossington offer just two accounts, among many others, of the callous social milieu that some residents fondly remembered. These opinions helped cement the process of differentiating which residents had rights and which ones could be murdered.

Judge Wells's account and the oral histories conducted with Campbell and Rossington exemplify south Texas residents' common encounters with widespread violence. Whether witnessing the violent act of extralegal executions, participating in them, or merely stumbling upon a decomposing corpse, residents of the Texas–Mexico border region could not escape the reality of violence in 1915. Those killed often remained nameless victims of the ongoing climate of anti-Mexican violence on the border. And yet neighbors and relatives of the victims noticed their absence and mourned their death and disappearance.

WITNESSING A DOUBLE MURDER

Unlike the lynching of Antonio Rodríguez in Rocksprings, the double murder of Jesus Bazán and Antonio Longoria did not result in an extensive paper trail of police reports, court records, international investigations, or newspaper sagas to lead researchers to the tragic events of September 27, 1915. Local newspapers did not report on the double murder or even acknowledge that a shooting took place on the Guadalupe Ranch in September 1915. Historical documents that acknowledge the murder of Bazán and Longoria are rare. Their deaths are not recorded in city, county, or Texas Ranger records. Texas Ranger captains were expected to record arrests or encounters with suspects in monthly reports. Instead, in his scout report for September 1915, Captain Ransom reported spending the majority of the month in south Texas but neglected to document the double murder. On September 27 he traveled from the town of Harlingen to Edinburg, left to scout west, and camped at a Ranger station in Monte Cristo on September 28. The next day he traveled from Monte Cristo to La Gloria Ranch to Jarachinas to Pinto Ranches to El Toro and finally camped in the town of Pharr on September 30. Ransom meticulously detailed where he traveled each day, noted the mileage traveled from each location, and even included a monthly tally (in September 1915 he traveled 1,460 miles).[57] Although he noted being at the Monte Cristo Ranger station (which neighbors the Guadalupe Ranch), he never mentioned encountering, shooting, or witnessing the murder of Antonio Longoria or Jesus Bazán.

The absence of historical documents makes it difficult to gather a clear motive for the double murder. One local account explains that the men were shot simply as a result of mistaken identity. According to this account, Ransom had been looking for a man named Eugenio Longoria, accused of participating in a local raid. When Ransom met Bazán and Longoria, he took Antonio for Eugenio Longoria. The shared last name provided cause enough to shoot both men in the back.[58]

One historical record offers an even more sanguinary reason for the double murder and the erasure of the event from public record. Hidden in 1,600 pages of a 1919 state investigation into state police abuse is a reference to the double murder. Instead of being a source of protection, their social status, in this period, made Bazán and Longoria vulnerable to state violence. Both were ranchers in an era when Mexican landowners were part of a dwindling minority. The success of Bazán and Longoria reminded both Mexican residents and newly arrived Anglo settlers that, in Texas, Mexicans had until recently been the colonizers of the region, the group that wielded the most political, economic, and social influence. Eliminating them, and other residents like them, helped Anglos secure supremacy in the region and industrialize agriculture.

Additionally, skyrocketing property prices made ranchers especially susceptible to land companies trying to buy up big ranches, divide them into parcels, and then resell the smaller plots for farming. The two property owners may have become targets for offering to testify on behalf of an ethnic Mexican neighbor fighting to maintain his property against an Anglo land company owned by developer S. W. Seabury. After they were killed, the land case was dismissed.[59] Certainly, challenging an Anglo land company's expansion would raise Bazán's and Longoria's profiles as obstacles to the agricultural colonization of the Southwest. In addition, Longoria was an active participant in the local political machine. Bilingual, educated, and socially influential, he was an affront to growing waves of Anglo farmers who believed that Mexicans had no place in politics or business. At a time when Juan Crow segregationist social policies were being cemented in the region, residents like Bazán and Longoria were a problem. Their deep roots resisted the encroachment by Anglo farmers. They remained thorns in the side of these social transformations.

The absence of written records helped hide the grim deeds of the Rangers and vigilantes. Instead, we know of this act of extralegal violence because of the friends and neighbors who were left to pick up the remains of Bazán and Longoria. After they buried the dead, these people preserved the details of the event and remained unsettled by the injustices they witnessed; not only did they mourn the loss of the two men, they shared that loss with the next generation.

Roland Warnock grew up in south Texas and worked on ranches as a young adult. He vividly remembered the environment that made residents fear for their safety. Sam Lane, for example, armed every employee with a high-powered Krag rifle, 400 rounds of ammunition, and a six-shooter pistol. He ordered Warnock and others to always carry a loaded firearm. Anticipating assaults by both Anglo and Mexican raiders seemed the greatest priority to Lane.[60] According to Warnock, raiders, Mexican and Anglo, crossed both national and private borders, eluding Texas Rangers and the US Cavalry alike. He explained, "There were a lot of white men that certainly didn't sprout any wings. . . . It was both races that played that border country."[61] While fear of Mexican banditry fueled the murder of ethnic Mexicans in south Texas, Warnock noted that blaming ethnic Mexicans for social banditry ignored the prevalence of theft at the hands of Anglos in the region.

Warnock also had specific memories of the abuse of power he saw at the hands of law enforcement agents. "It was some mighty dirty work going on then," he lamented, "There were so many innocent people killed in that mess that it just made you sick to your heart to see it happening." The sight of victims executed and tossed into the south Texas brush remained vivid in his memory. "If those ranchers caught a Mexican with a bunch of cattle, they didn't ask him where he got them, they killed him. I knew of one time when they hung eighteen men in a grove of trees. A man's life just wasn't worth much at all."[62]

Witnessing a widespread lack of respect for human life remained with Warnock throughout his life. Encountering dead bodies was especially troubling when the victims were not strangers. Warnock sympathized with Jesus Bazán and Antonio Longoria's precarious position, stating, "You felt sorry for them. One of these men I knew real well, sixty-seven-year-old Jesus Bazán." He continued, "These Mexicans were afraid that if they told the Rangers anything, the bandits would kill them, but if they hadn't helped the bandits, then the bandits would have killed them. They were right in the middle of it and didn't know what to do."[63] Warnock remained bewildered. No certain course of action could protect his neighbors from meeting violence.

The double murder, however, was just one of many violent acts Warnock witnessed that year. At the time, his father, Frank, worked for John Hammond, who owned the Melando Land Company near Monte Cristo, Texas.[64] Hammond partitioned up the land and cultivated citrus farms to sell to Anglo farmers moving into what was known as "Magic Valley." Farmers and developers relied heavily on engineers and mechanics to design and perform maintenance on machinery for industrial farming.[65] The Melando Land Company used multiple machines, including water pumps for irrigation and cotton gins for the removal of seeds from harvested cotton. Frank Warnock worked to keep the machines running. As part of his compensation, John Hammond ran a two-inch pipe to Warnock's home to transport water for the household.

After some time, Hammond turned a portion of the Melando properties over to brothers William and Edward Arthur Sterling, who came from a wealthy family, to see whether they could improve his investment.[66] Donning their usual cowboy boots, spurs, and leggings only helped the brothers, at six and a half feet tall, tower over local residents. Now in charge, they ordered Frank Warnock to work day and night under arduous conditions. Tensions between Frank Warnock and the Sterling brothers steadily increased, but the breaking point of the relationship arose over a malfunctioning cotton gin.[67]

One day during harvest season the Sterling brothers ordered Warnock to fix a cotton gin that broke at 3:00 a.m. As Roland Warnock told the story, "They only lacked two or three bales of cotton finishing, but Papa told them, 'I am just give out. It's going to take about two hours to fix this and I'm so tired I just don't feel like it. Let's shut it down and we'll fix it in the morning.'" The brothers refused and insisted he fix the gin. Warnock responded, "Well, gin it then"; he quit the job on the spot and left the men to fix the machine themselves. The Sterlings ordered two laborers to disassemble the pipes delivering water to the Warnock home. After discovering the problem, Warnock guarded the spot with his Winchester rifle. Otto Woods and Frank Lamb returned in the morning to finish the job, but Warnock told them to leave the pipes in place. He ordered them to tell "those long legged sons of bitches to come back here and take it out themselves." Frank Lamb ignored the warning and removed the pipe. Frank Warnock shot him and, as Roland remembered, "killed him dead right there."[68] Warnock drove into Edinburg and turned himself in to county officers. He was indicted for the murder of Frank Lamb and released on bond.[69]

Just two days after Roland Warnock helped bury the bodies of Jesus Bazán and Antonio Longoria, he went into Mission to meet his father.[70] The father and son stood outside a hardware store visiting with friends. The Sterling brothers soon walked down the sidewalk and approached Frank Warnock from behind. Before Roland Warnock could react, he saw the Sterlings "come around this corner with automatics in their hands and they hadn't taken no more than about three long, big steps, and they emptied their guns. Papa never did know what hit him. They put nine bullets in his back. He just fell right across in front of me."[71]

Roland Warnock escaped with only a minor bullet injury to his arm, but his father's body tumbled forward. Roland ran home in fear to tell his mother. She ran out the door to see her husband's body in downtown Mission. "I begged her not to go then, but she went anyway. She met the Sterlings as she left the house and started up the street. They didn't bother her, but they came right by the house. I still didn't have a gun. I just had to stand there and watch them pass . . . I have always blamed myself for that."[72] On the morning of October 2, 1915, Roland Warnock and his mother left south Texas accompanied by the body of his father. They buried Frank Warnock in Christoval, near the town of San Angelo, in north Texas.[73]

The shooting caught the attention of local journalists enthralled by two prominent ranchers shooting a local farmer in broad daylight in the business district of town. The Sterling brothers were arrested and charged with murder but released on $2,500 bond. Local newspapers covered the trial nearly a year later. The state retained Judge W. R. Jones to assist the local district attorney in the prosecution, and the law firm of Judge James B. Wells represented the Sterlings. One local resident took the stand to testify that Warnock was unarmed at the time of the shooting and that he had urged the farmer to remain armed while in town. Texas Ranger Paul West claimed the opposite. West testified that he witnessed Warnock reaching for a gun before the brothers fired a shot. The *Brownsville Herald* reported, "West was certain that Warnock had a gun." The jury found William and Edward Sterling not guilty on the grounds that they acted in self-defense.[74]

Roland Warnock left with images in his mind of the murders he witnessed. It seems probable that he mourned the death of Bazán and Longoria not only because he witnessed the cold-blooded killing, or because he knew the ranchers, but also because their deaths were intimately tied to the death of his own father in time, location, and the presence of William Sterling. After witnessing the murder of Bazán, Longoria, and his father all within a week of each other, he became overwhelmed with the blatant disregard for the value of human life. Those like Warnock who witnessed residents, alongside local and state police, commit acts of violence and walk about without care or worry carried fear with them. The sight of violence was not easily forgotten. Warnock later lamented, "For a long time I couldn't sleep at night. I could see it just as plain as if it were yesterday, and it was 46 years ago last fall." Unlike the shootings of Frank Lamb and Frank Warnock that resulted in arrests and trial, the double murder of Jesus Bazán and Antonio Longoria, without any public investigation, unsettled Roland Warnock.

For the Bazán and Longoria families, what options were available for redress? Without judicial investigations they had to chart out how to live in a climate that made their families vulnerable to violence. It is likely that the two widows knew that a Mexican did not stand a fair chance in a Texas courtroom. If sociologist Paul S. Taylor's early work serves as any indicator, in Hidalgo County, as in Nueces County, it was probably common knowledge that a woman would, at best, not be taken seriously in a court of law.[75] At worst, if an ethnic Mexican challenged law enforcement agents for committing a crime, violence could be a real consequence. After weighing the options, protesting these acts of violence seemed too risky.

By 1915, ethnic Mexicans were overwhelmingly relegated to manual labor in Texas. The numbers of ethnic Mexican landowners were shrinking, and they remained vulnerable to efforts to remove them from their property.

When legal channels failed, violence became an expedient method. "You don't buy from the husband, you buy from the widow" became a popular saying. It gestured to a widespread practice of executing landowning men to force the sale of land by their widows through threats of physical violence.

In this climate, Epigmenia Treviño Bazán, age sixty-five, Antonia Bazán Longoria, age thirty-eight, and their children continued to live on the ranch in the aftermath of the double murder. For one source of income, Epigmenia Bazán leased out portions of her property to relatives, and the two widows baked goods to sell for extra money.[76] Antonia Longoria was well known for making corn tortillas daily from scratch, *empanadas de calabaza* (pumpkin turnovers), and special *jícama* candies.[77] Bazán's adult children—Pedro, Jesus Jr., Gregorio, Petra, Enemencio, Luisa, and Mercedes—helped their mother remain on the property until she passed away on November 18, 1938, at eighty-four years old.[78] After the double murder, the Longorias' oldest children lived in nearby towns: Adela worked as a bookkeeper at the Edinburg courthouse and for the Hidalgo County clerk, and Pedro eventually owned two dry goods stores in the towns of Mission and San Benito. In 1920 Antonia moved to Donna and lived there for four years.[79] Her nieces, nephews, and grandchildren called her "Mama Toncha," in part for her habit of making a home for family members and close friends. She was known as a strict disciplinarian, and several of her siblings' children lived in her home while they attended school or worked in town. Long after she moved to Donna, Longoria practiced *remedios,* or folk medicine, and local residents frequently called on her to deliver babies or to cure *susto* (fright) or *mal de ojo* (evil eye) or to be anointed with *aceite de palo* (an herbal ointment) to heal scratches, cuts, and bruises. In 1924 Antonia and her family moved to Mission, where she lived in the same house until her death in 1966.[80] With the exception of a portion of land Epigmenia Bazán donated for the cemetery where Jesus Bazán and Antonio Longoria were buried and for the Guadalupe el Torero Cemetery, the Bazán and Longoria widows passed the property down to their children.[81] By keeping quiet the widows were able to remain in the region. They would, however, share the story of the double murder with trusted friends and relatives.

The children of Antonia and Antonio Longoria led active lives in south Texas as business owners, policemen, and members of local churches and

Epigmenia Treviño Bazán *(center left)* stands on her porch with surviving family members. Her daughter Petra stands on the left with her daughters Luisa *(hand on hip)* and Mercedes to the right. The baby in front is Eloisa, daughter of Antonio and Antonia Longoria. Despite violence and intimidation, the women decided not to leave their ranch, ultimately passing it on to their children. Courtesy Norma L. Rodriguez. Photo provided by the Bullock Texas State History Museum.

civic organizations. The civil services provided by Antonio before his death and the contributions of Antonia and her children were publicly recognized in Mission nearly a century after Antonio's death. On June 30, 2006, the Mission Historical Museum posthumously awarded Antonia Bazán Longoria the President's Pioneer Award, in recognition of her family's long-standing contributions to the early Rio Grande Valley region.[82] The celebration made no mention of the violence the families had suffered. Perhaps in another context, the family's success would be an example of the American dream of prosperity through hard work, determination, and diplomas. For the Longoria and Bazán families, however, theirs was a story of resilience in the face of intimidation and state terror. The public recognition and award stands in stark contrast to the erasure of the 1915 double murder from official records. That the family survived the hostile climate and maintained their property does not ease the long legacy of violence. Their success did not answer or resolve the relatives' lingering questions about the double murder, the denial of justice, and ongoing failures to grapple with racial violence in Texas.

INHERITED LOSS

Racial violence transformed the daily realities of entire communities in 1915. It shuttered businesses and shattered families and spread fear throughout the region. Amid these convulsions, however, residents preserved the memories of those they lost. They also passed on oral accounts of murder to friends and relatives. Younger generations would have their lives interrupted by grisly details of men shot in cold blood. When they heard that Texas Rangers, idols of state history, had murdered their relatives with impunity, it shook their understanding of the past. When they searched for more information and found there were no records, the silence sent some on a quest to document the violence and leave a record of the murders.

Kirby Warnock and Norma Longoria Rodriguez are two Texas residents who separately learned about the double murder in conversations with relatives. Neither of them grew up knowing the history, but in both cases they stumbled upon the double murder in their own surveys into family history. The two represent a larger group of residents who have found ways to make histories of racial violence available to the public. To preserve memories of the murdered, lynched, and dispossessed, they operated with a sense of urgency to keep these histories from being forgotten. These vernacular history-making practices give faces and names to victims and communities and cast an alternative light on state violence.

In 1973 Kirby Warnock interviewed his grandfather for the Institute for Oral History at Baylor University while he was a student. From this interview he learned the "dark history" of the Texas Rangers. He became eager to raise awareness of this fraught history. The eighteen-hour interview became the primary source for the published oral memoir of Roland Warnock, titled *Texas Cowboy* (1992), and the documentary Kirby completed a decade later, *Border Bandits* (2004). He also made his research and the full oral history with his grandfather available on his website.[83] Warnock screened the documentary in Texas communities starting in 2004 on what he titled the "Texas Justice Tour."[84]

The documentary opens with the Ramirez Family Band's Spanish version of the Eagles' popular hit "Desperado." The band's sorrowful performance audibly situates the viewer in a very familiar version of south Texas, but the opening testimony of Roland Warnock makes clear that the perspective of the narrative will be anything but familiar. As the camera pans slowly across the desolate scrub brush of south Texas, we hear in voiceover Warnock telling his grandson about burying Jesus Bazán and Antonio Longoria. He was a ranch hand at the Guadalupe Ranch in Hidalgo County. In an assertive voice he declares that the men were unarmed when the Texas Rangers shot them in the back and that no formal investigation took place. Warnock's narrative is then joined by the perspective of his grandson Kirby, two generations removed from the event.

The intertwining of these two perspectives introduces the reader to a narrative structure that moves back and forth between past and current accounts of the 1915 murder. Although the two voices remain distinct, the transitions between the two perspectives are fluid. For example, during the opening scene Kirby's account is synchronized with his grandfather's, so that as Roland tells the story his voice fades and eventually his grandson, presumably reading from the transcript of the oral history, completes the thought. This stylistic editing blurs the two distinct temporalities from which the narrative voices speak. The editing also makes it difficult for the viewer to distinguish whether they are hearing testimony from Roland's memory, from the memories of the story Kirby has internalized, or from the historical research Kirby conducted.

The documentary plays with temporality and history as nuanced forms of storytelling. This is most clearly exemplified when Roland recalls burying Bazán and Longoria in September 1915, as we see two repeating photographs of the graves in the present day. The film then again disrupts linear time in the closing scene, when the description of Roland burying the bodies overlays the image of his grandson visiting the grave sites. The viewer hears and watches as both men simultaneously lament the deaths. The film produces a narrative of a lived memory that continues to evolve, a memory carried in the body. In key moments like these, the film reminds us that this violence cannot be relegated to the past. Though the film is clearly a retelling of historical events, the viewer is consistently reminded that past events continue to be felt in present-day Texas.[85]

In making the film Kirby Warnock searched for family members of Bazán and Longoria who remained in south Texas. He filmed interviews with Heriberto Longoria, the one-year-old son of Antonio Longoria at the time of the double murder. With sorrow, Heriberto described the challenges of going through life without a father. He also lamented that the families never received a day in court. No investigation and no prosecution meant that the family had to live with the sense of injustice for generations. Heriberto F. Longoria Jr., who worked as assistant attorney general for the state of Texas, stared into the camera, a deadpan expression on his face, and talked about the grandmother who used to tell him about the death of his grandfather. Each time, he explained, she would become overwhelmed and begin to cry. In editing these interviews, Kirby Warnock carefully highlighted the long-lasting consequences of the double murder for generations of Bazán and Longoria descendants.

In the absence of judicial resolve, the descendants had to make sense of the tragedy in their own terms. The great-grandson of Jesus Bazán, Jon Bazán, works as a physician in the south Texas town of Harlingen. In the film he vehemently states, "I believe that the Texas Rangers were to the Mexican Americans and the Native Americans what the KKK was to the African Americans, and the only thing is that [the Rangers] were legal."[86]

As Dr. Bazán compares the practices of the Texas Rangers to the organized racial terror used by the Ku Klux Klan, he invokes a longer history of state violence against ethnic Mexicans living in Texas as well as state and vigilante terror against indigenous and black communities throughout the United States. He also points to an important distinction between members of the KKK, who hid behind white masks, and the Texas Rangers, who committed extralegal acts in broad daylight and in front of witnesses. The Texas Rangers carried state badges and acted in the name of the law. In both cases, local courts failed more often than not to prosecute this extralegal violence. Bazán's account highlights the intersecting histories in Texas often overlooked in public memory and by historians alike.

The documentary pays special attention to naming the agents of violence. During a segment of *Border Bandits* titled "The Killers," Warnock introduces the viewer to the Rangers Roland Warnock identified as men who rode together that day. The names of Captain Henry Ransom, Paul West, and William W. Sterling, the three men who collaborated to shoot Bazán and Longoria in 1915, are described as agents of violence. Linking the double murder to the death of his own great-grandfather, Warnock made a clear effort to document both the names of the dead and of those who took their lives. Likewise, the injustice Roland Warnock expressed at seeing Sterling walk free despite his involvement in a series of gruesome events is evident in the documentary.

Roland Warnock remembered with disbelief that William Sterling joined the Texas Rangers in 1918 and went on to an illustrious career. He rose to the highest rank and eventually served as the Texas Ranger adjutant general. Warnock would later read Sterling's memoir, *Trails and Trials of a Texas Ranger*. He explained to his grandson, "You would think that Bill Sterling was sprouting wings to read that book. Oh, a lot of what he said was true, but a lot of it was just wind. Our name was never mentioned, or that killing."[87] In his memoir Sterling posits that he worked diligently throughout his career as a Texas Ranger but retired without taking one single life during his tenure. Although Sterling was not a Texas Ranger at the time of the shootings in 1915, Roland Warnock's account remembers him as a man with blood on his hands. That Sterling conveniently erased Frank Warnock, Jesus Bazán, and Antonio Longoria from his memoir left Roland Warnock unsettled.

In the documentary, Kirby Warnock is careful not to conflate the murder of Jesus Bazán and Antonio Longoria with the murder of his great-grandfather. He memorialized the murder of Frank Warnock by publishing his memoir, which he hoped would disrupt the celebration of Sterling's legacy and make a wider indictment of the judicial system for protecting those with access to power and social clout. Yet in the film he is careful to explain that the execution of Jesus Bazán and Antonio Longoria represented an injustice of another sort. His grandfather's killer had at least been tried in court. The press, too, took notice of the shooting, the death, and the trial. Although Bazán and Longoria were landed Tejanos, their race outweighed their class. For these two ethnic Mexicans, there was no investigation, no trial, and not even a public acknowledgment of the double murder. This represented an even graver form of injustice; the loss of life was disrespected and ignored by the press and the local judicial system. Kirby Warnock, moved by what his grandfather witnessed, made the double murder and anti-Mexican violence the central focus of the documentary.

Border Bandits asks viewers to question the public memorials that celebrate Texas Rangers who participated in racial violence. The film ends by describing the graves of Henry Ransom and William Sterling, allowing the reader to visualize the disparity between the lives of Bazán and Longoria on one hand and Ransom and Sterling on the other, as they continue even in death. Sterling, who died in 1960, rests in Corpus Christi. His grave is decorated with a historical marker celebrating his service as a Texas Ranger. In contrast, the grave sites of Jesus Bazán and Antonio Longoria have tombstones, but neither is dignified with a historical marker. In the absence of the public recognition of past social injustices, Warnock mourns the legacy of racial violence in Texas.

During an interview with the *San Antonio Express News* in 2004, Warnock described sharing the controversial history with local residents. He explained, "This is a Western, but it's not a romantic [film] like most Westerns. It's dark. It doesn't have a happy Hollywood ending."[88] In particular, unlike in Westerns that romanticize and celebrate vigilantism and state agents, Warnock attempts to expose the brutalities of Captain Ransom and others. These screenings, often to sold-out crowds, attracted academics, local historians, and the wider public. The film *Border Bandits* became so popular that in San Antonio the Alamo Draft House movie theater held encore viewings to meet audience demand.[89]

Perhaps most interestingly, the screenings drew people who shared a common history with the Bazán and Longoria families. For some in the audience, the screenings became a public space to vocalize how the past continued to influence their lives. Warnock frequently traveled to the screenings and answered questions from the audience. The exchanges frequently turned into testimonials in which audience members explained their own relationships to tragic histories of death at the hands of Texas Rangers or famous ranch owners.[90]

Some viewers found solace in the company of others with similar troubled histories, but some who identified with the Texas Rangers had reactions of their own. In 2004 Tom Vinger, a spokesman for the Texas Department of Public Safety, explained that the events of 1915 had no relationship to today's Texas Rangers. The film made no insinuation that current state agents bore responsibility for the violence of the past. To the contrary, Kirby Warnock went to painful lengths throughout the documentary to describe the state police as elite officers. He was, perhaps, overly cautious of how his film might be perceived. The film begins with a printed disclaimer that reads: "It is the stated opinion of the producers of this film that the Texas Rangers are an elite law enforcement organization. The events portrayed in this production took place in 1915, and would not be possible today because of safeguards enacted by the Texas legislature and the Ranger force."[91]

Still, Vinger interpreted the film as unfairly staining the reputation of the state police. He argued that past events have no current social relevance. Without refuting any of the events covered in *Border Bandits,* he stated, "There's zero correlation."[92] For Vinger the crimes remained relegated to the past; he missed an important opportunity to participate in the public dialogue sparked by the documentary.

Vinger was not alone in quickly dismissing the documentary. Two years later, a *San Antonio Express News* journalist interviewed Jim McAllen, a relative of the McAllen family portrayed in the film and a supporter of the Hidalgo County Historical Museum. McAllen, like Vinger, refused to acknowledge the state police's collusion with vigilantes. Instead, he offered the clichéd observation that there are two sides to every story and that *Border Bandits* showed only one side. "I won't go there. [Warnock's] got a vendetta against the Rangers."[93] By describing Kirby Warnock as merely feuding with the Texas Rangers, McAllen dismissed the historians who contributed to the documentary, the archival documents it displayed, and the testimonies provided by generations that worked to preserve the history.

In circulating the documentary, Kirby Warnock helped demystify the heroic myths surrounding law enforcement agents and unsettle assumptions of people labeled as "bandits." He asked the public to reimagine the Texas frontier as a fraught social context, in which state officials and civilians devalued the life of ethnic Mexicans. In this same light, screenings of the documentary created opportunities for local residents to share their own histories and to publicly bemoan Texas's violent past.

In 2006 Warnock again encouraged the public to acknowledge the history of anti-Mexican violence in Texas. In an interview with the *San Antonio Express News* he described the use of violence to intimidate and forcibly remove ethnic Mexican landowners from their property in the early twentieth century. Warnock addressed the dispossession of land that underlay the racial tensions:

> They used this bandit thing as an excuse to go relieve almost all the Hispanics in the Valley of their land. The Rangers would kill tons of Mexicans, pile their bodies up and take pictures of them. . . . They had a saying, you don't buy from the husband, you buy from the widow. And I'm not saying strong-arming happened for every ranch down there, but it happened for quite a few of them.[94]

In the documentary and in subsequent interviews, Kirby Warnock made efforts to remind the public that the double murder of Jesus Bazán and Antonio Longoria reflected a widespread phenomenon of land displacement through violence and intimidation.

The documentary points out that the stories in *Border Bandits* exist because a grandfather told his grandson what he saw during his young adult life and then asks the viewer to consider the following: "Imagine a grandfather telling a grandson that his father was shot . . . imagine that multiplied by hundreds if not thousands."[95] The film thus prompts the viewer to think about the magnitude of generational storytelling. If the murder of Bazán and Longoria affected the surviving relatives and witnesses for more than a century, and hundreds if not thousands of murders occurred during this period, then we should assume there are other families living with similar traumas. For them the state's icons are not heroes but painful reminders of past violence. The long-standing effects of these stories are then exacerbated by the disavowal of this period of state terror in public history exhibits, popular culture, and public school textbooks.[96]

Norma Longoria Rodriguez was a Texas resident who learned from her father that Texas Rangers had been involved in the murder of her great-grandfather and grandfather. After searching for historical records of the deaths in state and university libraries and coming up empty-handed, in 1992 she interviewed her surviving aunt and uncle, Ernestina Longoria Martinez and Armando Longoria, who witnessed the initial robbery and the actions of their mother and grandmother after the double murder. She consulted with cousins to recover family papers and created a private archive of documents and photographs. Rodriguez studied her collection and used what she learned to write and publish poetry and historical essays online and in local newspapers. Generational memory, in this case, worked to preserve narrative accounts of the double murder, fill gaps in institutional archives, challenge social scripts provided by mainstream narratives, and draw our attention to the surviving relatives who made lives in the aftermath of violence.

In the mid-1970s, Rodriguez traveled with her father, Heriberto Longoria, to the grave sites for Jesus Bazán and Antonio Longoria. She lived in San Antonio, but on trips home to see her family she would go with her father to the family homestead in Hidalgo County. On one trip she noticed a discrepancy on the tombstones for Antonio Longoria and Jesus Bazán, which suggested the two men died on different days. According to Rodriguez, her father frankly told her, "Well I don't know why it's different, they were both murdered on the same day. . . . Killed by the Texas Rangers."[97] What would have been just another trip to pay respects at a family grave site shook Rodriguez. Despite spending time growing up with her grandmother Antonia Longoria, she had never heard of her relatives being murdered. As a child, Rodriguez's mother attempted to shield her from the family tragedy. When she was four or five years old, Rodriguez remembered asking about her grandparents. Her paternal grandmother was still alive, but she wanted to know about the others. Her mother explained that her parents had passed away and that her father's father and grandfather were shot and killed in a case of mistaken identity. The two men, riding their horses on the McAllen Ranch, Rodriguez was told, were mistaken for bandits and killed. Perhaps her mother wanted to protect her young daughter from a frightful memory or keep her from feeling contempt or confusion. The account she learned from her father when she was nearly thirty, an adult with a family and a job as a teacher, was far more charged. He bluntly described state police murdering her grandfather and great-grandfather. This challenged her perceptions of her family history and Texas history more broadly.

In her own words, "I went home and I went straight to the library."[98] Nearly sixty years after the event, Rodriguez began a search for more information about the double murder. She began traveling to Austin to conduct archival research at the University of Texas and at the Lorenzo de Zavala Texas State Archives. After years of searching, she still found no institutional records in public libraries, court archives, or newspaper accounts that mentioned the double murder or referenced the names of Antonio Longoria and Jesus Bazán. She became especially frustrated that no death certificates existed.

Turning to family memories, at first, was not easy. Rodriguez realized that her father was only one year old at the time. What she could learn from him would be secondhand. Shortly after her trip to the graves in 1973, she turned to interviewing her two aunts, who were eight and thirteen years old at the time of the murder. In an interview with me, Rodriguez said that when she started researching her family history, she did not know what she was doing. She simply sat her two aunts down together and asked them frankly to tell her the story about the double murder. She continued her research periodically throughout the years, while working full-time as a public school teacher in San Antonio and raising a family.[99]

As the years passed, Rodriguez regained momentum in researching the event. She focused on three tasks: to document the resilience of her relatives by conducting oral histories that highlighted her family's survival; to pass on her family history by narrating the story to her children and other family members; and to document the deaths of her grandfather and great-grandfather by publishing essays and poetry that honored them.

In the 1990s Rodriguez decided to interview her relatives again. She started with her aunt Ernestina, who opened up about the double murder. Rodriguez took notes by hand and typed them up. She realized it was important for her to get the story on record, so she purchased a recorder and, without any training, in 1992 sat with her aunt and uncle, Ernestina Longoria Martinez and Armando Longoria, the children of Antonia and Antonio Longoria. She eventually made a transcript of the entire interview.

Rodriguez asked what, if anything, the relatives had done to protest the double murder. She found that in the days following the violent tragedy, many visitors and family members came to offer the family their condolences, pay their respects, and ask Antonia Longoria whether she planned to pursue the assailants in court. Antonia worried especially for the vulnerability of her brothers, whom she believed would be the next targets of violence. Ernestina remembered overhearing her distraught mother responding to inquiries by saying, "'What would be the point in my making other children orphans?'"[100] Rodriguez read broadly the history of this period and eventually realized why her grandmother and great-grandmother kept their protests private. She explained to me simply, "The penalty of death. That's what would happen if they found that a man was lynched. The rest of the family was also in danger, especially the men. That's when they fell silent."[101]

Rodriguez learned that the women in her family had kept the story from the younger children in the years following the double murder. No one discussed the details of the killing with Heriberto or the other children in the family in the immediate aftermath because they feared that naming the Texas Rangers involved in the murder would bring further violence to the family. Antonia Longoria must have known that her children needed to know the truth. She waited until Heriberto was eight years old. She sat him down and shared the details of how his father and grandfather died at the hands of Texas Rangers.

Rodriguez concluded that the threats of violence kept her relatives from publicly challenging the murders of Bazán and Longoria. The threat of violence also shaped when relatives decided to talk about the event and when to keep quiet. Silence offered one means of protecting the family. Antonia Longoria's fear of "making more orphans" is as a reminder that women, too, could be victims of racial violence. During her research Rodriguez learned of other families—entire families—that had been killed. "It wasn't just men killed," she continued. "I've been reading cases of whole families, small children, killed or hung. Lynched . . . there was a lot of unrest and the [Mexican] Revolution made it easy to disguise killings . . . just say 'bandido' or 'sympathizer.'"[102] The thought of lynched children stayed with Rodriguez. As her journey through the past continued, she carried these other histories of violence along with her as she tried to make sense of her own family history.

From her family history Rodriguez learned that in the days following the double murder the family recovered one stolen colt, but neither the rest of the stolen horses nor the robbers returned to the ranch. When asked whether the family feared the return of the thieves, Ernestina replied emphatically, "Afraid? You are asking if we were afraid to be at the ranch? No, not mother. She was not afraid. She was brave." According to Ernestina, raids on local ranches stopped soon after the incident and the family continued living on the ranch for another five years before finally moving to Edinburg. Her brother Armando explained, "We left and the ranches remained alone . . . [as] witnesses."[103]

Although Norma Rodriguez grew up spending time alone with her grandmother Antonia, she never heard the details of the events directly from her grandmother. While investigating this case as an adult, however, she learned that her brother heard the story from their grandmother at a young age: "She just opened up to him."[104] Rodriguez remembered the relationship between her grandmother and brother as a "special kinship," a deep relationship. Perhaps her brother had a semblance of his grandfather Antonio, or perhaps Antonia believed young ethnic Mexican men needed to be warned of the dangers of race relations in south Texas.

Rodriguez was both amazed and frustrated by her family's actions following the double murder. She recognized the climate of violence and intimidation that shaped her family's strategic decisions to discuss or remain silent about the family history. Still, Rodriguez remained uneasy by what she described as the "code of silence" the Bazán and Longoria widows bore to protect their children from danger. In her essay "Silence of the Heart," she expresses grief for one of the consequences of this silence: "Unfortunately the silence on the part of the family and the community gave credence and perpetuity to the myth that the Rangers were 'above the law.'"[105] Given the climate of racial animosity toward ethnic Mexicans, Rodriguez sympathizes with Antonia Longoria and Epigmenia Bazán, who chose to "undertake a code of silence regarding the fate of their husbands. Whether this code of silence was borne out of sorrow, or self-imposed to protect themselves and their children from harm, or as a means of continuing with their lives as all women of every generation and culture have done, or a combination of all three possibilities, is indeterminate." Contextualizing the actions of Antonia and Epigmenia in a longer history of gendered survival and resilience, Rodriguez understood her grandmother and great-grandmother as "doing what they had to do to survive . . . especially for their children."[106]

Nearly 100 years later, Rodriguez decided the silence had to come to an end. She recognized the need to disrupt patterns of erasure and silence. She took on the task of documenting the stories of people who lived in the aftermath of state violence. While the histories Rodriguez had read of this period described families that left their homes in fear, never to be heard from again, she knew that these histories did not account for the multiple strategies borderlands residents used to challenge state violence, including remaining on their property. Rodriguez noted that even in Kirby Warnock's documentary *Border Bandits,* he depicted the Bazán and Longoria families as disappearing and abandoning their property. She and her family members drove to different cities in Texas screening the documentary and expressed gratitude to Kirby Warnock for his work. But she made a point to correct his characterization: "Warnock says the family left and disappeared, but no, we are everywhere. . . . In our case it didn't happen that way. My grandmother never sold anything."[107]

Rodriguez decided to write her own account of the double murder. In her publications, she demands, "These stories can no longer be ignored, minimized or covered up by explanations that conveniently protected the guilty parties and justified their actions."[108] Rodriguez's writings underscore how the double murder affected her family for generations. She helped reinscribe Antonia Longoria and Epigmenia Bazán as active residents able to maintain their property and livelihood after being widowed. She published both "Silence of the Heart" and a biography of her grandmother Antonia Bazán Longoria on her cousin Hernán Contreras's website, Los Tejanos. The piece received attention from the organizers of a genealogical website who republished Rodriguez's essay on their website, *Somos Primos*.[109] Transcriptions of the interviews she conducted with her aunt Ernestina Longoria Martinez and uncle Armando Longoria are available on the Los Tejanos website in both Spanish and English. They give insight into growing up without a father or grandfather and with a mother who had navigated threats of intimidation and violence marked their childhood. Rodriguez also honored the memories of Jesus Bazán and Antonio Longoria by publishing poetry in the *San Antonio Express News* on the anniversary of the double murder.[110]

In some memorials Rodriguez kept the violent history private. For example, in November 2008 she dedicated her poem "The Old Windmills / Los Papalotes," to her grandfather and great-grandfather on the ninety-third anniversary of their deaths. In describing the old windmills of south Texas she writes,

> Though assaulted by time, they stand stoic,
> like ghostly, battle-weary knights in tarnished armor.
> Abandoned relics of the last century,
> they linger precariously on the landscape:
> mute witnesses to secrets of long-ago kingdoms.[111]

The dedication did not mention the circumstances of their deaths. Perhaps Rodriguez sought an opportunity to remember the loss of her grandfather and great-grandfather, to restore some dignity, without addressing the double murder that ended their life. And yet the last stanza is a reminder that past histories are embedded in the south Texas land-scape. Even when histories of violence are not named explicitly, they are present.

Rodriguez continued to tell her family's history. In November 2014, she published a literary *ofrenda,* (offering) to her grandfather Antonio Long-oria in a special *Ofrendas y Calaveras* issue of the magazine *La Voz de Esperanza,* a publication of the Esperanza Peace and Justice Center in San Antonio. Here Rodriguez memorialized Antonio's legacy as an educator. He was certified to teach primary school in 1896, 1898, 1900, and 1902 and turned a storeroom adjacent to the family homestead into a classroom. When people asked Antonio how long he would continue teaching, she wrote, he would answer, "Voy a dar clases aquí hasta que venga alguien que verdaderamente sepa lo que esta haciendo. (I am going to continue teaching here until someone comes along who really knows what he or she is doing.)"[112] Rodriguez described the double murder in 1915 and praised her grandmother Antonia and great-grandmother Epigmenia for their fortitude and for continuing Antonio's legacy by encouraging the next generation of children to embrace education. The two buildings on the homestead, both of which he built from *sillar,* a mixture of lime and clay, are still standing.

Rodriguez dedicated this memorial to a living family member—her cousin Richard Martínez, Antonio's grandson, who restored the home-stead. She visited the schoolhouse and described her experience. "As I cross the threshold, I imagine I hear children's voices. In my mind's eye, I see the schoolchildren in *la escuelita.* They are seated around a long wooden table as Antonio teaches the three R's." Rodriguez relished the opportu-nity to imagine her grandfather alive in the idyllic place where he taught children the alphabet, spelling, and math. Standing in the schoolhouse and informed by her archival research, the teaching certificates she found, and the memories of her aunt and uncle she preserved, she pieced together a living memory of the grandfather she never met. By restoring the school-house, her cousin provided a memorial that honored Bazán and Longoria in life, not just in death. She thanked her cousin for restoring the build-ings "where his mother was born, and *la escuelita* on his ranch in memory of our ancestors."[113] Rodriguez has a painting of the schoolhouse on dis-play in her home.

Rodriguez publishes these narratives so that the stories of her loved ones cannot be erased, and she shares the story with her own children. Mario,

Bianca, Marco, and Roberto all know the family history and have all shared the burden of its weight. Two of her sons wrote about the double murder for courses during their undergraduate education as an attempt to further document the events and to process how their family responded to the violence. Describing how her children also grapple with this history, she explained, "It's always there. It's a part of their life I think. It's an injustice. It never leaves you. It's inherited loss." Despite never directly knowing her murdered relatives, the injustice of their deaths continues to affect her and her children four generations later. "I didn't really know the story, but once I knew it affects you very deeply. Then when you know it was multiplied many times, this is just two of them. There are so many others."[114] By describing the injustice she learned about as a feeling that "never leaves you," Rodriguez offers a glimpse into the mixed emotions of loss and indignation that cross generations.[115]

For Rodriguez, the first step in reckoning requires a recentering of the bodies and identities of subjects of state violence. During an oral interview, Rodriguez reflected on having forty years of her life interrupted by this inherited tragedy. She did not express anger. Instead, she reflected on her deep sense of remorse that she did not have an opportunity to meet Roland Warnock before he passed away. Her relatives held important information, but Warnock witnessed the shootings. If Rodriguez and Kirby Warnock had met earlier in their archival searches, she could have asked his grandfather the most intimate and lingering questions about the murder of Jesus Bazán and Antonio Longoria. "That has been my biggest regret," she lamented. "They could have asked [Roland Warnock]. We could have asked him, 'Did they die immediately?' We hope they did. We assume they did."[116] Among the many unanswered questions, those about the last moments of Bazán and Longoria are the most haunting for Rodriguez. Her questions are saturated with worry for a grandfather and great-grandfather she never met. She hopes that death came quickly and that they did not suffer in pain.

She found some solace in the accounts of Roland Warnock and Martiriano and Timotea Cantú, who were crucial in helping restore some respect for the two men by delivering them to a final resting place. In a climate in which law enforcement agents, vigilantes, and spectators alike disregarded the humanity of ethnic Mexicans, this civil act resisted the efforts of state terror to refuse residents the right to mourn the dead. For mourning survivors, remembering friends that had risked defying Ranger orders offered a moment of condolence.

By circulating alternative histories of this period, residents also teach the violence of racial conflict to the next generation. When asked why she dedicated so much energy over decades to documenting the murders, Rodriguez replied, "I wanted it in writing. I wanted my children to know the story, and I wanted them to pass it on."[117] Rodriguez offers "inherited loss" as a concept to articulate her family's intimate connection to this period of anti-Mexican violence. By attending to pain passed from generation to generation, Rodriguez has departed from the code of silence practiced by some in her family and embraced vernacular history-making to reckon with silenced histories of violence.

The continued circulation of the history of the double murder of Jesus Bazán and Antonio Longoria in 1915 shows that living in a period of racial violence is not a memory that is easily erased. Memorializing both the casualties and the survivors of violence remains a crucial motivating factor that inspires efforts to keep the history alive. Indeed, documenting the violence, mourning the loss of relatives gone more than a century ago, and sharing the story became one means to reckon with violence.

Residents like Norma Longoria Rodriguez and Kirby Warnock are shifting the circulation of generational memory by making these histories of violence available to the public. Their work disrupts patterns of anonymity, challenges the ongoing criminalization of the dead, confronts historical narratives that justify the violence inherent in nation-building practices, and makes evident the violent histories of border policing. Their vernacular history-making efforts have helped encourage a public dialogue about the history of state violence and injustice in Texas.

Efforts to memorialize the violence continue. In an article published in the *New York Times* in 2004, a journalist suggested that the documentary *Border Bandits* and the publication of historian Benjamin Johnson's book *Revolution in Texas* worked to "reopen old wounds."[118] The testimonies of Roland Warnock, Ernestina Longoria Martinez, Armando Longoria, Kirby Warnock, and Norma Longoria Rodriguez show us that these wounds had never healed to begin with.

The documentary caught the eye of Texas elected officials. After seeing the film at a screening in Harlingen, Texas state representative Aaron Peña of Edinburg announced that he planned to introduce a bill that would create a historical marker and monument at the grave sites of Jesus Bazán and Antonio Longoria. In addition, he described plans to introduce two more bills to memorialize the deaths; one would rename the stretch of road on FM 1017 where the men died as Tejano Memorial Highway, and the other would create a Tejano Heritage Day in Texas public schools. The memorials and the heritage day were aimed at initiating a discussion in schools about Texas's violent history. Representative Peña grew up in a household that told stories of treacherous Texas Rangers who terrorized Mexican communities. He explained, "the emotion has been tapped for so many years, and it's just exploded. It's taken on a life of its own." In analyzing the impact of contested Texas history, he explicated, "I think what happened down there goes to the root of the distrust between Anglos and Hispanics in Texas. It goes to the deep mistrust of law enforcement."[119]

The efforts to memorialize the double murder of Jesus Bazán and Antonio Longoria have been slow to materialize. In addition to submitting the application for a historical marker recognizing the lynching of Antonio Rodríguez in Edwards County in 1910, in 2014 I collaborated with the Hidalgo County Historical Association to submit a historical marker application for the 1915 double murder. The application highlighted the timely need to memorialize the 100-year anniversary of this tragedy and for a much-needed public acknowledgment of the widespread loss still felt in communities in south Texas. Persistence, in this case, paid off. The Texas Historical Commission rejected the application in the summer of 2014 and again in 2015, but finally in 2016 the commission approved the proposal. In the summer of 2017, the commission started coordinating with the Hidalgo County Commission to finalize the narrative for the plaque and to begin planning the historical marker unveiling ceremony.

CHAPTER THREE

Denial of Justice

IN WEST TEXAS, on the northern side of the Rio Grande just across the river from Chihuahua, Mexico, is a barren region known as the Big Bend. This region is lodged in a peculiar crook of the river, where the Rio Grande meets the southern tip of the Rocky Mountains and abruptly bends, shifting from a southeastern to a northeastern course. As a result, people living in the Big Bend are cradled on three sides by Mexico, from the east, south, and west. The desert climate averages an annual rainfall of only fifteen to seventeen inches. At 3,000 feet in elevation, the region avoids the scorching 100-plus-degrees summer temperatures found in south Texas, and the winter winds bring an uncharacteristic chill. The Big Bend runs from Candelaria on the Rio Grande fifty miles eastward to Marfa; the region's northern border runs parallel to the Southern Pacific Railroad tracks for over 100 miles through the rural towns of Alpine, Marathon, Sanderson, and Dryden.

The area has been a longtime destination for travelers looking to hike in stunning ravines and camp under a blanket of stars. The dusty landscape was once decorated by movie stars such as Elizabeth Taylor and James Dean, who took up residence in a hotel in Alpine while they filmed *Giant* (1956), an epic tale of west Texas cattle ranchers and oil tycoons. The desolate landscape again drew Hollywood when it became the backdrop for the neo-Western thriller *No Country for Old Men* (2007). Moving by car through west Texas, drivers can see ahead for miles on end. Because of the unbroken vistas, the landscape plays tricks with visual perception. Barbed-wire fences at great distances are invisible to the moving eye. When drivers get closer, the sun-scorched divisions of property become visible. Mountaintops that from a distance look like a mere blip on the horizon eventually tear into the sky and swallow the highway. Drivers share the road with eighteen-wheelers hauling goods, border patrol officers policing the vast region, and occasionally school buses of children traveling for sporting events. The communities that stand today are relics of earlier ones from a century ago.

The establishment of Fort Davis in 1854, outside of El Paso, brought the first Anglo cattle ranchers to the region. Some of the earliest Anglos in the region were Texas Rangers and former US cavalrymen stationed at Fort Davis to guard railroad survey teams. As the railroad moved west from Alpine to Marfa, eventually to link with El Paso, new residents arrived in the region. The fertile soil, rich with grama grasses, shrubs, trees, and edible cacti, provided enough water and vegetation for cattle ranching. However, early ranchers struggled to move their beef to nearby markets because of the mountainous terrain and regular periods of drought. Within a generation, miners began moving to the area, eager to excavate the region's rich mineral resources. The mining industry flourished in small towns like Shafter. By 1913, for example, a 300-ton mill allowed 600 tons of ore to be treated in twenty-four hours.[1]

The unforgiving desert and mountainous terrain that rendered the Big Bend difficult to explore also made the region notoriously difficult to police.[2] One Pecos County delegation claimed that the region "is a favorable resort of the murderers and desperados driven from other sections of the state."[3] This is not to say that all residents in the harsh climate supported criminal activities. But in the early twentieth century, lawmakers, ranchers, and state police would argue the opposite. They treated all Mexican residents of the region with suspicion.

In the early morning of January 28, 1918, Company B of the Texas Rangers and four local ranchmen—Buck Poole, John Poole, Tom Snyder, and Raymond Fitzgerald—surrounded the residents of Porvenir, a rural ranching community situated in the northeastern quadrant of the Big Bend region. With the help of the Eighth U.S. Cavalry Regiment, the Rangers and cattlemen woke up the residents and separated the fifteen able-bodied men and boys from the women, children, and elderly men. The posse then searched the homes for weapons. Ranger Captain James Monroe Fox then dismissed the cavalrymen. Without conducting interviews, the Rangers proceeded to execute their fifteen prisoners, who ranged in age from sixteen to sixty-four years old. Cavalry private Robert Keil later described what he witnessed: "For perhaps ten seconds we couldn't hear anything, and then it seemed that every woman down there screamed at the same time. It was an awful thing to hear in the dead of night. We could also hear what sounded like praying, and, of course, the small children were screaming with fright. Then we heard shots, rapid shots, echoing and blending in the dark."[4]

On the day preceding the Porvenir massacre, Texas Rangers rode into the camp of the Eighth Cavalry looking for Captain Harry Anderson. After dinner the captain introduced the Rangers to the gathered soldiers as men from Captain Fox's company at Marfa. The Rangers presented a letter from a Colonel Langhorne, which instructed the cavalry to assist the Rangers in searching the people of Porvenir, seizing all weapons, and ensuring that no one escaped inspection. When asked by the Rangers how many men lived in Porvenir, Captain Anderson replied that as many as twelve men were there at a time, because most worked on neighboring ranches throughout the year, in Marfa, Alpine, Valentine, and Van Horn.[5] Robert Keil remembered Captain Anderson disagreeing with the orders, especially the decision to search the residents at night, but he obliged the colonel's request. At approximately 10:30 p.m., Keil and others followed orders to leave for Porvenir.

When the soldiers arrived in Porvenir at 2:00 a.m., they carried out the Rangers' orders to wake the residents and gather them outside. In his memoir, Keil described trying to reassure the family members not to be alarmed as he woke them. However, his attempts seemed futile. Mere mention of the word "Rangers" inspired fear among the residents. He wrote, "this story will prove, I believe, that the terror was more than justified."[6] Soon after the Rangers asked the soldiers to withdraw, Captain Anderson asked the soldiers to hold their positions, as sounds of screaming, prayer, and gunshots echoed through the night. Captain Anderson then ordered the soldiers to return to the bluff. They arrived to hear the Rangers yelling, "We got him, Captain, we got him," before riding away on their horses.

As the soldiers reached the survivors, some women prayed, some cried, and a few pointed toward the bluff. Keil's memoir described the scene:

> At the foot of the bluff we could see a mass of bodies, but not a single movement. The bodies lay in every conceivable position, including one that seemed to be sitting against the rock wall. As soon as we were close, we smelled the nauseating sweetish smell of blood, and when we could see, we saw the most hellish sight that any of us had ever witnessed. It reminded me of a slaughterhouse. A hospital corpsman who was with us went over the bodies, but not a breath of life was left in a single one. The professionals had done their work well.[7]

In detailing the carnage, Keil noted that the arm of one of the young boys lay five feet from his body, while his other arm remained attached by only a thread of skin. An old man had his entire face blown away. Eulalia González Hernández found her husband being shot in the head and having been mutilated by stab wounds.[8] The entire bluff was stained with blood and human tissue.

The survivors reported that the fifteen victims were made to group together, facing the bluff. Standing three feet away, the Texas Rangers opened fire. After the victims fell, the Rangers emptied their guns into the bodies on the ground.[9] As Keil and his fellow cavalrymen tried to make sense of the carnage, the women made clear what had happened and why:

> The women crowded closer and our interpreter, who had her little boy in her arms, began to cry out what had happened. She told us they had first tied all the men together with a rope, then hit one with a pistol, knocking him down. They kicked and shoved them over to the bluff, and when she—the interpreter indicated another woman—tried to protest, she, too, was knocked down by the men. Then the interpreter corrected herself. "No! Not men—beasts, criminals! They had questioned no one at all," she said, "and their first words were threats, but when they were shooting the men, they asked each one, sneering, 'Are you Chico Cano?'"[10]

Years earlier, Chico Cano and his brothers José and Manuel were accused of killing three men, US Customs inspectors Joe Sitters and J. A. Howard and a cattle inspector, J. W. Harwick. The men had arrested Chico Cano for horse theft, but his brothers organized a raid and helped him escape.[11]

Cano continued to evade arrest and made a mockery of Rangers by causing turbulence in the region. Hunting for alleged bandits remained a common excuse for extralegal violence in 1918.

Captain Anderson acted quickly following the massacre. He sent a group of soldiers to get word to Colonel Langhorne, and a second group went to retrieve a priest twenty miles away. In the isolated terrain, residents would have to wait for a priest to bless what remained of their loved ones.[12]

A local schoolteacher, Harry Warren, took the survivors' statements. His father-in-law, Tiburcio Jácquez, was one of the murdered men. He noted that the group of survivors included women, children, elderly men, and two pregnant women.[13] Upon Warren's arrival, both Juan Flores (son of Longino Flores, one of the men killed) and John Bailey (the only Anglo man living in Porvenir the night of the massacre) showed him the bodies.[14] Only eleven years old, Juan Flores took on the enormous responsibility of helping identify his father and the other men for Warren's records.[15] The dead included Antonio Castañeda, Longino Flores, Alberto García, Eutimio González, Ambrosio Hernández, Pedro Herrera, Severiano Herrera, Vivian Herrera, Macedonio Huerta, Tiburcio Jácquez, Juan Jiménez, Pedro Jiménez, Serapio Jiménez Manuel Morales, and Román Nieves.

Following the Porvenir massacre, Harry Warren reflected on his conversations with the survivors. He wrote,

> The women and children then ran to the Mexican side of the river to a desert country where there wasn't a house or a sign of habitation, without a canopy to shield them from the pitiless winds of January and without a change of clothing and without a morsel to eat. There they stayed and the quiet little village of Porvenir with its peaceful farms and happy homes was no more! The Rangers and the four cowmen made 42 orphans that night.[16]

As accounts of the Porvenir massacre were circulated and published in the days, weeks, and months following the tragedy, competing interpretations of the Mexican ranching community emerged. State agents falsified reports and profiled the small ranching community as bandit sympathizers. They portrayed the massacre as a successful act by Texas Rangers to suppress a pocket of border unrest. Newspapers, like the *El Paso Times*, described the victims as Mexican peons and suspected bandits.[17] Witnesses to the violence—neighbors, soldiers, and relatives—gave competing testimonies and recorded their own accounts. Harry Warren's account, for example, draws our attention to the survivors, the widows and orphans, and the brutal decisions they faced: how to go on and how to live with the consequences of violence. Widows, children, and friends collaborated to hold the assailants accountable for their crimes and sought justice for loved ones. These witness accounts created the opportunity to charge the state for the unlawful practices of local and state police and US soldiers. Examining the Porvenir massacre and its aftermath reveals survivors who traversed national boundaries and navigated court systems and international commissions to seek justice.

In 1918 Texas courts failed to prosecute the Texas Rangers and civilians who participated in the massacre. Rather than accept this failure, residents utilized their Mexican national citizenship as a means to seek justice through international tribunals. By asserting their rights as Mexican nationals, widows, mothers, grandfathers, and brothers found a way to charge the US government with responsibility for the murders of their relatives. This group of survivors recognized the limits of American citizenship and sought to exploit the inequities of American law to gain some measure of justice.

The events in Porvenir show that anti-Mexican violence persisted well after the brutal repression in 1915 and that it extended across the state. By 1918 the violent militarization of the border reached a crescendo in west Texas. The epitome of this violence was the lethal force used to displace landowning ethnic Mexican families like Manuel Morales, which in turn provided opportunities for Anglo ranchers. Porvenir also shows how racial violence elicited multiple responses from survivors, one of which entailed recognizing the limitations of American citizenship, turning away from the US government for support, and utilizing the Mexican consuls to seek redress. Legal claims filed by relatives of those murdered in Porvenir, long overlooked by historians, reveal that residents resisted violent nation-building practices on the US–Mexico border and made efforts to hold nation-states accountable for the wrongful deaths of their relatives.

Five families filed claims through the General Claims Commission of 1923. They charged the United States with the wrongful deaths of residents, denial of justice for surviving relatives, unlawful use of firearms, and international delinquency on the part of the government. In the days, months, years, and decades following the massacre, survivors and witnesses testified in local courts, for diplomats, and for international tribunals. Their statements directly challenged efforts by Texas Rangers to justify the massacre. They spoke to the past, to their present, and to future efforts for redress. Cultural theorist A. Naomi Paik calls attention to the significance of testimonies that describe, name, and contest state violence. "The giving of testimony," she writes, "constitutes an event of its own, beyond the mere recounting of what has happened: it forms part of a strategy of survival and self-construction, and it attempts to seize the listener, to insist that we engage."[18]

In listening to the testimonies of widows, children, and other witnesses of violence, the limitations of courts to reckon with violence becomes apparent. In the end, court indemnities could not adequately reckon with the lasting influence of such violent events. After all, how could a state, which sanctioned the terror in question, be the site of redress? The families of Juana Bonilla Flores, Harry Warren, and Robert Keil continued to be affected by the massacre for generations. Preserving memories became a strategy of resistance against historical inaccuracies and social amnesias. The family histories expose the heavy burden on those who carry the load of a traumatic past.

BEFORE THE MASSACRE

In the 1910s in Presidio County, most Anglo residents lived in the towns of Candelaria and Marfa, while Mexicans resided primarily deep in the rural ranching and farming communities. In Porvenir, located in the northwestern district of Presidio County, Mexican residents worked their land as farmers. In 1910, of the 105 families living in the area, twenty-four families owned their homes while the rest rented property. Census agents identified nineteen of those homeowners as Mexicans who worked either as farmers or ranchers raising livestock. The occupations of other Mexican heads of house included farming and laboring on local ranches.[19]

At the time of the massacre, the residents of Porvenir were landowners, not the squatters and bandits the Texas Rangers, newspapers, and later historians described. Aside from ranching, residents made use of the arid desert soil for farming and raising animals.[20] Women raised children, managed domestic duties, and cared for livestock and crops while their husbands traveled to other ranches for work. Women also bartered by washing clothes for other families or by trading vegetables and other goods from personal gardens.[21] Residents occasionally bought goods at the closest general stores in Valentine or Brite, but mostly they lived off their cows, pigs, chicken, and goats. They also grew corn, wheat, pumpkins, and beans. They used surplus food and supplies to trade with their neighbors. Harry Warren took diligent notes on his financial transactions and trades with neighbors. He also recorded important farming and ranching accomplishments. At the time of the massacre, Warren noted that one family had raised an impressive forty acres of wheat. The residents made use of every resource, making homes in a desert region whose rough terrain was considered uninhabitable by most people.[22]

Porvenir residents assisted each other by bartering labor, tools, goods, and produce. Some days a neighbor might help a local family by trading work animals for tools. Manuel Morales, for example, frequently lent two of his work mules to Harry Warren and in return borrowed the public school teacher's plow for his own fields. The farming community relied on each other for buying goods, too. When someone made the arduous trek to Valentine or Brite for coffee, sugar, flour, corn, or tobacco, they bought items for their neighbors. Tiburcio Juárez and J. J. Bailey frequently traveled with lists and money from their neighbors. In some cases, they bought goods for neighbors who lent mules to help pull the wagons for the trip.[23] Local residents also borrowed from each other's technical and agricultural knowledge. In 1914 Harry Warren gave Manuel Morales $20 worth of goods from Valentine in exchange for his engineering skills and help building an embankment across Warren's ditch to divert water to irrigate his fruit trees. Mrs. Morales also helped wash Warren's clothes and gave him pumpkins from her garden to help round out their transaction of $20 worth of goods for engineering and labor.[24]

On his sixty-six-acre property, Harry Warren maintained a public school for local families.[25] Education became a vital institution in the social life of the rural community. Approximately twenty students, boys and girls, attended classes. They came from the Morales, Flores, Bonilla, González, Jaquez, Lares, and Nieves families.[26] Most residents spoke primarily Spanish, and most landowning men could both read and write in Spanish.[27] A few residents spoke English, including a young mother of two who attended school in Valentine as a child. Her bilingual skills became particularly helpful when she later acted as interpreter and translator for the US Cavalry.[28]

Morales and the other residents not only owned their farmland but also evinced an entrepreneurial spirit. In the mid-1910s Morales initiated a new venture to keep pace with the agricultural development taking place in other parts of the state. To maintain his property in the midst of rising costs, Morales started integrating farming into his ranching routines. In particular, he tried his hand at raising cotton, successfully irrigating his crops by diverting water from the Rio Grande. Still, Morales hoped to expand his enterprise. Three brothers who died the night of the massacre did not live in Porvenir but instead resided in Pecos, Texas. They visited the Morales ranches temporarily to help residents improve the irrigation system to expand the cotton crop.[29] Other successful farming attempts helped motivate local residents. In April 1912 J. J. Kilpatrick, who farmed near Candelaria, hauled thirty bales of cotton from his border property to Marfa, where it would be transported to buyers in Houston. Kilpatrick's enterprise steadily grew in 1913 when he bought an old cotton gin. In 1917 his status in the region grew when he purchased a more efficient gin.[30] Morales was not the only successful cotton farmer in the Big Bend, but his irrigation system helped him expand his venture and quickly captured the attention of local ranchers and farmers.[31] For the arid climate this was no small feat. It signaled to nearby residents that the land in west Texas could be financially viable for farming.

Families in Porvenir lived off their yields, and even developed a reputation for sharing their food with US Cavalry scouts who patrolled the US–Mexico border.[32] Frequently on the route back to camp, scout soldiers stopped in Porvenir to buy surplus goods and eat a home-cooked meal before continuing. Juan Bonilla Flores also sometimes rode his horse to the Cavalry camp to buy coffee or sugar when the residents ran low. Over time the residents developed friendships with soldiers and offered them generous hospitality.[33]

The memoir by Robert Keil, *Bosque Bonito: Violent Times along the Borderlands during the Mexican Revolution,* is the only published firsthand account of the massacre. Aside from chronicling the tragic events, Keil carefully detailed his warm feelings for the residents. He noted that the day of the Porvenir massacre he visited the farming community and bought

In the decade after the Porvenir massacre, cotton continued to be harvested from west Texas in increasing quantities. University of Texas at El Paso Library, Special Collections Department, PH010, Francis King Duncan photographs.

six dozen eggs for the mess sergeant. When he returned to camp and learned that Texas Rangers had concerns that the residents harbored arms as well as a bandit named Chico Cano, he initially found the news amusing. He wrote, "We knew the people living in Porvenir better than I know my next door neighbor today, and we were sure they wouldn't harbor outlaws, and that Chico Cano was as unfamiliar to them as he was to us."[34] The amicable relations between Porvenir residents and soldiers of the Eighth Cavalry did not protect them.[35]

During the Mexican Revolution, battles reached Ojinaga, Chihuahua, just south of US border towns in the Big Bend. Residents in west Texas became tense with anticipation. Mexican refugees and defeated soldiers alike sought shelter across the border, in towns such as Candelaria, Marfa, and eventually El Paso. Texas and military officials quickly organized to guard the vast 500-mile Big Bend region.

Texas Rangers and military officials came to suspect that some residents were being recruited into rebel segments. On March 9, 1916, when the revolutionary Pancho Villa organized a raid on the isolated New Mexican town of Columbus, fear spread through rural areas along the Southwest.[36] The proximity of the raids to the invasion of Columbus and the attack on US soldiers prompted President Woodrow Wilson to send General John J. Pershing into Mexico after Pancho Villa. His efforts, however, did not prevent the raids that followed shortly after.[37] Two months later, on May 5, a group described as Mexican bandits raided Glenn Springs and Boquillas, two border towns in west Texas. As many as eighty men plundered the cavalry camp and general store at Glenn Springs. This small community hosted the headquarters of the candelilla wax factory owned by W. K. Ellis and C. D. Wood and housed approximately fifty Mexican laborers and their families, who lived in a segregated community called Mexican Glenn Springs.[38] The raiders attacked a detachment of nine men from Troop A of the Fourteenth Cavalry, leaving Private William Cohen, Private Stephen J. Cole, and Private Hudson Rogers dead.[39]

In the wake of the attack, vigilantes and the US military alike often violated neutrality laws. Colonel George T. Langhorne, chief of the military district in Big Bend, described his orders in a telegram: "You may be sure that the soldiers never injured good citizens and I have orders to pursue the criminals and malefactors on either side of the river, until they are *exterminated* and good order is restored. The civil officials are taking steps to catch all criminals on this side."[40] Historian Ronnie Tyler wrote that in pursuit of adversaries in the Big Bend region or Mexico, US soldiers, Texas Rangers, and vigilantes "forgot about due process of the law and the rights of their victims." In west Texas, Mexican landowners living near the Rio Grande were accused of harboring bandits and were violently policed. The frequent violation of suspects' rights soon gave the Big Bend region the nickname the "Bloody Bend."[41]

The state police publicly made concerted efforts to show they were capable of rectifying border disturbances. In cases where Anglo residents died at the hands of raiders, state agents vowed vengeance. The morning of December 25, 1917, a deadly raid took place at the Brite Ranch in Presidio County. An estimated forty-five men participated, and a shootout ensued. Mickey Welsh inadvertently arrived at the ranch as the raid was unfolding; he and his two Mexican passengers were killed.[42] On December 29,

1917, Texas Ranger captain James Monroe Fox wrote to Adjutant General James A. Harley. Just returning from the river, he reported that after chasing thirty bandits he and his company had "good luck" and killed about twenty-five of the bandits. He assured General Harley that after their chase all remained quiet on the border.[43] It is difficult to tell what proof existed to warrant Captain Fox's company killing twenty-five men. The report made no mention of when the chase took place, what happened to the remains of the twenty-five men, the names of the dead, or identifying information. Labeling the dead men "bandits" seemed to be sufficient for state records.

Killing twenty-five men would further launch Fox's social prominence in west Texas and win him favor with the state administration and local ranchers alike. Considering the prominence of the Brite family, he must have felt pressure to act quickly. Or perhaps the attack on a prominent ranch enabled Fox to kill at will.

L. C. Brite became a member of the executive board of the Cattlemen's Association in Texas in 1912. He sold approximately 1,000 bulls annually. In 1914 the Brite Ranch headquarters became the county's designated voting precinct, housed the local post office, and had a flourishing general store. In 1915 the family founded Brite, Texas.[44] This regional prominence epitomized practices of farm colonization in the border region.

The raid on the Brite Ranch, therefore, signaled a trespass on one of the most prominent and well-secured ranches in Texas. Following the Christmas Day raid, the Brite family rallied the local sheriff, Texas Rangers, and family and friends—in a total of thirty cars—in a fierce attempt to follow the raiders.[45] The brutality of the event struck a note of panic with local residents; it was clear no expense would be spared in seeking revenge.

The Rangers kept up efforts to track down more assailants. Killing twenty-five alleged bandits did not appease calls for bloody justice. The Texas Rangers settled for revenge by proxy and continued a reign of terror that gripped the region. They turned their eyes toward Porvenir. Nearly a month after Captain Fox reported killing approximately twenty-five raiders in connection with the Brite Ranch raid, he reported to General Harley that he had killed fifteen more men. He reported that on the night of January 28, he and eight Texas Rangers, in the company of four ranchers, scouted the river region, where they encountered several Mexicans. After they gathered the Mexicans for questioning, he claimed, the assembly came

under fire by a second group of Mexicans and a general gunfight took place
in the dark. He reported that the next morning he returned to find fifteen
dead Mexicans. Conveniently, he informed the adjutant general that the
Rangers found several items from Brite Ranch among the residents' be-
longings, but he did not detail them.[46] Again assuring the general that all
appeared calm, he wished him a happy new year and concluded the letter.
On February 18 Fox submitted a second report that was a bit more forthcoming. He admitted to traveling to Porvenir to search the residents the
night of the massacre, but explained that this investigation was interrupted
when "some of their comrades who were not in this bunch of Mexicans
fired into the Rangers." The Rangers, he suggested, "immediately lay
down returning fire on all moving objects in front." The men, he explained, did not know how many Mexicans were killed until the next day
"on account of the darkness."[47]

These reports would later prove to be fabrications. Fox made no
reference to Company B's collaboration with the US Cavalry and four
ranchmen to search and disarm the men of Porvenir and did not reference
the family members who witnessed the events. For his first report he
submitted a story about a casual encounter that ended in violence. An un-
planned search of a group allegedly led to the Rangers being caught in a
shootout with unidentified Mexicans. In Fox's second report he admitted
to conducting an investigation in Porvenir in complete "darkness" but
again portrayed the events as being instigated by some unidentified "comrades" hiding in the brush and firing at the Rangers. According to Fox,
the dead were criminals. He claimed that the men had participated in the
raid on the Brite Ranch and therefore reported the incident as a fortuitous
event: fifteen more dead Mexicans.

Ranger Bud Weaver and ranchers John Poole, Raymond Fitzgerald, and
Tom Snyder submitted affidavits that repeated the claims Fox made in his
second report. Ranger Weaver confirmed that the Rangers arrived at Porvenir at 2:00 a.m. and that they rounded up the residents for an investigation. He claimed that during their investigation "a volley of shots were fired
at us behind and a little to the right of where we were." Ranchers John
Poole, Raymond Fitzgerald, and Tom Snyder gave the same account. The
men reported that they answered Fox's request to help investigate the residents of Porvenir. During the early morning search a group of unknown
parties fired at the group. The ranchers suggested that they merely fired

their guns in self-defense. Poole, Fitzgerald, and Snyder also went on to characterize the residents of Porvenir as "thieves, informers, spies, and murderers" that scouted the region for "the bandit gangs across the river." The ranchers alleged that the residents did not own property, had no farms or livestock, and that their only viable way to make a living was by assisting bandits in theft and robbery.[48]

Fox repeated these claims when he faced the Presidio County grand jury investigating the massacre. After hearing that the Rangers had allegedly killed bandits in self-defense during pursuit, the grand jury decided not to indict the assailants. None of the Texas Rangers and civilians who participated in the brutal massacre of fifteen unarmed men and boys ever faced judicial prosecution.[49]

In the years preceding and following the massacre, Texans tolerated, even celebrated, Captain Fox's reputation for killing Mexican men. One of Fox's gory deeds is preserved in one of the most infamous photographs of racial violence in the Southwest. Alongside Texas Ranger captain Henry Ransom and ranch foreman Tom Tate mounted on horseback, Captain Fox poses with Mexican corpses as if dragging the remains through the Norias Division of the King Ranch in south Texas.[50] Some Anglo ranchers certainly celebrated his presence in west Texas. During a survey of the political climate in the Big Bend region after the massacre, Texas Ranger investigating officer Captain William M. Hanson noted that Captain Fox enjoyed great popularity, especially at the Cattlemen's Club. Hanson observed, "the ranchers were quite satisfied with the work of Captain Fox in teaching the river Mexicans a lesson."[51]

If the fabricated statements by Fox, Weaver, Poole, Fitzgerald, and Snyder remained the only documents to account for the Porvenir massacre, we would be at a loss. Fortunately, the survivors gave testimonies of the tragedy they witnessed. On the day of the massacre, survivor Juan Méndez wrote an official testimony of the massacre for General J. C. Murguía in Ojinaga in an effort to seek the protection of the Mexican government. He wrote, "as testimony of the men assassinated at Porvenir, Texas and to represent them as a suffering people seeking refuge on the soil of our Mexican home land. . . . General: all the suffering women and families who have become orphans ask aid of you and our Government." By February 1, 1918, Consul Cosme Bengoechea received a copy of the telegram from General José C. Murguía with an account of the Porvenir massacre, a list of the murdered men and boys, and confirmation that the surviving residents were under his protection and care. Murguía also telegrammed Colonel George H. Langhorne asking for an investigation into the massacre. On February 18 and 28, Colonel Librado Flores, the temporary commanding officer of Chihuahua, Mayor M. M. Hernández, and C. Eleutario Contreras, the second judge of the locality convened proceedings in Ojinaga to collect statements. Seven written and translated statements of Juan Méndez, Luis Jiménez, Pablo Jiménez, Rosenda Mesa, Seberiano Morales, Gregorio Hernández, and Cesario Huerta were just the start of the growing Mexican consul investigation.[52]

The testimonies denied that any of the residents were acquainted with Mexican bandits.[53] They described the execution of the fifteen Porvenir residents on the night of January 28, 1918. In addition, the testimonies detailed a key incident with Texas Rangers four days prior to the massacre. Juan Méndez remembered being asleep with his family in Porvenir when three armed men entered his home at 1:00 a.m. and woke everyone. The unidentified men searched for weapons and without asking questions moved him toward a group of his neighbors, who were guarded by about thirty men armed with rifles and pistols. After collecting guns and ammunition from the residents, the men ordered the families to return home but took Méndez, Román Nieves, Nutemio González, and Manuel Fierro with them as prisoners. For two days the unidentified agents led the men through the mountains, interrogating them and threatening to kill them. On January 26, after two torturous days in Ranger custody, the Rangers released the prisoners, only to visit them again on the night of January 28. Fortunately, Nutemio González and Manuel Fierro were not in Porvenir when the men returned. The posse did not execute the elderly Juan Méndez, presumably because of his age, but they carried out the threats they had made to Román Nieves.[54]

The accounts recorded by survivors and their neighbors expose false statements by state agents and offered motives for the massacre. Harry Warren, for example, concluded that on the night of the massacre, the Texas Rangers collaborated with four ranchmen—Buck Poole, John Poole, Tom Snyder, and Raymond Fitzgerald. For a motive, he alleged that rancher Tom Snyder misinformed the Texas Rangers about the residents at Porvenir harboring bandits who had participated in the earlier raid on the Brite Ranch. Labeling the Porvenir inhabitants as bandits helped deflect attention from the unlawful behavior of Anglo ranchers themselves. Warren alleged that Snyder had earlier stolen mares and colts belonging to the farmers at Porvenir and sold them in Valentine. Fearing prosecution, he then gathered the Rangers to eliminate and intimidate witnesses.[55]

The testimonies also reveal the involvement of Mexican consuls, soldiers, and officials in helping the survivors following the massacre. Once across the border the survivors sought the aid of Mexican soldiers. Colonel Eduardo Porcayo and Mexican troop leader General José Murgia came from El Comedor, Mexico, to examine the bodies. The reports showed that the men had suffered a barrage of bullets to their bodies and that each had taken a bullet directly in the head. They took the names of the victims before the families buried them in a mass grave in Mexico. With the help of Mexican officials the residents received additional permission to take to Mexico some animals, family utensils, and a small amount of grain. The vast majority of their property, however, remained in the United States.[56]

Despite the grand jury decision not to indict the assailants, the brutality of the Porvenir massacre proved so egregious that international investigations started immediately. By February 15 the Mexican embassy filed a formal protest with Secretary of State Robert Lansing and asked that the State Department charge assailants with responsibility and "to apply to them a well-earned punishment." Lansing responded that he sent the formal protest to Texas governor Hobby, ordering him to investigate the massacre. On March 6 Bonillas replied and sent evidence of the massacre, including sworn witness statements, and preliminary reports that cleared the victims of any connection to local raids. On April 5 the United States responded by taking their own statements with survivors. Survivors were asked to return to west Texas to testify in Candelaria, just miles from the site of the massacre, before US investigating soldiers. Felipa Castañeda, Juana Bonilla Flores, Eulalia Hernández, Rita Jácquez, Librada Jácquez, Estefana Morales, Francisca Morales, and Alejandra Nieves. These preliminary investigations were damning.[57]

US soldiers who witnessed the massacre also wrote to Governor Hobby with information. Captain Harry Anderson of the Eighth Cavalry wrote with an account of what he described as the "midnight murder" when Rangers and ranchmen "took out the owner of the ranch and fourteen others—all farmers and small stock owners and shot them to death. *There was not a single bandit in the fifteen men slain* . . . two of them were boys."[58] The residents, he explained, were terrified and would not return to their farms. Terror in the region continued. Following the massacre Texas Rangers arrested Guadalupe Torres and murdered him near the gates of the Brite Ranch for allegedly attempting to escape. Panicked, Anderson pleaded with the Governor. "The object of this appeal is to call your attention to this unprovoked and wholesale murder by Texas Rangers in conjunction with ranchmen—Rangers who instead of maintaining peace are committing murder by the wholesale and to request Your Excellency to have these Rangers removed at once. . . . *No matter what white-washed report may have been made to you or to the Adjutant General, the facts herein are true and can be proven*."[59] To help investigate the massacre, Anderson included the name of another witness, Sergeant Bruin of the Eighth Cavalry, and listed the names of the fifteen victims. He explained that the widows and forty to fifty other witnesses could be contacted in Mexico.

With mounting federal and diplomatic pressure, the Texas governor had to respond. On June 4, 1918, Hobby disbanded Company B of the Texas Rangers, firing Andrew Charles Baker, Max Herman, Bud Weaver, Allen Cole, and Boone Oliphant, and transferring J. R. Bates, O. C. Dowe, S. H. Neill, A. H. Woelber, A. G. Beard, N. N. Fuller, and Frank Patterson to Company D.[60] He also pressured Fox to resign.

On June 11 Fox wrote a heated resignation letter. In the letter he amended his original accounts of the massacre. He wrote that he had ordered a raid on Porvenir because he believed the residents harbored Mexican bandits. In particular, he clarified, he had hoped to find Chico Cano. Fox criticized General Harley for giving in to pressure from the Mexican government and accused the governor of playing politics to secure the Mexican vote in future elections. Frustrated by the uncharacteristic hostility toward Company B's actions, he wrote, "The five men you have discharged are good men and were the best of officers. . . . It hurts me to be treated in this manner."[61] Fox's letter exhibited his refusal to respect Mexican life and his frustration at the shifting policy towards his extralegal policing methods. His brutality in the past had gained him respect and notoriety. The public condemnation from the adjutant general, who in other matters protected such acts, left Fox enraged.

According to the rules governing the Texas Rangers, all Rangers were expected to know the criminal laws of the state and to act accordingly, and at no time did they have permission to act without authority of the law. In reference to arresting individuals for inspection, rule thirteen stipulated, "Prisoners must always be accompanied by at least one Ranger, who will be held responsible for his safety, and must be delivered to a proper officer, taking his receipt, signed officially, therefore." Nowhere in the rules were Texas Rangers given authority to judge or punish subjects suspected of committing crimes. Because the men were disarmed and bound, Fox and others could not fall back on the usual explanation that the men were shot while trying to escape arrest.

The international implications of claims to American ideals of democracy during World War I, then raging, were not lost on Adjutant General Harley. He decided to publicly condemn Fox's extralegal actions. On June 12 Harley wrote a scathing letter to Fox accepting his resignation. The letter, released to the press and published in English in the *Brownsville Herald* and the *El Paso Times,* and in Spanish in the *Laredo Record,* stated that an extensive investigation had concluded that "15 Mexicans were killed when they were under the custody of your men and after they had been arrested and unarmed. This was proven by all kinds of evidence, even by the confession of those who took part and by reports collected by this office and by Agents of the Government of the United States." Harley continued that if peace officers denied any person, "whether he be white or black, yellow or brown," the constitutional right to a trial by jury, then they were illegally constituting themselves as both the judge and executioner. With "all kinds of evidence" the adjutant general condemned the massacre.

Harley described Fox's behavior as entirely unacceptable: "the calamitous rangers and violator of law must not be on the frontier where there may arise political complications which can occasion serious damages to our country and prevent the development of the war in Europe." Harley condemned Fox for killing men "defenseless and unarmed." He continued, while the US fought in World War I "to overthrow ruthless autocracy," the state of Texas would not "propose to tolerate it here at home." The adjutant general explained, "your forced resignation came in the interest of humanity, decency, law and order, the laws of the constitution of this state must be superior to the autocratic will of any peace officer, and that vandalism across the border can best be suppressed by suppressing it on the Texas side first." Harley publicly cautioned against the national risks associated with "trouble-maker and lawless Rangers" that complicated international relations for the United States.[62] Fox's forced resignation offered a rare occasion when state police faced reprimand and dismissal for extralegal violence.

By publicly disciplining Captain Fox for the massacre, Adjutant General Harley exposed the contradictions in Texas law enforcement. Despite years of encouraging Rangers to enforce a reign of terror in the Texas borderlands, by 1918 Texas administrators struggled to rein in the number of high-profile extralegal executions. Shooting ethnic Mexicans in the rural sections of Texas, in some cases, caused public alarm that reached the state governor's office, but for the most part it went unnoticed or ignored by the administration. But wholesale massacres of entire communities were harder for the state to ignore or explain away, especially when Mexican diplomats started communicating with Washington, DC. When Mexican nationals were involved, state killings made the federal government liable for the violence.

On July 19 Mexican ambassador Ignacio Bonillas wrote to Secretary of State Lansing regarding Harley's letter. He attached a copy of the letter published in the *Brownsville Herald* and pressed his hopes that "in the judicial investigation there may result not only the resignation of the Captain of the rangers, J. M. Fox, but the punishment which he and the others who are found guilty merit, because this is demanded by justice and the good name of the Federal authorities and of the State of Texas."[63]

Local politics, too, undoubtedly influenced Adjutant General Harley's actions. By 1918 protests against state violence had gained momentum. Texas state representative José T. Canales, Mexican consuls, and the survivors helped force Harley's hand. In 1919, when the Texas legislature convened an investigation to consider abuse of power by state agents, Canales introduced the Porvenir massacre as the final charge brought against the state police. He submitted depositions, news clippings, Ranger correspondence, and reports by Captain Hanson, the Mexican embassy, and US soldiers, including the letter to Governor Hobby from Captain Anderson. Despite the damning evidence, including confessions, the committee members did not ask questions or call witnesses to discuss the massacre, nor did they call for the prosecution of the agents, soldiers, and civilians involved. Calling for prosecutions would have challenged the reputation of the state police.[64] Instead, dismantling Company B satisfied the committee for the massacre of fifteen innocent men and boys.

As the Mexican ambassador had worried, asking Rangers to resign and offering sharp comments in print proved to be little more than a slap on the wrist. The adjutant general's office, in failing to file charges against Fox for orchestrating the massacre and for submitting false reports, allowed the captain to continue a career in law enforcement and eventually rejoin the state police force. Forced retirement for James Fox and Bud Weaver following the Porvenir massacre placed them both on only a brief hiatus from the state police force.[65] In 1922 Bud Weaver reenlisted as a Texas Ranger. Weaver's enlistment papers described his occupation before returning to the state police as "peace officer." In June 1925 James Fox reenlisted in the Texas Rangers as captain of Company A, stationed in Travis County. Again in February 1934, at the age of sixty-six, Fox reenlisted as a special Ranger. After being discharged from the state police, Boone Oliphant found employment on the Brite Ranch, while Andrew Charles Barker received a federal post as a US mounted customs inspector.[66] A more sinister interpretation of the adjutant general's actions is that disbanding the company allowed these men to continue their policing efforts while protecting the state from future accountability.

SEEKING REDRESS

In the late nineteenth and early twentieth century, many ethnic Mexicans throughout the borderlands took on the arduous task of pleading for common justice. As long as anti-Mexican violence continued to stain the Texas–Mexico border red, residents sought redress. In some cases there were long and laborious legal procedures.[67] When victims were Mexican nationals, their survivors could appeal to Mexican consuls. These procedures required the support of neighbors, lawyers, and diplomats. One case in particular gives insight into the possible avenues for seeking justice for the survivors of the Porvenir massacre.

On October 6, 1895, Florentino Suaste and Juan Montelongo traveled in two wagons with their wives and children through Lasalle County in south Texas to visit family in Mexico. That same day a local rancher, Mr. Saul, and a local deputy sheriff were pursuing assailants who allegedly stole livestock. The two groups crossed paths. Shortly after the meeting, the rancher and the sheriff exchanged gunfire with the two Mexican families. When the dust finally settled, Saul, Juan Montelongo, and the young

Pedro Suaste, son of Florentino and Nicolasa Suaste, lay dead from gunshot wounds. Florentino and Nicolasa Suaste suffered bullet wounds but
survived. Arrested and charged with the murder of rancher Saul, the surviving Montelongo and Suaste family members awaited criminal trial in
the county jail in Cotulla. The local deputy sheriff did not face charges for
his role in the death of Montelongo and the young Suaste.

Florentino Suaste never had his day in court. Days after the shootings
four men removed him from his county jail cell. With his wife, two
daughters, and the widowed Casimira Montelongo watching, the men shot
the injured Suaste and hung his body from a mesquite tree in the town
square. Someone later returned the body to the jail, where the rest of the
family had remained. The next morning the surviving relatives watched
as the wife of the county jailer came to clean the blood from the floors.[68]

As we have seen, lynch mobs commonly took prisoners from jail even
though courts would likely have sentenced them to execution. Local grand
juries often failed to indict or prosecute the assailants.[69] This judicial neglect is apparent in the 1895 lynching in Cotulla. The string of deaths, all
precipitated by accusations of a violation of private property, soon found
their way into Texas criminal court.[70] In May 1896 a Lasalle County grand
jury convened to consider the lynching of Florentino Suaste. They heard the
testimony of the jailer, Nicolasa Suaste, and Casimira Montelongo but did
not issue any indictments. The failure of the Texas judicial system to apprehend the assailants prompted the Suaste and Montelongo widows to
seek justice through civil courts.[71]

Approximately a year later, on October 3, 1896, Nicolasa Batista de
Suaste and Casimira Reyes de Montelongo filed separate cases through
their attorneys. Casimira petitioned for damages against Deputy Sheriff N. A.
Swink in the western district of the circuit court for the murder of her
husband, Juan. Nicolasa petitioned for damages against Swink, Lasalle
County jailer Louis Underwood, W. L. Hargus, Andrew Armstrong Sr.,
and Andrew Armstrong Jr., for their participation in the lynching of her
husband Florentino. Each woman asked for $20,000 in damages.[72]

In his final report dated September 13, 1897, US consul general
Joseph G. Donnelly in Nuevo Laredo, Mexico, found the following: "Crime
it was, deliberate and indefensible. The court had not passed on his alleged
offense. He was in the custody of the law, and therefore in the law's protec-

tion. His dead friend, his dead child, the wounded mother of his children, his own condition, shot as he was in four places, all the circumstances made the act particularly cruel and revolting."[73] Donnelly found that Texas authorities left the prisoners without adequate protection, especially after he discovered that three times in the years prior to this incident, mobs had removed prisoners from the same jail and lynched them in broad daylight, with "the whole populace onlookers or participants." In each of these previous lynchings, the grand jury delivered not a single indictment.[74] Even J. G. Smith, editor of the local newspaper, believed it impossible for a man to be taken from jail in the middle of town, shot, and hanged without leaving traces for indictment. In his testimony to the diplomat, Smith explained that one of the grand jury members had openly accused Sheriff Hargus of collusion with the lynchers. He said, "It is hard to get people to talk in the matter, particularly if you are a Ranger. No one wants to get in trouble. But if the authorities had acted honestly and energetically the truth would have come out."[75] This testimony speaks to the climate in Cotulla, where local law enforcement officers created conditions that made prisoners vulnerable to mob violence. Witnesses in the town later chose to remain silent to avoid trouble with local authorities or mob participants.

This hostile environment, however, did not dissuade the widows from bringing charges against the law enforcement agents and mob participants. Nicolasa Suaste and Casimira Montelongo bore the painful burden of testifying repeatedly throughout the investigations by Mexican consuls, US consuls, and Lasalle County officials. Nicolasa Suaste, on at least four separate occasions, described the string of deaths.[76] Even her daughters Martina and Concepción testified before the Lasalle County justice of the peace. They were asked to testify to both the lynching and the earlier death of Juan Montelongo, Pedro Suaste, and rancher Saul.

The claims by Montelongo and Suaste provide rare insight into the process survivors faced when testifying or giving a deposition. We have a glimpse into questions and exchanges from a transcribed interview of one of the Suaste daughters by attorney J. S. McLeary. Asked candid questions, witnesses had to reflect on an unbelievably traumatic life experience. In response to witnessing the death of her brother and Pedro Suaste, one of the daughters was asked, "What did your folks do?" She replied, "We all just stayed there crying."[77]

These testimonies were pivotal in challenging official reports by local police. In several cases state officials claimed that the men who participated in the lynching could not be identified, but as the testimony of a Suaste daughter reveals, she and her family did identify the assailants.[78] She identified a heavy-set man with white hair and a red beard named Armstrong. She described him as having entered the jail with three other men to remove her father. She testified that the jailer willingly opened the door and let the men into the cell. Next, the group carried her injured father outside. The questioning concluded as follows:

> Q: Did you see him when they hung him, or did they take him off?
> A: They took him off.
> Q: You heard the shot?
> A: Yes.
> Q: How long was it before they killed him?
> A: They killed him at once, as soon as they took him out, and then threw a rope around his neck and drug him off.
> Q: Did they kill him on the ground?
> A: Yes; and then hung him to the mesquite tree.
> Q: About what time was this?
> A: Twelve o'clock at night.
> Q: What day was this?
> A: Friday, the 11th day of October 1895.[79]

During the testimony, one of the Suaste daughters explained that one day while begging on the streets of Cotulla, she saw Andrew Armstrong and recognized him as one of the men who participated in her father's lynching.

In the aftermath of such violence, the Suaste and Montelongo families had no intention of making a life in Cotulla. They had left their homes and jobs in San Antonio only temporarily to visit family in Mexico. The widows and their remaining children had little means to live in Cotulla, and as a result the Suaste daughters were left to beg for money from the same residents who had gathered to celebrate the lynching of their father.[80] Sitting on the sidewalks, asking for help, the daughters encountered both the men who had helped kill their father and the men who failed to prosecute them.

The young Suaste's account coupled with the testimonies of the two widows ultimately led to Andrew Armstrong and his son being included in the charges filed by Nicolasa Suaste. They directly challenged the testimony of Cotulla jailer Louis Underwood, who claimed that he was overtaken by the mob, and the justice of the peace in Lasalle County, who reported that "the death of the deceased was caused by his being hung and shot by persons unknown."

Nicolasa Suaste filed charges accusing jailer Louis Underwood, Andrew Armstrong Sr., Andrew Armstrong Jr., W. L. Hargus, and N. A. Swink of organizing a mob for the purpose of killing Florentino Suaste.[81] The case stated that the accused, by reason of a malicious and willful act to kill Suaste, deprived Nicolasa of the support, protection, affection, and companionship of her husband. It also described Florentino as an able-bodied workingman who otherwise would have been fully capable of supporting his family.[82] By testifying in front of grand juries, to their attorneys, and to investigators, the Suaste and Montelongo survivors helped document the death of Juan Montelongo and Pedro Suaste. They also charged local authorities with committing or enabling the crimes and inflicting damages on the surviving relatives. Mexican consulates soon took up the charge in the investigation and demanded that the US government provide the Suaste family with an indemnity.

Mexican consuls used assumptions of female vulnerability in the claims. By alleging that the assailants denied Nicolasa Suaste's family the support, protection, and companionship of her husband, the case ascribed to patriarchal notions that described women as dependent on their husbands. Courts and diplomatic consuls saw widows and the heirs of victims of mob violence as socially vulnerable subjects. The Suaste case leveraged such assumptions to file damages against the state agents and local residents who participated in the mobs.

The gendered basis of the claims at one point threatened to undermine the case. When US investigations revealed that the Suastes had never been legally married, Mexican consulates went to great lengths to prove that they lived as a married couple and satisfied the state's common law marriage requirements. They had to provide evidence that the couple lived together, raised three children together, and referred to one another as husband and wife in public. Likewise, Mexican diplomats had to provide

THE INJUSTICE NEVER LEAVES YOU

US investigators with evidence that Nicolasa Suaste was a Mexican national in order to file a claim on her behalf. Had US officials decided that she was not married, not a Mexican national, or not financially vulnerable as a result of the lynching, Nicolasa Suaste would have been denied grounds to claim an indemnity from the US government. Proving her partnership with Florentino and her vulnerability must have been an especially painful and insulting task under the trying conditions she faced following the lynching.

With the citizenship and the marital status of the plaintiff settled, the consul general's investigation into the lynching continued for years. In his final report, Donnelly himself questioned the effort by state agents to prevent the incident from occurring in the first place. The actions of the grand jury, the district attorney, Ranger Brooks, Sheriff Hargus, and Deputy Sheriff Swink led him to charge authorities with "negligence so gross as to well arouse suspicion of collusion. They knew the threats. They knew the sanguinary record of the town. . . . It would have been some palliation of their failure to prevent the lynching and would have done much to suppress talk of collusion had there been active and earnest efforts made to find and punish those who were guilty of it."[83] Donnelly definitively argued that Texas law enforcement agents, courts, and LaSalle residents effectively sanctioned the lynching.

On December 6, 1900, President McKinley responded to the two cases filed by Nicolasa Suaste and Casimira Montelongo, thanks in part to the pressure brought by Mexican officials and to the findings of Donnelly's investigation. The president followed the outcomes in the cases of three Italian subjects lynched in Hahnsville, Louisiana, on August 8, 1896, and the lynching of Luis Moreno in Yreka, California, and recommended that Congress appropriate $2,000 to be paid to the government of Mexico for the widowed Nicolasa Suaste.

Florentino Suaste's status as a Mexican national living in Texas with his family at the time of his death allowed the Mexican government to be involved in holding Texas state officials accountable for the lynching. Had he been an American citizen, the failure of the local courts to prosecute the assailants would have ended the hopes for retribution. This case outlined a redress strategy for surviving Mexican nationals living in Texas whose families were victims of state-sanctioned violence. However, although the international investigation into the lynching of Florentino

Suaste elevated the case to a presidential priority, the vast majority of acts of anti-Mexican violence continued without concern from state or federal officials.

For local residents in the wake of the Porvenir massacre, the risks for speaking out against the state police were still high two decades after the Montelongo and Suaste widows filed claims. Anyone who challenged the Texas Rangers came under quick suspicion and risked being ostracized. For example, the reputations of both Harry Warren and Judge James J. Kilpatrick suffered because of their help to the survivors in challenging the police. Although an Anglo transplant from Mississippi, by 1914 it appeared that Harry Warren had been integrated into the rural Mexican community. Born on July 17, 1859, in Waterford, Mississippi, to Dr. William Calloway Warren and Mary Jane Bradford Warren, Harry attended the University of Mississippi and in 1882 began teaching in Maverick County, Texas. Throughout his career he taught in New Mexico, Arizona, and in Texas public schools in Carrizo Springs, Eagle Pass, and Porvenir and even across the border in the tiny town of Pilares in Mexico. Aside from working as an educator, he served as an attorney and counselor-at-law for Maverick County, as a justice of the peace in Presidio County, and temporarily as a US Customs inspector.

In 1910 Warren married Juliana Jácquez, the daughter of Tiburcio Jácquez, one of the men who would be killed eight years later. Jácquez and Warren together had three children: a son, Anacleto, born July 13, 1911; a daughter, Mary Nancy, born March 20, 1915; and another daughter, Helen Rosalie, born January 9, 1919, at the Morales Ranch near Pilares.[84] Aside from being related through marriage to one of the victims that night, the men killed in the massacre were in many ways Warren's peers and extended family. He taught the children of four of the men killed. In more than one way, he was intimately tied to both the victims and the survivors of the massacre.

Warren's life made him suspicious to Texas Rangers. His interracial marriage, his commitment to the community both as a teacher and lawyer, and his support of the survivors of the Porvenir massacre all signaled an apparent disregard for the racial segregation zealously guarded by many of his fellow Anglos. His integration with the Mexican community was permitted, if frowned upon, prior to the massacre, but afterward his position became more threatened. Both Texas Rangers and some US soldiers made it difficult for him to find employment elsewhere. Military officials chastised Warren after he tried to contact the survivors in Mexico to help them file a suit against the US government. In one letter, Lieutenant Leonard F. Matlock wrote that Warren "is a dangerous man in that he agitates the Mexicans on both sides of the river and keeps the situation at the boiling point. . . . Mr. Warren is now in Candelaria and I have forbidden him to talk to the Mexicans across the river until this matter can be adjusted."[85]

Military apprehension soon took the form of intimidation; the county school superintendent was forced to terminate Warren's teaching contract in Presidio County. In a report to Ranger headquarters, Colonel Langhorne dismissed Warren as a troublemaker whose son, he mistakenly alleged, was his only pupil in school. Langhorne continued, "in the community of Porvenir, he lived like the Mexicans and urged upon them the advisability of keeping all other white men out of the community. He is one of the three white men in this County that has failed to work with the others for the preservation of order."[86] The colonel chastised Warren and other Anglo men for being race traitors, breaking the boundaries of racial segregation and instead "living like the Mexicans." Langhorne went on to describe Warren as an educated man who had lost his reason to drinking and was disturbing the preservation of a racial order. In this case, US officials participated in policing both the political border between two nations and the racial divisions between Anglo and Mexican relations in the United States.

On July 21, 1919, Warren wrote to Colonel Langhorne asking him to expunge from his records a letter that criticized the teacher for his "companionship with bandits." Warren had witnessed the consequences of being labeled a bandit sympathizer. He accused the colonel of slandering his name and demanded that the original letter and any copies be removed from military files and destroyed.[87] When the colonel refused, Warren rallied supporters to defend his reputation. James J. Kilpatrick wrote to the Texas attorney general to call the military "assassins of character."[88] Texas state senator B. J. Pridgen, former US consul to Mexico, tried to help Warren get a job by writing a letter to recommend him for a teaching position in Eagle Pass, Texas.[89]

Aside from trying to help Warren, Kilpatrick and his wife, Lula, came under public scrutiny for his continued attempts to prosecute assailants in the Porvenir massacre. Despite intimidation by the state police and military officials, the Kilpatricks refused to keep quiet. In one account Kilpatrick wrote to US representative Thomas L. Blanton, "From the best information we can obtain, none of the fifteen dead Mexicans had anything to do with the Brite raid. And now the general belief is that the Mexicans were killed in order to strike terror in the hearts of the bandits and thieves for the purpose of putting an end to the raids and the stealing."[90] Kilpatrick's letter, it seems, did little to gain support from Blanton.

After interviewing the survivors and helping them with their plight, Justice of the Peace Kilpatrick described the sense of loss that lingered in west Texas. He wrote, "The waters of the Rio Grande in the upper Big Bend, as they flow to the sea, are ever murmuring the funeral dirge of innocent human beings cruelly slain; and in the soughing of the night winds among the rock hills, or in the lonely valleys, their sepulchral voices are heard pleading for common justice."[91]

DISAVOWAL

The survivors of the Porvenir massacre continued to seek redress years after the initial tragedy. They turned to diplomatic procedures and filed claims through the US–Mexico General Claims Commission of September 8, 1923. The Mexican and US governments bilaterally created the commission to settle the majority of claims of both Mexican and US nationals arising between July 4, 1868, and the start of the commission. Between 1875 and 1910 the Porfirio Díaz regime oversaw a period of tranquility for Americans residing in Mexico, and complaints were usually settled through diplomatic channels. With the start of the Mexican Revolution, however, war and political instability led to a calamitous rise in claims filed against the Mexican government by American nationals. Negotiations to initiate a General Claims Commission began as early as 1912, but the two nations did not agree on terms for the commission until the summer of 1923. The commission aimed to settle amicably any claims by citizens of each country against the other. It was composed of one person selected by the president of the United States, one person selected by the president of Mexico, and one person who presided, mutually decided upon by both nations.[92]

Although the local courts in Presidio County neglected to bring charges against the assailants, the General Claims Commission opened a door for

surviving relatives who wanted to charge the US government with liability
in the death of their relatives. In June 1926, eight years after the event,
Mexican attorneys filed separate claims against the United States on behalf of Concepción Carrasco de González, Jesus García, Victoria Jiménez
de García, Librada M. Jácquez, Eulalia González, Juana Bonilla Flores, Rita
Jácquez, Severiano Morales, Alejandra Nieves, Francisca Morales, Pablo
Jiménez, and Luis Jiménez. The claimants included widows, parents, grandparents, and brothers of the fifteen murdered men and boys.[93] They gave
memorandums that laid out the basic claims of the massacre, described the
injustice, and listed their nationality, relationship to the deceased, the nationality of the deceased, and any dependent children.

Asserting Mexican citizenship and claiming economic vulnerability
gave the descendants due protection from the Mexican government and
enabled them to challenge violence at the hands of Texas law enforcement and US soldiers. Although some of these claimants were longtime
residents in Texas, they used their legal status as foreigners in the United
States to seek justice.[94] For example, in her memorandum Concepción
González, forty-nine years old, described the massacre as a "savage act" and
a "monstrous crime" committed by Texas Rangers. She gave an account of
her family at the time of the massacre. Her husband, Eutimo González,
was a Mexican citizen, a native of El Mangle, State of Chihuahua, Mexico,
and baptized in the Parish of Ojinaga. She clarified that her husband had
"never changed his citizenship nor taken oath of loyalty to any other nation" and that her husband's death left her in a vulnerable position. She
wrote, "My said husband was assassinated at forty years of age, leaving me a
widow with nine legitimate children of our legitimate marriage . . . named
Francisca, Pedro, Santos, Refugio, Luciana, Andrea, Gerónimo, Blasa, and
Micaela." The massacre itself was sufficient, she declared, "to stain with
shame the leaders who committed it and whom the Government of this
country could not or did not wish to punish." She and the other descendants
appeared together, before the Justice of the Peace in Candelaria, Texas,
she wrote, "to ask for an explanation and justice."[95]

More than seventeen years after the massacre, and after collecting over
100 pieces of evidence on behalf of the survivors, on February 15, 1935,
Mexican attorney Oscar Rebasa filed a claim, *Concepción Carrasco de González,
et al. (United Mexican States) v. the United States of America,* combining the
separate claims into one case. The Mexican attorneys made three charges:

the Texas authorities did not give due protection to the men arrested by the Texas Rangers; the local authorities were the material authors and accomplices of the crimes committed at Porvenir; and the state authorities denied justice by failing to apprehend, prosecute, and punish the persons responsible for the murders.[96] The claimants requested $700,000 for losses and damages.[97]

To file a claim through the commission, claimants asserted foreign citizenship and charged the foreign government with international delinquency. The General Claims Commission laid out the terms for defining international delinquency for denying foreign nationals justice in the case of *L. F. H. Neer and Pauline Neer (United States of America) v. United Mexican States* (1926).[98] The case claimed lack of diligence and lack of intelligent investigation on the part of the Mexican authorities in investigating the murder of American citizen Paul Neer, who lived in Mexico. The tribunal decided on the three following terms: (1) that in international law the acts of a state should be judged by international standards; (2) that to constitute an act of international delinquency, actions (or inactions) of a government must fall so far short of international standards as to be recognizable by any impartial man as insufficient; and (3) that with regard to the liability of a government for a wrongful act, it was immaterial whether the act was derived from either the fact that authorities administering the municipal law did not comply with the law or that the municipal law did not allow them to act according to international standards. In particular, the last term argued that a government could not claim it acted according to municipal laws and therefore should not be judged by international standards.[99]

Filing the claim would prove to be just one of many steps for the claimants. After all, some of them had given testimony in February and April 1918. The proceedings stretched out for more than two decades. While the Mexican attorneys tracked down records relating to the Porvenir massacre in both Mexican and US governmental records, the claimants gave sworn testimonies describing the massacre. Moreover, they had to show proof of their Mexican nationality, their relationship to the dead, and that they were financially dependent on the victims of the massacre and suffered in their absence.

Each of the claimants required extensive documentation. For Juana Bonilla Flores's claim, for example, Mexican attorneys submitted certified copies of the birth certificates for her sons Narciso and Juan Flores. On

February 2, 1926, her friends José Chemali and José Torres swore before a notary public that they knew Juana Bonilla Flores and that she was in fact a Mexican national; that they knew her husband Longino Flores, murdered at the massacre, and that he was a Mexican national; that they knew Juana was the legitimate wife of Longino; and that she lived exclusively on the personal labor of her husband. For Alejandra Nieves's claim, Mexican attorneys had to file no less than thirteen affidavits to prove that she and her children maintained Mexican citizenship. She also had to prove that her husband had Mexican citizenship at the time he was murdered. Collectively, claimants provided testimonies, birth certificates, marriage certificates, baptism records, and witness testimonies to prove they had a right to file a claim.

These records are an eerily intimate archive of birth dates, baptisms, marriages, and the names of friends and relatives who testified to the lives and marriages. In another context they likely grieved for their murdered friends, but in these files, under oath, they gave factual testimonies, not about the life of the murdered or the loss friends and neighbors experienced, but of occupations, dates of marriages, and the citizenship of the deceased. These records served the purpose of verifying a legal claim to hold the US government responsible for a massacre.

On April 26, 1935, the US attorneys filed its response to the commission, denying the Mexican nationality of the claimants and the dead victims, denying the relationship between the claimants and the victims, and maintaining that the murder of the fifteen men and boys at Porvenir was justified. Regarding the charge of denial of justice, the attorneys invoked the US and Texas investigations and the convening of the Presidio County grand jury as fulfilling the duties of the United States for investigating the massacre.[100]

Mexican attorneys responded on July 5, 1935, submitting a fifty-page brief on behalf of the survivors of the Porvenir massacre. It argued that the United States was internationally responsible for the death of the fifteen Mexican citizens murdered by the Texas Rangers in Company B because it did not properly apprehend and punish the US citizens who had murdered the Mexican nationals. Mexican attorney Rebasa argued that of the thousands of claims it received, the Porvenir massacre was by far the most violent the commission would consider. The brief argued that the Presidio County grand jury decision not to indict the assailants was a wholly inadequate form of justice. Rebasa quoted Adjutant General Harley's letter condemning Captain James M. Fox's role in orchestrating the massacre. After finding Fox and the Texas Rangers under his command culpable, he should have prosecuted them for murder. Dismissing the Texas Rangers did not constitute justice. Finally, in the brief the Mexican lawyer also expressed outrage that the US attorneys would malign the character of the victims and their families. Submitting testimonies and reports by Texas Rangers and US officials that had allegations later determined to be false, according to the Mexican attorneys, constituted an attempt to cover up the crimes of the Texas Rangers.[101]

US attorney Bert L. Hunt responded to the Mexican claims by filing an incendiary reply brief for the United States on September 13, 1935. It disputed the Mexican claims that described the victims of the massacre as honest and honorable men and continued to disavow the rights of the survivors to file the claim. The US attorneys justified the Porvenir massacre as an example of violence by authorities to quell violence at the hands of Mexican bandits in the region. Attorneys listed seven raids by "Mexican bandits and outlaws" in the years preceding the massacre. The brief included defamatory letters, including one from Colonel Langhorne, dated March 12, 1918, that described Porvenir as a "rendezvous of bandits and generally bad characters." It also included testimony from Dr. G. D. McGregor that alleged the Porvenir residents "pretended to farm." They were "thieves and smugglers. . . . Their place was a rendezvous for thieves and bandits and also slackers," he suggested.[102]

Although US attorneys did not deny that Texas Rangers participated in the massacre, it suggested that "disciplining the participants by dismissing them from service" demonstrated that the state of Texas had investigated and acted in the wake of the massacre. The brief argued that justice had, indeed, been served by the dismissal of Captain Fox. In an inexcusable and misguided move, despite Fox's reports admitting to his role in the massacre, the brief claimed that he had not participated in the massacre, stating that the adjutant general "also obtained the resignation of Captain Fox, who had not, however, been personally present."[103]

This amount of deceit, in legal documents, is striking. Perhaps what is even more unsettling, however, is that in a sweeping rebuke of the hundreds of pages of evidence submitted for the claimants, the reply brief disputed the Mexican nationality of every claimant and charged they had no standing to file a claim against the US government. Regarding the claims of Librada M. Jácquez and Severiano Morales, the attorneys for the United States wrote that the Mexican government had submitted testimonies from "wholly incompetent witnesses" who had "worthless character" and thus could not be accepted as proof of Mexican nationality. They also dismissed illiterate witnesses such as Manuel Quinos, who "could not *even sign his name.*"[104] Moreover, in a callous addition, the attorneys disputed the claims by Rita Jácquez, widow of Macedonio Huerta, and Librada M. Jácquez, widow of Tiburcio Jácquez, because the women died before the claims were heard by the commission (Rita Jácquez died in 1930 and Librada Jácquez died in 1933). The attorneys tried having the claims dismissed despite having contacted the next of kin, Filomeno Huerta, the son of Rita and Macedonio Huerta, and confirming that he was still waiting for the claim to be decided. On March 8, 1935, US attorneys also sought the help of the US War Department to see if any of the fifteen victims had registered under the Selective Service Act, and if so claimed to be American citizens. The report showed that "the result of the search seems to be entirely negative." These results did not stop the US attorneys from trying to have the claims dismissed.[105]

The effort to smear the character of the victims and the overall lack of respect for the claimants is all the more damning when considering the internal records of the US attorneys. In a report filed by C. M. Bishop on September 13, 1926, the US attorney outlined the facts of the case developed by correspondence: that the Rangers and ranchmen had visited the residents of Porvenir on January 24, four days prior to the murders, arrested some of the residents and disarmed them; that on January 28 about thirty Rangers and civilians participated in the massacre; that Captain Fox and five more Rangers were dismissed from the service for their participation; that none of the "Rangers or ranchmen were ever prosecuted for their part in the affair."[106] In considering whether the commission would likely offer an award for the claimants due to the failure to apprehend, prosecute, and punish the assailants in the cases filed by Porvenir survivors, Bishop concisely concluded, "Yes."[107] To avoid paying a hefty indemnity, the US attorneys did what they could to have the claims tossed.

In response, on November 18, 1936, nearly twenty years after the massacre, the commission wrote to the Mexican attorneys requesting additional evidence from the claimants. Attorney Roberto Cordova, again, had to return to the private records of the victims of the massacre. He coordinated with the municipal president of Ojinaga Chihuahua. On behalf of Juana Bonilla Flores, Cordova submitted a certified birth certificate for Longino Flores and the sworn testimonies of Martin Medrano, Anastácio Romero, and Julio Aranda. The three men gave testimonies on December 9, 1936, confirming that Juana was born in the Mexican town of San Jose in the municipality of San Pablo Meoqui. They testified to knowing Juana's family since she was a young girl and that they also knew her husband Longino, also a Mexican national. Martin Medrano, for example, described Longino as a close friend with whom he had worked while living in San Jose.[108]

The claimants had a strong legal argument for an indemnity, but they were one of several thousand waiting for a decision. Under the jurisprudence of the General Claims Commission, American citizens filed a total of 2,781 claims against Mexico while Mexican citizens filed 836 claims against the United States. The majority of claims filed by American citizens against the Mexican government involved property disputes by ranchers and mining companies. The original convention of September 8, 1923, required the disposition of all claims within three years from the date of the first meeting.[109] Successive conventions extended the life of the commission in 1923, 1927, and again in 1929. By August 30, 1931, the commission had granted awards to American claimants in eighty-nine cases with sums amounting to $4,607,926.59. The commission granted awards to Mexican claimants in only five cases with sums amounting to $39,000.[110] Despite the commission's decisions on this batch of cases, claimants did not receive their indemnities until nearly fifteen years later. Legal scholar Herbert Briggs, writing in an international law journal, concluded that the commission was "one of the most dilatory, inefficient, and unfortunate in our history."[111]

We won't ever know what the commission would have decided. At a convention of November 19, 1941, the two governments decided on an en bloc settlement of the general claims by which Mexico agreed to pay in total $40,000,000, in installments of $2,500,000, while the United States agreed to pay $533,668.96.[112] The national debts accrued through decisions of individual claims resulted in Mexico being so financially indebted to the United States that the commission had to negotiate a deal between the two nations. The deal, on paper, agreed to stabilize the Mexican peso; the

United States agreed to purchase Mexican silver, and it would extend credits through the Export-Import Bank to Mexico for the construction of the Inter-American Highway. In other words, resolving individual indemnities took the form of international debt negotiations. The deal eventually helped the United States gain access to Mexican natural resources under favorable conditions. The construction of the highway linked the neighboring nations and literally paved the way for future trade and the future movement of goods and people across international borders.[113] This resolution heightened the national disparities in power relations between the two nations. A year later the United States strong-armed Mexico in negotiating the exploitative guest worker arrangement called the Bracero Program.[114]

The restricted time frame outlined by the convention protocol did not allow the General Claims Commission to hear all the cases before it adjourned. While the en bloc settlement signaled the "amicable" settlement of national tensions created by the claims, the settlement occurred at the expense of survivors of the Porvenir massacre and other claims that remained undecided by the tribunal. In the end, the US attorney's strategy to delay a hearing worked. In total, the commission failed to consider over 1,000 claims before the protocol expired.[115]

Although we are left with questions about how the commission would have decided in *Concepción Carrasco de González, et al. (United Mexican States) v. the United States of America,* it did make decisions for similar cases. Of the total 3,617 claims filed, at least thirty-two claims charged states with failure to apprehend or punish assailants, failure to punish adequately, denial of justice, wrongful death, unnecessary use of arms, or direct responsibility in the death of a relative. Five cases in particular filed by Mexican claimants with similar circumstances to those of the Porvenir survivors deserve our attention. They constitute only a small portion of these cases, but they are invaluable because they expose the larger phenomenon of relatives who sought justice for their loved ones in the face of intimidation and negligence on the part of the US judicial system. In the end, they offer an important insight into how the commission may have decided in the case of the Porvenir massacre.

Both *Teodoro García and M. A. Garza (United Mexican States) v. United States of America* and *D. Guerrero vda. De Falcon (United Mexican States) v. United States of America* involved charges that the United States held direct responsibility for the deaths of children at the hands of US soldiers. In 1919 Concepción García, a Mexican national, was living in Texas in order to attend school. That same year, Lieutenant Gulley of the US Cavalry patrolled the US–Mexico border. Concepción became ill and attempted to return home on April 8. While crossing the river to Mexico on a raft, the young girl, her mother Maria, and her aunt found themselves under fire. Her father, Teodoro, looked on from the Mexican bank as Gulley shot and killed his daughter.[116] The lieutenant's firing at an unarmed group necessitated an investigation, and on April 28, 1919, a court-martial sentenced Gulley, dismissing him from military service. However, President Woodrow Wilson, acting on the advice of the board of review, the judge advocate general, and the secretary of war, reversed the findings, ordered the lieutenant released from arrest, and restored him to duty in September 1919.[117]

Concepción García's parents charged the state with the wrongful death of their daughter and denial of justice for failing to punish a US border agent who shot and killed their daughter while she crossed the Rio Grande. Hearing the case on December 3, 1926, the General Claims Commission discussed the duty not only of municipal and federal authorities but also of soldiers to eliminate any reckless use of firearms. For US soldiers on the US–Mexico border, the commissioners referred to US Military Bulletin No. 4 of February 11, 1919, stating that "firing on unarmed persons supposed to be engaged in smuggling or crossing the river at unauthorized places, is not authorized." Moreover, General Order No. 3 dated March 21, 1919, outlined that "Troop commanders will be: held responsible that the provisions of Bulletin No. 4 . . . is carefully explained to all men." The commissioners found that states should be punished for "such offenses as unnecessary shooting across the border without authority."[118] The commission obligated the US government to pay an indemnity on behalf of Teodoro García and Maria Apolinar Garza. In deciding the amount, it considered reparations for financial loss and for indignity suffered by the claimants. The tribunal decided, "An amount of $2,000 without interest, would seem to express best the personal damage caused the claimants by their killing of their daughter by an American officer."[119]

In the case of *D. Guerrero vda. De Falcon (United Mexican States) v. United States of America,* heard by the commission on November 16, 1926, the court reviewed the details of the death of Gregorio Falcon. On the morning of May 5, 1919, Falcon, a Mexican citizen, bathed in the Rio Grande with a

man named Félix Villarreal. Two US soldiers suspected Falcon and Villareal of smuggling goods across to the American side of the river. The
soldiers unloaded a barrage of approximately fifty rounds of bullets at the
men, resulting in Falcon's death. Without bringing the soldiers to trial,
the US military police declared them innocent of any crime on the grounds
that they acted in the discharge of their duty to prevent smuggling. Mexican authorities conducted their own investigation and found no evidence
of smuggling.[120] Again the commission found that the soldiers disregarded
both American military regulations by directing fire against naked and defenseless Mexican nationals. It decided that the US government should
pay an indemnity of $7,000 on behalf of Dolores Guerrero, widow of
Gregorio Falcon, and Bartolo, Apolonio, Domingo, and Monica Falcon,
children of the deceased.[121] The two cases showed that the US government
could be held liable for the actions of soldiers and state agents against
Mexican citizens.

Other claims pursued by Mexican nationals through the General Claims
Commission showed that the US government could also be held liable
for crimes committed by Texas law enforcement agents. For example, in
the case of *Francisco Quintanilla (United Mexican States) v. United States of
America*, Francisco and Maria Inez Perez de Quintanilla, father and mother
of Alejo Quintanilla, charged the government with denial of justice, direct responsibility for acts of minor officials, death during custody, failure
to apprehend or punish, and measure of damages for wrongful death of
their son, who died in the custody of local police in Edinburg in 1922.[122]
Court records indicate that on July 15, 1922, Tom Casey lodged a complaint with local authorities accusing Quintanilla, his employee, of ha-
rassing his daughter. Sam Bernard, the Edinburg deputy sheriff, traveled
with three other men to arrest Quintanilla. The prisoner never made it to
the county jail. Three days later, around noon on July 18, 1922, his corpse
was found near the side of the road, three miles outside of Edinburg. The
Mexican consul intervened and accused Deputy Sheriff Bernard and
Walter Weaver, a civilian, of murdering Quintanilla. The grand jury of
Hidalgo County never heard the case.[123] The commission found that
under international law, when a government takes prisoners, hostages, or
interned soldiers into custody it is responsible and obligated to account for
them. Ultimately the commissioners found that the US government was

obligated to pay $2,000 to the Mexican government on behalf of Francisco and Maria Inez Perez de Quintanilla.[124]

Similarly, in 1927 the mother of Adolfo Pedro Galvan filed a claim for the failure of Nueces County officers to apprehend or punish assailants who murdered her son in 1921. Despite eyewitness accounts that Hugh Kondall shot Galvan twice, Nueces County Criminal District Court rescheduled the trial a total of twelve times over a period of five years. By April 1927 the Criminal District Court of Nueces County had still failed to try the case against Hugh Kondall.[125] Commissioners who later reviewed the case stated, "There is no reason to suppose that the legal machinery of the state of Texas is so defective that in a case in which a preliminary trial reveals that there were at least five eye witnesses to the shooting of Galvan the authorities during a period of six years later found themselves unable to conduct a proper prosecution."[126] The commissioners found that in the case of *Salome Lerma De Galvan v. United Mexican States* (1927), the US government was obligated to pay the Mexican government $10,000 on behalf of the Galvan family for failing to punish the murderers of Adolfo Galvan.

All these cases showed that the US government could be held liable for the actions of US soldiers, civil authorities, state police, and local courts. In the Porvenir massacre brief filed in 1935, Mexican attorneys cited many of these cases as precedent. All the cases demonstrate that the murder of Mexican nationals in Texas in the early twentieth century did not go unnoticed or uncontested by their families. Even in the midst of mourning, parents and widows sought justice for the dead. They called on their consulates to ask for justice on their behalf. The legal records also help illustrate the active work of military officials, law enforcement officers, and county courts to justify excessive use of force, to defend agents who did not follow protocol, to delay criminal trials of Anglo men, and in some cases to cover up for local police who left Mexican prisoners vulnerable to vigilante and mob violence.

In his 1943 report, Herbert Briggs concluded that the General Claims Commission eventually allowed American nationals awarded indemnities to receive "substantial justice."[127] These claims primarily resolved loss of property. His review invites further inquiry into how to gauge "substantial justice" for Mexican claimants whose cases involved indemnities for the deaths of their relatives. Even if the claimants succeeded in winning an indemnity, the financial amounts calculated by the commissioners could not constitute "substantial justice" for the surviving relatives.

As a measure for assigning indemnities, the committee officially considered not only the "reparation of pecuniary loss" but also "satisfaction for indignity suffered."[128] Calculating the financial loss owed a claimant with the victim's probable life expectancy and potential income throughout his working life created the conditions for these financial awards to reflect the class status of the victims. Figuring someone's worth based solely on income was a devaluation of human life. Moreover, in determining the indemnity, commissioners did not prescribe a formula for calculating personal loss or indignity suffered by the surviving relatives. How was the commission calculating grief? Additionally, within the structure of the claims commission, tribunals were restricted to fining national governments. This meant that the systematic sanctioning of reckless use of firearms by soldiers and local state agents, the denial of justice for residents, and the failure to prosecute assailants involved in the wrongful death of residents all continued unimpeded. Thus, although the international courts determined in the preceding cases that agents participated and bore direct responsibility in the death of residents or that courts had failed to apprehend assailants, the commission could not prosecute parties involved in state crimes.[129] While the commission masqueraded as a mechanism for justice, it may have appeased some claimants with indemnities, but it simultaneously left violent systems of policing in place. Moreover, the rulings were delivered decades too late to curb the widespread violent policing methods in the early twentieth century.

For widows and other family members—including Concepción Carrasco de González, Juana Bonilla Flores, Jesús García, Victoria Jiménez de García, Pablo Jiménez, Luis Jiménez, Eulalia González, Librada M. Jácquez, Rita Jácquez, Francisca Morales, Severiano Morales, and Alejandra Nieves—filing a claim did little to help them reckon with the Porvenir massacre. In her study of truth and reconciliation commissions in the twentieth century, political theorist Sonali Chakravarti argues that when commissions make room for personal testimonies, these accounts have the ability to "educate, empower, and hold others accountable." But, she continues, truth commissions and institutions of transitional justice must redefine what we think of as justice. In her words, "justice" must go beyond "accountability and punishment in order to include the emotions of victims and the legacy of suffering that affects entire societies after war, not just perpetrators and victims."[130] An important endeavor indeed. The descendants of the Porvenir massacre, however, are still waiting for accountability, punishment, and an acknowledgment of the heavy memories they carry.

THE BURDENS OF MEMORY

The survivors of the Porvenir massacre were denied legal, financial, and symbolic forms of redress. Though the possibility of the commission held out hope for a far more substantive form of redress than anything that came in our previous two cases, the 1910 lynching or the 1915 double murder, the end results were the same. There was no immediate sense of justice or redress. And residents continued to grapple with the consequences of the massacre long after 1918. As we trace the struggle to remember across multiple generations, we see how an entire community was affected by the tragedy. Relatives who witnessed the event and escaped death, neighbors, and even the soldiers unable to stop the massacre all remained gripped by memories of that night. Unsettled by the injustices they witnessed, a few Porvenir residents built their own archives and wrote their own histories of the massacre. Vernacular history-making offered them the chance to find some form of consolation. It also preserved the possibility that there might be justice in the future.

Some of the chief history-makers were Henry Warren and his daughter Nancy Elmendorf, Robert Keil and his daughter Linda Davis, and Juan Bonilla Flores and his daughter Benita, son John Flores Jr., and son-in-law Evaristo "Buddy" Albarado. In documenting the tragic events of the Porvenir massacre, this network of survivors developed a narrative of events that challenged the accounts of state officials. They recounted their memories in both oral and written form across nearly a century after the tragic events and in the process created archives both public and private. These archives give us access to the lives of those who were lost in the massacre and challenge the accuracy and authority of Texas Ranger records along with the criminalization of the dead. They also provide a window into the lives of those who survived the massacre and tell of their long struggle to live in the aftermath of violence. They endeavor to make visible the consequences of violent policing practices by state agents. To reckon with the

Narciso *(left)* and Juan Flores witnessed the murder of their father, Longino, during the Porvenir massacre of 1918. Juan, eleven years old, helped identify the bodies of the slain men. At the age of ninety-seven, he shared the story of the massacre with his daughter Benita Albarado, returned to the location of the massacre, and helped preserve the history. Courtesy Evaristo and Benita Albarado. Photo provided by the Bullock Texas State History Museum.

tragedy of the Porvenir massacre, residents turned to mourning, remembering, and retelling the story of that tragedy. In turn, their reckoning became a political act.[131]

For example, in 1934, Nancy Elmendorf approached Clifford Casey, then a history professor at Sul Ross State Teachers College in Alpine, for legal advice. She told him about the case filed through the General Claims Commission by the survivors of the Porvenir massacre. Her father, Harry Warren, had died two years earlier, but the lengthy legal proceedings continued, and Elmendorf sought legal help to figure out whether she was entitled to a certain portion of the potential indemnity, for her father's help in filing the case. Her father's archive included nearly 9,000 leaves of documents, including financial records, legal documents, school records, biographical materials, and printed materials. On February 1, 1935, the West Texas Historical and Scientific Society purchased the Harry Warren Papers from his children, Anacleto Warren, Nancy Elmendorf, and Helen Rosalie Warren.[132]

This collection inspired Casey's interest in the event and led him to write to the Claims Courts in Washington, DC, and Mexico City as well as to the US and Mexican consulates for more information. He also hired a research assistant, Elaine Carney, a Porvenir resident, to begin conducting interviews with anyone who knew about the massacre. Months later, on December 6, 1938, Carney wrote to the professor with news. She had interviewed an unnamed Mexican woman in town who had allegedly lived through the tumultuous period. She protected her household by keeping on hand a double-barreled shotgun to ward off any trespassers, including Texas Rangers. Carney had also met with an unnamed Mexican man who described another tragic event with the Texas Rangers that resulted in death. The man found his father's body lying dead two or three days after his murder. She continued her account: "They just dug a hole and rolled him in a tarp, and there the grave is today. This raid was all up and down Rio Grande. The Rangers just killed and left them laying."[133] Correspondence between Casey and Carney lasted for months, and letters between the professor and the lawyers helping Nancy Elmendorf continued until 1946.[134] Although Elmendorf and the other Warren heirs did not receive financial compensation, her efforts resulted in Harry Warren's archive being preserved and made available even today at what is now the Bryan Wildenthal Memorial Library at Sul Ross State University.[135]

Another relationship that helped preserve the history of the Porvenir massacre was that of Robert Keil and his daughter Linda Davis. Born in Dubois, Pennsylvania, in 1898, Keil dreamed of joining the US Cavalry. He realized his goal by running away from home at the age of fifteen. He bypassed enlistment requirements by changing his name from Kiel to Keil, lying about his age, and claiming he had no relatives. For over six years he lived in the Big Bend country, serving in the US Cavalry and later working as a civil service packer for pack-master Charley Coward. In the preface to Keil's memoir, *Bosque Bonito,* editor Elizabeth McBride described this period in west Texas as "the happiest and wildest years of his life. Yet they were also years of violence, and he would remain haunted throughout his life by the tragedies he witnessed."[136]

Memories of the massacre stayed with Keil into adulthood. In his later life, he dedicated countless hours to preserving his account of the massacre and defending the reputation of the victims. In 1963, forty-five years after the event, Keil began corresponding with archivists at the Texas State Archives, searching for official documents regarding the massacre. He disagreed with historian Walter Prescott Webb's depictions of the Texas Rangers as heroes and inquired about the 1919 congressional investigation of the Texas Rangers. In a three-page letter he gave his account of what he witnessed in Porvenir and explained,

> That was the incident Captain Fox and his company were fired for, but the truth has never been published. The Porvenir Massacre was only one of many similar incidents Fox had a big hand in, and it was he who kept the Upper Big Bend red hot. When he was fired there was no more trouble on the river. . . . I had looked at all of the victims . . . none were bandits.[137]

Keil mourned those who died in the massacre and insisted they were not bandits. While clearing the names of the victims, he wanted to condemn specific Texas Rangers rather than a broader practice of state violence. Throughout the letter, Keil criticized Fox and also quoted rancher Ed Nevill, who blamed the Texas Rangers for causing conflict in the region. By Nevill's accounts, "every time them damn Rangers do go to Ruidosa or Candelaria they ambush somebody and then run back to Marfa and leave us here on the river to face the trouble they stirred up." Keil also openly criticized historians' failures to accurately narrate the conflict in the region.

In 2002, the Center for Big Bend Studies posthumously published Robert Keil's manuscript. Elizabeth McBride had spent time with Keil's family and learned of his long efforts to publish his account. She wrote, "The beauty and tragedy of Keil's river experience were powerfully impressed upon him; and they continued to hold him captive as time and again he wrote the story, sought to have it published, and time and again, he was disappointed."[138] Recognizing the historical importance of the manuscript, Keil's daughter, Linda Davis, had attempted on her own to publish her father's writing.

Although they lived in Tucson, Arizona, Keil had frequently returned to west Texas, visited with surviving friends, and relived his memories as a cavalry scout.[139] Davis grew up hearing stories from her father about his days in the US Cavalry and the injustices he witnessed. She learned about the pain and horror he carried with him. As she described it, she lived through the memories with him. As a child she watched her father cry at his typewriter. Reflecting on his struggles, she compared his trauma to that of Vietnam veterans who suffered posttraumatic stress disorder. Her father, too, was haunted by the memories of the violence he participated in during his national service. In his case, however, he was troubled by the violent massacre not of a presumed foreign enemy but of an unarmed group of civilians on US soil, civilians he knew well.

Keil started writing *Bosque Bonito* when his daughter was six, and he finished it twelve years later. She explained, "My dad would cry and say, 'Linda those poor people. . . .' One time he told me he could get killed over writing the book. And I thought, 'Okay, you're getting strange, Daddy,' but it was the truth. Probably were some Texas Rangers out there still." Through the stories Davis heard from her father, she developed an appreciation for the relationship he had with the victims of the massacre. For Keil the murdered men were more than just residents he met on patrol. On multiple occasions Davis referred to them as his family, people who welcomed and nurtured him with tamales, homemade tortillas, and burritos. She explained, "He loved those people." According to Davis, the residents of Porvenir took care of her father, then just fifteen or sixteen, as he traveled on scout patrol. She expressed gratitude and exclaimed, "Those people fed him everyday. Those people were his family. He was just a kid."[140] When the book was finally published in 2002, Davis was flooded with memories of her father's torment. She described to me opening the package with the first copy of the book and falling to her knees. She realized at that moment that she, too, had been carrying the burden of these memories.[141]

In the process of editing the book, Davis and McBride joined a tour of sites led by Joyce Means, a west Texas resident who grew up on the border and wrote local histories. Means took visitors through the "hushed beauty of the country" but also included a visit to the site of the massacre and to various ranches that had been raided in the early twentieth century. On the tour, Linda Davis met Benita and Evaristo "Buddy" Albarado. The daughter of Juan Bonilla Flores—who narrowly escaped being murdered and survived the execution of his father, Longino Flores—Benita Albarado traveled with her husband and father to Alpine to search for records that would confirm her father's stories. According to Davis, the Albarados initially questioned Davis's motives and assumed that Keil had willingly participated in the massacre. Davis gave the Albarados a copy of *Bosque Bonito,* and eventually Benita called to thank her for publishing a book that publicly acknowledged her family's suffering.[142]

Benita Albarado, like Linda Davis, witnessed her father struggle with memories of the Porvenir massacre and felt the burden of that night, even decades later. As a young girl she remembered that her father woke in cold sweats and had nightmares that the Texas Rangers were coming to kill him and his family. Unlike Linda Davis, Benita Albarado did not know what events caused her father such turmoil until she was an adult.

Juan Flores carried the burden of these events in silence, hidden from his children, until 1998, when he began describing the traumatic events. Eleven years old on the night of the Porvenir massacre, Juan witnessed not just the massacre itself but the way it unraveled his family. In the years after the massacre, his mother, Juana Bonilla Flores, was consumed by flashbacks. In retelling these events to his children, Juan recalled that his mother, traumatized by that night, frequently woke in the middle of the night screaming that the Rangers were coming to kill her family. To protect her from harming herself, the family kept their hunting rifles locked in a chest. One day in 1935, his mother found the chest unlocked. She loaded a rifle, leaned over the barrel of the gun, and fired. Juan Flores, who seventeen years earlier had witnessed the execution of his father, found the body of his deceased mother.[143] The graphic details of the massacre in 1918 and lasting image of the tragic death of Juana Bonilla Flores in 1935 were passed down to Benita Albarado by her relatives.

Benita Albarado did her best to piece together information about her grandmother. She spoke with relatives, some of whom were willing to share their memories, while others demurred. Her father, she remembered, "never wanted to talk about it." Juan Flores chronicled the events of the massacre for his children but did not want to discuss his mother's suicide.

From conversations with relatives who were more forthcoming, she learned that her grandmother shot a bullet into her heart.[144] After nearly ten years of research, they eventually located her death certificate.

The gravity of Juana Bonilla Flores's death is all the more troubling considering that while she was in the throes of insurmountable sorrow, the US attorneys succeeded in having the US General Claims Commission question her nationality and marriage to Longino Flores. Just two months before her suicide, on September 13, 1935, the brief filed by US attorneys tried to deny her legal standing. By December 9, 1936, when Martin Medrano, Anastácio Romero, and Julio Aranda traveled to Ojinaga to give testimony, under oath, about Juana as a young girl and her marriage to Longino, she had already taken her life.

I do not have any evidence that Juana Bonilla Flores had been informed about the US reply brief. Despite that, the proximity of the banal legal procedures to her death emphasizes just how far removed the cold procedures were from the ongoing suffering of survivors of the massacre. It also raises questions about the indignation that Medrano, Romero, and Aranda may have felt when answering callous questions about her life.

In retelling the history of the Porvenir massacre, Benita Albarado described her grandmother as another victim of that night. Seventeen years later, the effects of the tragedy consumed Juana Bonilla Flores and her mental health deteriorated. Albarado, saddened by the details she learned from relatives, whispered, "She went crazy. She would run around at midnight, knocking on the doors of other people telling them to run for their lives because the Rangers were coming to kill them."[145]

Witnessing the execution of his father and finding the body of his mother also had devastating effects on Juan Flores. He was troubled well into adulthood. The Albarados describe Juan Flores as having a photographic memory. In his old age he could recall all the names of the residents in Porvenir and their children. When he visited the sites on Joyce Means's tour, he even corrected the location she described as the mass grave of the Porvenir victims. Benita Albarado, like her father, grew up in a household with a parent who suffered from frequent nightmares and flashbacks of past traumas.

In 1950 Flores admitted himself into the Texas State Hospital in Big Springs to receive psychiatric care. Speaking only Spanish, he was unable to communicate with the English-speaking hospital staff. Unable to swallow the medication usually provided before a treatment, Flores later told his daughter that during his six-month stay, he underwent shock therapy a number of times without tranquilizers or pain medication. The Albarados were troubled by the inability of the hospital to provide Flores with basic care. Undergoing shock therapy seemed like another form of torture. After discussing his father-in-law's attempts to seek help to cure his nightmares, Buddy Albarado shook his head and explained, "There's nothing you can do for that. It's stuck in your brain."[146]

Benita Albarado and her husband continue to confront the consequences of her family's inherited loss by investigating and keeping alive the story of the Porvenir massacre. As I finished writing this book, the couple was still dedicating long weekends traveling to archives and reading the latest historical accounts of the period. They have paid over $1,000 to researchers at the National Archives of the United States in College Park, Maryland, to locate and make copies of relevant federal records, including any documents related to the claim *Concepción Carrasco de González, et al. (United Mexican States) v. the United States of America.*

They preserve a collection in their home that spreads across multiple rooms and closets. Copies of documents from state and university archives, family records, photographs, portraits, maps, recorded interviews, and more are preserved in their private archive. The Albarados transcribe most of these documents for ease of reading and reference. They are up to date with blogs that discuss the history and stay informed about other families' efforts to retrieve their own histories and grapple with inherited loss. If the Porvenir massacre is referenced in a newspaper article, they know about it.

They are committed to documenting the Porvenir massacre as well as the broader practice of anti-Mexican violence in the early twentieth century. In November 2006, the Albarados traveled to Regan Wells, approximately thirty miles north of their home in Uvalde, to take part in a memorial service organized for Marine Gararez, a Mexican laborer lynched on May 11, 1914.[147] Local residents gathered to install a plaque at the site of the lynching, and Buddy Albarado was there to film the memorial. Four years later, in November 2010, he drove to Rocksprings for the memorial for Antonio Rodríguez and Effie Henderson. Their private collection also includes a copy of the documentary *Border Bandits.*

When the couple travels to book talks or other events, they take copies of documents related to the Porvenir massacre and share them with historians and audience members. In addition to transcribed documents, they sometimes include photographs of the Texas Rangers who participated in the crime and quotes of callous depictions of Mexicans by state agents. In their efforts to educate more people about the massacre, the Albarados include the names and the ages of the Porvenir massacre victims. They refuse to allow the victims to remain anonymous.

I first learned about the Porvenir massacre and of the long efforts of the Albarados in the fall of 2008 when my uncle, Rogelio Muñoz, mailed me a package of documents. The Albarados had gathered copies of historical documents relating to the massacre and asked Muñoz for his legal advice. They briefly described the massacre and the General Claims Commission of 1923. They described their frustration that the assailants were not prosecuted and that the survivors did not receive an indemnity. Further, they wanted to know whether they had any legal grounds to file a new claim against the US government for the denial of justice in the wake of the Porvenir massacre.

As it was outside his legal expertise, Muñoz offered the names of other lawyers to call but also offered to share the package with me, a historian who might have an interest in researching the case. The package included letters of correspondence, the first page of the claim filed by the survivors of the Porvenir massacre, and newspaper clippings from the *El Paso Times.* The descendants had also reached out to other historians, scholars, and filmmakers. In 2002 the Flores descendants started collaborating with filmmaker Gode Davis from Rhode Island. Davis was producing a film *American Lynching: Strange and Bitter Fruit,* and after learning of the massacre he wanted to feature Juan Bonilla Flores as a survivor of a massacre. Flores, at ninety-seven years old, sat for an hour-and-a-half interview on film. As most interviews begin, he listed his age and place of birth, gave his parents' names, and described his childhood. But five minutes into the interview, he started to describe the events that changed the course of the lives of the residents of Porvenir. He described the participation of Evan Means and Bob Evans and the involvement of US soldiers in the massacre, names left out of the historical records. He remembered notifying Harry Warren the day of the massacre, helping to identify the mutilated bodies, and the fear by the residents in the aftermath. He remembered his mother as strong and hard-working. She worked on the farm and then, after the massacre, worked wherever she could find a job. But he also remembered her struggling with sadness. She cried every day.

When asked if he was afraid following the massacre, he explained that everyone was afraid, and as a result they abandoned their homes and all scattered across Mexico and Texas. He also described the sadness in not knowing who to turn to for aid. "Yes. Everyone of us collapsed, crying. There was nothing we could do. There was nothing that could help us. To whom could we complain?" Even the US soldiers that they had known and broke bread with participated in rounding up the residents. They no longer trusted the soldiers in the wake of the massacre. In remembering the experience of burying the dead, Flores answered frankly, "Well, what could we do? We could only weep and all, everyone there. Then we put them into a wagon. And we went and buried them. All of them were put in a single pit. But the person who stayed after Juan got them down was Mr. Nevill. He couldn't tear himself away; he stared at the bodies." Local ranchers that knew the victims, like Ed Nevill, Jenkin Pat, and another Flores referred to as "El Doc," came to help with the burial. Their neighbors, too, were shocked by the tragedy.

Flores described a life with nightmares and the great sadness of his memories. The massacre itself was horrific. He described the injustice of unarmed men being rounded up, bound, massacred, and mutilated. He also carried the burden of the realization that murderers walked around free. The impunity they enjoyed further pained the survivors and intimidated other residents. He described the nightmares he suffered throughout his life, and he also described the lasting sadness when he remembered the injustice of the massacre. "Oh, yes, it's very bad. We can never forget it. Not until we die. My mother thought about it a great deal and cried seeing how well off we had been and how we had been ruined overnight. Well, everyone there was ruined, each of those little villages where we had lived so tranquilly and so comfortably."[148]

To help tell the story on film, Flores also traveled with his family and the film crew to the site of the massacre. On film his son, Juan Flores Jr., asked his father questions about the location of the homes, the farms, and the site where the fifteen residents died. At ninety-seven years old, Flores made a pilgrimage. He withstood hours of travel on Texas highways, on farm-to-market roads, and finally off road to where he lived when his family remained complete. He withstood the sun and the rocky terrain to share his account of the lives lost and the horrors of the massacre on film.

Recognizing the taxing process of recalling the memories under these conditions, the interview captured a touching exchange between father and son:

> *Flores, Jr.:* How do you feel now, Dad? I know these questions are very
>   painful. It's painful for me too.
> *Flores:* Of course it is. How could it not be?
> *Flores Jr.:* But, how . . . how do you feel coming back to your birthplace?
> *Flores:* Well, I remember.[149]

The emotional toll of the memories and answering a series of questions was taxing on everyone involved, but Juan Bonilla Flores, nearly one hundred years old, and his family were committed to remembering the loss in order so that others would not forget. Gode Davis eventually released a trailer of the documentary that featured his interview with Flores. When Flores died in 2007 Davis added a memorial to his website. He concluded his thoughts, "I was touched by his sense of humor and civility, but most by his courage . . . I will miss this gentle human being greatly. Most of all, I lament the bitter truth that we could not complete our production before he died this year at age 101."[150] Despite his best efforts, Davis himself died before the documentary came to fruition. The family preserved their correspondence with Davis and preserved the transcripts of the interviews in the hopes that one day more people would have access to the accounts Flores preserved and shared.

These efforts to bring their historical findings to light offer a glimpse into the sometimes episodic nature of the effort to memorialize the tragedy. In between their own children graduating from high school and college, getting married, having children of their own, and family illnesses, the Albarados make time to preserve this history and make it publicly available. They have taken on the task of preservation. In their spare time and with their own resources, and with great persistence.

An indemnity from the US government could not have fully ameliorated the suffering and trauma experienced by the generations of descendants. A critical part of the injustice is the fact that no assailants were prosecuted for their involvement in the massacre, that the 1919 legislative investigation into the Texas Rangers did not allow for the committee to hear evidence of the role of the state police in the massacre, that the

General Claims Commission of 1923 also did not hear the case filed by relatives of the victims, and that the state of Texas has failed to recognize this history as a tragedy.

Harry Warren, Robert Keil, Juan Flores, and the other survivors affected by the Porvenir massacre remembered what they witnessed. Some may not consider Robert Keil to be included in the category of survivor because his life was not at risk and he was not the intended target of the Rangers' violence. But the need to remember and reckon with the violence cut across racial lines in a way that may not initially have been anticipated. For survivors like Juana and Juan Flores, remembering the event, in the form of flashbacks, had devastating consequences.

These burdensome memories came at great costs to their families for generations. For some who learned the history of the massacre, remembering became a political act of resistance that contained the possibility of shifting public dialogues and historical narratives. The efforts to narrate these events and challenge state-sanctioned violence also carried an implicit effort to find some form of redress. There are no simple solutions that will bring total or complete closure, but the efforts to document the past and to remember offer some form of resolution.

Publishing *Bosque Bonito* helped Linda Davis find some closure in carrying out her father's wishes. She continues to circulate the book at local history conferences, and in 2010 during a family reunion she held a book reading for her extended family.[151] For the descendants of the Porvenir massacre, closure seems farther away. They want answers as to why, given all the evidence of this case, the assailants were never prosecuted. They want a judicial court to hear evidence and to rule that the United States was liable for the wrongful death of fifteen men in Porvenir in 1918. Officially recognizing the massacre as a state crime would go far in bringing some consolation. In 2016, after two previous attempts, the Texas Historical Commission finally agreed to identify the site of the Porvenir massacre with a state historical marker describing the injustices of the Texas Rangers. By the time this book went to press, the marker had yet to be unveiled.

The generational practice of documenting the past, the troubled lives of survivors, the court testimonies of members of the Suaste and Montelongo families, and the cases brought before the General Claims Commission all testify to the long-lasting effects of racial violence on communities at large. As in the case of the double murder of Jesus Bazán and Antonio Longoria, mourning and trauma in the wake of state-sanctioned violence deeply affected ethnic Mexican and Anglo residents; the wounds of a former era do not heal merely with time. On the contrary, the legacy of violence in the early twentieth century is traceable through its long impact on generations of residents, as well as through the ongoing failures to prosecute police abuse and reform policing regimes on the Texas–Mexico border.

CHAPTER FOUR

Cultures of Violence

ON JULY 26, 1918, President Woodrow Wilson publicly denounced the pervasive lynching culture in the postwar United States. True democracy, he proclaimed, insisted upon "ordered law and humane justice." He continued, "It cannot live where the community does not countenance it."[1] As soldiers returned from service in World War I, he linked mob violence at home to tyranny abroad: "Germany has outlawed herself among the nations because she has disregarded the sacred obligations of law and has made lynchers of her armies. Lynchers emulate her disgraceful example. I, for my part, am anxious to see every community in America rise above that level with pride and a fixed resolution which no man or set of men can afford to despise." Seizing postwar momentum, Wilson invoked a higher moral ground as the foundation of American superiority to Germany. The lyncher, he continued, "Is no true son of democracy, but its betrayer." He called on the nation to harness the energy it had once placed into World War I and to redirect its efforts toward keeping America's "global reputation untarnished."[2]

Possibilities for civil rights, women's suffrage, and labor rights filled the air. Working class activists leveraged wartime labor shortages and made strides in their organizing, but when US servicemen returned to the work-force, the swelling labor market complicated organizing efforts. Servicemen returned to find the Midwest and the Northeast transformed by the Great Migration of African Americans from the US South. In the Southwest, recent Mexican arrivals who had crossed the border during the deadly civil war in Mexico also changed the complexion of the workforce. Con-flicts erupted. During 1919 approximately four million workers went on strike. As the world witnessed the success of the Bolshevik revolution, attempts by governments and employers to quell the rise of labor unions took on a particular urgency. One strategy included inspiring fear of com-munism in the United States. While a particular version of American democracy—all-embracing, possibility-laden—was being broadcast across the globe, at home the categories of belonging felt increasingly narrow. Along with the rise of the Red Scare, other ways of encouraging divisiveness—particularly racism, eugenics, and xenophobia—gripped the nation.[3] As unions advocated for more power, and women and minorities of all kinds demanded more rights, the social unrest was palpable. The ideal of an inclu-sive American democracy looked more and more like a myth.

Wilson's speech labeled "the lyncher" a betrayer of democracy, but he also offered an implicit defense for his refusal to act against lynchers. Rather than submit federal legislation to help eradicate lynching culture in the United States, Wilson placed individual responsibility on all Americans to end the brutal practice.[4] This was, after all, the same president who started his presidential tenure by segregating federal employees in Washington. Raised in the South, Wilson ushered Jim Crow into the White House. He was also keenly aware of the power of states to set the tone for social norms. Extralegal violence thrived in the United States because state administra-tions and law enforcement officers allowed, endorsed, or even participated in such acts. He called upon governors and local law officers to cooperate "actively and watchfully to make an end to this disgraceful evil"; he also surely knew that a speech alone, absent legislation, would do little to change the violence across the country, especially in states like Texas.[5]

The federal government watched as racial violence swept the nation. At the conclusion of the war, states and local communities sought to reim-pose racial hierarchies. The nation witnessed the resurgence of the Ku Klux Klan. The group—anti-black, anti-Mexican, anti-Semitic, anti-immigrant, anti-Catholic, and anti-union—inspired fear across the United States and included politicians, judges, and bankers in its membership. Violence continued to be a means for policing social boundaries.

In 1919 Texas governor William P. Hobby's administration was confronted with two efforts to transform cultures of racial violence in Texas. The first effort, led by State Representative José Tomás Canales, sought to investigate violent policing regimes and reform the state police. The second effort, organized by the National Association for the Advancement of Colored People (NAACP), challenged the widespread lynching culture in the state.

Sitting at his desk in January 1919, the governor was at a crossroads. He could heed the calls of the NAACP and pass anti-lynching legislation. He could also work with the legislature to hold the state police accountable for their brutality, reform the force, and prosecute police for past crimes. Or the governor could curtail any further gains in civil rights.

In 1919 the violence that had long targeted African American and ethnic Mexican communities converged on the capitol grounds in Austin. Although histories of anti-black and anti-Mexican violence have been segregated in popular memories of this period, the ideologies that condoned violence in Texas against those communities mutually informed and justified one another. To fully comprehend the culture of impunity that allowed anti-Mexican violence to thrive in Texas, it is necessary to consider the ongoing history of anti-black violence in the state.[6] Both these histories emerged from ideologies of white supremacy that took particular forms across the American South and West. Both, in turn, helped state authorities justify extralegal violence. These histories converged and coalesced in Texas, a state built by conquest and slavery. When studied together, the histories help dispel long-held distinctions traditionally made between vigilante violence and state violence. Instead, extralegal violence comes to the fore as a common and sanctioned practice of state policing in the twentieth century. These converging histories show that anti-black and anti-Mexican violence mutually informed one another. Texas Rangers who abused their power targeted both ethnic Mexicans and African Americans.

In late January 1919, for the first time, a committee of state legislators would investigate police abuse, rights violations of residents in the border region, and the state's role in inciting terror. State Representative Canales introduced legislation that aimed to reform the state police force by reducing its size, increasing agent salaries, and placing agents under bond. The Canales Bill, as it was known, called for a deep investigation into Ranger conduct going back to the peak of anti-Mexican violence in 1915 and sought to document acts of extralegal violence by the state police. Throughout weeks of testimony, witnesses provided accounts of Texas Rangers who collaborated with local police and civilians to commit murders, torture prisoners, and intimidate residents. Moreover, Canales showed that state administrators called for and sanctioned these acts of violence. Denial of the civil rights of ethnic and racial minorities, in other words, was not the work of a few unrestrained or rogue agents. This was a key characteristic of state policing.

Meanwhile, anti-black violence continued unabated. The same month the investigation began, one of the most brutal lynchings of an African American occurred in the east Texas town of Hillsboro, under the watch of Texas Rangers, just 140 miles north of Austin. The lynching prompted the NAACP and the National League on the Urban Condition Among Negroes to intensify efforts to pressure the Texas state administration to end the lynching culture.

The role of states, courts, and local police in allowing mobs to enact violence with impunity came into clear view in 1919. While Canales was documenting abuse by the state police in Texas, anti-lynching activists were calling attention to the ongoing collusion of local police with mob instigators of violence. At least thirty-four lynching victims in 1919 were removed from the custody of officers, taken either in transport or from jails. That local and state police officers sometimes colluded with vigilante groups was no surprise to ethnic and racial minorities, but Canales and the NAACP made these practices visible to a wider audience. The NAACP called for an end to the brutality and asked that police fulfill their duties to protect citizens. Moreover, they declared, when local police failed to uphold their responsibilities, they should be held accountable. As the 1919 investigation showed, the state police failed to protect the rights of both ethnic Mexicans and African Americans.[7]

These battles for civil rights forced the Texas administration to reveal whether it would function as an arbiter of social change or as an institution that would preserve the status quo, allowing racial violence to continue unabated. In January demands by the NAACP for an investigation into a lynching and the investigation into the Texas Rangers led by Canales coincided, bringing the interconnected Texas traditions of racial violence to the fore. The Hillsboro lynching provided an important reminder that while the murder and intimidation of Mexican residents was under examination, the brutal practice of lynching black Texans continued. John R. Shillady, the secretary of the NAACP, sent a letter to Governor Hobby to ask for a full investigation into the most recent lynchings. The Shillady request would sit on the governor's desk unanswered until Shillady made a trip to Austin that summer. Mob violence against African Americans loomed over the Texas Ranger investigation. In 1919 state administrators ignored President Wilson's calls for "ordered law and humane justice" and requests to transform the cultures of violence in Texas.

CULTURES OF VIOLENCE IN TEXAS

In the early twentieth century, southwest Texas and east Texas, separated by hundreds of miles, seemed worlds apart in regard to their landscapes, economies, demographics, cultural practices, and racial politics. Residents in southwest Texas had closer relations with residents in Mexico than with their fellow statesmen in the east, who were more closely tied, both economically and culturally, to Southern states. Although the two regions were connected by the railroad in 1904, travel remained limited to those who could afford a train ticket, those who owned a private automobile, or those who could weather the long trip on horseback or by wagon. Land promoters created pamphlets and postcards to help entice farmers to relocate to south Texas.

These pamphlets gave the public a curated image of life on the US–Mexico border. Few Texans from the central, northern, or eastern regions, however, had traveled to the southwestern edges of the state. Promotional photos gave residents an imagined sense of border life. Postcards showcased the region's fertile grounds, recent advances in infrastructure, and docile workforce, all in an effort to portray the region as an entrepreneurial paradise.[8] In January 1919 the state legislature would become fixated on

LOWER RIO GRANDE VALLEY OF TEXAS

© Gardner's Studio

PICKING GRAPE FRUIT IN JANUARY   1353-30

Anglo growers stand proudly next to bountiful boxes of produce. In the background, Mexican laborers holding up grapefruits pose as dutiful workers. Photographers portrayed idyllic scenes to entice Anglo farmers to move to south Texas. Such images were in direct contrast to the widespread violence and turbulence of the era. Robert Runyon Photograph Collection, RUN12693, The Dolph Briscoe Center for American History, University of Texas at Austin.

learning more about this region. Instead of a growers' paradise, they would learn of racial hostility and death. Postcards of agricultural possibilities circulated alongside postcards of dead Mexican bodies.

Despite the geographic separation, the grip of mob violence could be felt across the state. The culture of violence was one reality that linked the state together. Chapters of the NAACP in Texas cities, ranging from as far east as Beaumont to as far west as El Paso, gained strength and influence, with 2,652 members in 1918. In total, Texans organized thirty-three branches of the NAACP, making the state an organization stronghold. The largest chapter in San Antonio reported 1,228 members; Houston was second, with 414 members.

In the postwar period, civil rights organizations such as the NAACP focused on anti-violence advocacy in the absence of federal or state solutions. The NAACP had been founded less than a quarter century earlier, in 1896, during Reconstruction. By 1919 it had become the premier advocacy group for civil rights, with hundreds of branches across the United States. Its leaders believed that, as a strategy, numerical research could offer empirical evidence of the widespread horror of vigilante violence and implore the American public, as well as state and federal legislators, to combat it.[9] Inspired in great part by the research of Ida B. Wells-Barnett, who worked to dispel racial myths with statistical research, they utilized statistics as a means to introduce the crisis of lynching to the broader public. By telling the stories of lynching victims, they tried to dislodge popular assumptions about links between race and violence and crime. In her 1895 statistical opus *The Red Record: Tabulated Statistics and Alleged Causes of Lynching in the United States,* Wells-Barnett commanded, "Can you remain silent and inactive when such things are done in our own community and country? Is your duty to humanity in the United States any less binding?"[10]

In 1919, more than two decades later, the NAACP recorded a total of eighty-three lynchings across the nation. Seventy-seven of the lynching victims were African American, four were listed as white, and two were Mexican. Adding further to the gravity of these numbers, the NAACP reported that even soldiers were not protected from the brutality of mob violence. Ten of the African American victims were US soldiers who had returned from serving in World War I.[11] To make matters worse, mobs were using increasingly gruesome methods. In six different states, eleven victims were burned alive. Three other victims were murdered before their corpses were ceremoniously burned in front of crowds. In its annual report, the NAACP raised the alarm about this increased brutality, what they called the "monstrous crime of burning men alive."[12] Of all the states in the union, Texas maintained a national profile for having a long and rampant history of lynching. In 1918 alone, Texas mobs lynched eleven victims, second only to Georgia, where mobs claimed nineteen victims.[13] In 1919, when the NAACP released a list of the top ten states with the highest rates of lynching since 1889, Texas came in third with 335 victims, behind Georgia and Mississippi.[14]

In the heart of this longtime hotbed of lynching, members of the NAACP in Texas faced severe intimidation; they were framed as Northern agitators bringing instability to the region. In the face of pressure to stop organizing, local members continued to make strides and even garnered the support of major newspapers. On August 4, 1918, for example, the *San Antonio Evening News* offered to pay a reward of $1,000 for each conviction of mob participants if the victim was "Negro." The newspaper also agreed to provide a $500 reward if the victim was "white." The difference in reward amounts showed that the newspaper viewed vigilante violence in general as a social menace but maintained particular moral outrage at racially motivated lynchings.[15] The newspaper's efforts received wide publicity throughout the NAACP branches. Deep in the heart of Texas, the newspaper reward served as a symbol of a shifting public tide.

On January 13, 1919, the San Antonio newspaper called on the Texas commonwealth to "Hold up the lyncher before the eyes of decent men, in law and in fact, as a political and social pariah, an outcast!" Mob participants, the newspaper continued, acted as "an institution of lawless license, not of divinity and humanity and lawful liberty." The newspaper proposed that the Texas legislature amend the state constitution so that no man convicted of participating in a mob could be eligible to serve in public office.[16] These calls would fall on deaf ears. A week later the Hillsboro mob would take the life of Bragg Williams. No Texans claimed a reward. Instead, mob participants continued to enjoy a culture of impunity.[17]

Under the leadership of Secretary John Shillady, the NAACP published *Thirty Years of Lynching* (1919). The pamphlet included a state-by-state breakdown of lynching rates by year and listed the lynchings in each state chronologically with information on the alleged reason for the murder. The publication included only a small number of victims of anti-Mexican violence, and details of the events were rarely included. For example, it notes that on July 29, 1915, a mob lynched Adolfo Muñoz in Brownsville for murder. The remaining list of Mexican victims, however, continued without names. The publication showed that on August 20, 1915, six Mexicans were lynched at San Benito for "pillage and murder"; on September 3, 1915, three Mexicans were lynched at an unknown location for murder; on September 14, 1915, six Mexicans were lynched at San Benito and in Edinburg County for banditry; and on October 10, 1915, ten Mexicans were lynched near Brownsville in Cameron County for "train wrecking and murder."[18] Unnamed victims are rare in the publication, as the NAACP made great efforts to document the names of victims and the circumstances of their murder. The organization gathered data on lynchings primarily from newspaper accounts and did not consult the Spanish-language press. Most English-language newspapers did not consistently report on violence. In 1915, for example, even the *San Antonio Evening News* had reported that accounts of finding dead Mexican bodies were so common they would no longer report on these sightings as news. As a result, the NAACP had limited access to reporting on the lynching of ethnic Mexicans.[19]

When the English-language press did describe anti-Mexican violence on the US–Mexico border, reports often referred to the killings as a measure of local and national security.[20] Moreover, the fact that the violence occurred at the hands of state police and US soldiers alike wrapped the killings in a cloak of official state action leading to minimal questioning about the brutality of policing practices. The successful criminalization of Mexican residents in the press prohibited both the broader public and anti-lynching activists from seeing the ongoing crisis of violent policing regimes on the border as related to broader systems of racial violence.

By the end of the decade, however, the NAACP started to take notice. In 1922 the NAACP publicly acknowledged its inability to report on the motives for these acts of anti-Mexican violence and noted the need for more attention to the topic.[21] For the time being, the NAACP would stay busy documenting the brutal acts of anti-black violence in Texas.

THE LYNCHING OF BRAGG WILLIAMS

In January 1919 in the east Texas town of Hillsboro, the Hill County court convicted Bragg Williams of the murder of Mrs. George Wells and her child at Itsaca on December 2, 1918. At the request of the Hill County district judge, Texas Rangers guarded the courtroom during the trial, quickly removed Williams from the courthouse, and transported him to a Dallas facility. The agents then departed, leaving him unprotected. On January 20, 1919, when the local police transported Williams from Dallas back to Hillsboro for sentencing, they did so without protection from Texas Rangers. Judge Horton Porter, in front of a courtroom filled with residents from Itsaca, sentenced the prisoner to be hanged on February 21, 1919. His defense attorneys quickly filed notice of appeal, which sent the residents of Itsaca into a fury. A mob formed, declaring Williams should suffer immediately.[22]

Newspapers reported that county officers attempted to control the mob, to no avail. At noon on January 20, mob participants cut down a telephone pole and charged through the jailhouse door. Upon entering the county jail they seized Williams and dragged him out to the public square, where they chained him to a concrete post. Participants gathered boxes, barrels, and other materials and saturated the pyre in coal oil. Approximately 400 men, women, and children gathered to watch Williams burn at the stake. He reportedly endured the flames for five agonizing minutes before he perished. The crowd watched for forty more minutes until the flames had completely consumed his bodily remains.[23]

The particular brutality of the public burning caught the attention of the NAACP. Shillady sent a letter to Governor Hobby. In the name of the NAACP he requested information regarding efforts by Texas authorities to prosecute mob participants. He reminded Governor Hobby of the address by President Wilson the previous summer, in which the president implored state governors, local officers, and US citizens to keep "America's name without a stain" and to end lynchings, the "disgraceful evil" that continued to plague the nation. Since that address, mobs had lynched twenty-one black citizens, four in Texas.[24] The Texas governor did not respond to Shillady's query.

In February 1919 the grand jury of Hill County failed to return any indictments against persons who participated in the mob. The failure to prosecute at the county level prompted Attorney General C. M. Cureton to act at the state level. He named twelve mob participants who were allegedly in contempt of the court of criminal appeal. The attorney general announced that on January 20, when Williams's legal team appealed his conviction by the trial court, his case was thereby placed within the jurisdiction of the higher court. Conviction for contempt of the court of criminal appeals could result in a fine, imprisonment, or both without limitation.[25]

The investigation shined a light on the role of state police in the Hillsboro lynching. During the grand jury hearing, larger questions started to circulate about the circumstances that allowed the lynching. In particular, the absence of Texas Rangers during Williams's sentencing at Hillsboro raised concerns. Questions loomed about why state police would guard Williams during the trial, then leave him unaccompanied during sentencing. When the attorney general announced the possibility of charging twelve participants with contempt of court, he also made efforts to quell growing concerns about the Rangers. He dismissed claims that the state agents deserted Williams. According to Adjutant General Harley, the Rangers did not transport the prisoner back to Hillsboro because they had no further responsibility to protect him. This explanation satisfied the attorney general. Despite the negligence of the Hill County judge and the failure of the Texas Rangers to extend their duties, neither Judge Porter nor the officers received official blame for creating conditions that left Williams vulnerable to vigilante violence.[26]

Contrary to the adjutant general's defense, Rangers worked with complete autonomy when they patrolled their regions. They made decisions about how and when to complete their investigations and also had the authority to extend their assignments when they deemed necessary. Testimony during the investigation showed that state agents did not operate by official mandates from state or local authorities.[27] In 1918, for example, Sheriff W. T. Vann of Cameron County requested that Captain Stevens and his company be removed from his county. According to the sheriff, Stevens and his agents collaborated with local residents to unlawfully disarm Mexican residents and were inciting racial tensions. In addition, he complained, they regularly violated procedures by arresting men in Cameron County but placing them in neighboring county jails. Captain Stevens refused to meet with the county sheriff and denied his requests to stop making arrests and disarming local citizens. It took a formal directive from the adjutant general to remove Cameron County from Stevens's jurisdiction.[28]

State agents did not regularly take orders from local police or judges. They were fully able to aid in protecting Bragg Williams during his sentencing and would not have needed a formal request to do so. Instead, despite the racial tensions permeating Hillsboro, the agents left Williams at the mercy of local police. Their negligence would not result in any disciplinary action. The lynching of Bragg Williams would linger in Hillsboro and loom over Austin during the months of January and February. The tragedy, however, did not slow the investigation of the Texas Rangers. To the contrary, the lynching would prove instrumental for lawyers who justified extralegal violence in defending the state police.

RESTRICTIVE PROCEDURES

On January 31, 1919, the Joint Committee of the Senate and House convened to investigate the Texas Rangers. The committee included State Representative William Harrison Bledsoe (chairman), Senator Paul Dewitt

Page (Vice-chairman), Senators Robert Lee Williford and Edgar E. Witt, and State Representatives William Madison Tidwell, Dan Scott McMillin, Thomas J. Tilson, and Samuel Cabell Lackey. José T. Canales introduced nineteen charges against the Rangers, submitted evidence, and questioned witnesses. For each set of charges brought before the committee, Adjutant General Harley had an opportunity to write a response. Dallas attorney Robert E. Lee Knight represented the Adjutant General Department during the proceedings, cross-examined Canales's witnesses, and called witnesses of his own. In addition, the Texas and Southwestern Cattle Raisers Association (CRA), one of the civilian organizations that filled the state police with their own inspectors, furnished their own lawyer, Dayton Moses, to aid in the Ranger defense.[29]

The investigation developed into two competing representations of violence on the Texas–Mexico border. Representative Canales called witnesses who described the state police as instigating violent conflict by abusing local residents. In the turmoil of the Mexican Revolution, residents of the border region were exposed to both the chaos of the civil war across the Rio Grande as well as the violent acts of state police, local authorities, and vigilantes. The pattern of abuse by state police led to a widespread mistrust of the state government in general. Canales had the challenge of convincing the legislative committee that the state-sanctioned practice of killing ethnic Mexicans and terrorizing residents was a moral outrage. He presented evidence of Texas Rangers' use of extralegal violence and abuse of power and the resulting loss of innocent life in the border region. He hoped the evidence that showed Rangers denying residents the right to trial and assumption of innocence would inspire drastic reform.

Knight took every opportunity to undermine Canales. He portrayed Anglo Americans living near the Mexican border as vulnerable in a time of undeclared war against violent ethnic Mexicans. These residents, Knight and his witnesses suggested, relied on the Texas Rangers for protection from ongoing attacks from so-called Mexican bandits. Knight called witnesses who described the Texas–Mexico border region as a harsh and foreign terrain inhabited by desperate Mexicans. According to the state's defense, the region was lawless; the only hope for guaranteeing the survival of Anglo Americans was the strong presence of state police. Knight portrayed Mexicans as a class of criminals who roamed the region posing an ever-present threat to Americans and their property.

These competing versions of the violence on the Texas–Mexico border would come into direct conflict. Canales and Knight each called witnesses who described their version of events. The investigation would become a battle between the representative and the state attorneys to successfully convince the committee, state legislature, and visitors watching the proceedings that either the Texas Rangers or ethnic Mexicans were the cause of violence.

On behalf of the state, Knight and Moses developed a number of strategies to defend the state police force. First, the attorneys made efforts, in some cases successfully, to get charges against the force dropped. Knight worked especially hard to have the seventeenth charge stricken from the record. Convinced that the adjutant general's office justified Ranger actions rather than discharging agents for extralegal actions and excessive uses of force, Canales filed the charge specifically against Adjutant General James Harley and investigating officer Captain William M. Hanson. Both, Canales argued, were "wholly incompetent to discharge the duties of his office."[30] Captain Hanson had the duty of investigating complaints of Texas Ranger misconduct. Representative Canales argued that Harley kept agents who were "notoriously bad men" on the force and that he used Rangers for political favors for the state governor. Hanson, he suggested, routinely investigated Ranger activities with the sole purpose of defending and justifying their violence. Under their leadership, there was no hope of ending abuse by the state police.

Canales encouraged the committee to recommend that the governor remove Harley from the adjutant general's office and "select for said office someone capable of exercising duties of the office with dignity and economy and with honor to the state."[31] Agent abuse continued when state procedures allowed a captain to investigate the alleged crimes of his peers. Rangers should not investigate Rangers. The problems of the state police were not only in the agents' actions but in the justification of their acts by the adjutant general's office.

The implication of the governor's involvement proved to be too much for the committee to entertain. Soon after Canales introduced the charge, Chairman Bledsoe explained that the recommendations fell beyond the scope of the resolution under which the committee operated. Senators Willingford and Page agreed and moved to have the charges stricken from committee review. In response Canales challenged the committee, "I saw the General's tactics. He thought I was going to file—to shoot rabbits, little rabbits here, and say this man and this—this is what he thought." He continued, "I have reliable information, you will see, from my answer, that the 'higher-ups' were responsible for this transaction. . . . So I took this matter up with members of the house as to whether this committee was within the scope. . . . The whole matter of the Ranger force is being investigated. The Adjutant General is at the head of the Ranger Force."[32]

Adjutant General Harley did concede that the ability to hire and dismiss Rangers fell to his discretion, but he interrupted the representative to remind the committee that the Texas governor sat at the head of the Rangers. Harley cautioned, "I have been acting under his instructions. That is what it amounts to."[33] He suggested that if the committee investigated the adjutant general's office, they would also have to investigate Governor Hobby. The committee took heed of Harley's warning and moved to avoid implicating the governor's office, striking the charges against the adjutant general.

Despite the committee's decision, Canales provided evidence that Harley and Hanson knowingly kept "desperate characters" on the force who terrorized Texas residents.[34] Canales argued that the state regularly commissioned agents with violent reputations, which gave insight into the culture of policing and the personnel decisions made by state administrators. He filed a charge that the state hired an agent previously convicted of murder in Marfa. Ranger Horace "Hod" L. Roberson had a bloody reputation. In 1911, shortly after becoming a Texas Ranger, Roberson shot and killed a Mexican man in El Paso who reportedly was drunk and had threatened him with a knife. In 1915 he had also been charged with the murder of Carlos Morales Wood, the editor of the Valentine newspaper *La Patria Mexicana,* which printed articles condemning abuse at the hands of the state police. Roberson faced charges for murdering Wood, but a jury acquitted him.[35] He had also been indicted for murdering Henry Foote Boykin in Hudspeth County in west Texas. In January 1915 Roberson shot the unarmed Boykin, a well-known cattleman of the region, and also shot innocent bystander Walter Sitter.

A court in El Paso convicted Roberson of murdering Boykin, and he received a twenty-year prison sentence. Roberson's attorneys filed for a mistrial. A second trial in 1916 found Roberson guilty of manslaughter and sentenced him to five years in prison. After an appeal the case was sent back to El Paso and was retried in 1919. A jury again convicted Roberson of manslaughter but gave him a reduced two-year prison sentence. Roberson's attorneys moved for a fourth trial and were successful in receiving a new trial in a new venue. Throughout these proceedings Roberson was released on bond and allowed to enlist in the Texas Rangers in April 1914 and again in May 1916.[36] Another Ranger, W. B. Sands, who joined the force in December 1915, had also previously escaped a murder conviction by the narrowest of margins. In 1917 Sands, in a state of intoxication at the Coney Island Saloon in El Paso, shot and killed Sergeant Owen Burns, a soldier of the US Army for almost twenty-five years. Although Sands was indicted for murder, the local trial resulted in a hung jury and officials decided not to retry the case. Feeling the pressure of the investigation, the adjutant general discharged Sands from duty before the start of the investigation.[37]

Lawyers for the state police argued that the charges that mentioned Rangers Roberson and Sands needed to be stricken from the record because, conveniently, neither of the agents served on the force at the time of the investigations. Canales disagreed. If he could not investigate the adjutant general and the investigating officer, he would enter into evidence their hiring practices and the character of the men serving on the force.[38]

The early motion by the committee to strike charges from the investigation foreshadowed the tone of the proceedings. Canales also had trouble filing accusations made by residents who feared violent retribution at the hands of the Texas Rangers. Some residents refused to sign their names to charges or to appear in public to testify before the committee. Remaining anonymous, they believed, offered the only hope of protection from Texas Ranger retaliation. Residents from Cameron, Hidalgo, and Starr Counties provided specific incidences of agent abuse and criminal acts, but they asked Canales to keep their names private. He remembered several pleading, "Please don't reveal my name, because I know what will happen to me."[39]

Canales agreed that the adjutant general's office regularly failed to reprimand abusive Rangers, instead "put[ting] the Rangers on notice that charges were made." Subsequently the Rangers harassed and intimidated residents. People who reported Ranger abuse, Canales argued, "have hell to pay for it." Residents had lost faith that filing charges would reform the force. For that reason, he continued, "peaceable and law abiding citizens would not make charges against the Rangers knowing the character of the men on the force."[40]

Lawyers for the Texas Rangers demanded a list of residents' names, but Canales refused, explaining that he would not betray local confidence. The chairman allowed Canales to keep the names of the residents out of the public record, but the committee then summarily refused to admit the letters into evidence.[41] In one swift decision the letters submitted by private citizens were removed from evidence. The committee did not preserve the number of letters or charges in their records.

The decision to exclude the anonymous charges troubled Canales, who empathized with residents' fears. His wealth and position as a state representative elected to four terms did not protect him from facing great risk for leading the investigation. Weeks before the hearing began, in December 1918, Ranger Francis Augustus "Frank" Hamer confronted the state representative in San Benito. Hamer, who stood six feet, three inches tall and weighed about 230 pounds, has been described as a "hulking Ranger."[42] His stature was matched by his reputation as the "Angel of Death" in south Texas. Ranger William W. Sterling added to the mystique when he confirmed that Hamer had some twenty-six bullets in his body from all his shoot-outs with "bandits and thieves and desperados."[43]

Upon seeing the representative in San Benito, Frank Hamer asked Canales for the name of his relative who had charged the Texas Rangers with abuse in October 1918. When Canales refused to share the name, Hamer threatened, "You are hot-footing it here, between here and Austin and complaining to the Governor and the Adjutant General about the Rangers and I am going to tell you if you don't stop that you are going to get hurt."[44] When the representative sought counsel from Sheriff Vann, the local officer advised him to carry a double-barrel shotgun and kill Hamer. The sheriff even offered to assign an officer to accompany the representative for the job. According to Vann, no jury would convict a man for killing another in self-defense. Canales declined.[45]

Fearing that reporting the incident to the adjutant general would only worsen the situation, the state representative attempted to bypass the adjutant general's office by reporting Hamer's threats directly to Governor Hobby. The governor took no interest in the complaint and instead passed the telegram to the adjutant general. Harley then wired Frank Hamer on December 23, 1918:

> Under Governor's orders you are instructed not to make any threats against the lives of any citizens especially J. T. Canales and that he is to be given proper protection as a citizen. Complaint has been filed that you have made some threats. Without going into the truth of the matter you are instructed to be careful and courteous at all times and not to make a personal matter of your official duties. Undertake to adjust differences as best you can without causing any trouble. Answer. Harley, Adjutant General.[46]

Harley showed no interest in doing any actual investigating. The telegram, however, served two purposes. By instructing Hamer not to intimidate citizens, the adjutant general technically followed the governor's instructions. The telegram also subtly provided Hamer with the name of the citizen who filed the complaint.

Inciting Hamer could prove lethal, as his reputation suggested. Canales described Hamer's intimidation tactics and called on witnesses to testify to his character during the investigation. Dayton Moses, who served as the attorney for the CRA, took the stand in 1919 and described Hamer's reputation as an inspector as unnecessarily violent. According to Moses, when Hamer joined the Texas Rangers as a special Ranger, many residents disagreed with his harsh treatment of suspects and brutal interrogations.[47] Texas Ranger William W. Sterling, who had known Hamer since 1912, testified that although tough, Hamer's methods of intimidating suspects did not constitute a crime. To the contrary, Sterling described Hamer as one of the best agents on the force, with a good reputation in his former hometowns in east Texas. Residents of Navasota allegedly applauded his efforts as city marshal for some years. Sterling, however, conceded that if Hamer made a threat to kill someone, he was a fellow likely to make good on his threat.[48]

Hamer continued to intimidate Canales despite, or because of, the telegram. In the days before the investigation, he stalked the representative around Austin. The tactics took their toll. As Canales's relatives later remembered, both the representative's wife, Anne Anderson Wheeler Canales, and friends in the legislature carefully escorted him into the capitol to protect him from feared assassination attempts.[49] According to

J. C. Machuca, an early organizing member of the League of United
Latin American Citizens, at one point during the investigation the representative's peers hid him in a local jail and stood guard to protect him from
threats by Ranger supporters.[50]

Canales withstood the intimidation and continued the investigation.
While Hamer and Texas Ranger supporters intimidated the state representative outside the state capitol, inside the building the attorneys for
the adjutant general's office took to attacking his character during the
proceedings.

Knowing the tide was against him, Canales took the witness stand and
presented himself to the committee as a fellow Texan, a servant of the court,
a peer in the state legislature, and a committed supporter of the Texas
Rangers. Public audiences filled the room of the Railroad Commission,
where the investigation was being held, to see Canales testify. Newspapers
advertised the day as a marquee event. People without seats stood in the
back of the room and spilled into the hallway. Latecomers were forced to
stand outside on the capitol grounds and peer through the windows. The
public nature of the accusations added insult. Canales found himself on display and on trial.[51]

Canales began his testimony:

> I was born in the old county of Nueces very near to the present town
> of Kingsville. I am forty-two years old, will be next month. I went to
> public schools of my country, came to Austin and attended business
> college. From here I went to Kansas City, Kansas and from there I went
> to Michigan and graduated from the University of Michigan in 1899,
> and have been practicing law in the State of Texas ever since then as a
> general practitioner, criminal as well as civil law.[52]

Canales proceeded to show his deep family roots in Texas and his long
career of service to the state. He was elected state representative from Cameron County in 1904, 1905, 1907, 1909, and 1916. He continued serving
in the legislature until 1919. Since 1904 he had lived in Brownsville on his
family property. Known as the Cabra Ranch, the land had been a haven
for Texas Rangers patrolling the region. Canales described his family's hospitality toward the Rangers and expressed having known and respected
many officers of the state. He had a particularly high regard for men such
as Captain Wright, Captain Hughes, and Captain Rogers. In the nineteenth

This photograph of a young José T. Canales was used for his state representative composite. Canales was forty-two years old at the time of the investigation of the Texas Rangers. 35th House Composite; Detail: J. T. Canales, CHA 1989.530; Photographer: Eric Beggs, 12/14/98, post conservation. Courtesy The State Preservation Board, Austin, Texas.

century, he stated, agents held such high character "that their own conscience was a self-restraint."[53]

The representative then reiterated his motivations for bringing charges against the state police force. His actions were "not prompted by malice . . . but for the purpose of enabling the Committee to investigate the abuse permitted in the present Ranger force in various sections of the state."[54] He offered a nostalgic admiration for honored Texas Rangers of the past and directly contrasted their methods with those used by current agents. He was trying to help return the force to a period of former glory when, as he described, Texas Rangers were noble men.[55] To further show his allegiance, the representative described his independent efforts to help police the border region. In 1915 he personally financed his own vigilante group of residents, known as the Canales Scouts. Witnesses also testified that Canales provided resources to support the local police and state agents in the valley.[56]

Canales's autobiography failed to sway his opponents, however. Knight sought to undo Canales's opening statements. He publicly undermined the representative's character, demeaned his family, and cast him as having deep-seated sympathies with bandit activities. To do this, he brought the discussion of race to the forefront of the investigation. It was Canales, not the Rangers, he argued, who needed to come under investigation.

While cross-examining the state representative, Knight argued that Canales did not accurately portray the crisis in the border region. He asked the committee to consider why the representative had not introduced evidence of the violent banditry plaguing border residents. To this Canales interrupted, "This is a Ranger investigation and I am telling of outrages committed by the Rangers, where they have done things they ought not to have done, and not an investigation to gather data as to what was done by the bandits."[57]

Throughout the proceedings Knight made his attacks increasingly more personal. He profiled Canales as a foreign other with unconscious sympathies for Mexican bandits. In one exchange Knight claimed that the representative did not support Rangers, deputy sheriffs, and citizens taking the laws into their own hands for the "merited punishment of any of the banditti" because Canales's foreign characteristics led him to have unconscious leanings toward the plight of other Mexicans, including those participating in raids and revolutionary activities.[58] Recognizing that Knight had crossed a line, Chairman Bledsoe stepped in and said, "That is absolutely inexcusable." Mr. Curtis interjected on behalf of Canales that the accusations were immaterial and irrelevant.[59]

Despite the objections, Knight continued, "Mr. Canales, have you not consciously, or do you think it is possible, unconsciously permitted yourself to be worked into a condition where you are prone to minimize the outrages perpetrated and magnify the casual mistakes of those struggling with the situation down there, about which you have testified."[60] Canales asserted that he knew well of violent attacks on Anglo Texans. He declared, "No sir, I did not minimize it at all. . . . I say here that the men who killed the Austins and others down there committed cold blooded murder—the ones in the attack on the Galveston Ranch committed cold blooded murder. I don't justify any of them, but I do say that that is no reason why innocent people should be taken on suspicion and murdered and killed in cold blood—that's what I state."[61] Canales refused to be called a bandit sympathizer simply because of his assumed racial difference.

Knight also asked inflammatory questions about Canales's loyalty to the American government. He attempted to portray the representative as having sympathies with German wartime efforts. Canales argued to the contrary that he actively helped authorities arrest German sympathizers living in the valley, including one German priest.[62] Likewise, he argued that he had done everything in his power to support the efforts of local police, the Texas Rangers, and the US military in their efforts. He replied to the accusations that "through our efforts we have caught some of those bandits, have caught some of those robbers, have caught some of those murderers, and we have hung some of those murderers that killed the Austins, and I have done everything within my power—certainly more than you have done or more than anybody else in Dallas."[63]

The representative thus challenged efforts to defame his character by offering up his own frontier bravado. He strategically distanced himself from revolutionary activities and identified as a fierce American patriot willing to take the law into his own hands for swift delivery of justice. Canales claimed not to have strict reservations against vigilantism but rather portrayed himself as acting to curb the indiscriminate killings he saw as egregious. The contradiction—condemning extralegal violence by state agents while admitting to participating in vigilantism in response to the murder of an Anglo father and his son—seemed to escape the committee. The general acceptance of vigilante violence that ran throughout the proceedings, and was even exhibited by Canales, however strategically, would ultimately prohibit the investigation from bringing real reform to the policing regimes in Texas.

In a second attempt to discredit the representative, Knight's concerns became apparent. He was inspired by eugenic anxieties about blood purity.[64] Knight asked, "Now, Mr. Canales, you are by blood a Mexican are you not?" The representative at first refused Knight's attempt to categorize him as Mexican. He responded, "I am not a Mexican, I am an American citizen." Canales's demand that he be recognized as an American citizen did not slow Knight's interrogation. To clarify, Knight asked, "By blood?" On display in front of his peers in the state house of representatives and before the committee, Canales was forced to address how his racial and ethnic markers of difference cast suspicion on his motivations. Canales conceded on the stand that his family history, culture, and heritage placed him in an alternative category: "Well, Mexican, you may call it, that's true, a Texas Mexican."[65]

Although all ethnic Mexicans in the United States who maintained American citizenship were legally recorded as white, being ethnically Mexican socially distinguished one as belonging to a different, inferior race to Anglo Americans, subjected to segregation and discrimination. Some members of the Tejano elite class—landed, educated, and influential in politics in the border region—had been able to continue to operate at the top of social hierarchies well into the twentieth century. But as we have seen, by 1915 class and privilege did not protect one from being a target of violence and discrimination. In a climate of crisis on the border, ethnic Mexicans, regardless of citizenship status or class, were portrayed as a foreign threat and deserving of violent repression. The suspicion wrapped around Canales for his Mexican blood was on full display throughout the proceedings. It became an insurmountable obstacle for Canales.

Knight continued to portray the representative as someone with an unconscious allegiance to Mexican bandits. He asked Canales about his family history, what relatives came from Mexico, and if he had any "blood relatives" still living in Mexico. The representative affirmed that his father had come to the United States before he was born and that he did have relatives in Mexico. In a blatant move to discredit the representative's reputation and undermine his patriotism, Knight named a relative who had avoided registering with the US government during World War I and instead fled to Mexico. To show he placed patriotism above familial connections, Canales responded, "Some have gone, yes, and we have disclaimed them as being absolutely unworthy of our relationship."[66]

Despite Canales's willingness to correct Knight, not all committee members entertained the accusations. Senator Willingford interrupted Knight and asked frankly, "You want this Committee to assume that because Mr. Canales has some relatives in Mexico that he is disloyal?" Knight responded,

> No sir, I do not. I simply offer it under the ordinary rules of proceedings of his character. Hear me a moment, it will not do any harm. There is a saying that blood is thicker than water, and Mr. Canales has stated on the stand that he had a member of influential clients on the other side

through whom he could receive information. Now then, I want to show, of course, that his clients and relatives on the other side whose names are in the hands of the Rangers, and whose vigilance and work along the border are keeping them over there, I think it would have some influence upon the ordinary human mind as to whether uncon-sciously, I am not accusing the gentleman of consciously having motives that are not worthy—but I say that might unconsciously influence him in this matter. . . . Can't the committee be assisted by seeing the leaning of the witness, either consciously or unconsciously?[67]

Knight exploited the same assumptions many Rangers made while on patrol, presuming that all Mexican residents were guilty by association and open to suspicion. The investigation was intended to expose the state po-lice force's practice of assuming the guilt of any ethnic Mexican in the re-gion, and yet Canales found himself the subject of investigation. Having been criminalized and racialized as a foreign threat—an American citizen with Mexican blood in his veins—he was deemed untrustworthy by the state attorneys.

Canales's family also played into his colleagues' mistrust. Many must have been dissatisfied that the representative traveled to Austin with his wife, Anne Anderson Wheeler Canales, an Anglo American. The inter-racial marriage flew in the face of legislators who stood for strict segrega-tion. His family, his wealth, his degrees, his interracial marriage, and his political stature must all have enraged those who worked to instill Juan Crow in south Texas and erase the economic and political influence of Mexican residents in the state. Canales was a reminder of the vibrant pres-ence of non-Anglos, a long-standing part of Texas culture that many longed to erase.

Knight took pride in embarrassing Canales and dehumanizing his family more broadly. More members of Canales's family came under scrutiny and questioning. In October 1918 a relative of Canales, Santiago Tijerino, who maintained a ranch on the border of the Rio Grande in Hidalgo County, had a hostile encounter with a group of local police, federal agents, and Texas Rangers Frank Hamer and Lee Rosser. By Tijerino's account, the Texas Rangers in the group flogged, verbally abused, and intimidated him on his own ranch in Hidalgo County while he looked for stolen cattle that had been taken across the border into Mexico. The agents reported that they were on Tijerino's property looking for smugglers and they became angry when the rancher allegedly gave away their position. Tijerino was born in Texas and had lived all his life in Texas, but motivated by fear he wanted to abandon his property and move to Mexico for his safety.[68]

Captain Hanson investigated the matter but dismissed Ranger involvement. Instead, he wrote a report that demeaned Canales's family. Knight asked Canales to respond to the report: "And Captain Hanson told you he had investigated the matter and taken the affidavits of parties present, and that your relative and his two sons were caught in the field as they went there—that they went down sneaking, as he expressed it, like a coyote, slipping and climbing trees, and these men who were there to catch smugglers were given away by your relatives and they abused them for giving them away?"[69] Likening Tijerino and his sons to wild coyotes prompted Canales to strike back, "I said if those men thought it was their duty to put him in jail, arrest him and put him in jail all right, but they had no right to abuse him in order to provoke a difficulty and then murder him for resisting arrest." Canales continued, "I know the methods of those officers in always pulling together and covering any crimes, and they will always testify the same way. . . . No man has a right to abuse a prisoner at all— have a right to arrest him, but not to abuse or curse him."[70]

If a member of the state legislature could be profiled as a disloyal foreigner in a room of his peers, and in front of a public audience, the victims who came forward with charges would assuredly have faced the wrath of the lawyers defending the adjutant general's office. Politicians, landowners, and longtime residents alike found themselves at the mercy of state police. Despite the personal attacks on Representative Canales and his family, the proceedings continued. He would build his case against the state police and bring to light the reign of terror brought upon residents in the border region.

EXTRALEGAL VIOLENCE ON PUBLIC DISPLAY

In an effort to expose the culture of impunity enjoyed by state agents, Representative Canales identified 1915 as the beginning of the outrages committed by the Texas Rangers. That year, he explained, "the service began to degenerate."[71] According to his account of the conflict, revolutionary activities spilling into Texas from the Mexican Revolution, the threat of German propaganda being circulated in south Texas, the ongoing exploitation of Mexican labor, and the mischaracterizations of "the Mexican character" led to what was referred to as the "bandit troubles" and a period of extralegal state repression. The representative argued that in his opinion, "the large majority of Mexican people along the border were and are law-abiding and rather timid people."[72] They were citizens, not the criminals portrayed by Hanson and others. He continued that had it not been for violence against Mexican residents by Texas Rangers, conflict between local residents and state agents would not have escalated.

Canales pointed to trouble in the summer of 1915. He noted that the murder of two brothers, Lorenzo and Gregorio Manríquez on July 24 while in police custody, and the lynching of Adolfo Muñoz days later, taken from police custody while in transport, served as watershed events that sparked racial tensions. State policing violence was at the center of the controversy. Texas Rangers Daniel Hinojosa and Frank Carr would come under scrutiny during the investigation. Residents believed they made a calculated decision to transport Muñoz from San Benito and move him to the Brownsville jail, twenty miles away, at eleven o'clock at night. In the process of transporting Muñoz, a group of men took him from Ranger custody, tortured him, and lynched him, hanging him from a tree about a mile and a half outside of San Benito. Evidence of torture was seen on Muñoz's remains.[73]

The representative emphasized the state agents' blatant disregard for the prisoner's safety. He argued that they intentionally traveled at night to leave the prisoner vulnerable to vigilante violence. "They could have taken him in the morning, they could have taken him on the noon train, they could have taken him on the afternoon train, they could have taken him safely in an automobile in the afternoon," he exclaimed, "but they started with him about eleven o'clock."[74] In south Texas it was common knowledge that Rangers Hinojosa and Carr conspired with local residents, some of whom were leading citizens of San Benito and Harlingen, to coordinate the lynching. This served as only one example of the brutalities committed by Hinojosa and Carr. This lynching initiated a period of fierce conflict.[75]

Ethnic Mexicans were stricken with widespread fear. Canales stated, "they did not believe that the officers of the law would give them protection guaranteed to them by the Constitution and the laws of this State. The immediate effect, then, was that all men who were charged with crime would refuse to submit to arrest."[76] In 1915 residents feared being questioned by police or local agents and considered that any interaction with a Texas Ranger made them vulnerable to being the next victim of the police or local mobs.

Representative Canales continued presenting evidence that the Texas Ranger investigating officer, Captain Hanson, had full knowledge of these violent methods that struck fear in Texas residents. A few key cases help to highlight the lengths taken by some Rangers to circumvent legal procedures. For example, in August 1918 in Hidalgo County, José Hernández reported being flogged and horsewhipped by Texas Rangers in Captain Stevens's company. The agents accused Hernández of theft and used torturous tactics to obtain a confession. Ignacio Bonillas, Mexican ambassador to the United States, wrote to Secretary of State Robert Lansing in Washington, DC, on August 31, 1919, regarding the abuse. In a report about the growing hostility toward Mexican citizens in the area, he noted the torture of José Hernández, a Mexican citizen laboring on a ranch approximately ten miles near Donna. Hernández testified that Rangers, whose names he did not know, came to his house and took him and his ten-year-old son to a grove of trees. They tied the arms of both Hernández and his son before they began their interrogation. The Rangers threatened Hernández that if he did not confess to stealing property, they would hang him and his son from the tree limbs above them. When Hernández refused, the Rangers placed a rope around his neck, threw the other end over the limb of a tree, and lifted Hernández so that his feet barely touched the ground. With another lariat the Rangers flogged him until he fell unconscious. In an act nothing short of sadism, the agents forced Hernández's son to witness his father's torture. Mexican consul, José Z. Garcia, visited Hernández and reported that black and yellow bands still marked his body from his waist down to his knees six days after the violent beating. He wrote, "The lashes could still be seen well marked. The condition in which the man was about [sic] such that he could neither sit nor lie down for several days."[77]

In the case of the torture and interrogation of José Hernández, Captain Hanson reported that a local deputy sheriff in Cameron County, Fred Winn, confessed to the flogging. Canales disputed this confession. He pleaded with the committee not to be convinced by a Hanson cover-up. He continued, "I knew that Capt. Hanson was up to his old tricks—he either tries to justify the actions of the Rangers or shield them."[78]

The defense for the Texas Rangers referred to an account by a local druggist in Donna, Thomas Hester, who met with a notary public on October 13, 1918, to give a competing account of the recent events. According to Hester local residents believed José Hernández had been stealing or had knowledge of the theft. Although he had no firsthand information about the incident, Hester claimed, "I am very positive that the Rangers had absolutely nothing to do with this whipping, and if this man was whipped at all it was done by those who had suffered losses in that immediate section where this man Hernández lived." Hester repeated the often-spoken excuse that Mexican residents blamed any act of violence on state agents. If the Texas Rangers were involved in a crime, he added, Mexican consuls were more likely to be involved in the investigation. "This class of outlaws are afraid of the Rangers, and do not fear any other class of officers, and they try on all occasions, to make it as hard as possible for the Rangers."[79]

Hester, without direct knowledge or evidence, summarily characterized Hernández as a thief. He swiftly portrayed any Mexican resident who filed complaints of abuse with the Mexican consuls as "outlaws" looking for protection from the Mexican government to slow down Ranger activities. The criminalization of residents who brought charges against the Texas Rangers became a strategy to discredit claims. Knight used these accounts to undermine victims who reported being abused by the Rangers. Rather than sympathizing with the plight of victims of violent crimes who attempted to end abuse at the hands of the state police, Knight and his witnesses clouded these residents in suspicion.

Representative Canales continued to present evidence of officers abusing their authority and the efforts by Captain Hanson to protect them from prosecution or being dismissed from the force. According to some, Rangers needed only one qualification for serving on the force: that they had previously worked as gunmen and killed ethnic Mexican residents. Some of the agents who came under close scrutiny included special Ranger Daniel Hinojosa and Rangers Frank Hamer, John J. Edds, A. B. Hodges, and Graham Meyers. In all cases Canales went on to show that the crimes and abuses committed by the Rangers had been covered up or justified by the state administration.[80]

The career of Ranger John J. Edds offered one of many opportunities to show negligence on the part of the state administration. He had a record of violence before joining the Texas Rangers and continued to use lethal force as a state officer. Prior to being a Ranger, Edds had worked for four years as a deputy sheriff in Wilson County, southwest of San Antonio, under Sheriff William L. Wright. During the investigation, Wright gave a glowing character assessment for Edds. Canales questioned Wright directly and asked how many men Edds shot and killed before he joined the Rangers. It turned out that in his duties in Wilson County, Edds shot a Mexican man in the leg for attempting to avoid arrest. He also killed an unarmed black Texan. Captain Wright alleged that Edds shot the Mexican and killed the African American in self-defense. "That is the only one he shot except this negro—a bad negro in a fight at a restaurant, the negro shot at him."[81] Although Edds had already shot one man and killed another, state authorities did not question his qualifications for service. To the contrary, Wright and the attorneys for the Texas Rangers criminalized his victims and, in contrast, repeatedly referred to Edds as a boy, innocent of any wrongdoing. Wright praised Edds's conduct as an officer: "Just as honest as can be . . . I consider him among Mexican people—to handle Mexican people one of the best officers I ever saw." Edds's methods for "handling" ethnic Mexicans and African Americans earned praise from his supervising officers. With two shootings under his belt, Edds joined the state police in September 1915 at twenty-four years old.[82]

Edds first joined the force as a Ranger under the supervision of Captain Henry Ransom, but he would eventually be reunited with his former boss William Wright, who became a Texas Ranger captain in command of Company K. On September 3, 1918, Edds, as an agent in Company K, placed a prisoner in the custody of two civilians. He authorized two Mexican ranch hands, Sabas Osuna and Federico Lopez, who worked on a ranch owned by special Ranger Eduardo Izaguirre, to transport a prisoner named Jose Ma Gomez Salinas to the Jim Hogg County Jail in Hebbronville, Texas.[83] With the prisoner in handcuffs and mounted to a horse, the three men rode to the jail, located approximately forty miles away. Edds testified before the committee, "He got within four miles of jail and was killed. They took him about thirty miles, I guess."[84] Osuna and Lopez later testified that they each rode behind the prisoner to keep an eye on his movements. When the group neared Hebbronville, Gomez Salinas allegedly spurred his horse and attempted to dash into the brush. Each man took one shot, both hitting the prisoner in the back. Gomez Salinas fell off his horse and died near the side of the road, with his hands still in handcuffs. The ranch hands later testified that they believed it was their duty to shoot at the prisoner to prevent his escape.[85]

Upon hearing of the incident on September 12, 1918, Adjutant General Harley wrote to Captain Hanson asking for an investigation and stating that if he found Edds "responsible for turning the prisoner over [to] the irresponsible parties, Edds will be held accountable. We cannot stand for that kind of dealings in the Ranger force."[86] More than a mere breach of protocol, the investigation exposed Edds's egregious policing practices. In addition to turning the prisoner over to civilians, he deliberately denied the prisoner his legal rights. In his written statements Edds explained that he had turned the prisoner over to two trusted civilians because he needed to be in district court in Rio Grande City the next day. He did not want to take the prisoner with him to the Rio Grande City jail because he feared that Judge James Wells would release the prisoner on bond. Instead, he wanted the prisoner to be in jail in Hebbronville, where he could leave orders that the prisoner not be released on bond and trust that his request would be met. When he released the prisoner to the care of Osuna and Lopez, he sent with them a letter addressed to Ranger Paul Perkins and Mr. Oscar Thompson of Hebbronville, explaining that the prisoner would arrive with two ranch hands. He wrote, "This man has been stealing for some-time and if they make bond fro [sic] him arrest him again and hold him until I can get the evidence in shape. . . . I did not want to take to Rio Grande City to jail as I was afraid Judge Wells would get him out on a writ of Habeas Corpus. [I]f they attempt anything like that slip him out of jail and take him to Laredo as this is too important a capture to let get away just for lack of getting our evidence in shape."[87]

Edds's letter demonstrated his overt attempt to deny Gomez Salinas the right to make bond. He wrote his goal, to deny the prisoner bond, in the letter without hesitation. He further instructed Ranger Perkins and Oscar Thompson, if necessary, to "slip" the prisoner out of jail in Hebbronville and take him to Laredo to give Edds more time to collect evidence for the indictment. This letter was a smoking gun in Canales's effort to show Texas Rangers blatantly abusing their authority.

The Texas Rangers investigating officer Captain Hanson would defend these actions. After reviewing statements from Edds, Captain W. L. Wright, Special Ranger Eduardo Yzaguirre, Sabas Osuna, and Federico Lopez,

Hanson did not cite Edds's behavior as violating either the prisoner's rights or legal procedures. Instead, Hanson focused his investigation on the two men who shot the prisoner. He gave two possibilities for the killing. First, he suggested that Osuna and Lopez killed Gomez Salinas to prevent the prisoner from escaping custody. His second theory suggested that the two ranch hands might have been the actual thieves and murdered Gomez Salinas to eliminate a witness. To support this theory Hanson pointed out that the victim's body had curiously been found in the middle of the road, still handcuffed, and not in the brush, as Lopez and Osuna had claimed. A local grand jury did not indict either man.

Rather than finding fault with Edds for placing Gomez Salinas in the custody of two civilians, men who may or may not have had motive to kill the prisoner, Hanson described Edds as a "splendid officer" who would not knowingly be party to the murder of a prisoner. Hanson overlooked the Ranger's written statements that he intentionally acted to deny the prisoner's rights: instead, he went on to criminalize the prisoner, not the officer. He reported that other Texas Rangers had information that Gomez Salinas, alias Jamaica, had been implicated in another raid and had a reputation as a thief. He concluded his report: "I further believe that the American citizens, including the District Judge of that District, believe the Mexicans did a good job in killing this man."[88]

Despite Gomez Salinas's never having been indicted for theft, Captain Hanson, Ranger Edds, Captain Wright, and even a district judge portrayed him as guilty of theft and considered his murder a favor to local residents. The grand jury summarily accepted testimony that claimed the region was better off without Gomez Salinas. They decided not to indict Lopez or Osuna.

Although the adjutant general had previously instructed Hanson to hold Edds accountable if it was proved he broke regulations and turned a prisoner over to civilians, Edds faced no punishment for his actions. In an unconvincing attempt to show that he made some efforts to correct Rangers' behavior, following his investigation Hanson assured the adjutant general that Captain Wright gave clear instructions to his company that they must never turn a prisoner over to civilians. Edds continued his service as a Texas Ranger without any correction to his policing practices. The culture of impunity that allowed the murder of a resident to go unpunished overrode judicial procedures and guiding policies of the state police. Hanson allowed that murder, in this case the shooting of Gomez Salinas, was a necessary means for maintaining state civility and social life in the border region. He found that the region was a better place without men like Gomez Salinas. In the end, the local district judge and the Texas Ranger investigating officer collaborated to officially sanction an extralegal execution and cloak the act as a public good.

When Edds took the stand before the committee, he brazenly defended his actions and stood by his practice of breaking police and judicial procedures. He admitted to taking conscious steps to deny Gomez Salinas his rights to due process.[89] Rather than express remorse for the prisoner's death, Edds explained that in his long career as a Ranger he believed he had a right to summon citizens as a posse to assist in the execution of the law. In fact, he stated, he had done so on many occasions. He went on to describe Gomez Salinas as "a very dangerous thief, who had been depredating on the good people of that country for a good while."[90] Moreover, he boldly described his deliberate efforts to deny ethnic Mexicans their civil rights in the name of securing the property of "good people."

The failure to reprimand Edds had deadly consequences. Only a month after Gomez Salinas was shot and killed Edds would again come under scrutiny for shooting and killing an unarmed Mexican laborer, Lisandro Muñoz. Edds confessed to killing the laborer as he woke from sleep before daybreak on October 6, 1918, in Rio Grande City.[91] According to a written statement and his testimony before the committee, Edds and Rangers Monroe Wells and R. W. Lawrence surrounded the home of Jesus Sanchez, located just 300 yards from the Rio Grande at the Los Saenz Ranch. The Rangers came in pursuit of Sanchez's son, Alonzo, who reportedly attempted to desert state military registration by fleeing to Mexico. A local source allegedly informed Rangers that Alonzo Sanchez, described as having a dark mustache, had recently crossed back into Texas. They reported that his brother, Zaragoza, had a clean-shaven face. With these vague descriptions guiding their approach, Edds stationed Wells and Lawrence on the perimeter of the property and proceeded to search the grounds.

Upon getting closer to the home, Edds found two men sleeping outdoors on cots: one with a dark mustache and one with a clean-shaven face. Edds testified that he walked within four feet of the man with a mustache and woke him by calling the name Alonzo. When the man asked what he wanted, the Ranger alleged that he asked his name. Edds reported that the man did not answer his question. He explained, "He could not answer me. I guess he seen the rifle cocked—I don't know what struck him, he got to where he could not talk to me. He got up from his cot, I said, 'Sit down. I want to talk to you.' Suddenly he reached and grabbed my rifle by the barrel." After describing a scuffle for control of the gun, he concluded, "I shot this man. The gun was right up against him when I shot him. It burned a big hole in his drawers and badly powder burned his flesh; it shot him right in the groin."[92]

The gunshot woke Zaragoza Sanchez, who asked Edds whether his cousin was dead or alive. Edds testified that from this question he learned that he had mistakenly killed Lisandro Muñoz, Zaragoza's twenty-three-year-old cousin, who had been visiting the Sanchez family. The gunshot also woke the rest of the family sleeping in the house. Jesus Sanchez, his wife Gabriela Garza, and their five daughters, Carmen, sixteen, Isabel, fourteen, Ernestina, twelve, Anita, nine, and Maria, seven, gathered outside. Despite the family's concern and efforts to tend to Muñoz, Edds reported that he did not allow the family to approach the body. "We stayed right there and didn't let anyone come near the body so they would not put out the tracks [footprints], you know, because there were the signs where we had scuffled plainly visible, and I wanted the Justice of the Peace to come there and hold an inquest."[93] Concerned less that he had killed an innocent man in the close range of his aunt, uncle, and young cousins, Edds decided to preserve the scene for investigators who would come to evaluate whether he had warrant to kill Muñoz.

From just before daybreak until Captain Wright and local authorities arrived at 10:30 a.m., the body of Lisandro Muñoz remained out in the open in the backyard of the Sanchez home. His relatives could only look on and wait in fear for officials to arrive before they could tend to the dead and mourn the loss.[94] In no portion of the testimony or written statement provided by Edds did he describe remorse for killing an innocent man. He also did not express sympathy for the family members who witnessed the event. Instead, he mentioned the relatives only when explaining that Jesus Sanchez confirmed that his son Alonzo had been on his property but had returned to Mexico just after midnight. Edds expressed regret only for missing the opportunity to arrest Sanchez.

During his testimony about the incident, Edds described being puzzled by Muñoz's refusal to speak. Committee members took pause at his confusion. It seemed obvious that waking up to a cocked rifle in the face would likely cause anyone to freeze in fear. Senator Willingford questioned Edds about his poor choice, "Why would you get up close enough to a strange man to grab your rifle?" Edds responded that he never thought the sleeping man would attempt such an act. The senator pressed Edds and accused him of lying about Muñoz grabbing the agent's rifle. "Don't you know he wouldn't do it," Willingford challenged. Edds insisted, "No. He did." "You were a Ranger in the night, arresting a desperate man and got close enough to him to grab your weapon?" Edds only responded, "It was just daylight; you could see a little."[95] In disbelief, Senator Willingford stopped questioning the agent. The careless killing of Muñoz in pursuit of Sanchez, wanted not as a dangerous criminal but for avoiding a draft registration, seemed to surprise even the committee members. At once criminalized as dangerous and yet wanted for service in the US military, Sanchez embodied the contradictions for ethnic Mexicans with American citizenship.

The local county attorney and sheriff came to the scene and after conducting a brief investigation decided not to place Edds under arrest.[96] Hanson followed suit and did not dismiss Edds from the force, instead claiming that he acted to protect his own life. Representative Canales could not make sense of Hanson's decision. He argued that Edds's written testimony showed that he should have been indicted for manslaughter, if not murder in the second degree.[97] Even Judge James B. Wells, a friend of the Edds family and one who described John Edds's uncle, Henry Edds, as "one of the finest men we have in Texas," found the agent's actions a criminal offense.

At the conclusion of his investigation into the shooting, Captain Hanson turned to Judge Wells for legal advice and presented Edds's written testimony for his review. Wells testified before the committee that he reached a level of indignation when he read the testimony. He remembered yelling at Hanson, "What goose or what fool got that boy to make that statement?"[98] According to Judge Wells the written statement could have been used as evidence to convict Edds for the murder of Lisandro Muñoz. In the judge's opinion, Edds had signed a statement that was tantamount to a confession to murder. Despite the legal opinion, Hanson reported to the adjutant general, "I am thoroughly convinced that Sergant [sic] Edds was compelled to kill this man in order to save his own life. . . . I do not believe that Sergant [sic] Edds is in any way to blame." Hanson continued, "I do not believe that there is a jury in the United States that would convict him of anything in connection with this, taking into the circumstances of the killing."[99] Convinced that a grand jury would not indict Edds if he was later arrested, Hanson decided not to dismiss the officer or order any punishment for his actions. Edds continued his service as a Ranger without interruption. Again, as investigating officer for the Texas Rangers, Hanson officially sanctioned the behavior of Rangers who overstepped the boundaries of the law.

By 1919, however, under the scrutiny of the pending legislative investigation of the Texas Rangers, Hanson was forced to reconsider his support of extralegal violence. The adjutant general's office changed course at the last possible hour. Just one day before Ranger John J. Edds testified before the committee in Austin, on February 6, 1919, Harley officially suspended him from duty. The evidence admitted for the investigation proved to be so incriminating that during his testimony Edds received word that he had just been indicted for killing Muñoz. Before Edds could testify, Chairman Bledsoe warned that any statements he made could be used against him in court. Emboldened by his belief that he had nothing to hide, he testified before the committee without legal representation. He remained steadfast that before a jury of his peers, his actions would not be seen as criminal; rather, they would be affirmed.[100]

John Edds's past record of shooting and killing a "bad Negro" prior to joining the state police was not the only reference to state police intimidating and abusing African Americans in the discharge of their duties. Although Representative Canales primarily introduced evidence of anti-Mexican violence, residents submitted their own accounts of Texas Rangers abusing African Americans and denying them their civil rights. The terror at the hands of Rangers extended far beyond the borderlands.

Thomas A. Johnson of San Angelo experienced police abuse firsthand. He worked at a wholesale and retail dry goods store, the Baker-Hemphill Company. He was one of several African American men arrested on suspicion of stealing goods from a railroad shipment. Rangers A. B. Hodges and Graham Meyers arrested Johnson on a Saturday in early February 1918 and interrogated him in a local hotel in the company of San Angelo police and residents. Johnson testified that a Mr. Futch "cursed me around and abused me a whole lot. . . . He called me bastards [sic] and everything, bad names he could think of, and so I just sat there, I never said anything for a while because they were strangers, I didn't know either one of them, only Mr. Simmons at the time. He talked to me and abused me around a little bit." Not knowing his accusers added to Johnson's fear. The posse threatened him with violence and menacingly shared details of the abuse they had bestowed on another man arrested for theft.[101]

When Johnson was being transported from the hotel to the San Angelo jail, he spotted an African American man on the street. He asked the man to relay a message to his wife that he had been arrested. The Rangers intervened and threatened the man if he delivered the message. When Johnson's wife later learned of the arrest, she found his bosses and went with them to meet with local police, asking that they release her husband on bond. Local officers explained that they did not have authority to release him because the Texas Rangers had taken him into custody.

On Monday, after having Johnson in custody over the weekend, and without gathering a confession, the Rangers transported him by train to a jail in Sweetwater, seventy-five miles north of San Angelo. Johnson again tried to send a message to his wife with someone he passed on the street, but the Rangers would not tell him where they were taking him and instructed the resident not to call Johnson's wife. When Johnson arrived in Sweetwater, the abuse continued. The local jailer did not provide him with a blanket, and without heat, he suffered through the cold. During his time in Sweetwater, the jailer provided Johnson with only one meal. In addition, the interrogations became more violent. Employees for the railroad company entered the jail freely and interrogated Johnson. He denied any involvement and refused to confess to the crime. One unnamed jailer even threatened Johnson with mob violence. Johnson testified that the jailer said, "well we are going to get you and you better be kind of easy, because I am going to come through there in a few days and bring my crowd over, and I am going to pick you up and you will never know what became of you."[102]

While Johnson was in jail, his wife panicked. She asked local police to release her husband. When they refused and would not tell her where Texas Rangers had moved him, she hired San Angelo lawyer W. A. Anderson to help her figure out where her husband was being held and on what charges. Anderson located Johnson in Sweetwater and helped coordinate his release. When his attorney arrived in Sweetwater, the Rangers removed Johnson from the jail and transported him back into the custody of San Angelo police. There his wife and his bosses delivered the bond for his release. The Texas Rangers never filed charges against Johnson. Another man described by the state's attorneys as a "darkey" was found to have stolen the goods in collaboration with a white employee of the Santa Fe Company. Both were arrested, but only the African American man was charged with theft.[103]

When Johnson was released, he was sick and too weak to work. It took him two weeks to recover from his time in Ranger custody. According to his lawyer, Johnson had been swept up in a disagreement between different mercantile companies and the railroad company. The companies reported that their goods were being lost in transport. Rangers responded by arresting African American men who worked for retail companies and attempted to make them admit to stealing the goods. For their involvement in his abuse and explicitly denying him access to a lawyer, Anderson filed a complaint and requested an investigation into the Rangers' conduct. He never received notification that Rangers Hodges or Myers were investigated or even that the adjutant general had received his complaint.[104]

During the investigation Knight took little interest in Johnson's treatment. The questions Knight asked attempted to show that local police in San Angelo, jailers in Sweetwater, and railroad employees had intimidated and mistreated Johnson, but not the Rangers. He even suggested that Johnson had little room to file a complaint because Rangers Hodges and Myers only verbally threatened him. Johnson insisted that they had denied him a phone call to alert his wife and had prevented others from informing her. Knight belittled his accusations and asked, "Did he use any violence on you at all—just talking to you roughly?" Johnson responded, "Yes, sir, it was awful *roughly*."[105]

When Anderson testified before the committee in 1919, he found himself a character witness for Johnson. Chairman Bledsoe asked the attorney, "what kind of a negro is he?" Anderson replied, "As good a negro as you will find, and he is one that his house will make any kind of a bond for." Describing Johnson as a "good Negro," Anderson also bolstered his characterization by describing Johnson's class status. Thomas Johnson was a homeowner in San Angelo, with a concerned wife and caring bosses who, believing him innocent, helped ensure his release from jail. At the end of Bledsoe's questioning, Anderson told the committee that Johnson was present and available to testify before the committee. He knew the details of the abuse better than the attorney. Anderson must have been concerned that the committee would look upon Johnson with suspicion, that they would assume he was a "bad Negro" and doubt his claims. Without being prompted, Anderson added, "I will say this, that he has the reputation of being [an] honest, truthful and law-abiding Negro."[106] This charge showed the committee that Rangers also arrested African Americans merely on suspicion, without evidence, and abused their authority to intimidate prisoners in their custody. Rangers placed prisoners in jails with local police who would collaborate in denying them bond and threatening them with violence. In Sweetwater, they even threatened African American prisoners with mob violence. And by keeping relatives confused about the location of their loved ones, Rangers also tormented the families of their prisoners.

EMBRACING MOB VIOLENCE

The testimony of witnesses during the investigation eventually grew to more than 1,600 pages of transcription. Examples abound of police abuse and extralegal acts of violence. Knight and Moses argued that state senators and representatives from the central and northeastern part of the state had no grasp on the volatile climate on the border. They described an ongoing and increasingly aggressive undeclared war in which Mexican bandits allegedly targeted vulnerable American property owners near the border. In addition to stealing livestock and goods, the alleged bandits also threatened the lives of white women and children. The state lawyers argued that the Texas Rangers were justified in using any violent means necessary to protect white American citizens. To convince the committee, they relied on racial tropes commonly used to justify mob violence against other racial and ethnic minorities in Texas.

In the investigation, Knight and Moses harnessed existing white supremacist ideas that justified the abuse and execution of racial minorities without proper investigation. On numerous occasions the attorneys asked the committee to agree that Texas Rangers should be able to act outside the parameters of the law. More specifically, they suggested that suspending legal procedures and regulations was necessary to protect Anglo American citizens and their property. US congressman Claude Benton Hudspeth, the namesake of Hudspeth County, representing the Sixteenth District of west Texas and a former Texas Ranger, became a star witness. He supported

Knight's argument that ethnic Mexicans in the region were bandits and demanded that Rangers act with brute force. In his opinion, the character of Mexican residents necessitated this tactic. Cloaked in his authority as a US congressman, he stated, "a Ranger cannot wait until a Mexican bandit behind a rock on the other side shoots at him three or four times. . . . [Y]ou have got to kill those Mexicans when you find them, or they will kill you, as they did Joe Sitter and Mr. Hulen down there."[107] To the congressmen, any Mexican, on either side of the border, posed a dangerous threat.

Hudspeth advocated for local residents taking the law into their own hands. He explained, "The people raised up and surrounded those bandits, and when they rounded them up and killed them. . . . You cannot handle those Mexicans with kid gloves, not when they come twelve miles below El Paso and steal a milk cow every night or two."[108] Perhaps recognizing that his statements were supporting extralegal murder by state agents and residents alike, Hudspeth later clarified, "I don't believe in murdering people, but there are a bad class of men along the River that have to be handled in a certain way."[109] His sensational testimony continued with descriptions of the brutality of the people he described as Mexican bandits. Droves of bandits, he explained, waited just across the Rio Grande ready to raid and pillage. Fear of the Texas Rangers, according to him, was the only element that kept thieves at bay. Their brutal methods were an important element in creating an intimidating force. Fear made the agents effective.

The congressman's sweeping criminalization of an entire population sanctioned the use of violence as a strategy for policing the border region. When asked to consider what would happen if the number of Rangers was reduced, he responded, "I think this, those bandits, and there are hundreds of them on the other side of the River now . . . if the Ranger force was materially reduced, they would immediately make incursions into this country in all the Big Bend, murder the people and take off their live stock. They would know it almost as quick as the people in this portion of the State."[110] Moreover, Hudspeth suggested, local Mexican residents had an information network that spanned the border and fed news to bandits across the river. He described them as an ever-present threat, waiting for the right moment to attack. If the state reduced the agents, he believed, the consequences would be swift and violent. His account proved vital in convincing legislators from other regions of Texas that the border region demanded violence to maintain peace.

Intrigued by Hudspeth's emphasis on a persistent threat on the border, Chairman Bledsoe asked whether he believed Rangers known to have participated in cold-blooded murder ought to be allowed to stay on the Ranger force. The congressman explained, "If he killed him in cold blood, no, but those bandits over there don't give a snap for your life." Bledsoe attempted to help Hudspeth refine his statements and asked, "That is as long as they are in fighting trim. . . . You are talking about a condition before they surrender?" Hudspeth continued, "Yes, but I don't believe in this, Mr. Chairman, in extending very much clemency to men who come across the River and murder our wives and children." The congressman did not linger on agents committing cold-blooded murder. Instead, he shifted the focus back to those aggressors he believed threatened white women and children—icons of vulnerability that since Reconstruction had been used to justify mob violence against ethnic and racial minorities.[111]

"Now I am going to be candid with you," the congressman continued, "talk about the mob law, if I had it in my power I would lead a mob in a minute against them, and if you reduce these Rangers or curtail them to the extent that they cannot cope with the situation and they continue to come across there and murder men and women like they did old Mickey Welsh and the little boy down at Glenn Springs and Glen Neville, there will be people that will respond, and I will come back from Washington to lead them if I am needed. We are going to protect our property." He later reiterated his comment about a bad class of men along the river.[112]

Hudspeth went on to describe a meeting in April 1918, in which approximately 300 Texas residents gathered to meet with him and US soldiers. Their hope was to seek protection from the alleged raids by a Mexican bandit named Chico Cano. He explained, "The condition of the public mind was so disturbed they had brought their wives and children and old Texas women with their sun-bonnets on had come there to that meeting."[113] According to Hudspeth the conditions were so tenuous that residents even suggested surrendering US territory and moving the US–Mexico border north of the Galveston, Harrisburg and San Antonio railroad in west Texas to escape the threat of violent raids. While the federal and state governments sought to control the international border through force, the congressmen and others thought the government might as well cut its losses and surrender the region to lawlessness.

Knight and Moses called witnesses, like Hudspeth, to testify that state brutality was a necessary means for dealing with Mexicans who, as a group, were criminal in nature. Despite their legal training, both Knight and Moses described Mexican residents as not having the legal protections or rights guaranteed to American citizens and foreign nationals. For example, in his examination of Representative Canales, Knight ignored federal laws of presumed innocence. He asked for a list of innocent men murdered by Texas Rangers. The representative argued that all men executed by Texas Rangers without investigation were legally innocent because they had not been proven guilty. Knight, however, asked, "Do you know that they were not guilty?" Collectively Bledsoe and other committee members began an exchange with Knight. The members quickly grew impatient with Knight's disregard for legal protections. The exchange is quoted here at length:

> The Chairman: Under the laws of our state, they are presumed to be innocent until their guilt is proven—are they not justly entitled to be tried by our courts before their guilt is established?
> Mr. Knight: He said the Rangers committed wholesale executions of innocent people, and I asked him to name a single one that was innocent.
> The Chairman: The presumption of the law is that they were innocent.
> Mr. Knight: If that's the ruling of the Committee, I yield.
> The Chairman: It is not only the ruling of the Committee, but it is the well-recognized law of the state.
> Mr. Knight: Mr. Canales has made frequent complaints here about injuries done to Mexicans—I asked him to state the name of an innocent man, regardless of that presumption of the law, and I don't think it should be excluded on that ground.
> Mr. Tidwell: Under the law of this state, it does not make any difference whether a man is guilty or innocent, if he is taken out and killed without the due process of law.[114]

Chairman Bledsoe reminded Knight that the province of the committee was only to investigate the activity of the agents on the force, not alleged Mexican bandits. He encouraged Knight to ask instead whether he knew any men executed by Rangers without due process of law. The guilt or innocence of the executed parties, he insisted, was immaterial to the investigation. Knight continued to insist that he took issue with descriptions of murdered Mexicans as innocent victims. Tidwell impatiently responded, "To take a man and shoot him, whether he is guilty or innocent—what difference does it make whether he is innocent or not?" Curtis joined the exchange: "I want to add to what has been said—it makes no difference how guilty a person may be, when he is taken out and executed without authority of law, an innocent man for the purpose of this investigation has been executed."[115]

Knight again refused to accept the committee's clarifications and continued to cast suspicion on Mexican residents living in the border region. To convince committee members and those in the audience who did not live in the border region to justify state-sanctioned violence against ethnic Mexicans, Knight and Moses relied on excuses used to support mob violence against black Texans for alleged crimes against white Texans. The lawyers for the Texas Rangers declared that during the crisis of a war against bandits and revolutionaries, extralegal violence was required. Dayton Moses went so far as to liken the extralegal acts by Texas Rangers to those of Anglo mobs that lynched African Americans. Rather than describe state agents as acting within their authority, he conceded that they were analogous to vigilantes acting outside the law. Lynch mobs became his barometer for agent behavior. Moses argued,

> We will agree that no prisoner ought to be killed—that no officer ought to let a prisoner be killed, and also that a Negro who is charged with an outrage on a white woman ought not to be mobbed, but they do it just the same. If Mexican soldiers on the other side of the river murder our soldiers when they capture them or our people when they take them over there, it would arouse a feeling of ill will and anger on the part of men on this side.[116]

In likening the actions of officers who murdered and abused prisoners with the vigilante acts of Anglo mobs, Moses publicly sanctioned extralegal acts at the hands of state agents. He described these acts as part of daily life. He even added that while these acts were illegal, the committee should be sympathetic to the emotions motivating the practice. According to Moses, crimes by state agents targeting ethnic Mexicans ought to be condoned because residents felt anger at Mexicans who committed robberies and murder. Revenge by proxy, according to Moses, was a reasonable method of policing.

Public support of acts of extralegal violence against Mexican residents, Moses suggested, were in line with public support for Anglo mobs that targeted African Americans. He elaborated, "And while it would not justify it, it would palliate it to some extent, just like the people who mobbed that Negro up at Hillsboro in broad, open daylight. While it is not justification, yet you don't feel in your heart that condemnation which you might feel." Before Moses could continue his inflammatory endorsement of mob violence, Chairman Bledsoe hastily interrupted, "There may be conditions under which we may go into that, but I don't think we have the authority to do it at this time."[117] Just as quickly as the lynching culture in Texas, palliated by members of the investigation, arose at the proceedings, the chairman swiftly moved the conversation rather than allow the exploration of linked cultures of police and mob violence.

In asking the committee, and those in the audience, to provide clemency for extralegal executions by state agents and the lynching of African Americans by Anglo mobs, Moses aligned the proceedings with white supremacy and excuses for mob violence. His casual reference to the lynching of Bragg Williams is a reminder that the broad culture of racial violence throughout the state at the hands of state police and mobs was on the minds of the committee and witnesses. Moses endorsed both. This support for violence informed the outcome of the proceedings. The attorneys for the adjutant general used the ideals of white supremacy, and the right of Anglo Texans to deny rights to ethnic Mexicans and African Americans, to unite the committee in excusing the crimes.

"VINDICATION COMPLETE"

Despite the witness testimonies, the investigation did not shift the culture of impunity enjoyed by state agents and local vigilantes who participated in racial violence and intimidation. Changing the culture of the judicial system fell far outside the bounds of the committee. The legislation that initiated the proceedings restricted the investigation to a fact-finding commission that could neither prosecute assailants nor hold state administrators accountable for their role in sanctioning these acts. In this way, the investigation acted similarly to some truth commissions in the latter part of the twentieth century: in South Africa following apartheid; in Argentina following the disappearances of people between 1976 and 1983; in Guatemala following human rights violations during thirty-six years of violence; and in the United States following calls to reckon with the 1898 Wilmington race riot, the 1921 Tulsa race riot, the internment of Japanese Americans during World War II, and the Greensboro massacre of 1979. These entities had varying abilities to initiate judicial procedures to prosecute assailants for violence. In the case of the Historical Clarification Commission in Guatemala, the commission had no authority to subpoena witnesses or even name perpetrators.[118]

Truth commissions and reconciliation commissions, however, make efforts to confront traumatic histories by investigating past crimes and creating a clear and undeniable historical record for the public. The records left by the 1919 investigation of the Texas Rangers, on the other hand, leave a clear record of state crimes but also a record of state agents justifying violence. There is no admission of guilt or wrongdoing by the state. To the contrary, during the investigation, lawyers for the Rangers and their witnesses defended Ranger abuse and supported brutal methods of policing that denied both American citizens and foreign nationals in Texas their civil right to judicial procedures.

The state legislature would officially sanction the policing practices in an opinion delivered in the thirty-sixth legislative session. On February 19, nearly a month after the investigation began, Chairman Bledsoe presented the investigating committee's findings to the Texas House of Representatives. The committee delivered a unanimous opinion that the ongoing conflicts along the border region necessitated the state police. They also found that Texas Rangers should be compensated accordingly to support their efforts. The committee thanked the Rangers force for its service and declared that the agents could not receive credit enough for the discharge of duties under dangerous and "trying conditions."[119]

The committee specifically thanked Adjutant General Harley in its report to the legislature. Far from Canales's calls for Harley to be replaced, the committee found that he deserved "commendation" for the "able, efficient, impartial, and fearless" manner in which he commanded the Ranger force during a time of great turbulence. The committee similarly praised Captain Hanson.[120] The adjutant general's office was elated with the opinion. Captain Hanson wrote to Ranger C. J. Blackwell and declared, "committee report was all we could hope for. Vindication complete."[121]

The proceedings did effect a noticeable change, however. The investigation resulted in a drastic reduction in the number of active agents. The state legislators shrank the state police to just sixty-eight Rangers. The commission found charges of misconduct and "unwarranted disregard of the rights of citizenship" to be "established by sufficient and competent evidence." The proceedings did not, however, change the procedures of the state agency, nor did it call for the prosecution of any Rangers, local police, or civilians suspected of having committed murders, abusing their authority, or fomenting racial tensions. These practices, in Hanson's words, were "vindicated."

Captain Hanson, riding high on the committee's report, received a promotion. That summer he left the state police to work as a chief investigator for the US Senate investigation into US and Mexican affairs.[122] Texas Rangers who came under scrutiny for policing techniques conveniently left the force shortly before the proceedings began but often transitioned into other roles as local law enforcement agents. As we saw earlier, James Monroe Fox, the Texas Ranger captain who orchestrated the Porvenir massacre of 1918, resigned from the force and worked in local law enforcement in Travis County. After a short stint in local law enforcement, he would again serve as a Texas Ranger in 1925 as a captain of Company A and reenlisted again as a special Ranger in 1934.[123] Horace L. Roberson, another Ranger who came under investigation during the 1919 proceedings, had no trouble finding employment. When he was not a member of the state police Roberson served as an inspector for the Texas Cattle Raisers Association, a foreman for the T. O. Ranch in west Texas, a Midland County deputy, and a deputy US marshal.[124] As sheriffs, as deputies, as prison guards, or later as border patrol agents and federal employees, these former Rangers, despite their histories of brutality and abuse of authority, continued careers in law enforcement.

Texas legislators who participated in the 1919 investigation and those who sat in the audience interpreted the testimonies based on the social and political norms of their home constituencies. In this light, white supremacist ideologies that condoned anti-black vigilantism helped justify the documented anti-Mexican violence at the hands of state agents. During debates on the use of force, legislators would lean on popular rationales about mob violence to justify their understanding of the use of force against ethnic Mexicans. Racist assumptions of "bad Negros" would support the continued racist depictions of the Mexican bandit. Texas legislators would maintain the racial ideologies of the frontier South that embraced violence as a means for preserving racial hierarchies. They would continue to mark the bodies of racial and ethnic minorities as available for violence at the hands of mobs or law enforcement officers.

ONGOING RACIAL VIOLENCE IN TEXAS

The Texas Ranger investigation ended in late February, but—no surprise—racial tensions continued. The NAACP continued to examine the widespread lynching culture and abuse by local and state police toward anti-lynching activists. The summer months of 1919 proved tumultuous around the nation, as racial conflicts erupted in places like Elaine, Arkansas, and Omaha, Nebraska.[125] Approximately thirty riots nationwide were reported. This led to the months from May to October 1919 being called the Red Summer.

In July the east Texas town of Longview erupted in conflict. The rural community, with a cotton and lumber economy, had a population of 5,700 residents, approximately 30 percent of whom were African American. Tensions in the community continued to rise as two prominent community leaders—Samuel L. Jones, a schoolteacher, and Calvin P. Davis, a doctor—helped organize black farmers to bypass local white cotton brokers and sell directly to buyers in Galveston. Their efforts to help farmers escape social and economic oppression caught the attention of local Anglo residents looking to maintain the racial and economic hierarchies of the town.

Longview had recently demonstrated a dark reputation for policing interracial relationships with violence, when on June 17, 1919, a white mob removed Lemuel Walters from the Gregg County Jail and lynched him for allegedly having a relationship with a white woman from nearby Kilgore. The allegations that the white woman consented to romantic relations with a black man kept racial tensions in the community high. They boiled over on July 10 when the *Defender,* the influential African American Chicago newspaper, reported the lynching of Lemuel Walters and described his romantic relationship with the unnamed white woman. The newspaper quoted the woman as saying that she and Walters had been in love and that if they had lived in a Northern state they would have married. That same day a white mob accosted and beat Samuel L. Jones, who worked as a local correspondent for the *Defender* and was assumed to be the author of the article. Not satisfied with the beating, a mob of fifteen white men returned to Jones's home in the middle of the night. In anticipation of a mob gathering, local supporters came to stand guard.

When the Anglo mob entered Jones's yard they were greeted with gunfire. Three members of the mob received nonfatal injuries from shotguns, but one member who hid under the porch was later discovered and severely beaten. The mob dispersed quickly after exchanging gunfire with Jones's defenders. Some went to recruit more participants, while others went to a local hardware store and stole guns and ammunition. When they returned to Jones's home later that night, they found it empty.

The mob set fire to the home and continued searching the town. They set fire to the homes of other residents who publicly supported black farmers. They burned the home of Davis, the black physician who helped organize local farmers, then moved on to burn the homes of other prominent black residents. To further intimidate and insult black residents, the mob also burned the local black dance hall.[126]

On the morning of July 11, 1919, the county judge and sheriff called on Governor Hobby to send aid. He sent Texas Rangers and 100 Texas National Guardsmen to help local authorities regain control of the town. Despite the military presence, the violence continued to escalate. On July 12, the local sheriff, E. M. Meredith, instigated more violence when he shot and killed Davis's father-in-law, Marion Bush. Anticipating a backlash, the town mayor requested an additional 150 guardsmen from Governor Hobby. When the additional guardsmen arrived on Sunday, July 13, they placed the town under martial law. All Longview citizens, including local law enforcement officers, were required to turn in their firearms. Texas Rangers arrested seventeen white men and twenty-one black residents on charges of attempted murder. Additionally, nine white men were charged with arson. The white men were released on bond and the Rangers transported the twenty-one black residents to Austin jails to prevent an Anglo mob from storming the local jail. By July 18, Brigadier General R. H. McDill, who commanded the guardsmen in Longview, consulted with Hobby and they agreed to end martial law. Anglo residents were allowed to pick up their firearms the following day. The black men placed in custody in Austin, in contrast, would be detained for more than a month.[127]

The racial conflict in Longview caught the attention of the NAACP in San Antonio and in Austin. When word of the black residents transported to Austin reached the branches, local members visited the men in jail while they were in custody. In the NAACP annual report of 1919, the organization documented the string of racial conflicts throughout the country, listing Longview as one of the most spectacular examples of anti-black violence. Arnold Rampersad accurately described the climate, writing, "Blacks had fought for their country in Europe, but discrimination and de facto segregation was the order of the day almost everywhere."[128] In Longview the lynching of Lemuel Walters and the subsequent violence took the region by storm. As a result, the town suspended a reception planned to honor the homecoming of African American troops. Rather than coming home to a celebration, soldiers arrived to a full-blown attack on black residents, especially those transgressing racial borders or fighting for civil and labor rights.

The conflicts in Longview and in Knoxville, Tennessee, were described as being "in reality attempts at lynchings." Anti-black violence required residents to respond with violence in self-defense.[129] By this account, in response to the lynching of Lemuel Walters in June and the subsequent attempts to lynch of Samuel L. Jones and the murder of Marion Bush, residents took up arms to defend themselves from white mobs and police forces with sanguinary reputations. Accordingly, the report described the clashes in Knoxville and Longview as just two more cases in which the lynching culture in the United States could be seen as part of a broader social menace.[130]

The death of Marion Bush, likewise, enhanced calls to curb police violence. In the long struggle against racial violence in the United States, the NAACP had made some strides at the state level and cooperated with state legislators and governors to pass anti-lynching legislation. They celebrated examples of some state and county police officers who prevented the lynching of residents in police custody. The police in Texas, however, had not yet earned such accolades. To the contrary, state agents in Texas met the NAACP with blatant hostility and targeted local branches and national representatives with threats of violence. Their efforts were supported by the state administration.

CALLING ON VIOLENCE

Governor Hobby's actions during the investigation of the Texas Rangers should not have come as a surprise to anyone. In 1914 he was elected to state office as the lieutenant governor for Governor James Edward Ferguson. Serving under Ferguson, Hobby observed a governor who militarized the border, expanded the state police force, and called for the repression of Mexican residents. When the state legislature successfully filed twenty-one articles of impeachment against Ferguson, including the misapplication of public funds, Hobby found himself the twenty-sixth governor of Texas at only thirty-nine years old. The young governor would continue his predecessor's legacy of increasing the military presence in the state. Texas maintained half of the country's military camps, and Hobby would help meet the demand for more servicemen by setting up a military draft in Texas. He charged the state police with the responsibility of apprehending men attempting to dodge the draft. The governor also built a reputation for suppressing labor strikes, maintaining racial segregation, and showing force on the US–Mexico border. Some of his public statements, however, might lead one to think otherwise.[131]

On January 22, 1919, in the wake of the Hillsboro lynching, Governor Hobby made public demands for change in Texas. In addition to increasing funds for public schools and universities and increasing taxes on wealthy Texans, Hobby proposed that the state legislature pass laws "so drastic lynching will be forever stamped out."[132] Despite the public statements, the governor ignored requests from the NAACP encouraging him to write anti-lynching legislation and to order investigations into lynchings in Texas. His private sentiments toward the civil rights organization would later be revealed.

While the public address in January may have given others a sense of false hope, NAACP secretary John R. Shillady had his doubts. Before he reported to Texas to investigate ongoing mob violence and the intimidation of branch members, he reached out to his colleagues and asked, "Do you think there is any danger?"[133]

On August 21 Shillady traveled to Austin to meet with state authorities to propose state anti-lynching legislation and to discuss the forced closure of NAACP branches in Texas. Newspapers reported that the NAACP asked Assistant Adjutant General W. D. Cope about Texas Rangers intimidating and investigating black Texans as a result of the Longview conflicts. The Rangers concluded that associations advocating racial equality had incited racial tensions in Texas. The state police, in other words, blamed the NAACP and black labor organizers. This finding led to continued aggression toward anti-lynching activists and NAACP branches in Texas.[134]

Early in August 1919, Governor Hobby directed Texas Rangers to investigate the local branches of the NAACP, under the auspices that the organization might be circulating Bolshevik propaganda. The agents' effort to help the governor and slow NAACP progress proved successful. The Rangers found no ties to communism, but they claimed that the NAACP branches did not have the proper state charters. The agents pressured the branches in Texas to disband.[135]

Hobby agreed with the Texas Rangers' findings. Rather than condemning lynching practices throughout Texas, the administration blamed civil rights organizations for inciting racial conflict. In direct contrast to his public statements about the need to end the lynching culture in Texas, the governor blamed attempts for racial equality as a root cause of the tensions. He called for the suppression of these efforts and met the NAACP with open hostility. Upon his arrival in Austin on August 21, Shillady was hauled before County Judge Dave J. Pickle in the Travis County Court. Pickle declared that the NAACP secretary had been "inciting negroes against the whites'" and warned him to leave the state. Shillady stayed and held a meeting with local residents. Upon returning to his hotel, Judge Pickle, Constable Charles Hamby, and Ben Pierce accosted and severely beat the NAACP secretary. Judge Pickle later reported to the press that before the beating he asked Shillady why he was "stirring up more trouble than Austin citizens can get rid of in ten years." When Shillady suggested the judge merely did not see things from his point of view, Constable Hamby boasted, "I'll fix it so you can't see" and struck Shillady in the eye.[136]

Pickle admitted that he and Pierce joined Hamby in beating Shillady until his face bled freely. He bragged that the NAACP secretary pleaded for mercy. The posse escorted Shillady to the train station and forced him to purchase a ticket out of state. They warned him not to detrain until he left Texas. When the train stopped in Waco, Shillady spoke with reporters to explain he had hoped only to discuss anti-lynching legislation with Governor Hobby and Attorney General C. M. Cureton. Newspapers reported that the visibly bruised secretary had no plans to get off the train in Texas.[137]

When the secretary reached New York, his colleagues described him as being badly beaten, shaken, and having lost his spirit. The NAACP leapt into action. The chairman of the board of directors wired Governor Hobby to directly request an investigation into the assualt and to confirm that the officials who participated would be prosecuted. Rather than denouncing the participation of members of the court and local police in beating Shillady, the governor rebuked the NAACP for interfering in state matters in a telegram: "Shillady was the only offender in connection with the matter referred to in your telegram and he was punished before your inquiry came. Your organization can contribute more to the advancement of both races by keeping your representatives and their propaganda out of this State than in any other way."[138]

In light of Hobby's rebuke, the NAACP board became increasingly concerned with the official and public responses to the Shillady beating. Both state administrators and newspapers approved of the actions by the local police and a county judge. Further, the organization attempted to secure Texas counsel to prosecute Pickle, Hamby and Pierce. The NAACP searched, but no lawyers in Texas would take the case. The attack and subsequent failure to prosecute the assailants became a symbol of fierce systemic violence. In 1919 the NAACP published a brief pamphlet, *The Mobbing of John R. Shillady,* describing the attack and including a statement from Shillady. The organization printed 6,000 copies of the pamphlet that year, just 200 short of the number of the pamphlet *Burning at the Stake.*[139]

The beating at the hands of Texas authorities and the sanctioning of this violence by Governor Hobby left Shillady deeply troubled. In addition, Shillady continued to be chided by state governors. In the spring of 1920, Mississippi governor Lee M. Russell sent a telegram warning Shillady not to visit his state or to do so at his own risk. In June 1920, nearly a year after he had been violently accosted in Austin, seeing Governor Hobby overlook the actions of the Texas mob and continuing to face violent hostility from states in the South, Shillady left his post as secretary of the NAACP. The efforts to curb lynching in the United States would continue without him.

The violent attack on Shillady is a reminder of the many forms vigilante violence took. Extralegal violence did not always end in lynchings. All violence motivated by racial difference sought, in one way or another, to instill fear and encourage silence. The agents of the state who sought to dismantle the growing strength of the NAACP in Texas did their work well. By the end of 1921, all but seven of the original thirty-three NAACP branches in Texas had disbanded.[140] The threats against Representative José T. Canales by a Texas Ranger, the organized defamation of his character during the investigation, and the beating of Shillady by a Texas county judge show that state agents participated in acts of intimidation and mob violence with the tacit consent of Governor Hobby. Moreover, they stand as reminders of the danger civil rights activists faced when publicly challenging state-sanctioned violence. Contrary to popular notions that mob violence took place at the hands of marginal populations under cloak of night, in Texas violent crimes took place in broad daylight, with witnesses, and by prominent citizens. Indeed, the governor himself, as well as a variety of men charged with upholding the law, played key roles in creating a climate of fear. Rather than help turn the tide, authorities turned a blind eye to the Texas tradition of state-sanctioned violence.

The casual reference to the lynching of Bragg Williams at Hillsboro in the 1919 investigations of the Texas Rangers helps expose the widespread lynching practices in Texas towns, the circulation of these events in the media, the failure of local courts to prosecute mob participants, and the limited action by the state to hold local judicial systems accountable. The frequency with which victims were taken from police custody and lynched highlights the role of local and state police in allowing acts of vigilantism to occur. It also provides the deeper history of the forces that have shaped the long-standing mistrust of local and state police by racial minorities.

State agents who abused their prisoners and left them vulnerable to vigilante murders proved to be a concern in the legislative investigation of the Texas Rangers. Yet 1,600 pages of evidence documenting the widespread practice of extralegal violence by Texas Rangers did little to persuade the state to change the culture of policing. Lawyers for the state administration successfully convinced legislators that the stark period of anti-Mexican violence was justified as a necessary means for controlling the border region. They criminalized the Mexican residents of Texas and convinced legislators from the far reaches of the state of the existence of an ever-present crisis on the Texas–Mexico border. In the name of securing the border and Anglo property, the loss of Mexican life was celebrated as a symbol of American progress. Governor Hobby, his administration, and the Texas legislature moved to maintain a culture of vigilantism and systemic racial violence in the Texas judicial system. Authorities embraced the Texas tradition of state violence and the culture of impunity enjoyed by police.

Racism would continue to shape the daily life of Texans and inform how future generations remembered this part of the state's history. The 1919 investigation would be archived and kept from the public. Historians would gloss over the crimes committed by the state police. The federal government, too, helped shift the focus from investigations into police abuse by coordinating an investigation into the violence suffered by American citizens in Mexico during the turbulence of the Mexican Revolution. Rather than investigating violence targeting racial and ethnic minorities in the United States, just months after the Texas Ranger investigation the US Committee on Foreign Relations deflected attention from police abuse. The Investigation into Mexican Affairs interviewed over 257 witnesses in nine different cities between September 8, 1919, and May 20, 1920. William Hanson, who as a captain of the Texas Rangers had justified abuse and murders at the hands of state officers, worked as the chief investigator for the commission to inquire into the loss of property and life by Americans in Mexico during the revolution. In this context, he was committed to documenting loss of life and property. He provided a "murder map" showing the location of the deaths in Mexico and included "American citizens killed on American soil through attacks by raiding Mexicans" but made no mention of the deaths of ethnic Mexicans, Mexican nationals or Americans citizens, killed on American soil at the hands of vigilantes, local authorities, state police, or US soldiers.[141] Historians have noted that in running the commission, Senator Albert Fall weighted the proceedings with witnesses who provided "anti-Mexican interpretations and pro-intervention sentiments." In his preliminary report, Fall suggested that the United States should send a police force or the US military into Mexico to protect American citizens from depredations.[142] His calls to march US soldiers into Mexico were not followed, but the investigation provided another opportunity to restage arguments that portrayed Mexicans as inherently violent and the Mexican government as corrupt and volatile.

In the years following the investigation, former Rangers with bloody reputations were brazen in their support of each other, even those facing prosecutions. In the summer of 1920, a group of twenty current and former

Rangers gathered to support their friend Horace L. Roberson, profiled in the 1919 investigation, as he stood trial again for the murder of Henry Boykin and Walter Sitters in west Texas in 1915. Previous courts had found Roberson guilty of murder and manslaughter, but his lawyers succeeded in having those convictions overturned and appealed. Finally, in the summer of 1920, a Travis County court acquitted him of all charges.

In celebration, the group joined Roberson for a photo. The men chose to pose at the foot of a monument honoring Terry's Texas Rangers, the Eighth Cavalry that fought for the Confederacy. The group posed in solidarity with an earlier era of Rangers who fought for slavery, sedition, and white supremacy during the Civil War.[143] Men the likes of Frank Hamer and James Monroe Fox stood alongside venerated Ranger captains like John Hughes, who recruited Roberson to the state police, and Roy Aldrich, who served as the Texas Ranger quartermaster from 1918 to 1947. The group stood dressed in suits, hats, and ties staring at the camera with stoic expressions. James Monroe Fox, standing in the middle of the back row of Rangers, opted not to wear a tie but instead wore a gleeful smile, and Frank Hamer stood casually with a cigarette in hand. The 1920 photograph taken outside the state capitol is a visual reminder of the lasting law enforcement careers of Texas Rangers accused of murder and abuse and the even longer history of a state police force entangled in state violence and white supremacy.

The new decade of the 1920s began with a bloody start. Texans witnessed continued lynchings, and more residents lost their lives to mobs, local police, state agents, and border enforcement officers. The 1920s saw the reemergence of the Ku Klux Klan and its move into state and federal administration. In 1922 Texans elected Earl Bradford Mayfield, a card-carrying member of the Ku Klux Klan, to the US Senate. The board of the Texas State Fair, which declared October 23, 1923, officially Ku Klux Klan Day, encouraged all Texans to honor the racist and xenophobic organization.

In 1924 Congress passed the Johnson–Reed Immigration Act of 1924, the first comprehensive restrictive immigration law in the United States. Designed by eugenicists, the act excluded Chinese, Japanese, Indians, and other Asians from immigration. It also established numerical limits on immigration from European nations and created a national origin quota system. The act did not, however, place numerical restrictions on migration from Mexico. Instead, US congressman Claude B. Hudspeth, a former

In the months and years following the 1919 investigation into Texas Ranger abuse, many Rangers felt vindicated. Some, including James M. Fox and Frank Hamer, were brazen in their support of peers facing prosecution for murder. In the summer of 1920 a group assembled in Austin for the trial of former Ranger Horace L. Roberson. They posed at the foot of an Austin monument honoring Terry's Texas Rangers, the Eighth Cavalry that fought for the Confederacy during the Civil War. E. A. "Dogie" Wright Papers, di_04832, The Dolph Briscoe Center for American History, University of Texas at Austin.

Texas Ranger, pushed for a rider to the appropriations bill providing $1 million to establish a "land border patrol" to police the US borders with Mexico and Canada.[144] With the reduction of the number of Texas Rangers, former agents dispersed into local law enforcement to work as police officers, sheriffs, and prison guards. They also went on to join the US Border Patrol in 1924. The first border patrol agents grew up with the violence of the Texas Rangers and witnessed the culture of impunity that protected agents of the state. According to historian Kelly Lytle Hernández, the agents were primarily working-class Anglo Americans "who often used law enforcement as a strategy of economic survival and social uplift in the agricultural-based societies of the borderlands." "And they had grown up," she continues, "with white violence toward Mexicanos. . . . [T]he early officers of the Border Patrol enforced US immigration restrictions according to the customs, interests, and histories of the borderland communities where they lived and worked."[145] The story of the early years of the US Border Patrol and its policing regimes in Texas is firmly rooted in the violence of the borderlands.

Official Texas history, too, would celebrate the racist legacy of the Hobby administration. In the years after 1919, icons of racism would be memorialized for future generations as pillars of the state. Governor William Pettus Hobby would go on to run several newspapers. At the end of his term he worked for the *Beaumont Enterprise,* bought the *Beaumont Journal,* and worked for the *Houston Post-Dispatch.* In the 1930s Hobby acquired the Houston Post Company, which included the radio station KPRC, the television station KPRC-TV, and the *Post* newspaper.[146]

When Hobby died in June 1964, a state historical marker was erected in his birthplace in Moscow to honor his life. In 1967 the Houston International Airport was renamed William P. Hobby Airport. Just as the civil rights movement to desegregate schools, resist labor exploitation, and end inequality gained momentum in the state, Hobby would again intervene. The renaming honored a governor who stood for stark segregation, opposed labor unions, and endorsed state violence as a means for quelling advances in efforts for labor rights and civil rights. For residents with memories of this history, the airport is a reminder of how deeply entrenched racism is in state institutions. In Texas there is no shortage of public celebrations that honor icons of state violence. For too many, it is racism memorialized and celebrated in plain sight.

CHAPTER FIVE

Idols

SABINAL is a rural town located sixty miles west of San Antonio. Like much of the wide-open rural stretches of Texas, places to gather are few and far between. People see each other in church and at school. But more often, people gather in restaurants. The local Dairy Queen, for example, offers more than just fast food gratification. It is a site of sociability: old men gather for coffee in the early morning; friends meet for ice cream; teams unload from school buses to fuel up after athletic competitions. And in a town short on cultural institutions, the Dairy Queen is also a place of community remembrance.

In 2009, on a drive home to see family in the nearby town of Uvalde, I stopped at the Dairy Queen to stretch my legs and buy a sweet tea. What I saw stopped me in my tracks. In between advertisements for chocolate dipped ice cream cones and "Belt Buster" cheeseburgers was an exhibit honoring the Texas Rangers. Framed photographs of Company D, which patrolled the area in the late nineteenth and early twentieth century, were on display. The photos show rifles, horses, mesquite trees, cacti, and Rangers standing or mounted on horseback. These objects, nestled against the Texas landscape and surrounded by barbed-wire fences, evoke popular portraits of the Texas frontier.

In a Dairy Queen in Sabinal, Texas, a local resident put up photographs honoring the Texas Rangers. From at least 2009 until 2011, two images of a lynching were casually displayed above a trash can without context or information. One photograph shows eight men standing in anticipation of the lynching with the words "READY FOR THE HANGING." The detail from the larger display shows a man suspended from a roof by a rope. Casual displays of vigilante violence are unsettling to residents troubled by the cultures of impunity enjoyed by state police and vigilantes alike. Author photos, May 25, 2011.

I sipped my tea and scanned the images. They were identical to hundreds of images I had seen in historical archives, not to mention racks of postcards of old-timey photos that could be found at any south Texas tourist shop. As I walked toward the exit on the back wall near the rear exit just a few feet above a trash can, I saw two unsettling images. One photograph showed eight men standing in front of a wooden shack. In the bottom right corner of the image was printed the words "READY FOR THE HANGING." A few inches to the left was a second image: the crowd had disappeared, but in the center was a man suspended from the rickety roof by a rope tied around his neck.

Below these stunning images were two more photographs that seemed oddly casual next to a lynching scene. One shows a Texas Ranger on horseback gazing off into a distant horizon. His horse stands at attention and his rifle rests across his body cradled in his arm. In the bottom left

corner of the image was printed "HEAD OF COWBOYS 1900." In the second photograph fifteen men casually sit and stand around a campfire eating a meal. In front of these four photographs hung an advertisement, a cardboard cutout of a new frozen beverage called the "Moolatté," complete with whipped crème and chocolate drizzle.

I leaned in closer to look at the lynching photographs and then stepped back to place them in the context of a fast food restaurant, complete with the smell of French fries and the sounds of customers ordering in the drive-thru lane. I quickly turned around to see whether anyone else shared my confusion. These photographs did not belong in a Dairy Queen. But the other patrons were quietly talking among themselves, enjoying their meals and ice cream. Dismayed, and trying not to draw attention, I snapped pictures of the installation. When the counter was empty I talked to two young women working there and asked why photographs of a lynching adorned the walls of a Dairy Queen.

In the wake of the 1919 state investigation of the Texas Rangers, Texas legislators took a series of steps to ensure that the widespread use of extra-legal violence by state police would not undermine state authority in the region. Reducing the size of the force and dismissing unqualified officers were only the first steps in creating a public perception that the Rangers were becoming more professional. The atrocities committed by the state police and US soldiers alike, however, belied claims of American ideals and democracy in the wake of World War I. Early historians and state institutions would join the effort by creating a historical narrative that did not erase this period of violence but instead venerated the state police for bringing Texas into modernity. Their violent policing practices would be celebrated and immortalized as the embodiment of Texas masculinity and pride.

New works by historians have helped demythologize the state police and challenge the representations of the murder of ethnic Mexicans as justice served. These advances, however, are slow to alter popular perceptions. School lesson plans and public history are the terrain upon which the battle for historical representation has been and continues to be staged.

The dominant sites of public history in Texas obscure periods of state violence. From history textbooks to museum exhibits to state monuments, residents are presented with partial narratives of the past. Dominant groups have the potential to utilize collective memories to assert both cultural and social power over entire populations through the politics of memory. According to David Blight, "cultures and groups use, construct, or try to own the past in order to win power or place in the present." The authors of the anthology *Lone Star Pasts: Memory and History in Texas* attend to the politics of collective memory, documenting the prevalence of dominant Anglo Texan memory as a "suffocating power" used to control Mexican American residents.[1]

The cultural power of the past finds its strength in what historians describe as the "Texas creation myth," which instilled ideological principles of freedom and democracy into a simplistic racial narrative: Anglos are superior to racial and ethnic minorities. The history of Texas is narrated as a racial triumph. Anglo settlers are honored as pioneers who guaranteed Texas modernity by rescuing the region from threatening Indigenous nations and corrupt Mexicans. These myths, then, become part of the social fabric by being reinscribed through public school lesson plans, museum exhibits, and public memorials and celebrations. Through this process, minorities find themselves "racially excluded from the communal womb of Texas memory," argues historian Andrés Tijerina. "The Anglo memory serves," he continues, "to alienate Mexican Americans . . . every year when seventh-grade Mexican American students attend the required Texas history class in public schools across the state. They listen as the teacher recites the racially coded public texts, and they are categorically distinguished from their Anglo classmates."[2] As early as the 1930s, Texas history textbooks denounced the Mexican "character" and omitted ethnic Mexican contributions to the development of Texas.[3] For example, in one widely used 1932 textbook *Lone Star State,* author Clarence Wharton wrote about the colonization of Texas by Anglo settlers: "We are now at the real beginning of Texas history. All that happened in the 300 years after Piñeda sailed along our shores and Cabeza de Vaca tramped from Galveston Island to the Rio Grande was of little importance."[4] Erasing the violence of conquest and colonization shaped the narratives of belonging among the public.

Whereas in the early twentieth century Mexican students in Texas were denied the right to public education, in the twenty-first century they are still often denied the opportunity to imagine their ancestors as participants in the construction of Texas history or to learn alternative histories of conquest, colonization, and slavery. The disavowal of racial violence also helps obstruct possible critiques of the nation for past and ongoing crimes against minorities in the name of protecting national borders.

According to Fitzhugh Brundage, there is an urgent need to study the "architects of memory"—those who "wield power over the past and all those upon whom that power is exercised."[5] In Texas the architects of memory include photographers, journalists, politicians, historians, historical commissions, and cultural institutions such as museums. Indeed, there is much to be gained from examining how power is garnered from bestowing feelings of pride and a sense of achievement through the glorification of a history of state-sanctioned violence. Understanding the ambitions and frustrations of these architects sheds light on the power used to recall the past and "fix it on the landscape."[6] A full understanding of this cultural power requires examining the long-standing practices in Texas by cultural institutions and residents that refuse to grapple with racialized crimes against humanity, the institutions and groups that continue to memorialize Texas Rangers as models of American ideals.[7] We will also analyze vernacular histories created by local residents that align community understandings of the past with mainstream accounts. We saw earlier how vernacular history-making can reckon with histories of violence, but the practice can also result in individuals perpetuating oppressive versions of history. Vernacular histories are sometimes displayed not to bring about healing or to recover erased histories but instead to maintain unjust social norms and divisions.

RELICS OF VIOLENCE

Collections in small local and regional archives in Texas and in institutional libraries across the country contain scattered photographs of lynched Mexican men, decomposing corpses, and military prisoners lined up prior to execution. If you see a collection of Mexican Revolution–era postcards, the photos will most likely be filed there. Photographs of racial conflict in Texas between 1910 and 1920 are simultaneously parts of two phenomena: photographs of lynchings and photographs of war. The rise of amateur photography began in 1890 at the same time as the number of lynchings increased at a devastating pace. Between the 1880s and 1930s, the practice of photographing some of the 3,000 black men and women lynched by Anglo mobs became popularized.[8] By selling and circulating these images, photographers ensured that the moment of racial terror survived long after the event and continued to reassert this terror in the American South.[9] The photographs were thus both a bonding mechanism for those who shared the images and a continued method of racial intimidation.

By the twentieth century amateur photographers and entrepreneurs documented and sold images of atrocities of war. The Mexican Revolution (1910–1920) provided a rich subject for photographers on both sides of the border. Military conflicts just a stone's throw from American cities quickly became the subject of photographers' cameras, as did the militarization of the border. Robert Runyon, for example, lived in Brownsville in 1909 and opened a portrait studio, but he soon expanded and went off with his camera to capture the dramas of war. He amassed thousands of photographs of the Texas–Mexico border region.[10] Other photographers, such as Otis A. Aultman and Walter H. Horne, moved south to border towns at the start of the revolution to make a profit.

The war provided a lucrative subject as the revolution coincided with the golden age of the picture postcard. By 1910 Americans mailed approximately one billion postcards annually.[11] Walter H. Horne, owner of the Mexican War Postcard Company, is credited with making the most money

from selling pictures that captured violence on the border. He sold postcards in stores throughout the United States and even in Europe. By 1914
he had sold more than 30,000 postcards at about 2.5 cents apiece. His biggest customers were the 40,000 American soldiers stationed at Fort Bliss
near El Paso.[12] During their recreational time they bought and sold souve-
nirs to send home to friends and relatives to give them a sense of the landscape and people. Postcards became a convenient way to share a piece of
the borderlands with people back home. Images that captured the violence
of the time sold particularly well. Horne noted, "The more gruesome
photos sold even better."[13] One of Horne's photographs captures approximately fifteen Mexican bodies piled on top of one another. Arms, legs, and
torsos intermingle, seemingly impossible to disentangle individuality and
humanity reduced to limbs in a pile.[14] The place of death is not designated. They could have died fighting in the Mexican Revolution or in Texas.
This image and others like it, with little information about the dead or the
circumstances of their death, were reproduced on postcards for consumption and distribution.

Photographers commodified Mexican corpses and enabled the casual
circulation of their images. In 1918 a newcomer to west Texas mailed a
postcard to his mother, Mrs. Ruth Fairbanks, in Emmit, Kansas. Horne's
photograph of jumbled Mexican bodies is the image on the postcard. On
the back, the son, H. F., gives his mother an update on his efforts to find a
job in his new hometown of El Paso and composes a mundane sense of his
life on the border: "feeling pretty fair, the weather is fine here and pretty
warm."[15] He references his own well-being and assures his mother he will
remain in contact. Of the appalling image on the other side of the postcard he makes no reference. For H. F., Mexican corpses were a part of the
borderlands landscape and perhaps something to excite his mother—a tit-
illating glimpse of life on the border.

Photographs of executions, as well as those with American soldiers grinning while posing with dead or wounded Mexican prisoners of war, sold
well. These images frequently relied on racist and derogatory labels—
"greaser" and "bandit" were particularly popular.[16] In many of these
photographs, such as "The Body of Mexican Bandit Leader," a corpse is
surrounded by crouching US soldiers who smile at the camera as they prop
up the dead body as a trophy and a sign of their readiness to fight abroad.[17]
In similar images the corpses are bound by rope; some are disrobed with

On March 23, 1918, a newcomer to Texas with the initials H. F. mailed a postcard
to his mother, Ruth Fairbanks, describing his life in El Paso. He makes no
reference to the photograph on the front side of the postcard showing unnamed
Mexican corpses piled on top of one another. In the 1910s photographers such as
Walter H. Horne commodified Mexican deaths by selling such photographs as
postcards. Photographs from this era continue to circulate at book sales, on the
Internet, and at antique stores. Yale Collection of Western Americana, Beinecke
Rare Book and Manuscript Library.

their genitals in full view; others are covered haphazardly with a blanket. In some images the bodies have clearly been desecrated; others offer a hint of sexual humiliation.

These performances of wartime masculinity are coupled with a polyglot range of titles, captions, and descriptions. All present the dead as bandits, thieves, or greasers who deserved to die. In each, there is a presumption of guilt. Labeling the bodies as criminals kept viewers from feeling sympathy for the victim and, instead, instructed them to celebrate the violence by joining the soldiers in their voyeuristic delight. Moreover, the availability of these postcards for purchase encouraged their casual exchange.

American photographers of the Mexican Revolution did not portray the dead as victims of war. Rather, the anonymous dead represented a symbol of progress. The photographs were offered as evidence of American superiority and military power. Through such images, consumers gained confidence in the US ability to secure the border with Mexico. More dead Mexican bodies on the US–Mexico border meant safer conditions for Anglo settlement, consumption, and capital.

The portrayals of the dead as bandits and a menace to progress became the norm, but photographers did not, of course, invent these representations. As we have seen, politicians, local law enforcement, state police, vigilantes, and journalists described Mexicans as bandits and called for their killing. The state, its police, and the media developed the language and the justification. Photographers helped by visualizing these representations in print and making them available for the public.

When photographers turned their lens on violence in the United States, they captured victims of extralegal executions. Texas Rangers, local police, US soldiers, and civilians are shown in these photos. Indeed, it is the authority of a soldier's uniform or the presence of a Texas Ranger that lent credence for the deeds captured on them. Collectively, photographs of war in Mexico and scenes in Texas offer a glimpse into the climate of anti-Mexican violence. They offer us remains of ethnic Mexicans targeted with violence who suffered gross injustices and violations of their civil rights.

Robert Runyon is credited with capturing the most infamous image of anti-Mexican violence in south Texas. The raid on the Las Norias section of the King Ranch on August 8, 1915, by an estimated sixty Mexican men, resulted in a killing spree that left an estimated 102 dead.[18] The King Ranch in this period was known as the greatest symbol of Anglo domination on the frontier. The ranching empire maintained a staggering two million acres of land at its peak, with property across several counties.[19] Local and state officials ordered swift retribution.

In a series of eight photographs, Robert Runyon recorded some of the carnage.[20] Three of the images show the same four corpses, lying on the ground, alone in the barren landscape. The four corpses were arranged side by side on their backs. Runyon moved his camera around the bodies to photograph them resting on a bare landscape that stretches for miles; there is little more than a shrub in the background. The men's legs lay straight and their arms are tucked by their side; three of the men are facing one direction; the fourth body lies in the opposite direction. Their faces and hair are powdered with fine dust and their clothes stained with blood. Runyon labeled one of these photographs "DEAD MEXICAN BANDITS." With that swift caption, the men were marked as criminals, threats to American society in life, and, in death, spectacles.

For the remaining photographs in the series, six men on horseback took turns posing behind the bodies. In one photograph Texas Ranger Frank Hamer and another member of the posse sit on horseback, with smug expressions, holding a white sheet. In another photograph Runyon repositioned the men on the opposite side of the bodies, with two riders holding the sheet and a third joining the photograph. The men are dressed in gear appropriate for riding; Hamer is wearing a tie and jacket. The heads of the bodies are closest to the men on horseback and their feet point toward the camera. For the next photographs three different men rode their horses to the opposite side of the bodies so that the heads of the corpses would be closest to the camera. They show three men—Texas Ranger captain James Monroe Fox, ranch foreman Tom Tate, and an unidentified rider—mounted on horseback holding ropes tied to the corpses. Two of the bodies look untethered. One body was lassoed by two ropes at the leg, while the body lying in the opposite direction of the group had a lasso around the neck. For one photograph Runyon positioned his camera so that the body lassoed by the neck is in clear view. In each of these photos the men sat on horseback with the ropes pulled taut. There is so much tension on the ropes it appears that if a horse had taken even one step backward it would have dragged the bodies. The mounted men sat in a prideful pose of frontier bravado with their hands on their hip or on the saddle horn. In two groups of three, these men waited patiently for their time in front of the camera; they rode their horses around the bodies and posed while Runyon repositioned his equipment. Texas Rangers proudly posed next to the bodies like trophies, ensuring that Runyon would make a profit and that their reputations would be preserved. The intentionality and commitment of these men is eerie to contemplate.

In one of the photos the body closest to the camera is shown to have the man's left leg bent so far back that the man's shoe nearly reaches his left elbow. The body looks as if it arrived at this still position from being dragged by his right leg. In other photos his legs lie straight. Runyon did not seem short on ideas for framing the bodies. The photos were sold in Brownsville, on display in stores where relatives of the deceased may have seen them for sale.

During the 1919 investigation of the Texas Rangers, State Representative José T. Canales submitted one of the Runyon photographs, three men posing with the bodies tethered by ropes, as evidence of state police abuse.

On August 8, 1915, photographer Robert Runyon took a train from Brownsville to the Norias section of the King Ranch to photograph the bodies of Jesús García, Mauricio García, Amado Muñoz, and Muñoz's brother. He took eight photographs, five with Texas Rangers and local residents posing with the dead bodies. He arranged the bodies for the photographs, which would later be sold as postcards in Brownsville, where relatives of the deceased may have seen them for sale. These images were no doubt an intimidating sight for ethnic Mexicans in the region. Robert Runyon Photograph Collection, RUN00103, The Dolph Briscoe Center for American History, University of Texas at Austin.

Texas Rangers and a civilian sit on horseback with lassoes pulled taut around the
bodies of Jesús García, Mauricio García, Amado Muñoz, and Muñoz's brother.
One of the bodies has a rope around the neck. Runyon's photographs came under
scrutiny during the 1919 investigation of the Texas Rangers when José T. Canales
used them as evidence of Ranger abuse and intimidation. Robert Runyon
Photograph Collection, RUN00101, The Dolph Briscoe Center for American
History, University of Texas at Austin.

Canales described horror and indignation at such treatment of human beings. He viewed the images as someone who lamented the desecration of
humanity on display. His interpretation, however, was acutely refuted by
witnesses called by the state. During his testimony Lon C. Hill joked about
the photo and explained that the image merely showed Texas Rangers
clearing the ranch of the corpses to dispose of them. This act, he remembered, was quite common. William Sterling later wrote that Hill told the
committee, "Gentlemen, those horses and those ropes were nothing but
the Norias hearse. No regular funeral equipment was available."[21] Though
the transcripts do not have a record of that exchange, Sterling fondly remembered Hill's quip. Sterling mused that the room, filled with an audience of legislators, journalists, and curious residents, erupted in laughter.
Hill identified Captain James Monroe Fox and Tom Tate for the committee

but did not know the name of the man on horseback in the center. He described Runyon as a young photographer who arrived by train with his Kodak camera ready to take approximately a dozen photos. Hill insisted that Runyon did not stage the photograph but merely captured the men in action clearing the bodies from the ranch.[22]

These assertions quickly came under question by committee member Dan S. McMillin, who took note of the horses facing the bodies in the photograph. For this to be a photograph of the active removal of bodies from the ranch, the horses would have had to drag the bodies by walking backward. McMillin questioned customs inspector Joe Taylor, who also witnessed Runyon taking the photographs, "Is it customary for them to back their horses when they are drawing these dead men we have seen in the picture? . . . The heads of the horses are towards the body, aren't they? . . . I don't think though, it is customary for them to drag them in front of their horses and back their horses all the time." Taylor simply responded, "No, they don't do that."[23] McMillin's questioning made the staging of the photographs obvious, but the insight did little to change the course of the investigation.

The investigation offered one important detail about the deceased men in the photograph. Lon C. Hill identified one of the dead men in the photograph, Jesús García. When Hill arrived at the ranch, García was still alive. Knowing that he would die from his wounds, García called over to Hill to ask a favor. He wanted Hill to inform his family in south Texas that he had been killed. Hill testified that he delivered the message to García's family, but he made no comment about his interaction with the family or their names, nor did he offer any remorse for the treatment of a man Hill knew died worrying for what would come of his family. The three other men in the photograph are believed to be Mauricio García, Amado Muñoz, and Amado Muñoz's brother. These men too had families.[24]

The photograph continues to be the most widely circulated image in academic publications for showing the atrocities and extent of the violence of the period. It is also, however, sold on eBay, is a favorite of amateur historians, and makes its way into private collections. In 2017 Larry and Roy Todd, two brothers raised in south Texas, discussed a postcard with the image that belonged to their father, William Aaron Todd, who displayed it in his gas station when they were younger. Years later the brothers considered the photograph merely a curious memento belonging to their father, who maintained a small collection of historical memorabilia.[25]

The archives produced by photographers, state police, and the mainstream press must be read with caution. Analyzing these photographs requires a refusal to assume that the dead in the images were bandits or thieves or that they were justly killed. It requires a new consideration for the lives of the dead depicted on film, in state records, and in newspaper archives. As often as photographers criminalized the dead with their captions, Texas Rangers identified men they killed in their monthly reports and letters of correspondence with similar descriptions: "suspicious character," "Mexican bandit," or "unknown Mexican thief."[26] The English-language press printed articles that labeled victims this way. Cultural institutions, 100 years later, continue the same practice of circulating images that criminalize ethnic Mexicans.

MAKING HEROES

In the years following the 1919 investigation, the state legislature actively worked to undo any damage that had been done to the perception of the state police. The first step came when the records of the proceedings, testimonies and evidence of state brutality and horror, were filed away in the Texas State Archives in Austin. One Texan had access to the investigation following the proceedings. After graduating from the University of Texas at Austin with a bachelor degree in history, Walter Prescott Webb joined its faculty in 1918. In 1931 he published his first book, *The Great Plains,* and then turned to the 1919 investigation for his second book, *The Texas Rangers: A Century of Frontier Defense,* published in 1935. In Webb, the Texas Ranger legacy had a trusted guardian. After all, in his youth he was molded by the celebrations of the Rangers of the nineteenth century. He grew up in Ranger, Texas, and attended Ranger High School.

Webb's book helped create the myth of the Texas Ranger. He described the Rangers as possessing supreme mental and moral qualities. A Ranger, he insisted, was more than merely courageous; he had a "complete absence of fear. . . . This means he is free, with every faculty about him, to act in complete accord with his intelligence." Webb especially exuded admiration for Texas Ranger captains. A Ranger captain had the ability to anticipate danger. "He is all mind, and his mind works, not only in emergencies, but ahead of them; he anticipates the contingency and prepares for it." In addition to extraordinary intelligence and judgment, Webb praised Texas Rangers who were merciless in conflict. "A Ranger captain, to be successful, must combine boldness with judgment. Once he has decided to strike, having always only a small group, he must strike with such force as to devastate or completely demoralize his enemy."[27] In his praise, Webb encouraged readers to interpret the Rangers' brutality in demoralizing enemies as something to applaud and respect.

Webb contrasted the superhuman qualities of a state officer with the savagery of Native Americans and the corruption of Mexican enemies. For Webb racial supremacy was a matter of innate biological differences. Derogatory descriptions of Native Americans are abundant in his writing. Still, he believed they were incrementally superior to the mixed race of people he called Mexican Indians. In his first book, he described Mexican Indians as having blood, when compared with the blood of Plains Indian, like "ditch water." In his second book, he continued this racist diatribe describing Mexicans as having a "cruel streak in their nature," inherited in part from the Spanish conquistadors and in part from the Indian blood.[28] He described Representative José T. Canales as "a citizen of the Rio Grande Valley," but made sure to note that he was "a man of Mexican blood."[29]

From his work on the Texas Rangers, Webb would go on to amass great success. He remained an important member of the University of Texas at Austin's History Department from 1918 until 1963. He directed the Texas Historical Association from 1939 until 1946 and served as the president of the American Historical Association in 1958. In addition to his professional accolades, Webb's research received prestigious support, including two Guggenheim fellowships and a Ford fellowship.[30] Webb, a young member of the faculty during the 1919 investigation of the Texas Rangers, built his career and reputation on a version of Texas history that justified state violence.

In addition to social clout and institutional respect, Webb gained financially from his histories of the West. As a professor at the University of Texas at Austin, Webb made $2,850 in 1937. This annual salary was substantially supplemented by his book sales and his contracted work as a public historian. He also received between $2,500 and $5,000 each year in royalties from the early years of his publications. The National Park Service paid him $1,200 for a two-month assignment to develop a guidebook for a park in the Big Bend Region in west Texas. In 1936 his profits and acclaim grew when he received nearly $15,000 from the sale of the movie rights for his book *The Texas Rangers*.[31]

The rise of Webb's professional career fortuitously paralleled a major milestone in Texas history. The 1935 publication of Webb's ode to the Texas Rangers coincided with the centennial of the Texas Revolution. The Commission of Control for Texas Centennial Celebrations, created by the Texas Legislature in 1935, took on the charge of celebrating the anniversary of Texas's independence from Mexico. In the midst of the Great Depression, the state allocated more than three million dollars of state funds for the construction and placement of markers, memorials, and buildings to designate sites of historical significance. State funds also helped purchase land for celebrations, including stage pageants and expositions recognizing the industries that contributed to the state's economic growth. Each county received a historical marker indicating the source of the county name and the date it was established. Across the state fifteen museums and memorials, including Big Bend Historical Museum, the Ranger Memorial in San Antonio, and Panhandle-Plains Historical Museum in Canyon, received funding for permanent buildings. The state funded or supported approximately 1,100 exposition buildings, memorial museums, statues, and markers. To supplement the rising costs, companies sponsored exhibits and construction. Ford Motor Company, for example, paid $2,250,000 to build the Ford Motor Company Building at the centennial exposition.[32] In total fifty buildings made up the central exposition in Dallas. The commission coordinated the commemoration under the dual themes of history and progress. Cities across the state participated by hosting their own special observances starting in 1935, with the final celebrations closing in 1937. These commemorative efforts all fit a very particular narrative.[33]

Within the attempts to both celebrate and reinforce Texas's collective memory, two historical events are particularly important: the war for independence from Mexico in 1836 that resulted in the Republic of Texas and Texans' allegiance with the Confederacy in the Civil War.[34] Anglo residents in Texas in the late nineteenth century attempted to harness war memories to reclaim the valor of Civil War veterans despite the demise of the Confederacy.[35] By the early twentieth century, historians Greg Cantrell and Elizabeth Hayes Turner argue, the Battle of the Alamo during the Texas Revolution from Mexico provided a "more useful past, one that brought bravado and glory to the field of memories. Hence 'Remember the Alamo' replaced the rebel yell, at least superficially."[36] Historians writing in the early twentieth century, they contend, helped exalt figures like Stephen F. Austin, Davy Crockett, and iconic Texas Rangers. These narratives in turn "did not shape Texas memory so much as affirmed it."[37]

Webb became a key player in the production of a public Texas history. He and other architects of the centennial celebrations depicted the Texas Revolution and the efforts by Anglo settlers to maintain social and political control in the region as a racial clash of civilizations. Of these efforts, literary scholar John Morán González wrote, "Centennial discourses synthesized the historical elements of what historians now recognize as the iconography of Texas into a coherent narrative."[38] The successful defeat of Mexico in 1836 portrayed Mexico and its residents as tyrannical and uncivilized, thus the emphasis on memorializing and pledging never to forget the Alamo. Centennial narratives reinscribed race as the key element for determining which residents in Texas would be credited with bringing about modernity to the state. Native Americans and Mexicans were portrayed as obstacles to progress. The Texas Rangers and their acts of violence, on the other hand, were mythologized as icons that defeated treachery and secured Anglo civilization. The brutality of the state police was erased. Instead, residents were encouraged to celebrate their efforts. Webb, and the commission for the Centennial celebrations, above all, helped cement the Texas Rangers as saviors of Texas. To do this, they brought history out of the classroom and built markers and monuments, and coordinated celebrations to instill Texas pride in a prescribed past.

These celebrations of the Texas Revolution also instructed residents on how to perform state pride. Since Texas independence in 1836, the centennial history suggested, the Texas Rangers made Anglo success possible in the state. Two Western films released in 1936, *The Texas Rangers* and *Ride, Ranger Ride,* helped cement the image of Texas Rangers and make them Hollywood heroes. Texas governor James Allred named the song "Ride, Ranger Ride," recorded for the film, as the official "Ranger-Texas Centennial Song."

Written by Tim Spencer and recorded by the Sons of the Pioneers in 1936, the catchy song begins, "Ride Ranger Ride, From Red River to the sea you have written history." It claims that the Texas Rangers and their success in "conquering every foe since a hundred years ago" shaped the course of Texas history. In the song, the Texas Rangers are "loyal Texas sons," and the state, and by extension Texans, continues to need their protection. The song calls on the state police to continue to ride, protect the state, and honor those Rangers who fought before them. Roy Rogers and Gene Autry later recorded their own versions and performed them in film.[39]

In Dallas the W. K. Kellogg exhibition celebrated the Texas Rangers by providing an opportunity for children to become junior Rangers. After having their photo taken and reciting a pledge, kids signed their name and walked away with a certified junior Ranger card. "Like a good ranger," the pledge read, "I'll be brave, honest, obedient and always keep my eyes open for danger." By signing the junior pledge, children affirmed that Texas Rangers were the models of bravery, honesty, and obedience. They vowed to support the state police by being steadfast in fighting crime at home where they lived. They also committed to being loyal to the state. The commercial sponsorship of this exhibit at the centennial provides a glimpse into the well-functioning machine that turned this mythic icon of the Texas Ranger into a commodity for consumption.

The Texas Centennial became a key moment for state institutions to engender public pride and a communal sense of history, and members of the Texas Centennial Control Commission actively worked to maintain the status of its heroes after the anniversary. In 1939 J. K. Beretta of the commission wrote a letter to the *Southwestern Historical Quarterly* warning historians of the dangers of narratives that might whittle away at the idealization of these heroes. In response to researchers who questioned the script of heroic actions by William Travis and others at the Alamo, Baretta pleaded, "let us believe it"; he begged professional historians to let public history and Texas residents "keep our illusion of . . . Texas heroes as patriotic, loyal, and good citizens."[40]

The efforts to cement an official version of the past continued throughout the twentieth century. The Texas Historical Commission (THC), created in 1953, oversaw the selection of historical events, people, or sites that deserved recognition. It continued the tradition that started with the centennial celebrations and installed state historical markers across Texas. Throughout the latter half of the twentieth century, the THC marked the landscape with racially coded narratives of progress. Texas historical markers celebrated the founders of towns and cities and highlighted the history of military forts and, as we have seen, prominently displayed the history

During celebrations for the Texas Centennial, new generations were encouraged to acknowledge Texas Rangers as models of bravery, honesty, and obedience to the state. The Kellogg Company sponsored the W. K. Kellogg exhibit in Dallas, which served as the "headquarters" for junior rangers. Children signed the junior Ranger badge, which showed the junior Ranger pledge and a photograph of the child in a cowboy hat. By signing the junior Ranger pledge, children vowed to support the state police by fighting crime where they lived. DeGolyer Library, Southern Methodist University, George W. Cook Dallas / Texas Image Collection.

of massacres and raids against Anglo settlers by Native Americans. Native Americans remained the enemies of progress in these markers, while the role of ethnic Mexicans in conquest and as targets of racial violence is largely ignored.

In 1970 one such marker was erected on the side of the road outside of Uvalde. It narrated the history of what is known as the "Chalk Bluff Indian Massacre." On May 26, 1861, Henry Robinson and Henry Adams, identified as "two of southwest Texas' most feared Indian fighters," were "ambushed by a band of twenty hostile Indians." The marker notes that unidentified Indians "attacked Robinson's home" and then scalped the two men.[41] Seven years later, in 1977, in nearby Edwards County, the THC erected a marker highlighting the "Mackenzie Trail," which in 1852 connected the US Army forts Clark and McKavett. It described the need for the military to patrol the region and protect local settlers from Native Americans. These markers are consistently uncritical of the violent histories of displacement and colonization in Texas. Instead, they valorize Anglo settlers and cast anonymous "Indians" as the brutal enemies of a progress that needed to be policed.[42]

These markers were inspired by Walter Prescott Webb's histories. Those applying for markers relied on his work for the research essays submitted to the THC. And yet, as the thirty-year anniversary of *The Texas Rangers* neared, Webb felt the time had come to update his book, which would be reprinted by the University of Texas Press in 1965. He told the director of the press that he had failed to write a balanced history that accounted for ethnic Mexicans' experiences during the violence. He reflected, "If a man can't grow in thirty years, he may as well be dead." In 1963 Webb died tragically in a fatal car accident. The University of Texas Press decided to reprint the book, without revisions, but with a flattering introduction by President Lyndon B. Johnson, who, just the year before, had signed the 1964 Civil Rights Act.[43]

VENERATION

During the civil rights era of the 1960s and 1970s, academics, activists, and local residents were simultaneously questioning the history of the Texas Rangers and the current practices of the state police. In 1968 a US commission on civil rights held hearings in San Antonio to learn about institutional practices of discrimination in the state. One complaint was the small number of racial minorities represented as law enforcement officers in Texas. As of October 1968 the Texas Department of Public Safety employed nearly 1,650 uniformed and approximately 110 plainclothes law enforcement officers. Of these, there were twenty-eight Mexican American officers, only 1.5 percent of the total. The highway patrol did not employ a single African American officer. The state employed sixty-two Texas Rangers, but no Mexican Americans or African Americans wore the Ranger badge. These findings led activists to argue that discrimination during the hiring processes kept racial minorities from becoming law enforcement agents. Critics described this as a reflection of broader institutionalized racism, the effects of which could be felt throughout the state.[44]

Shifting the culture of policing, many believed, would prove impossible if the state refused to integrate the police itself. Amid civil rights organizing in Texas to remove racist depictions from history lessons in schools and to change patterns of policing, the THC recommitted to venerating Texas Rangers as icons.

The Texas Ranger Hall of Fame and Museum in Waco contributed by enshrining in popular memory the Rangers as heroes of the early frontier. From its inception the museum showed little interest in acting as a leader to calm racial conflicts in Texas. In 1968 the Waco City Council approved an ordinance declaring the First Street Cemetery "unkempt, neglected, and offensive." The city received a court order to relocate graves from the lower section of the cemetery to build Fort Fisher Park and the Texas Ranger Museum. This lower section of the cemetery contained the remains mostly of African American residents, including Shepherd Mullins, a former slave elected to the state House of Representatives in 1869; Asian Americans; and some European Americans. Despite the original agreements, during construction the headstones were removed, but the remains were not. When the museum started new construction for an education center in 2007, these mistakes were revealed. Construction workers disinterred the remains of more than 160 unidentified bodies. Archaeologist Fred McGhee exclaimed at the time, "You're talking about the desecration of hundreds of burials in a wanton fashion." Years later the city of Waco was still blundering to identify and reinter the remains. As late as 2015, the exhumed remains were reportedly stored at the Ranger museum in boxes.[45] The museum had its beginnings, quite literally, with skeletons in the closets.

In 1968 the Texas Department of Public Safety named the museum the official museum of the Texas Rangers, in 1973 it also became the site of the official Texas Ranger Hall of Fame, and in 1997 the Texas legislature recognized the museum and its research center as an official repository for state police records. In addition to funding from the state, the museum relies on city and county funds, visitor revenue, and private donations. With state authority to help, the museum has a two-part mission: "To disseminate knowledge and inspire appreciation of the Texas Rangers, a legendary symbol of Texas and the American West; To collect, preserve, study and exhibit artifacts, artwork and archives relating to the Texas Ranger service; To permanently document and honor the service of Texas Rangers past and present."[46]

Rather than calling into question the violence of policing techniques, the Texas Ranger Hall of Fame and Museum uncritically displays violence in its exhibits. The museum dedicates important exhibit space to the role of the state force in policing state borders and private property with violence. Officers are portrayed as heroes who enabled the creation of national borders that made way for the agricultural revolution in the late nineteenth and early twentieth century. Visitors are greeted on the front lawn by a statue honoring Major George B. Erath (1813–1891), a Texas Ranger and land surveyor.[47] Major Erath, cast in bronze, stands with a rifle in one hand, surveying equipment on the other, and a pistol tucked into his belt. When visitors enter the museum, one of the first displays highlights the role of Texas Rangers as guards for surveyors who mapped the state's borders with Mexico. The celebration of this role, of course, stands in for a more complicated history of securing private property and making international borders. The museum, charged with inspiring appreciation for the state police, frames even the most violent histories of the state police as achievements. In this sense, the museum functions as a permanent ongoing tool for image management and for hegemonic control of historical narratives.

At the museum, visitors are presented with a history of the state police, the evolution in the clothing and weapons they used, and, through an interactive exhibit, the far-reaching influence of the Texas Rangers on popular culture. Just a few of the many details offered in these permanent exhibits include the role of Stephen F. Austin in organizing the first company of Rangers in 1823; the role of the officers in protecting surveyors creating maps of the US–Mexico border in the mid-nineteenth century; the Rangers who patrolled the earliest ranches that fenced their property; the daily life of Rangers and their families living on the Texas frontier; and major accomplishments such as the capture of the infamous Bonnie and Clyde in 1931. The Texas Ranger as popular culture phenomenon also takes up a considerable amount of space at the end of the exhibit. Displays about the television series *The Lone Ranger* and *Walker, Texas Ranger* are larger than the museum's other exhibits on the history of the state police.

A key feature of the museum is the Texas Ranger Hall of Fame, planned in 1973 to commemorate the 150th anniversary of the state police and officially opened in 1976. The hall commemorates thirty Texas Rangers "who gave their lives in the line of duty or made significant contributions to the development of the service."[48] In a darkened hall the walls are lined with portraits of select Texas Rangers, each illuminated by a spotlight. Visitors move through the hallway slowly and with respect and with reverence.

Next to the portraits, firearms are the most prominent artifacts on display. The first room of the museum is dedicated to the history of firearms. Two display cases hold early models of the Colt Walker and the Colt Paterson repeating pistols—the guns of choice for early generations of Rangers—cradled in a fabric-covered box. The guns are massive. The accompanying caption explains that the first models weighed four pounds, nine ounces, and asks the visitor to imagine holding and aiming a gun that weighs nearly as much as a five-pound bag of flour. The exhibit showcases the evolution of firearms, especially the development of the Colt .44 revolver. Through an interactive display visitors are encouraged to practice assembling and reloading a Colt Paterson repeating pistol. A plastic replica gun is mounted to a flat panel and secured by three metal cords. A series of four smaller photographs sits below with step-by-step instructions for properly loading the gun. After practicing, visitors are asked: "Can you imagine trying to reload an early Colt Repeating Pistol while in a fire fight?"

Patrons marvel at the weapons encased in plastic and compare them to the photographs of Rangers posing with their firearms. Guns used by famous Texas Rangers act as surrogates for the men themselves. The prominent place of the history of these weapons in the museum, and the way it frames the history of violence as a heroic progression of guns, makes this a destination for gun enthusiasts and fans of Texas history alike.[49]

There is no shortage of displays that highlight guns and ammunition used in the late nineteenth and early twentieth century. The museum does little, however, to contextualize the use of these firearms or to make room for the histories of those who found themselves at the other end of the gun. Instead, visitors are called upon to imagine themselves as the one wielding a firearm. In asking residents to identify with Texas Rangers, the museum curators also encourage visitors to admire the Rangers and their skillful use of early firearms and to empathize with their position.

In this celebratory museum there is little room to reflect on the history of racial violence at the hands of state police. One exhibit case accounts for the decade between 1910 and 1920, when Rangers performed countless acts of anti-Mexican violence. By presenting this period as an expansion of the force in response to turbulence stimulated by the Mexican Revolution, this display decontextualizes the violence from the racial politics of the time. Instead, it interprets the role of Texas Rangers in this turmoil as merely protecting the lives and property of Anglo settlements under threat. Identifying Texas Rangers as providers of protection from the dangers of the frontier is a central theme in the museum more broadly. The museum curators frame Texas Ranger aggression as a defensive and protective measure, all done in the name of security.

In this display, only four captions describe the historical context. Collectively, the panels—"Border Troubles," "1919 Reorganization," "Ranger Transportation," and "Scouting for Smugglers"—give little insight into the importance of an era that would upend social relations in the region. (In contrast, the history of the *Lone Ranger* television series has no less than ten captions with historical information for visitors.) Nearly half of the items in the display of this pivotal period are guns, ammunition, and related objects used for policing. The torso of a mannequin dressed in iconic Mexican revolutionary garb is mounted in the center of the case. Dressed in a period long-sleeve shirt, the mannequin is adorned with a straw sombrero and two cartridge bandoliers forming an X across the chest. The mannequin, front and center, introduces the visitor to the figure of the Mexican revolutionary, portrayed as a racial threat to Texans living near the border.

The period items take center stage. Should visitors take the time to scan the labels scattered on the periphery, they would read a short description about the Texas Rangers being organized into four companies in 1901. Over the course of the decade, the narrative explains, Rangers were charged with preventing and investigating the following activities: (1) bandit depredations or raided ranchers; (2) sabotage against irrigation and agricultural production; (3) sabotage against the railroad; (4) liquor smuggling; and (5) possible invasion from Mexico during World War I. Without broader context, this list suggests to visitors that any use of the guns on display would be warranted. Presenting the arms in this way, detached from the violent consequences of conflict during this period, is a pervasive pattern throughout the museum.

The display includes another peripheral two-paragraph label titled "Border Troubles." The caption explains that the Mexican Revolution of 1910 created an unstable social climate in northern Mexico and that *El Plan de San Diego* (1915) heightened "an already tense atmosphere by creating distrust among residents along the Mexico-Texas border." According to the panel, revolutionary activity spread into Texas, "where the Rangers worked to protect life and property." After listing some raids, the label concludes that these events caused Texas governors to mobilize emergency companies of Rangers to "augment the small force already stationed in Texas." The labels and photographs highlight the need for Texas Rangers and identify a clear racialized threat.

The displays encouraged viewers to consider the bravery of the men but did not call attention to the consequences of their policing techniques. This description mimics the justifications for violence outlined by lawyers defending the state police during the 1919 investigation discussed in Chapter 4. In particular, two of the raids listed on the plaque, one on the Norias Ranch in 1915 in Cameron County and one on the Brite Ranch in Presidio County in 1917, resulted in some of the most well-documented cases of racial terror at the hands of the Rangers in the 1910s. Yet the exhibit makes no reference to the Porvenir massacre that followed the Brite Ranch raid or the indiscriminate killing that followed the Norias Ranch raid. Moreover, the broader histories of the role of Texas Rangers in state violence do not find a place in this display or anywhere else in the museum. Rather, a label describes the raids as causing "the Governor to declare martial law" and increase the number of Texas Rangers. In the brief reference to the governor, the panel did not explain that martial law in this period called for only Mexican residents to give up their weapons, making it a crime for a Mexican resident to possess a firearm, knife, or ammunition in 1918, thus leaving these residents vulnerable to raiders, vigilantes, and state police alike.

Instead, below this label is a photograph of Texas Rangers from Company A in 1918, pictured peacefully at their headquarters at the Norias Ranch. Directly under the photo of the leisurely gathering of Rangers is another titled "Mexican Revolutionaries, 1910" that floats without any text to accompany the title. The men are dressed in sombreros and boots, and one is draped in ammunition. Both men face the camera with shoulders squared to the photographer, and each holds a rifle in his right arm. This image is coupled with a second picture similarly titled "Mexican Revolutionary, 1910s." In this photograph, a man mounted on horseback stands in the foreground, and one woman and five other men face the camera from a distance. From some writing in the upper right corner of the photo-graph, it appears that this image was circulated as a postcard, but no infor-mation is provided for the viewer to assess who was being photographed and what, if any, relation they had to the Texas Rangers. In this display, photographs of Anglo Texas Rangers are accompanied by captions that identify the date, location, and the company at the very least. The photo-graphs of the Texas Rangers are deserving of historical details. For ethnic Mexicans, conversely, their images in these photographs are taken as self-evident, presuming that the viewers already know how to interpret the images.

The display does not address the extent to which Texas Rangers in this period participated in extralegal violence, but it does include a small label on the 1919 investigation of the Rangers led by State Representative José T. Canales. The label gives a vague and general account of the investiga-tion. The quick rise of special Rangers, it reads, resulted in unqualified Rangers joining the force and committing crimes. The "vigilante nature" of these new Rangers, the label suggests, led to the investigation and reor-ganization of the force, as well as to a reduction in the size of companies to no more than seventeen men. The label, however, does not detract from the overall celebration of the Texas Rangers, nor does it credit Rep-resentative Canales for attempting to challenge state violence. At no more than six by nine inches in size, the label does little to encourage visitors to think critically about violent policing. It suggests to visitors that, in the 1910s or elsewhere, the vigilante aspects of policing were peripheral, not a signature part of the policing regime. The panel does not make note of the atrocities committed by key captains of the force, such as James Monroe Fox and Henry Ransom. Nor does it lament the role of investigating of-ficer William Hanson in maintaining a culture of impunity for the police. To the contrary, Hanson's pearl-handled .45-caliber Colt revolver is promi-nently on display in the museum. The calls for violence by state legislators and governors that created the period of racial terror by the Texas Rangers are similarly absent.

Rather than being made to consider the social vulnerability of Native Americans or ethnic Mexicans, viewers are encouraged to celebrate Rangers with their guns and ammunition and to see Mexican residents, like those in the photos, as the source of violence. The pattern of criminalizing Mex-ican residents that took hold in the nineteenth and early twentieth centuries continues into the twenty-first century in Waco. Despite dozens of academic books that have documented the history of anti-Mexican violence and the role of the state police in this period of ethnic cleansing, this museum does not reflect this history. Like most museums that fall in line with state power, the display is out of line with current understandings of US history.[50] It replicates the simplistic narrative laid out by Walter Prescott Webb in 1935.

The website supported by the Texas Ranger Hall of Fame and Museum offers a bit more information on this topic, in its history of the force, under the section titled "Bandit Raids." In this account, the narrative reads: "Mexican raids into Texas in 1915–16 caused an estimated 21 American deaths; an estimated 300 Mexicans or Tejanos may have been killed in South Texas by the actions of Rangers, vigilantes and citizens. Some sources place the death toll as high as 300 and 3,000."[51] With its encyclopedic tone, this account avoids calling attention to this period as a tragedy in Texas and US history. The description attributes "American" death to the hands of Mexican raids and suggests that the unknown number of Mexican residents may or may not have come at the hands of Rangers, vigilantes, and citizens. These simplistic racial binaries leave the reader assuming that Americans in this period were exclusively Anglo and that Mexicans were exclusively foreign. With no clear aggressor to blame for the death of ethnic Mexicans, visitors are not provided with a narrative that would raise alarm for the dead. To the contrary, visitors to the museum and to the website will not find a place to lament extralegal violence targeting ethnic Mexican residents.

The museum in Waco and its online supplement do not give visitors or readers an assessment of the racial conflict or how it influenced social relations throughout the twentieth century. There is no space to lament the loss of life or to question violence at the hands of police. None of the names of the lost are recorded. The role of Texas governors, adjutant generals, inspecting officers, and captains of the force in calling for and orchestrating violence is erased. Instead, the blame for a period of racial terror is placed on unnamed rogue officers without proper training but doing their best in the face of a racial threat. The museum's mission to "inspire appreciation" for the Texas Rangers as a "legendary symbol of Texas and the American West" demonstrates that the museum is more invested in maintaining the folk image and allure of the Texas Ranger.

The museum introduces iconic officers to new generations by continuing the educational traditions that began during the Texas Centennial of 1936.[52] Still today, children can become certified junior Texas Rangers. After paying a $35 donation to the museum and taking a pledge, the same pledge drafted in 1936, children can have their name added to the museum's database of state police and receive a certificate signed by an active-duty Texas Ranger. A toy badge and four museum tickets complete the package.[53]

The complementary website expands these efforts to reach new generations. It provides lesson plans for educators, such as the "Crime Scene in a Box," which allows students to solve a mock crime scene and encourages them to "delve into the exciting world of the modern Texas Ranger and crime lab technicians."[54] The museum encourages teachers to learn the history of the Texas Rangers by reading *The Texas Rangers* by Walter Prescott Webb and *Savage Frontier Volumes I, II, II* by Stephen L. Moore.[55] Despite scholarship published since the 1930s that has challenged Webb and others who represented the Texas Rangers as defeating "savage" Natives and "treacherous" Mexicans to ensure the future of the Anglo race on the frontier, the museum continues to encourage educators to consult this outdated material. In this the museum honors the requests of J. K. Beretta of the Texas Centennial Control Commission, and others, that we should all work to maintain the status of the state police as heroes. After visiting the museum, resident beliefs in the "Texas heroes as patriotic, loyal, and good citizens" are reinforced without complexity.[56] But even more alarming, such beliefs are not just left unchallenged at the museum; in addition, the museum displays racist representations of the past.

A 2014 public television short called "History of the Texas Rangers," produced by C-Span, shows the urgent need to reimagine the mission of the Texas Ranger museum and its role in shaping public history. Executive Director Byron Johnson and the museum's marketing and promotions coordinator Christine Rothenbush gave a short history of the Texas Rangers and a tour of the museum. This account furthers simplistic and outdated understandings of Texas's past. The show begins with Rothenbush explaining that the 200-year history of the Texas Rangers "upholding values of law and order and justice" originated in "innocent beginnings of [the Rangers] protecting their friends and their family members from Indian raids." Stephen F. Austin, she continues, settled the region now known as

Texas and gathered volunteers to protect the 300 Anglo colonizing families from Comanche raids. After the removal of Native Americans, she continues, the Indian threat subsided and the Rangers went on to become an official state police force following the Civil War. She then swiftly changes the topic to describe state police duties in the early twentieth century. According to this account, protecting oil fields and being active during the Prohibition Era preoccupied state police responsibilities. Although brief, this reference provided the only quick mention of the Texas Rangers on the border. "Unfortunately, Texas borders Mexico," Rothenbush quips, "and Mexico has a lot of tequila [laughs], so the Rangers started acting as a border security, which is something they do today. Of course, it's not tequila, it's narcotics and other things they are working to protect Texans from. So, evolution really took place as the times and the era they were living in changed." Just as casually as Rothenbush dismissed the violence of Native American displacement, she erased the anti-Mexican violence at the hands of Rangers throughout the nineteenth and early twentieth century. She also marked the Texas–Mexico border as a site in need of ongoing policing.[57]

The oversight of the history of racial violence at the hands of the state police is all the more puzzling given the opening images that greet the viewer. Rothenbush's narrative begins with her voice overlaying a photograph of the Texas Ranger Hall of Fame and Museum, followed by the infamous Robert Runyon photograph that shows Texas Ranger captains Henry Ransom, James Monroe Fox, and ranch foreman Tom Tate mounted on horseback holding ropes tied to Jesús García, Mauricio García, Amado Muñoz, and Muñoz's brother. The dead bodies have been cropped from this use of the photograph, a literal example of the museum's selective view of history. But for those who are familiar with the image, this is a haunting opening. The use of this photograph, in fact, led me to believe that the museum would finally account for the history of Ranger violence. Instead, this violence continues to be disavowed by museum directors. The decision to include the photograph, without reference to the historical context and its significance in shaping racial divides in Texas, is another example of the long tradition of trivializing Mexican death at the hands of state police.

The mission and the strategies of the museum need serious reconsideration. Well into the twenty-first century, there should be no room for public cultural institutions, with the power to shape public understanding, to continue promoting histories that apologize for, erase, or celebrate violence. This is especially the case when the institution is paid for, in part, with taxpayer dollars and endorsed by the Texas Department of Public Safety, the Texas Legislature, the City of Waco, and the Texas Ranger Commemorative Commission. The people and city of Waco alone have donated more than $6 million to the museum since 1968.[58]

VERNACULAR PRIDE

The making of history happens in local communities, too, by residents who display their patriotism and local claims to belonging with vernacular history-making efforts. In rural areas in particular, homemade memorials and exhibits play important roles in shaping public relationships to the past. Tammy Gordon suggests that "the creators and users of these displays see these exhibitions as ways of bringing individuals together around ideas about the past."[59] They prescribe versions of history and create boundaries of belonging. Curators and coordinators express their personal views in informal settings such as restaurants, churches, beauty parlors and schools. These displays provide a medium for people to make their understanding of history public.

Dairy Queen is a chain of soft serve ice cream and fast food restaurants that is a subsidiary of Berkshire Hathaway. Since 1940 over 5,000 Dairy Queens have opened around the globe. Texans are the reigning customers, as the state houses the largest number of Dairy Queens in the nation. To entice patrons, the chain offers menus that are regionally specific. For example, in south Texas, restaurants offer fast food versions of local staples. Texas menus include chicken-fried steak finger baskets with fries, Texas toast, and creamy white gravy; Jalitos, fried strips of mild jalapeños served with ranch dressing; and three crispy beef tacos called Texas T-Brand Tacos with sliced pickled jalapeños on the side. In Uvalde, patrons can order weekly specials of taco salads and enchiladas, and in Victoria the Dairy Queen offers chili-smothered beef burritos. Historian Vicki Ruiz writes that racial and ethnic foodscapes are "markers of belonging and difference set within a larger frame of US inequality." She continues, "If food constitutes an 'ethnic borderland,' then in what ways are the boundaries permeable or fluid? Or to restate an earlier, perhaps more rhetorical question: Do foodways bring people together or serve as a signifier of otherness?"[60] Although the ethnic food options on the menus might at first glance signal an embrace of Mexican or Mexican American culture, in Sabinal the local decor, casually displaying the history of racial violence, interrupts any illusions about cultural and social integration in south Texas. Appropriating and enjoying Mexican food while holding anti-Mexican sentiments is a contradictory mixture all too common in the American Southwest.

In rural communities where restaurants provide some of the only communal spaces, owners give franchises a community flare by decorating their walls with the public school colors and mascots. Whataburgers, Dairy Queens, and Burger Kings seemingly become extensions of the city chamber of commerce or the local historical society by helping exude town pride through historical exhibits. Owners sponsor little league teams, support community events, and hang framed pictures of championship teams on their walls; the players sit and stand in two rows holding bats and gloves or soccer balls. Like the multicultural menu, the public displays create the appearance of community inclusion and unity. Instead of little league baseball players, though, the walls in the Sabinal Dairy Queen are decorated with group photographs of a team of another sort. In the late nineteenth and early twentieth century, Uvalde County hosted Company D's headquarters, and a number of local residents worked as Rangers. To reflect this local connection, photographs of Company D members are displayed throughout the restaurant.

During my initial visit to the Dairy Queen in Sabinal in 2009, the local ties to the history of Company D were memorialized on the walls. Instead of baseball teams, the Texas Rangers were displayed as the home team. For example, a photograph taken in the town of Realitos in 1887 showed Captain Frank Jones with his team of fourteen men; Rangers sit and stand in two rows posing with pistols and rifles in hand.[61] In total five photographs of the local company and two portraits of local Ranger captains from the late nineteenth century decorated the walls. Like restaurants that display photographs of local little league and high school teams, the exhibit displayed historic Rangers and created an atmosphere for patrons to celebrate the company as their own. Interspersed with these images were portraits of recent Texas Rangers, including Joaquin Jackson, John Aycock, Clete Buckaloo, and one group portrait of Texas Rangers of Company D wearing uniforms of starched white button-down dress shirts, Texas Ranger badges, ties, cowboy hats, boots, and khaki jeans. The attire today is more formal, but the staged photographs are still complete with Rangers holding their pistols in their belt holsters and rifles in hand.

The Dairy Queen exhibit also displayed memorabilia of another form that similarly celebrates local residents taking control of a dangerous Texas landscape. Scattered throughout the restaurant are photographs of residents displaying the enormous diamondback rattlesnakes that they have killed. One of the deadly venomous snakes, killed in December 2008 near Del Rio, measured just over seven feet long. In total, nine photographs showed men standing proudly, but visibly straining, to display the heavy carcasses that dangled from hooks and grabbers. The most prominent cluster of these images was displayed just feet away from the photograph series depicting a lynching.

Framed hunting photographs are common décor in the rural Southwest, and viewing these images alongside those of Texas Rangers and US servicemen contributes to an atmosphere of masculine pride and accomplishment in taming the landscape. The placement of lynching photographs, then, in close proximity signaled to the viewer that the photographs of vigilante violence are not mounted as a critical assessment of Texas's past. Instead, this exhibit suggested that there is an equal sense of pride in displaying the lynched body as there is in displaying the hunted rattlesnakes. Both represent the dominance of the Anglo male and celebrate his ability to kill. Indeed, these two kinds of visual images bear an awful kind of overlap. In analyzing lynching photographs, historian Amy Louise Wood observed, "The image of white men posed next to their black victims bears an uncanny resemblance to the familiar snapshot of a hunter with his prey."[62] At this Dairy Queen, the echoes of hunting imagery in lynching photographs are undeniable, as they sat on display in the same collection of memorabilia, on either side of the restaurant's exit.

Susan Sontag envisioned a world in which photographs of genocide would ensure "that the crimes they depict will continue to figure into people's consciousness." In south Texas, photographs of lynched bodies or piles of corpses have not been used to encourage a public consciousness of the evils of violence. To the contrary, photographs depicting mob violence continue to celebrate that violence in casual display.[63]

During my stop in 2009, I waited before leaving for an opportunity to talk to two young Mexican American women who worked behind the counter. I wondered what they thought of the photographs and if they knew anything about them. They said that they did not know much about the photographs. They did know, however, that they did not enjoy looking at or even being near them. While taking out the trash, one employee continued, she made it a point not to look at the graphic images, displayed above the trash can. Although they did not know if the photographs captured a local lynching, one employee explained that the images reminded her of the stories she heard growing up about lynchings in Sabinal of African American and Mexican men. To their knowledge, during their employment, no customers had protested the photographs. Although they did not know the origins of the lynching pictures, they both knew that Jim Ryan curated the exhibit. They gave his name and a customer gave directions to his home from the restaurant. "You can't miss it," one said, "It's the house with the Texas Ranger star and the big truck in the driveway."[64] The women described the former school superintendent as a regular, friendly customer. He would, they assured me, be happy to talk with anyone interested in local history or the Texas Rangers.[65]

They were right. Jim Ryan welcomed the opportunity to sit for an oral history. Ryan had dedicated his time over the course of decades to collecting and preserving the history of the Texas Rangers. His interest in publicizing Texas Ranger history had turned Ryan into an archivist, collector, curator, artist, and historian after he retired from his work as a school superintendent in the Sabinal public schools. He displayed his collection of objects with pride. He dedicated the large den in his home to an impressive personal archive of photographs, drawings, files, and Texas Ranger and Native American memorabilia. In fact, his collection spilled out into the living room and covered nearly every wall in the communal spaces of his home with photographs, drawings, or other collectibles. Saddles, headdresses, and period clothing were just the beginning.[66] One of Ryan's most impressive pieces was his collection of approximately 100 badges worn by now-retired Texas Rangers and local law enforcement officers. Ryan had turned his home into a private museum.

Ryan was a descendent of an early Texas Ranger in the area, Karl Ryan. In his opinion, all Texas residents owed their current freedoms to these early Rangers. To this end, in 1992 Ryan traveled to Austin to meet with the senior captain and chief of the Texas Rangers Maurice Cook with an idea to form a historical organization to publicize the history of the Rangers from 1874 to 1901. He became a member of the Texas Ranger Foundation and the Texas Ranger Association, and eventually became a director of the Texas Ranger Hall of Fame and Museum in Waco. To expand his impact he helped found the Badlands Texas Rangers, a living history reenactment group that put on public education events dressed in the attire of the Texas Rangers in the late nineteenth and early twentieth century.[67] Photographs of these reenactments can be seen through an online exhibit called "Frontier Battalion Texas Rangers Exhibit." Six men, including Jim Ryan, are shown dressed as Texas Rangers. Women and children also appeared in period clothing.[68]

County historical commissions support the reenactments. On July 9, 2011, members of the Frontier Battalion Texas Rangers organized a celebration of the history of the officers in the town of Goliad, who had patrolled the area from 1823 to the present day. Nearly 500 people gathered for the event. With support from the Goliad County Historical Commission, battalion members including Jim Ryan organized a display of Ranger pistols, Winchester and Remington rifles, handcuffs, leg irons from the 1870s and 1880s, objects from the Mexican Revolution, service items, photographs, and a selection of books. Texas Ranger Tony DeLuna made a special appearance at the event.

The group also taught a new generation about the contributions of the state police by making public appearances at Texas public schools. Ryan noted that he wanted new generations to recognize the role of the state police who lived on the Texas frontier and actively "protected settlers from bandits and marauding Indians," keeping the "peace in Texas while civilization sort of moved on."[69] The group walked into school gymnasiums packed with students, dressed in period clothing, and gave history presentations on the Texas Rangers that replicated simplistic racial narratives of brave Texas Rangers and threating Native Americans. These efforts were paused in the 1990s when state laws implemented zero-tolerance policies prohibiting guns and ammunition on school campuses. School administrators refused to allow the group to come onto campus with their Colt .44 revolvers. Believing the denial an insult to the legacy of the state police, the group refused to make appearances without their guns.[70]

To reach a wider audience, Ryan also embraced his creative license and started directing privately funded films. The Badlands Rangers performed in three films that chronicled the bravery and courage of early Texas

Rangers. Their movies, *Bass Outlaw, We Do Not Fight Draws,* and *Leander H. McNelly,* have been screened locally and sold in convenience stores, local shops, and at group reenactments in Sabinal and Uvalde.

The Badlands Texas Rangers have become a part of local Texas culture. They make appearances at local museums such as the Children's Discovery Museum in Crescent, at county fairs, and at community events like one called "Pioneer Days" in the south Texas town of Pearsall. The Badlands Rangers are also a regular highlight of the annual Wild Hog Festival in Sabinal that brings in statewide crowds. An online newspaper, the *Hill Country Herald,* distributed throughout Frio Canyon, Nueces Canyon, and Sabinal Canyon, wrote that the Badlands Texas Rangers' reenactments were "in all ways appropriate to represent the real men and circumstances they bring to life." The newspaper described the group as historically accurate. The performances, local journalists claimed, allowed spectators to celebrate "the legacy of men who stood, fought, and died . . . for us, and for this land." In addition, on promotional material the group states that they operate with approval from the Texas Ranger Hall of Fame and Museum in Waco and the Texas Department of Public Safety.[71]

This long tradition of celebrating policing without discussions of its consequences makes room for the casual display of photographs of lynchings. Ryan told me that customers frequently asked about the images of the lynchings in his exhibit. Primarily, they wanted to know if the lynchings happened locally. Ryan would explain that they were not local.[72]

Recognizing that this period caused many residents to fear the state police did not stop Ryan from including two photographs depicting violence. During our interview he revealed that the images on display at the Dairy Queen are not of an actual lynching in Texas but instead still images from a movie. The photos were displayed without any indication that they came from a movie. Unlike the other photographs that included printed captions, these were unlabeled. Their inclusion in an exhibit on the Texas Rangers and local history, combined with the lack of context, led customers to believe these were historical photographs.

The Dairy Queen exhibit raises concerns about shared histories of violence and individual efforts to glorify state police as the founders of national and regional security. In the exhibit, brutal violence was displayed as homage. The casual display of a lynching at once celebrates the violence, dehumanizes the dead, and disavows sentiments of loss for customers who lament histories of racial violence. The exhibit helps expose the tensions embedded in the way memories are framed and signals a need to confront long-standing frictions regarding the telling of history.

It would be easy to dismiss this exhibit as an outlier or the work of racist Texans in small rural towns. To the contrary, finding humor in extralegal violence is common throughout Texas. Patrons shopping at local boutiques selling Texas kitsch are greeted with celebrations of a long tradition of Texans using firearms to defend their property and businesses. For example, rusted iron signs featuring a revolver and the words "We Don't Dial 911" are popular. In fact, they are almost as common as decorations that celebrate Texas's independence from Mexico in 1836. As far as New Orleans, Louisiana, and Providence, Rhode Island, I have seen shopkeepers decorate their walls with posters that display a photograph of men waiting to be hanged accompanied by some variation of the same basic threat: that shoplifters will be prosecuted by the owner, not the police. The embrace of this frontier bravado is done without critical consideration for the racial minorities who are typically assumed to be the threat or for those whose lives became more vulnerable under the Texas state flag. In a climate in which histories of violence exacerbate unresolved racial tensions, vernacular exhibits by individuals, like the exhibit in Sabinal, further entrench social divisions.

Representations in the media, by historians, and by historical commissions that portrayed Native Americans as savages and ethnic Mexicans as bandits, criminals, and threats to Anglo society established the roots of a narrative that have been difficult to dislodge. Walter Prescott Webb created a historical narrative in 1935 that helped to exalt the Texas Rangers to mythic proportions. This representation became cemented in Texas public history by the Texas Centennial celebrations, films, music, and the Texas Historical Commission. I keep wondering, if the University of Texas Press published a new edition of *The Texas Rangers* in 1965 with Webb's revisions, would it have inspired public representations of Texas history that confronted state violence?

In the end, if Webb had revised the book, at the very least removing the inflammatory racist descriptions, it would not have changed the scope and interpretation of Ranger actions. What we do know is that despite academic publications, new and old, that have dismissed racist celebrations of violence, the Texas Ranger Hall of Fame and Museum in Waco continues to mimic outdated narratives in their celebrations of Texas heroes. The museum continues to encourage visitors and teachers to read outdated books, like *The Texas Rangers*. Jim Ryan's exhibit subsumed the violent history of the force within celebratory tales of its valor, courage, and dedication to protecting Anglo settlers in the face of perceived danger. The perspective espoused in the Dairy Queen is sanctioned not only by a long tradition of Western history that celebrated the Texas Rangers but also by state-sponsored historical organizations. However, this is symptomatic of a broader failure to grapple with the violent histories of conquest, slavery, and colonization that converge in the state. The contemporary disavowal of the long legacy of violence from this period continues to close off the possibility of critiques of the nation-state for past and ongoing crimes, which are erased in the name of protecting citizens of the state. The continued use of these limited perspectives has serious consequences. They continue to give credence to outdated and distorted depictions of histories of racial violence. By maintaining these narratives, the conditions are created so that residents literally stumble into depictions of racial violence in the most mundane places.

Reckoning with Violence

FROM THE SUMMER of 2012 until the summer of 2014 I lived in Austin and worked at the University of Texas at Austin as a postdoctoral fellow in the Center for Mexican American Studies (CMAS). I remember walking into the reception office for the first time and seeing a framed photograph on the wall of Américo Paredes, smiling, holding his guitar. This was the center that Paredes built while he taught at the university. In this center, and in Mexican American studies classes across the campus, he loomed large.

I also frequently bumped into the legacy of Walter Prescott Webb. Every day that I drove to campus I parked my car in a garage on San Antonio Street and made the long walk to my office at CMAS. I walked passed Walter Webb Hall, a building adjacent to the parking garage. In the spring of 2013, I gave a talk in the Walter Prescott Webb lecture room. I spoke about the Porvenir massacre with the portrait of Webb looking back at me. When the chair of the history department invited me to give the lecture, I noticed in the e-mail signature that the endowed faculty position was named in honor of Walter Prescott Webb.

Walking around campus in the Texas heat, I occasionally wondered what interactions that Paredes and Webb might have had in Austin. On at least one occasion Paredes was aware that Webb could possibly undermine his career. In 1957 Paredes become frustrated with an editor at the University of Texas Press, Frank H. Wardlaw. Considering *"With His Pistol in His Hand"* for publication, Wardlaw sent the manuscript to Walter Prescott Webb, then, chair of the press's advisory board, to assess the work. Paredes wrote in a letter to Wardlaw on February 21, 1957, that if he had known Webb was on the board, he would not have sent his manuscript for consideration. "Though I have not for a moment doubted his impartiality in judging what I have written, I do think I should not have put Dr. Webb in the position of passing on something that attacks his own work. There is no personal ill-will on my part towards Dr. Webb, of course. But I do feel that his work deserves rather strong criticism." Paredes was concerned that the recommendations by a biased board would defeat his purpose in writing the book. "I would rather not water it down," he explained, "I doubt I could revise the manuscript so that the faculty advisory board could accept it for publication."[1]

Wardlaw quickly responded pleading with Paredes to consider submitting a revised manuscript to the press. He assured Paredes that "although [Webb] ruefully finds himself the villain of the piece at several points," he recognized that the contribution was long overdue. Of Webb, Wardlaw wrote, "He said that he has always considered it a weakness of his book on the Texas Rangers that he was unable to give the Mexican attitude toward the Rangers, and their side of the border conflict, with any degree of thoroughness. He says he made an effort to get this material but was unable to do so largely because of the language barrier."[2]

Paredes would go on to make select revisions, and the university press would publish the book in 1958. The keepers of history opened the door that year, ever so slightly. More than half a century later, residents and scholars are trying to push it wide open.

On Thursday January 21, 2016, the Bob Bullock Texas State History Museum opened its doors to visitors attending a symposium for the exhibit *Life and Death on the Border, 1910–1920*. The flagship state history museum was literally too small to contain the public enthusiasm for the exhibit. Online registration for the event reached capacity within days of being announced. Over 200 people reserved seats and more e-mailed and called with requests for a spot on the waiting list. As word spread, the demand for seats increased. Guests who already had tickets e-mailed with requests to add two more or five more to their group. Even elected officials had to be squeezed onto the list. To meet the demands the Bullock staff coordinated a second faculty panel on Saturday, January 23, the same day the exhibit opened to the public.

Crowds were eager to see the exhibit not because they wanted to consume curated history, to see a collection of objects, or to learn a history they did not know. They came because they did know, because they had heard these stories from their fathers or their grandmothers. They came to witness a history long disavowed now on display in a state museum. People lined up at the Bullock because they had waited for over a century for the cultural institutions of Texas to officially recognize the role of the state police and politicians in enacting a reign of terror so devastating that the effects would reverberate for generations. They came to bear witness to that first public reckoning.

Many of those visitors were descendants of victims of racial violence. For over a century their relatives had been portrayed as bandits and threats to the nation. The memories they kept, the artifacts they protected, and their efforts to tell an alternative history made the exhibit possible. A history they helped preserve would finally be on display in a state museum. This was a historic moment for the making of public history, an important step in reckoning with histories of racial violence.

Some of the visitors also came to the symposium with skepticism and doubt. For over a century, state institutions had kept racial violence from public view or, worse, had celebrated periods of genocide, slavery, and extralegal violence as necessary steps toward modernity. Carved in the pink granite exterior, the Bullock museum façade welcomes visitors to explore "The Story of Texas," a singular official account of Texas's past. Visitors wondered, would the state museum finally tell a history that recognized crimes against humanity? Would the Bullock finally lament the dead?

Meeting official histories with a healthy dose of skepticism is a widespread practice for racial minorities and marginalized groups in Texas. Chicana cultural theorist Rosa Linda Fregoso described learning to question Texas history when she was young. She remembered that in her eighth-grade Texas history course, the instructor gave "heart-wrenching" lectures on Anglo–Mexican struggles for Texas's independence and juxtaposed Anglos portrayed as "noble" with Mexicans described as "villainous." While Fregoso learned at school about "the cruel streak in Mexican nature," at home her father gave her an informal education in vernacular history and introduced her to alternative accounts of the past. In her analysis of Pilar Cruz, the leading Tejana character in the film *Lonestar*, Fregoso writes that the character's countermemory of Tejas put her "in touch with a long tradition of opposition to racist discourse, with popular forms of knowledge, transgressive tales of resistance, subaltern practices of suspicion of official versions of history."[3] The museum exhibit would have to contend with the deep-seated suspicion that many visitors, like Fregoso, had learned from an early age.

The centennial of the peak anti-Mexican violence in 1915 provided an opportunity to insist that Texas cultural institutions finally acknowledge the dozens of new histories, literary works, and cultural criticisms that had dispelled the myth of the Texas Rangers. To be sure, shifting pervasive representations of the past would be impossible if state institutions did not participate. In the twenty-first century, public history became the terrain for efforts by scholars and residents alike to shift public understandings of histories of racial violence in Texas.

MEMORIALIZING VICTIMS OF STATE VIOLENCE

Residents who practice vernacular history-making have been calling for a public reckoning and a public dialogue about Texas's violent past. Their efforts confront public histories, like those at the Texas Ranger History Museum and Hall of Fame, that disavow state-sanctioned violence in the early twentieth century. In doing so, they continue the practice of what Américo Paredes described as "anamnesis," a praxis against forgetting.

After decades of researching these histories, many residents are increasingly impatient with the slow efforts by state institutions to encourage a new public understanding of the past. The Internet has enabled some people to avoid the usual mechanisms of state bureaucracy and make these histories public on their own. One is the website Los Tejanos, created by Hernán Contreras, a resident of Houston. By treating his family history as a window into Texas history, Contreras bypasses official venues for history-making and, instead, makes vernacular histories of racial violence accessible to the public. The website functions as a repository for primary sources, including letters, photographs, wills, court documents, certificates, land titles, maps, and journals. The site also records humorous stories of the region and preserves vernacular culture. One webpage shows a family tree that traces Contreras's family back to the Nuevo Santander settlement in Texas in 1748. The tree helps to reinforce the family roots in Texas and visualizes the long dedication by relatives to preserving records of the family. Although the website offers information primarily about Contreras's family, he encourages others to create their own family archives. He invites his visitors to stake their claim.[4]

In addition to documenting family histories, Contreras titled one section of the website "Essays." It includes the writings of his cousins Norma Longoria Rodriguez and Irma Longoria Cavazos as well as four essays written by Contreras himself. Although most genealogical groups in Texas celebrate pioneering men, Contreras's website also highlights the women in his family.[5] One of these essays, "Hispanic Women of the Mexican-American Frontier," describes women as "highly assertive and politically active" in shaping the history of the region.[6]

While situating the family as a part of the Spanish colonial past, the website departs from other regional history sites to include the history of racial violence. Alongside documents and essays that illustrate his family's long history in Texas are histories of racial violence suffered by his family. In the section titled "Reign of Terror," Contreras writes, "Tejano settlers in South Texas suffered unprecedented violence during the Border Wars (1910–1919) that went far beyond the violence of a frontier life. The Hispanic settler not only had to contend with bandits, rustlers, smugglers, gun runners but with Texas Rangers who indiscriminately killed thousands with impunity making this era truly a reign of terror." Contreras includes the Texas Rangers, naming specific agents, in his list of threats to local residents. Contreras's depiction of the era contrasts with the representation put forth by the Texas Ranger Hall of Fame and Museum which titles this period the "Bandit Wars." While the museum in Waco points to Mexican Revolutionaries and bandits as the cause of social turmoil in this period, Contreras highlights the Texas Rangers' practices of racial terror.

On this portion of the site, viewers see photographs from the Robert Runyon collection of Texas Rangers dragging the bodies of ethnic Mexican men following the raid on the Las Norias Ranch in October 1915.

Contreras included four images from the series. The photographs are accompanied by a paragraph that estimates that Rangers and vigilantes murdered 5,000 ethnic Mexicans. He also acknowledges the attempts of Representative José T. Canales to reform the force through the 1919 investigation. The photograph of Texas Rangers dragging Mexican corpses, coupled with the staggering number of victims, helps the viewer to imagine the atrocity of the crime. It puts forward an alternative interpretation of the Texas Rangers.[7]

To help preserve the names of some of the victims, Contreras includes a section dedicated to the case of Jesus Bazán and Antonio Longoria, murdered in September 1915. The page acts as a memorial for the deceased, includes a photograph of Antonio Longoria, and provides a short description of the double murder. It also includes histories written by Norma Longoria Rodriguez and her reflections on the impact of the double murder on generations of descendants. In addition, viewers can read transcripts in both Spanish and English of the interviews she conducted with her relatives who witnessed the events, as well as her essays on the life of her grandmother, who survived the incident. This page pays particular attention to naming the victims in this case and to recounting the long contributions of their families to south Texas communities.[8]

In a state with deeply entrenched narratives of progress, public spaces that allow residents to learn about and mourn racial violence remain scarce. Thus, the Internet is particularly important in allowing people to lament the dead and circulate these histories. Los Tejanos itself serves as an avenue to publish writings of the vernacular history makers. It provides a digital public record of the memories residents preserved for over 100 years. After being published on Los Tejanos, Rodriguez's essay, "Silence of the Heart," also received circulation through the website Somos Primos, which eventually was transmitted on an e-mail Listserv called Historia, facilitated by history professor Roberto Calderon from the University of North Texas at Dallas. The wider circulation of the essays supports Contreras's primary goal: to create broad access to these alternative histories. Los Tejanos, a digital lament, provides an important public space to record and memorialize the history of racial violence in Texas.

Sharing vernacular histories on the Internet allows for residents researching their family histories to connect online. Texas residents have located other descendants of murdered victims on the Internet and are attentive to historical accounts of the period in Wikipedia entries. Benita and Evaristo Albarado, for example, frequently monitor both Wikipedia and blog entries on the Porvenir massacre of 1918. In addition to learning how to conduct historical research and how to navigate institutional archives, they acquired digital skills. Buddy Albarado maintains a blog, *Porvenir Massacre, 1918.* In April 2009 he, with the help of his grandson Joe Leal, published their first post, a historical narrative of the massacre; the entry begins, "Did you know the Texas Rangers massacred 15 Mexican people in Texas in 1918?"

On October 1, 2011, Leal added an online memorial, a photograph of Juan Flores while accompanying his children and grandchildren to the site of the massacre. He stands against the backdrop of the west Texas terrain. The caption reads, "Juan Bonilla Florez, son of Longino Florez who was murdered at El Porvenir Ranch. Juan Florez witnessed the brutal murder of his father, and fourteen other men and boys in 1918 when he was 11 years old. Here in this photograph he is showing his daughter and son, where it happened."

On September 1, 2015, Joe Leal added an updated description of the massacre from Wikipedia and a political cartoon by Frederick B. Opper. The cartoon shows Lady Justice slumped in a chair, with her feet up on a desk, asleep. A mouse pulls at the hem of her dress, spiders have attached cobwebs to her crown with the inscription "JUSTICE," and the scales of justice are strewn on the floor. Outside the window of the room where justice has fallen asleep, a posse of snarling men with pistols have removed a prisoner from a jail and prepared a noose for a lynching. One man carries a flag that states, "Lively Lynchers." The caption for the cartoon reads, "Justice Out of a Job. Every Man His Own Lynch-Lawyer in the South and West." The cartoon was originally published in *Puck* magazine on July 4, 1883. The Albarados found a copy of the cartoon during a research trip to the Marfa public library. The depiction of sleeping justice reflected their sentiments that innocent lives were taken in plain sight. Justice, in the form of judicial recourse, had never been served for the victims or the survivors of the massacre.[9]

Glenn Justice, a regional historian and the managing editor for Rimrock Press, also took to the web and created a blog that focuses on west Texas history. He started his online forum "as an open effort to discuss Texas history in general outside the usual trappings and agendas of the academic world."[10] His historical entries invited residents to participate in history-making by posting their own histories. He also encouraged visitors to ask research questions to stimulate online discussion.

On February 2, 2007, Justice's post on the Porvenir massacre of 1918 caught the attention of local residents whose relatives were victims of the attack by the Texas Rangers. On March 21, 2007, Alexa Nieves Saucedo thanked Justice for his account of the massacre, because she had been independently researching the event for her family. Likewise, a few weeks later on April 1, Manuel Casas explained that his father had been born in Porvenir in 1924 and that some of his "kinfolks" were members of the Herrera and Flores family, victims of the massacre. These visitors to the site expressed enthusiasm at finding the online post as it helped their own efforts to research their family histories.

In 2008 Domingo Garcia Cano delivered the exchange the historian had hoped for. Rather than mere thanks or critique, Cano added to the account Justice published online.[11] Domingo Garcia Cano's comment, which exceeded Justice's original post in length, noted on the site that his great-grandfather, Chico Cano, was the man the Texas Rangers were supposedly searching for when they killed fifteen men at Porvenir. Cano described his relative as a participant in the Mexican Revolution who, like Emiliano Zapata and Pancho Villa, developed a reputation among the residents of the border region as a Mexican Robin Hood. The entry chronicled Cano's participation in the revolution as well as his efforts to defend and protect families living in Texas from vigilante attacks. The commenter gave a personal account of a man labeled a bandit by historians ranging from Walter Prescott Webb to Glenn Justice himself. He also eulogized his great-grandfather, who avoided execution and died in 1943 of natural causes. He wrote, "When he was elderly and on his deathbed, Cano was asked if he was afraid to meet his maker. He said, 'My father was my maker. Poverty was my maker. Distrust was my maker. I have met them all in my life.'" Like many of the comments on Glenn Justice's blog, Cano encouraged readers to continue researching and suggested a published family history on the life of his relative. The book *Bandido: The True Story of Chico Cano, the Last Western Bandit,* by descendant Tony Cano and Anne Sochat, he explained, offered an alternative account of Cano's long life in the borderlands.[12]

Justice's blog post and the comments that followed give just one example of a network of residents who have independently researched this period of racial violence and show how they have recently used the Internet to share their findings. For residents like Saucedo, researching the Porvenir massacre provided the opportunity to answer family questions about their past. For others like Glenn Justice, it helped satiate an interest in Texas history. For Cano, researching and participating in the online dialogue provided an opportunity to recharacterize his great-grandfather and complicate the "bandit" label from his family name.

These independent efforts, taken up in people's spare time, between work and family obligations, have become important venues for speaking back to the silences or disavowals in mainstream histories. And yet these vernacular histories of racial violence have to contend with a century of myth-making by historians, state history, and popular culture. Moreover, websites like Los Tejanos also compete with vernacular exhibits by residents who idolize the Texas Rangers, like the photographic display in the Sabinal Dairy Queen. As long as outdated celebratory representations of the past are bolstered by state cultural institutions, change will be slow in coming. State institutions that look to be leaders in critically reflecting on histories of racial violence would be well served by looking to vernacular history-making efforts that continually challenge mainstream accounts. There are untapped opportunities for collaboration in reckoning with histories of violence. If historians, state institutions, and vernacular history makers joined together to present a flawed narrative of Texas history, those who want to change the narrative will have to join together as well.

NEW MARKERS AND EXHIBITIONS

On February 23, 2013, as the centennial of the peak of anti-Mexican violence neared, a group of professors gathered at the National Association for Chicana and Chicano Studies' Tejas Foco annual conference in San Antonio. Under the name "Refusing to Forget," the group planned a commemoration. Professors John Morán González, Trinidad Gonzales, Sonia Hernández, Benjamin Johnson, and I came together to coordinate a series of events to foster a public dialogue on the lasting consequences of the long history of anti-Mexican violence in Texas. We each had published books or articles on this period of violence, but we were also aware that academic publications had done little to create a lasting dialogue or shift in public perception of the past. Lesson plans had not been updated, and cultural institutions in Texas had not revised their accounts to reflect advances in the field of US history. Reshaping the common understanding of Texas's past required working beyond the academy. We planned a multifaceted effort including an exhibit, some form of monument or historical marker, and lesson plans for K–12 classrooms. We hoped that with this multipronged approach we could reach a wide audience and make a lasting change to public history.[13] Why couldn't we unsettle state power over the narrative?[14]

Developing the agenda would have been impossible without input from residents who had been working to memorialize this history for years. On the day of our first meeting, Benita and Evaristo Albarado joined the group to discuss their efforts to memorialize the Porvenir massacre. The couple told the history of the massacre and, in typical fashion, brought copies of documents to share with the group. But they also asked questions. They wanted to know why we were working on the project, what goals we had, and our strategies.

When we shared ideas for an exhibit and a monument, the Albarados asked an important question. They wanted to know how the state was going to participate in the memorialization efforts. For them, books, exhibits, and monuments would not change public understandings if state institutions did not participate in the memorialization efforts. They were right. They had attended the screenings of *Border Bandits,* the memorial for Antonio Rodríguez in Rocksprings, and the book talks by Linda Davis. Working on the margins had been invaluable for preserving, lamenting, and commemorating these histories, but vernacular histories had made little progress in getting state institutions to teach these histories to the public. If state institutions continued to disavow histories of racial violence, how could broader publics come to relearn the history? Without state participation, the memorialization efforts risked allowing the state to maintain outdated narratives.

We agreed: even as professors—privileged with doctorates, university affiliations, and publications—we had some doubts we could find collaborators on the state level. We decided that by applying for Texas State historical markers through its Undertold History program, we could urge the Texas Historical Commission (THC) to memorialize state-sanctioned racial violence. Approved historical markers would help shift the public history landscape in south Texas. In the summer of 2014 we submitted five applications for historical markers to commemorate the lynching of Antonio Rodríguez in Edwards County, the double murder of Antonio

Longoria and Jesus Bazán in Hidalgo County, the civil rights efforts of Jovita Idar in Webb County, and the Porvenir massacre in Presidio County in 1918. In addition to these watershed historical events, we also submitted an application to commemorate *la matanza,* the peak of violence in Cameron County in 1915. The marker application described the period of terror as it was commonly referred to by local residents but also made a call for a marker that acknowledged the dead whose names had yet to be recovered.

In 2014 the THC approved the applications to commemorate *la matanza* in Cameron County and for Jovita Idar in Webb County. Prior to this, we had had high hopes that the marker application for Jovita Idar would be accepted. After all, she was a civil rights icon. It would be easier to celebrate an overlooked hero than to confront the state violence she criticized. The approval of the marker to commemorate *la matanza,* in contrast, revealed that the THC was genuinely interested in confronting controversial histories of violence. And yet, three of the marker applications, each with deeply researched narratives, had been rejected. The following year, the committee approved the application for the Porvenir massacre. Finally, in 2016, after the third Undertold Marker application and separate efforts by the Hidalgo County Historical Commission, the THC approved a historical marker for the double murder in Hidalgo County. As we saw earlier, the marker for the Rocksprings lynching was rejected three years in a row. Although the committee agreed that the event was historically significant and the most well-documented case of a mob lynching of an ethnic Mexican, without local support the committee decided not to approve the application.

The planning for these marker unveilings revealed that working with understaffed state institutions could also be painfully slow. As of the summer of 2017, the four approved historical markers were still in various stages of completion, but none had been unveiled. But the acceptance of four historical markers did signal a willingness by some branches of Texas public history to include histories of racial violence as significant and deserving of state memorialization. There continue to be real possibilities for changing public history at a local level. And our effort showed that academic historians are learning, with the help of community members, what it takes to change the popular historical narrative.

Finding a museum to host an exhibit also took a series of attempts. After months of correspondence with other cultural institutions and receiving polite declines, we found a collaborative spirit at the Bob Bullock Texas State History Museum. Margaret Koch, at the time the deputy director of exhibitions, agreed to meet with team members to discuss our idea for a temporary exhibit. As far as Koch and her staff could remember, we were the first group of professors to pitch a project at the Bullock. The museum regularly called on scholars to serve as consultants, but the staff generated the ideas for special exhibits and scheduled them out three years in advance. This collaboration would break the museum's mold.[15]

For most historians, the Bullock mold needed to be remade. When the museum opened in 2001, it received woeful reviews from Texas historians. Walter Buenger, for example, wrote, "As I left the museum after that first visit I pondered how it does and does not reflect the historiographic trends of the past fifty years. Creators of the museum carefully included prominent Tejanos, blacks, and women. Yet their approach to the Texas past is just as much from the top down and just as simplistic and celebratory as fifty years ago. The consensus approach looks different on the surface today because it includes minorities and women, but in key areas it remains the same. Over time everything grew bigger and better. Texans increasingly lived happily together."[16] The museum had smoothed over histories of violent and racial conflict and resuscitated an entertaining multicultural brand of history, a history for consumption but not critical thought.

In his review, Buenger raised alarm for the audiences that would move through the museum: "They want to sell tickets instead of challenging the public to think about the past . . . and so we should expect what we get from the Texas State History Museum. . . . To say that this was all we can expect does not minimize the potential impact of the museum."[17] Since the opening of the Bullock, its impact has been far-reaching. As of 2017, nearly eight million visitors learned Texas history by visiting the museum, and a great portion of them were schoolchildren. In 2016 alone, 600,000 people visited the museum, of whom nearly 90,000 were students, teachers, and chaperones.[18]

In 2013 and 2014, I took students in my courses to the museum for lessons on the politics of public memory. After a semester of reading histories of the US–Mexico War in 1848, of racial violence in Texas, and of civil rights movements throughout the twentieth century, we marched across campus to the museum. There we closely examined exhibit labels. Students located historical silences, erasures, and euphemisms. After discussing the exhibits, they reflected on the power of cultural institutions to shape generations of opinions about the past. While we were visiting the museum, we all noticed school buses of younger children on field trips to the Bullock for educational programming.

Thankfully, the museum audiences that visited in 2016 explored a museum that was shifting in its public interpretations of the past. In 2014, with the fifteen-year anniversary of the museum in sight, the Bullock staff planned a Texas Social Justice Series, which aimed to explore race, ethnicity, class, and gender throughout Texas history. The museum hoped to revise portions of its permanent exhibitions and host temporary exhibits to reflect the diversity of the state in its historical narratives. This concerted effort would address the visible gaps noticed since the museum opened in 2001.

I saw firsthand the potential of these efforts. In June 2014 I participated in a kickoff event for the series. I joined a panel of scholars for a discussion on the topic "The KKK in Texas: Ongoing Legacies." The event was inspired when a Texas resident lent a new object to the museum—a Ku Klux Klan grand dragon robe. The family had found the bright orange robe, complete with hood and cape, in the attic of a family member when they passed away. With intricately stitched embellishments (a black dragon and the letters G. D. Texas stitched on the chest and on the hood, red triangles along the hem, and black trim), the robe had been made with great care and attention. Recognizing the significance of the artifact, the family wanted to preserve the robe but did not want to keep it in their home. They wanted to donate it anonymously to a Texas institution. Although the Bullock is not a collecting museum, the staff decided to seize the opportunity and confront the history of racism and white supremacy in the state. They wanted to display the robe in the museum's permanent exhibit as a way to start a public dialogue.

The robe, as one would assume, came with its own set of challenges. To display this object required a considerable amount of historical context. How could the museum prevent the display from being misinterpreted as a veneration of the Ku Klux Klan? How could curators accurately portray the social, economic, and political influence of the white supremacist organization in Texas? The museum features three floors of galleries and displays a history spanning 13,000 years. Unfortunately, at the time of the donation, the galleries did little to display the violent histories of conquest, colonization, slavery, and segregation in the state or the state's long-standing ties with white supremacy. Under the leadership of museum director Dr. Victoria Ramirez, the staff decided to revise the permanent exhibit to explicitly address the pervasive history of racial violence in the twentieth century. The staff would not be able to display the robe in the public exhibits until those revisions were complete. They planned a public symposium on the history of the Ku Klux Klan in Texas as educational programming would be vital in contextualizing the robe.

The museum staff decided to display the robe, for one evening, at the June symposium in the second-floor lobby right outside the theater. As visitors arrived they were confronted with the illuminated orange robe. The intimidating object was striking. As I reached the top step of the grand marble staircase, it took my breath away. As I waited for guests to arrive, I lingered to listen. The crowd that gathered whispered about the bright orange color and the intricate stitch work. Most described the display as chilling or frightening. Others wondered what crimes the owner of the robe committed and why the family decided to remain anonymous. Had the donors been proud, ambivalent, or ashamed of their family leadership in the Ku Klux Klan? Were the donors coming to the event? Some broke the tension by making jokes about the height of the person who had worn the robe; the white supremacist who hid behind these pieces of fabric, the highest-ranking official of the Ku Klux Klan in Texas, was short, really short.[19]

The staff and the scholars were nervous at the start of the panel. Nobody was sure who would arrive or what their views on or their relationship to the Ku Klux Klan would be, but visitors filled the auditorium. After the panelists gave five-minute presentations on the history of vigilantism, white supremacy, and the Ku Klux Klan in Texas—a painfully short amount of time for professors—we turned to the audience for questions.

No one asked about the history of the Ku Klux Klan. Instead, the audience was interested in the present; they wanted to discuss strategies for ending racism, vigilantism, and police violence. They also expressed concern at the rising number of hate groups in Texas. I had anticipated that the audience would have questions about historical events or, worse, doubt

our claims. I had prepared copious notes, statistics, and talking points specifically for the question and answer session. But I had misjudged the Texas
audience. The questions about the present were refreshing but far more
challenging. Reflecting later, I realized that I should have been prepared
to cite the number of Ku Klux Klan chapters in both the early twentieth
century and the early twenty-first century.[20]

At the close of the panel, visitors and panelists funneled out of the theater to the lobby, where the museum sponsored a short reception. The robe
had been removed, the staff having decided that the lasting image from
this event should not be the haunting sight. Instead, visitors mingled, eating
and discussing ongoing racism in the state. Visitors left the event, walking
down the grand marble spiral staircase at the Bullock, having participated
in a discussion about racism not only as a thing of the past. In this event, a
robe had opened the door for a much-needed public dialogue facilitated by a
state museum. It signaled the possibilities for the Bullock to create a space for
conversations, informed by historical context, about ongoing social needs.

On July 25, 2014, the Refusing to Forget team met with the Bullock
team: Margaret Koch, Kate Betz, Toni Beldock, Jenny Cobb, James
McReynolds, and Tom Wancho. In advance of the meeting the professors
had drafted an exhibit proposal and outline for the exhibit script to share
with the staff. In a Bullock conference room, we gathered around a beautiful wood table, professors on one side and staff on the other. The group
drafted a mission statement, reviewed the proposal and exhibit outline,
agreed on the title *Life and Death on the Border, 1910–1920,* and planned
for a potential opening in January 2016. One e-mail, phone call, and conference call at a time, the project gradually came together.

A year later, on July 23, 2015, team members gathered again at the
Bullock museum for a second onsite exhibition meeting. By this time the
Refusing to Forget team had provided comments on a series of drafts of
the exhibition script, but we needed to do more to help the staff locate
artifacts in private collections to complete the exhibit. The same challenges,
gaps, and omissions in state archives that make it difficult for historians to
write about this history make it equally challenging for curators who rely
on the same institutions for their exhibitions. Texas cultural institutions
had Ranger memorabilia, guns and jackets, and artifacts from the Mexican Revolution, such as Pancho Villa's saddle. These objects, the museum

Pancho Villa saddles, circa 1915, on display at the Bullock museum exhibit *Life and Death on the Border, 1910–1920*. Although Pancho Villa did not spend a significant amount of time in Texas during the Mexican Revolution, the saddles drew a wide audience. A wall-length detail of a Robert Runyon photograph shows Texas Rangers on horseback with ropes tied to the bodies of dead Mexican men. The staff removed the bodies from this detail and instead focused on the agents. Photograph provided by the Bullock Texas State History Museum.

assured us, would help bring visitors to the exhibit. Objects like the saddle were breathtaking indeed. Pancho Villa commissioned a saddle that would catch the light and shimmer for the cameras of Hollywood's Mutual Film Company, which filmed him in battle.[21] It was embellished with silver thread and had a saddle horn made of silver with replicas of dogs on the sides complete with ruby eyes. Villa was famed for raiding towns in New Mexico and crossing into Arizona. He had not, however, spent significant time in Texas. The saddle was indeed impressive, but we were worried it would be distracting. The Texas Ranger memorabilia, too, risked visitors focusing their attention on the dress and the guns of the state police rather than the acts they committed.

Private archives became invaluable for ensuring that the exhibit made room to display personal artifacts that gestured to the gravity of human loss. I showed the Bullock curator, Jenny Cobb, photographs of some of the private artifacts I had studied in the homes of Benita and Evaristo Albarado and Norma Longoria Rodriguez. Cobb immediately recognized their value. She coordinated visits to the Albarado and Rodriguez homes and secured permission to transport and display the objects. These were the objects that would make it possible to tell a new version of Texas history, one that introduced visitors to the names and faces of victims and families impacted by state violence. Displaying the objects also provided an opportunity to showcase the efforts of local residents to preserve their own histories. The photographs, documents, books, and portraits the families lent to the Bullock were protected as invaluable objects alongside the Villa saddle and the Ranger memorabilia.

The resulting exhibit consisted of three sections: "Life," "Death," and "Legacies." The first section, "Life," showcased the economic and cultural diversity of ethnic Mexicans living in the Texas–Mexico border region. It displayed objects like a stylish lace cotton wedding dress bought in Corpus Christi and worn by Soledad Galván at her 1916 wedding to Nemecio Jiménez Sr. at McAllen Sacred Heart Church in Hidalgo County, the Bible that belonged to the Idar family, and a 1900 Cruz de Animas (Cross of Souls) crucifix, commonly found in Mexican homes to inspire reflection and prayer for family members who had died.

This section gave an overview of the economic changes, including ethnic Mexican land dispossession, that accompanied the arrival of the railroad and Anglo real estate developers.[22] Alongside the stories of landed Tejanos and the arrival of the railroad were photographs of laboring ethnic Mexicans clearing the region of mesquite trees to make room for farming and picking crops. A scythe, or swinging blade, used to clear canals of grasses and weeds was on display. The panel caption described the scythe by the derogatory nickname used by Anglo landowners: "the Mexican golf club."

The second section, "Death," gave an overview of the decade of anti-Mexican violence. Gallery panels described the history of resistance and revolution, the return of the US military to the border, and the policing practices of the Texas Rangers. It outlined a history of the Texas Rangers from 1915 to 1920 and described the role of Texas governors James Ferguson and William Hobby calling on the state police to patrol "suspected

Mexicans" and execute them without trials or convictions. Panels described
1915 as an exceptional year of anti-Mexican violence, including *la matanza*
(the massacre) of ethnic Mexicans. The narrative included journalists' accounts of the bloodshed and highlighted witnesses like Frank Pierce, who
attempted to document the brutality by keeping a list of murdered residents. The exhibit also avoided confining the Ranger abuses to a single
decade, because it had been a long-standing practice. One panel informed
visitors, "Originally a force of 10 men created by Stephen F. Austin in
1823 to protect the lives and property of Anglo settlers and businessmen,
the Rangers later earned the nickname *los diablos Tejanos* (the Texan devils)
from Mexicans for their ruthless and lethal attacks against civilian Mexican
populations during the 1846–1848 war between the U.S. and Mexico."

In this section the team and curators had debated what images of violence to include. The group agreed that photographic evidence could help
convince skeptical visitors of the brutality of the past, but there were tensions about how to do this without sensationalizing the violence. Ultimately
the team decided to display the Robert Runyon postcard of Rangers posing
with "Dead Mexican Bandits" in the wake of the Norias Raid in a small
shadow box. In a departure from the widespread use of this image in academic publications, the exhibit caption listed the names of the men on
horseback and the dead men on the ground.

Still, the designers considered how to use Runyon images for dramatic
visual effect. We considered a practice developed by artist Ken Gonzales-
Day in his series "Erased Lynchings." Gonzales-Day took lynching postcards from California but removed the victim and the rope from the image;
his purpose was to draw attention to the agents of violence. In removing
the dead, Gonzales-Day redirected the viewer's gaze to the perpetrators
rather than allowing the viewer to make a spectacle of the victim.[23] Leigh
Raiford's study of the use of photographs by anti-lynching activists to promote social awareness also offered an important reminder. Photography
does not do the work of consciousness raising alone: "Rather, depending
on the text and context, it can encourage these processes."[24]

The group agreed that one goal of the exhibit was to draw attention to
the mechanisms of state violence. The designers cropped the Robert
Runyon postcard, excising the four dead bodies but keeping the Ranger
Henry Ransom and ranch foreman Tom Tate on horseback, and they blew
up the image so that it filled one wall from ceiling to floor. I would have

preferred not to have the likes of Henry Ransom looming large, literally watching visitors at the exhibit. In this case, however, his was the face of violence, not veneration.

The giant wall graphic and the postcard display were accompanied by the original three bound volumes of the 1919 Texas Ranger investigation. For the first time, the claims against the state sat in a display case, and the testimonies were on view for the public. The exhibit included an interactive display that allowed visitors to read selected testimonies from the investigation on mounted tablets, to consider the histories of racial violence preserved in the volumes. This display helped make state violence a central component of the exhibit. In this section, José T. Canales received praise for his role in calling for the investigation into state police abuse. The exhibit labels highlighted the reforms to reduce the number of Texas Rangers and the investigation report that concluded that Rangers were "guilty of, and are responsible for, the gross violations of both civil and criminal laws of the state." Although the exhibit fell short of explaining that individual Texas Rangers did not face prosecution for the crimes, in its less than 200 words the panel was unequivocal in affirming that Texas Rangers had committed gross violations from 1915 until 1919.

The Longoria and Bazán double murder and the Porvenir massacre, two events discussed in the 1919 investigation, were examples of brutality on display. Panels that described the double murder and the massacre displayed aging but carefully preserved photographs of Antonio Longoria, Jesus Bazán, and a Bazán family portrait. Captions listed the people in the photos and described their place in the communities by occupation and land ownership. It also displayed an application for a cattle brand by Juan Bonilla Flores to give visitors a sense of how residents navigated state institutions and responded to the changing world around them. The captions helped to show that the dead were not nameless *bandidos*. As a strategy, curators drew attention to life before death.

The exhibit also created space for the survivors. While many people died during this period, many more lived. Life continued in the aftermath of state violence. These displays made important gestures to those left in the wake of violence, by including photographs of survivors. An oval wooden framed portrait of Juan and Narciso Flores, circa 1925, showed the two brothers as young adults, years after witnessing the Porvenir massacre. Sitting on a wicker chair and a stool, dressed in suits with matching blue ties,

wearing cowboy hats, the brothers sit with their left legs crossed. The composed portraits perhaps hid the family struggles. In another context, this
photograph would have looked like any old family photo. But these were
the faces of survivors of one of the most horrific massacres in US history.

Historian Edward Linenthal has considered the power of making names
and faces central in public memorialization efforts. He points to the Oklahoma City National Memorial and the United States Holocaust Memorial
Museum as two examples. He reminds us, "These memorial environments
do much more than just 'remember.' . . . They are acts of protest against
the anonymity of mass death in the twentieth century. Hence the emphasis
on names, faces, life stories."[25] We would also be wise to remember that
aside from the state-sponsored public memorials like those mentioned by
Linenthal, local residents have preserved alternative histories of racial violence that emphasize the faces, names, and life stories of the departed. *Life
and Death on the Border, 1910–1920* borrowed from their insistence that victims' lives and dignity be restored in the retelling of their tragedies.

More could have been done in this section to discuss the relatives who
filed claims against the US government. A fuller discussion of such efforts
would have enhanced visitors' understanding of the many lives gravely impacted by the massacre. Displaying court records, for example, would
have provided an opportunity to see the names of the survivors and to consider the role of the Mexican government in seeking some form of restorative justice for the victims of the massacre. A significant piece of US legal
history, this was a missed opportunity.

Even though I wanted more of the personal details, I realized that including any family portraits and artifacts was no small statement. Alongside local and national institutions—the Library of Congress, the Dolph
Briscoe Center for American History, the State Preservation Board, the
Texas State Library and Archives, and the Nettie Lee Benson Latin American Collection—Norma Longoria Rodriguez, Christine Molis, and Benita
and Evaristo Albarado received credit and thanks for loaning their artifacts.
Portraits of relatives and family documents helped ensure that visitors would
see at least some of the faces and names of those who survived, rather than
leaving with only images of the dead. The exhibition also laid bare the
absences in state archives and cultural institutions. Without these privately
curated histories, events like the double murder in Hidalgo County and
the Porvenir massacre would have remained hidden from the public in the

Texas Ranger memorabilia are preserved in archives and museums across the country. Foreground: jacket worn by John Coffee Hays, Colt Revolver first model Dragoon, and a Texas Ranger badge courtesy of the Autry National Center, Los Angeles. Background: the portrait of Narciso and Juan Bonilla Flores and documents from the Evaristo and Benita Albarado collection are on display. Without objects loaned from private collections, the museum would have been unable to show the impact on families of state-sanctioned racial violence in Texas. Photograph provided by the Bullock Texas State History Museum.

bound pages of the investigation, where their names are misspelled and the crimes themselves are discussed without moral outrage.

Instead of relegating anti-Mexican violence to a remote decade in the past, the curators developed a final section that turned visitors' attention to ongoing practices of racism and discrimination paired with efforts for civil rights. The final room of the gallery, "Legacies," displayed histories of racism and resistance throughout the twentieth century. A panel on Juan Crow segregation showcased a brand of Texas racism that continued long after 1920. In addition, galleries portrayed the efforts of civil rights pioneers such as Jovita Idar and the participants in El Primer Congreso Mexicanista in 1911. The cross-border organizing, journalistic traditions, efforts for women's suffrage, and challenges to racism and discrimination received recognition for creating a foundation for later civil rights organizations like the League of United Latin American Citizens, La Raza Unida political party, and the Chicano Movement. The literary, musical, artistic, and cultural traditions of ethnic Mexicans in the region, and the various strategies for attaining civil rights throughout the twentieth century, illustrated the continued work to end anti-Mexican sentiments and discrimination.

The concluding exhibit panel announced:

> The struggle to eliminate discrimination and racism continues today. For the historical narrative, the true numbers of those killed in the border violence between 1910–1920 is unknown. Current estimates range from several hundred to several thousand. Memories from survivors and descendants are being researched and recorded in academic publications, novels, documentaries, family memorials, and petitions for historical markers across the region from descendants of those killed. Their legacies illustrate the deep ties between Texas and Mexican history, and their resilience in the face of adversity calls for continued reflection on the impact of Texas's past on today's generations.

The conclusion spoke to the need to conduct further research, to learn from the past, and to continue memorialization efforts.

PUBLIC RESPONSES TO THE EXHIBIT

On January 21, 2016, after years of planning, the Refusing to Forget team gathered in Austin for the opening exhibit symposium and to brace ourselves. Our goal to display the history, account for state violence, and show respect for the dead would be assessed by the families that had carried that role for decades. Descendants filled the auditorium. The Albarados brought their children and grandchildren to the event. Norma Longoria Rodriguez and her children attended. My family too—parents, sister, *tías, tíos,* and cousins—came to see this new accounting of Texas history. And Trinidad Gonzales, a descendant of the violence himself, arranged for a bus to bring thirty-five high school students from south Texas to attend the symposium.

During the faculty panel, the team gave an overview of the historical context for the period of violence, discussed the failure of the state to correct crimes at the hands of state and local police, outlined the challenges in researching and documenting this history, and spoke to the importance of local families who had refused to let these histories be forgotten. Kate Betz, the museum's education director, turned the microphone over to the audience. In the question and answer session, the audience, as at the Ku Klux Klan symposium, did not ask specific questions about the history we described; they reminded us that they knew the history intimately.

Antonio Alfonso Longoria was the first person to speak. He stood up and described himself as a grandson of Antonio Longoria, murdered in Hidalgo County by Texas Rangers in 1915. He gestured to other Longoria descendants who had traveled to the exhibit, filling an entire row of seats. He offered thanks for the exhibit but expressed his frustration. The collaboration between residents, professors, and museum curators was too long in the making. He asked how the group and the museum planned to make this history more widely known to the public. In particular, members of the audience wanted to know when educators would start teaching this history in public schools. The history on display in the flagship state history museum was only the first step.

The questions about public education remained central. What would it take to convince public school educators to teach the histories of violence? How could Texans prevent more violence from occurring if they did not know this history? The audience spoke urgently about the need for scholars and the museums to commit to continued efforts to reshape public memory through the exhibit and beyond. Kate Betz described upcoming events exclusively for teachers, including a free event called "Evening for Educators: Changing Borders" on February 3, 2016. Refusing to Forget team member John Morán González gave a lecture on the role of *corridos* in ethnic Mexican communities, and the Bullock provided instructions on how to use their lesson plan "Corridos and Culture." The lesson helped middle and high school students analyze the lyrics of traditional *corridos*. In addition, the Bullock hosted educator events to provide teachers with more context and free materials, and developed a student and family guide to help facilitate public engagement with the content.

The symposium ended with anticipation to see the exhibit. In addition to the reception the museum offered a musical performance by a San

Antonio conjunto group. The Albarados brought pamphlets with information on the Porvenir massacre to give to visitors interested in learning more. Even with family artifacts on display, they did not miss an opportunity to share documents and evidence of the massacre. Through these pamphlets, they curated a narrative that was not mediated by museum workers or historians.

The symposium was unlike any the Bullock had facilitated before. Extended families reunited at the exhibit. They gathered and took group photos at the exhibit entrance, grandparents read labels out loud to their grandchildren, and families that lent artifacts for the exhibition posed next to the panels that displayed their family history. The Bullock staff stayed busy coordinating the reception but took the time to appreciate that this was a monumental occasion for the small group of Texas citizens who had worked to preserve this history, as well as for the much larger group of residents that came to see the exhibit.

Margaret Koch knew early on in the installation process that the exhibit had the capacity to start a public dialogue about the past. Before the faculty symposium she shared that during the installation she observed a printing contractor on a ladder leveling an exhibit graphic reading the panel captions. What he read prompted him to stop his work. He picked up his cell phone and called a relative to ask if they knew about the history he was reading. He then read the caption out loud over the phone. Koch had never seen an exhibit's content stop an installation in its tracks.

The emotions, the food, the music, and the crowds all combined to make it difficult for visitors to study the exhibition closely. I arranged with the Bullock staff to give the Rodriguez and Albarado families a private tour the following day, before the exhibit was officially open to the public. They had a chance to visit with the team that took care of their artifacts and displayed them, to read through the panels and check the accounts of their family histories, and to tour the exhibit without crowds and distractions. Of course, 75- to 150-word labels could not convey the significance of their family histories, but having the events that shaped their families' lives described as crimes and tragedies, having the names and the photographs of their relatives memorialized in the flagship state history museum, did bring some sense of relief.

After the tour, the families and I had lunch and took time to reflect on their efforts and the exhibit. These descendants-turned-researchers, historians, bloggers, and poets shared details of their struggles to piece together evidence of their family histories. Little of the conversation actually revolved around the exhibit. Instead, they shared stories about archivists who had dismissed their requests for documents, about the struggle to find evidence, and about the challenges of correcting racist assumptions about US history. They also talked about children and grandchildren and life beyond family tragedies. In an interview for the National Public Radio broadcast Latino USA, Norma Rodriguez shared that when she met Benita Albarado that weekend, the two had a common understanding of each other's struggles. She described it as being part of a sad club or community that neither of them wanted to be a part of.[26] And yet they remained connected by injustices suffered by their families 100 years before.

The symposium, the tour, the lunch, and the continued conversations were full of mixed emotions. The events felt at moments like family reunions and at other moments like a funeral or memorial service. The rooms were filled with joyous laughter and with deep sighs, words of celebration and solemn reflections. Christine Molis, a descendant of Jesus Bazán and Antonio Longoria, described walking through the exhibit as surreal, saddening, and a bit confusing. "I don't know how to put it into words, but you just stand there like, wow, that's my blood. That's part of me. . . . It's saddening to know what happened, and to think how did my family go through this? How did they survive it afterwards?" Molis knew the history of the double murder. She had helped preserve the history and lent family photographs from her private collection for the exhibit. When she saw the history on display for the public, familiar emotions and unresolved questions reemerged. But she expressed enthusiasm for the exhibit and a sense of pride for her role in telling the history: "I'm proud to know they're honoring him now and telling his story so that people know what really happened in those days."[27] The exhibit did not dispel sentiments of loss, but there was some relief in having Texas's flagship history museum acknowledge the injustice. In this way, the exhibit helped ease some feelings of indignation inspired by 100 years of public disavowal of this history.

The exhibit succeeded in attracting widespread attention. Media coverage highlighted the importance of the Bullock in finally recognizing the sentiments and histories of local residents. The exhibit marked a radical departure, but one that was welcomed by journalists. Cindy Casares of

Latina Magazine praised the work and described the importance of raising public awareness of these stories. She also remained critical of the long delay in a state acknowledgment of the violence. Casares astutely titled her piece "Texas Finally Acknowledges Rangers Killed Hundreds of Latinos."[28] Joe Holley of the *Houston Chronicle* likewise praised the efforts of local residents to preserve memories of this period of violence. Despite suppressed documents, silenced histories, and discarded bodies, communities remembered. Holley concluded, "At the Bullock these days, those memories have been given new voice."[29] Both Casares and Holley pinpointed the tensions on display in the exhibit. Wrapped in praise that the Bullock had finally participated in this memorialization effort was an explicit acknowledgment that state cultural institutions had disavowed this history for over a century.

The possibilities for such collaborations and sharing little-known histories were also revealed. Historian Linda Pritchard reviewed the exhibit for the *Journal of American History*. She wrote, "The most compelling stories in this exhibit are the kind whispered by family members to successive generations, not those usually told in a state's official history museum."[30] Tom Dart for the *Guardian* agreed. He interviewed Melba Coody, a descendant of Jesus Bazán and Antonio Longoria, and her daughter Christine Molis. His coverage of the exhibit was brief. Instead, he shared with readers the atrocities committed by the state police and gave an account of the double murder of Jesus Bazán and Antonio Longoria in 1915 and of the Porvenir massacre in 1918.[31] The private memories that gave an alternative accounting of Texas history had moved from conversations among relatives and trusted friends to the private archives in people's homes to the walls of the state flagship history museum and finally to the pages of the *Guardian*. Alternative histories were making the transition from marginalized and disavowed to acknowledged and lamented state crimes of the past.

Any sentiments of accomplishment, however, quickly developed into momentum for more work to bring the history to a wider public. The collaborators, descendants, scholars, and curators also spoke with certainty that this one exhibit was not enough to shift public perceptions of the past. After all, the Texas Rangers remained venerated icons in the state. There was, surprisingly, little public backlash from Texas Ranger enthusiasts compared to in the wake of the screenings of *Border Bandits* in 2004. Instead there was mostly silence. Worse even than the silence, there were no public acknowledgments by other museums, like the Waco Texas Ranger History Museum and Hall of Fame, of the need to amend their exhibits.

Life and Death on the Border was a temporary exhibit; we all knew that in April the panels would be packed away, artifacts would be returned to lending institutions and families, and the permanent laudatory exhibit would remain. But we also know that during the ten-week exhibition, over 40,000 visitors walked through *Life and Death on the Border*. Teachers, students, and board members from school districts across the state made special trips to Austin for the exhibit. The Bullock staff considered the exhibit a monumental success. Margaret Koch described the effort of engaging the Texas Rangers, "often seen as beyond reproach," as having great rewards. By curating a first-of-its-kind exhibit that "revealed the Rangers as the instigators of racially-motivated violence," the Bullock broke new ground in state public history. But more than that, she believed, the exhibit helped change the way visitors think about the museum itself. "In concert with programming that draws modern-day connections to the past, we analyzed a period of history once seen as myth and engaged a new audience: the previously under-represented Latino community."[32] Indeed, most visitors I spoke to consistently expressed surprise that the Bullock had taken on the task of shining a light on state violence. For racial minorities who often look at public projects by state historical institutions with suspicion, this exhibit was an important step in gaining their attention and potentially their future patronage.

Assessing the impact of this one exhibit is difficult because efforts to memorialize this period of violence continued after the exhibit came down. The exhibit emboldened calls for reforms to curriculum and changes to public history. It also shed light on the willingness of some state cultural institutions to lead by example and encourage critical reflections on histories of state violence. Then director Victoria Ramirez said that the exhibit was the sort of remembrance any reputable museum should take on. The Bullock was opening the door for critical engagements with histories of violence in Texas. She said, "We're not here to rewrite history. We're not here to tell people how they should understand history. What we want to do is help people gain a broader perspective on the world the way it is."[33] Ramirez is correct: these are the acts of remembrance reputable museums must take on.

The *Life and Death on the Border* exhibit at the Bullock showcased the need for more leadership by state institutions to reckon with histories of violence that have long been disavowed. The Smithsonian National Museum of American History has developed exhibits that confront histories of racial violence in America, such as *Bittersweet Harvest: The Bracero Program 1942–1964,* a traveling exhibit that examines the experiences of Mexican laborers working in the United States through a guest worker program. The exhibit was the culmination of a collaborative project between the Smithsonian, the Institute for Oral History at the University of Texas at El Paso, and Brown University. The group collected hundreds of oral histories with former braceros and their family members; the exhibit, and accompanying digital archive, offered one model for making use of community memory. Historian Mireya Loza, who helped lead the effort to collect oral histories, reflected on the reactions to the exhibit by visitors who were former braceros interviewed for the project, or who had relatives that were braceros, as they moved through the exhibit at the Smithsonian. Many of them were moved to tears when they looked at the photographs and the objects that testified to widespread abuse. For the Smithsonian to recognize the guest worker program as a history of exploitation and oppression was a moving experience for these visitors. Loza observed that the exhibit "validated their sacrifice through narratives of family uplift and opportunity,"[34] and some visitors felt newly incorporated into the fabric of America.

Public projects can be commemorative or educational, and can play an important role in community grieving. Of the new National Museum of African American History and Culture, director Lonnie Bunch explained that he hoped the museum could help the nation "grapple with its tortured racial past." He continued, "And maybe even help us find a bit of reconciliation."[35] The need for reconciliation with tortured racial pasts is all the more pressing in the twenty-first century. To bring some relief to aggrieved residents, to bring about healing, is an urgent task. And yet that goal can also seem to grate against the reality of ongoing patterns of racial violence. The act of state institutions creating spaces for community healing for past crimes in the midst of ongoing state violence is loaded with contradictions. Lisa Yoneyama poignantly asks of public efforts to recover marginalized or silenced experiences, "How can memories, once recuperated, remain self-critically unsettling?"[36] One important way to do this is to avoid commemorating state violence as a thing of the past. Rather, these projects should speak to ongoing and broader patterns of injustice. At the National Museum of African American History and Culture, for example, alongside artifacts of chattel slavery and the lynchings of African Americans, curators included a door from a home devastated by Hurricane Katrina and protest signs calling for justice for Trayvon Martin. Black lives continue to be made vulnerable by the state, and visitors are called to reflect on this as they leave the museum.

The power of remembering names of Mexican victims and speaking to ongoing violence is all the more important amid growing anti-immigrant sentiments and policies in the twenty-first century. The efforts to commemorate the centennial of this stark period of anti-Mexican violence came to fruition in, were marked by, and were made all the more urgent by ongoing violent policing in the United States and the continued criminalization of border residents and migrants. As a small gesture to the ongoing debates about immigration policing and the border, the curators at the Bullock included one 1987 sculpture created by Luis Jiménez in the "Legacies" section of *Life and Death on the Border.* The piece, titled *Border Crossing (Cruzando el Rio Bravo),* shows a man bearing his wife and child on his shoulders as they cross the river into the United States—a common sight Jiménez witnessed growing up in El Paso. It served as a reminder that the border region continues to be misrepresented as a threat to national security.[37]

Speaking to the *Guardian,* Christine Molis expressed hope that the exhibit would act as a reminder that racial tensions along the border and violent border policing existed long before "modern-day drug cartels and immigration controversies." She explained, "The violence has been there all along, it was just never spoken about before."[38] Reporters, too, placed the exhibit within the context of heightened levels of xenophobia and racism in the midst of the 2016 presidential campaign. Rebecca Onion, writing for *Slate,* considered the Bullock exhibit a glimpse of progress. "Belatedly, tentatively, Texas has begun to reckon with this bloody history," she wrote, "For a state that has long refused to come to terms with those years . . . it's something like progress, even if the legacy of this violence will require far more than exhibits to expiate."[39] At best, learning from crimes of the past will help inform current debate about immigration, policing, and national belonging. The lessons of the past, when forgotten, have devastating consequences.

Epilogue

ONE WEEK IN OCTOBER 2010, I spent day after day sitting at the long table inside the special collections reading room in the James C. Jernigan Library of the Texas A&M University–Kingsville campus. The library lobby was full of alumni who had returned for reunion weekend. Draped in the school colors, blue and yellow, the alumni enthusiasm and celebrations were an odd juxtaposition to the grim records I was reviewing. The staff of the South Texas Archives graciously brought to me box after box from unknown rooms. Files included letters, maps of south Texas, nearly 100 photographs and postcards, and seventeen oral histories with local residents, conducted by students from the university for class credit. On my last day in the collections, an archivist asked whether any of the oral histories I had listened to were particularly helpful. One oral history, labeled "Anonymous no. 237," had caught my attention. The archivist responded that she did not know about the interview but quickly discouraged me from giving much credence to the content. If interviewees decided not to make their name public at the time of interview, in her opinion, there was a high probability that the recorded stories might have been fabricated. The anonymity of this interview, she felt, rendered it unreliable.

The interview is a forty-one-minute-long testimonial in Spanish. It begins with the voice of the interviewer, who also remains unnamed: "In
partial fulfillment for Texas History 413, the following interview of a sixty-
six-year-old man was taken. This interview concerns his views and opinions
of the Texas Rangers here in the early 1900s." After this statement, with a
worn but still commanding voice, the interviewee begins:

> *Los [sic] voy a platicar una historia de los rinches de noveciento quince que yo*
> *alcancé a ver de la edad de nueve años. Perseguían a Tomás Garza de Mission,*
> *Tejas, hijo de Doña Virginia Garza. Los rinches los alcanzaron en un lugar que*
> *le decían Peladitas. Lo agarraron los rinches, lo amarraron a un mesquite con*
> *cadena, y le echaron cincuenta galones de gasolina, y vivo lo quemaron. Eso*
> *hacían los rinches en novecientos quince.*
>
> I'm going to tell you a history of the *rinches* in 1915 that I saw when I
> was nine years old. They were following Tomás Garza of Mission,
> Texas, son of Doña Virginia Garza. The *rinches* found him in an area
> known as Peladitas. The *rinches* grabbed him, tied him to a mesquite
> tree with a chain, and then they poured fifty gallons of gasoline on him,
> and they burned him alive. That is what the *rinches* did in 1915.[1]

Over the next forty-one minutes, the man continues almost without
pause. He describes brutal law enforcement methods, discrimination, segregation in south Texas, and example after example of acts of racial violence. In the words of the interviewee, state agents and local residents did
not hesitate to "kill Mexicans like rabbits." The interviewee made his goal
clear from the beginning. He wanted to give an account of a series of murders he witnessed or learned about: "*Eso hacían los rinches en novecientos*
quince. / That is what the *rinches* did in 1915." Sitting in front of a tape recorder, he testified to the history of racial violence as he lived it and
remembered it. He gave the names of victims along with the names or
titles of Texas Rangers, local law enforcement officers, and area ranchers
who participated in these extralegal executions. This was an act of anamnesis, a praxis against forgetting.

The anonymous oral history, conducted in the early 1970s, is one of
many examples of the will that has made this book possible: an individual,
long forgotten by history, who insists on recording his own truth; a will
that insists on documenting what has been disavowed; a will that hopes
future generations will reckon with the past. In this act of vernacular

history-making, the witness was careful to name the dead, to name the family members left in the aftermath, and to name the assailants who committed brutal murder. The anonymous interviewee thus left a trail of breadcrumbs—names, dates and locations—to aid people like me, future researchers hoping to recover erased histories.

The treatment of this oral history by a local archivist serves as a reminder of the relationship between historical narratives, memory, archives, and power. The truth of what happened can be suppressed by overt racism, by the intentional actions (or inactions) of a police captain, or a county judge, or a state senator. But history can also be disavowed by small, ordinary, and inadvertent details; by an offhand comment from an archivist that undermines the credibility of a memory; by an archivist who withholds folders from visitors searching for evidence of their family histories or guides researchers away from testimonials that seem officially troublesome; by a historian who chooses to focus on one story as opposed to others, who assumes that titled and long-celebrated employees of the state are good and that unnamed others are not. It is in this vast gamut of choices, of actions and inactions, of the conscious effort and the unconscious assumption, that histories of loss are disavowed.

Decades after the killings, when justice continued to feel out of reach, remembering the names of the dead proved an important means of grieving injustice. In describing these events, residents like the anonymous interviewee rejected the dehumanizing histories that ignored or celebrated violence. In the climate of ongoing racial tensions in Texas in the 1970s, a climate that encouraged him to remain anonymous, the interviewee must have known that the time for a public reckoning had not yet arrived. Nonetheless, he also knew that accounts should be preserved, in anticipation of days ahead with more possibilities. To dismiss the content of the interview is to foreclose those possibilities.[2] Passing histories along to future generations creates an opportunity and an anticipation of future efforts to reckon with histories of violence.

As this book has shown, people whose lives were interrupted by the tragedies they learned from relatives answered the call for a public reckoning with this history. Benita and Evaristo Albarado, Romana Bienek, Linda Davis, Norma Longoria Rodriguez, Kirby Warnock, and others preserved these histories and through vernacular history-making made them public. Their efforts inspired others, myself included, to hold to account state institutions in revising the stories they tell about histories of violence. One exhibit and a handful of state historical markers are only the beginning of reckoning with this history of violence. As we have seen, there are also many victims whose names still need to be recovered.[3]

In recognizing the strong impulse to remember the dead, we should also be cautious of unintended consequences of efforts to memorialize. On the one hand, the consequences of not reckoning with histories of violent border policing are profound. As Vicki Ruiz wisely reminds us, "Historical memory shapes affinities of belonging and claims of citizenship."[4] The failures to confront violent policing practices in the 1910s allowed a system of violence to go unchecked in the twentieth century. The failure to remember this history enables its perpetuation. On the other hand, public projects on histories of violence may lead some to conceptualize racial and ethnic violence as matters only of the past. Recognizing the significance of a violent historical period, writing about that history, and memorializing victims is not enough. Current efforts to reckon with histories of state violence are occurring in the midst of ongoing practices of police brutality both along the border and across the country. Remembering the past, then, is also about knowing the present.

In 1924 politicians and state agents who created the conditions for a widespread period of anti-Mexican violence went on to become the architects of the US Border Patrol and incarceration systems in the United States. Current federal and state policing regimes have deep roots in the violence of the borderlands—the regime of terror practiced a century ago on the Texas–Mexico border is crucial to ongoing conversations about police brutality and the carceral state. The history reminds us of the dangers of criminalization and unchecked racial profiling and police abuse.

More than 2.3 million people are incarcerated in American federal and state prisons, juvenile correctional facilities, local jails, Indian Country jails, civil commitment centers, military prisons, and prisons in US territories. Seventy-one percent of federal prison inmates are Black or Latinx. Since 2009, congressional appropriation laws have included language that sets a quota to maintain 34,000 immigration detention beds on a daily basis. US Immigration and Customs Enforcement (ICE) is the only law enforcement agency subject to a statutory quota. In 2015 the United States spent nearly $2 billion a year on immigration detention centers and relied on private prison companies to manage these facilities. In 2017 approximately 41,000 people were confined in immigration detention.[5] We are living in the midst of structures of containment. Bryan Stevenson reflects that mass imprisonment has "littered the national landscape with carceral monuments of reckless and excessive punishment and ravaged communities with our hopeless willingness to condemn and discard the most vulnerable among us."[6]

In addition to confinement, the US–Mexico border continues to be a hive for policing. Indeed, the US Border Patrol is the nation's second largest police force, after the New York Police Department. Since 2000 Border Patrol officers have made nearly twelve million apprehensions. Latinx populations accounted for nearly all, a staggering 92 percent, of these apprehensions. And reports of abuse, misconduct, and corruption are on the rise.[7]

Calls for an expanded Border Patrol in the twenty-first century have had dangerous results. When the Border Patrol expanded dramatically between 2006 and 2009 (adding 8,000 new agents), the number of employees arrested for misconduct (civil rights violations or off-duty crimes such as domestic violence) increased by 44 percent during the three-year span. The American Immigration Council reported that more than 100 employees were arrested or charged with corruption, including taking bribes to smuggle drugs or people, and many more have been charged with misuse of force, criminal misconduct, abuse of migrants, and violating constitutional rights. According to US Customs and Border Protection reporting, border agents killed fifty-one people between 2005 and 2015. Five of these killings involved police firing shots across the border.[8]

As we reflect on the centennial of the 1919 state investigation into Texas Rangers, worrisome trends of police abuse continue, and the requirements and oversight for border enforcement officers are starting to thin. In 2014 the United Nations High Commissioner for Refugees called for mandatory training for US border enforcement authorities in "fundamental principles of nondiscriminatory treatment" and "on the basic norms and principles of international human rights and refugee law."[9] Instead, in 2017 the Department of Homeland Security moved to ease training and enrollment requirements for Border Patrol agents, even as it sought to increase their numbers by hiring 15,000 new Border Patrol and ICE agents.[10] The call to rapidly expand the number of agents failed to consider the proven risks, historically and more recently, of having officers on a police force without the proper requirements. Despite the lessons learned, Homeland

Security officials suggested waiving a required polygraph test (required by the Anti-Border Corruption Act of 2010), removing language proficiency tests from Border Patrol entry exams, and removing one of two physical fitness tests for officers. Given the state of policing on the border, reforming police practices is an important struggle to engage. Transforming immigration policies and ending the criminalization of immigrants is the longer struggle ahead.

Policing strategies and incarceration, unfortunately, are merely one part of the brutal US security efforts. Strategies like Operation Gatekeeper, for example, inaugurated in 1994, strategically increased policing along the US–Mexico border in California, New Mexico, and Texas in order to funnel would-be migrants and refugees to the most dangerous area of the border, the Sonoran Desert, thus deterring them from crossing. Using the desert as deterrent did not work. These efforts did not curb migration but instead had dire humanitarian consequences. According to US Border Patrol statistics, over the past eighteen years, nearly 7,000 people have died of hypothermia, drowning, heat exhaustion, or dehydration attempting to cross into the United States.[11] Anthropologist Jason De León describes the federal plan simply as "a killing machine that simultaneously uses and hides behind the viciousness of the Sonoran Desert. The Border Patrol disguises the impact of its current enforcement policy by mobilizing a combination of sterilized discourse, redirected blame, and 'natural' environmental processes that erase evidence of what happens in the most remote parts of southern Arizona."[12]

The fact that hundreds die crossing into the United States every year, and that this is not considered a national crisis, speaks to the dismissal of immigrant life by US Americans on a daily basis. The US–Mexico border is again littered with bodies, transformed into what De León describes as "a land of open graves." Families and friends are returning to the borderlands to search the landscape for the remains of loved ones. Anthropologists and immigrant rights groups are helping to document and identify the dead. And the graves are not limited to Arizona.

In south Texas, too, groves of mesquite trees are again concealing dead bodies. Brooks County, for example, is described as a "death valley" for immigrants.[13] Since 2009, the remains of more than 550 undocumented migrants have been discovered in the county alone. In 2014 a group of archeologists from Operation Identification, a project at Texas State Univer-

sity's Forensic Anthropology Center, found a mass unmarked grave near the
inland border checkpoint in Falfurrias in Brooks County. What they discovered was harrowing. Some of the bodies were just tossed into the pit,
while others were placed in trash bags, shopping bags, or body bags. Some
bags had the bones of several different bodies. It turned out that Border
Patrol agents had collected the remains of unidentified people who died
attempting to cross into the United States. After they found them, they
haphazardly buried the dead.[14] The Colibrí Center for Human Rights is a
family advocacy organization working to end migrant death on the US–
Mexico border. Founder and forensic anthropologist Dr. Robin Reineke is
collaborating with families and forensic scientists to collect missing persons reports, help identify the dead, and return the remains to families
looking for their loved ones.[15] When immigrants are criminalized and
made the scapegoats of elected officials, the borderlands remain a place of
violent policing. Colibrí is collecting a twenty-first-century red record.

When I learned about these anthropologists discovering mass graves and
attempting to recover the names of the dead, I thought about the early work
of Ida B. Wells-Barnett, Jovita Idár, and Frank Pierce, creating records of
death and calling for social justice. When I contemplated the families
waiting to hear from loved ones after they crossed into the United States,
I remembered Miguel García in 1918 searching groves of mesquite trees in
south Texas for the remains of his son Florencio. When I learned that in
2010 Jesus Mesa Jr., a US Border Patrol officer, shot his gun across the US–
Mexico border killing fifteen-year-old Sergio Hernández, I thought about
Concepción García in 1919, shot and killed by a US soldier while crossing
the Rio Grande, returning to Mexico from school in Texas. When I heard
that in 2017 the US Supreme Court denied Hernández's parents legal
standing to sue Mesa for using lethal force, I thought about the descendants of the 1918 Porvenir massacre, waiting for decades to have their claims
decided by the US-Mexico General Claims Commission of 1923, only to
learn in 1941 that the commission would not hear the case.

When I consider how long it will take for families, advocates, and communities to recover from the injustices they are witnessing today, I think
about Norma Longoria Rodriguez, Benita and Evaristo Albarado, and Juan
Flores Jr., who still carry sentiments of loss 100 years after their relatives
were murdered by the state police. Recounting these myriad acts disrupts
popular assumptions that violence is followed by reconciliation, that the

dead were likely criminals anyway, that the mere passage of time can heal wounds. Answering calls for justice requires remembering the names of the departed, acknowledging the lives lost, and confronting disavowed histories of violence. In calling for redress, descendants are in the company of other social luminaries like Mamie Elizabeth Till-Mobley, Jennicet Gutiérrez, las Madres de la Plaza de Mayo, the Safe Women Strong Nations project, Mothers Against Police Brutality, Justicia Para Nuestras Hijas, and the Missing Migrant Project.

These calls serve as a reminder: reckoning with the past is intertwined with current efforts for social justice and transformation, for freedom and full humanity. We live in a world that needs to be reconstructed. The more people understand the long consequences of violence, the more likely we will be to intervene against—to denounce outright—the violence and death that continues today.

Notes

INTRODUCTION

1. Oscar Dancy, testimony, "Proceedings of the Joint Committee of the Senate and the House in the Investigation of the Texas State Ranger Force," Adjutant General Records, Texas State Archives, Austin, 543–544. The term "ethnic Mexican" is used in this book to refer to Mexican nationals and Mexican Americans living in the United States.

2. Dancy, testimony, "Proceedings," 543–544; H. J. Kirk, testimony, "Proceedings," 597. Kirk identified Florencio's father as Miguel and his brother as Isadoro, but did not name his mother or wife.

3. Dancy, testimony, "Proceedings," 543–544; H. N. Gray, testimony, "Proceedings," 1059–1061.

4. Ibid.

5. Las Tranquilas Ranch was also known as the Piper Plantation. Reports noted that Chas Stark Jr., a US Army private, accompanied the Rangers as a guide along with two sons of Atenojenes Uribe. Report from Hon. Andres G. García, Inspector General Charge'd Affairs, El Paso, Texas, May 24, 1918, evidence, "Proceedings," 807–809. Records show that Champion received permission from a local Judge Edwards.

6. Chas F. Stevens, testimony, "Proceedings," 1432; "Servicio Consular Mexico, Consulado General en El Paso, May 24, 1918," "Proceedings," 810; Dancy, testimony, "Proceedings," 543–544.

7. Dancy, testimony, "Proceedings," 557.

8. Florencio García, May 1918, certificate number 19810, State Registrar Office, Austin, FHL microfilm, 2,073,216. It appears that the number 189, a code for unidentified cause of death, was added in pencil or a different pen. The number looks to have been added after the certificate was filed on May 27, 1918.

9. "Rangers Are Charted with Man's Death," *Brownsville Herald,* May 28, 1919; "Accused Rangers Waive Hearings: Saddler and Lock Remanded to Custody of Their Captain—Bond Fixed at $3,000," *Brownsville Herald,* June 1, 1918; "Dos Rangers Fueron Acusados de Homicidio," *La Prensa,* June 3, 1918; "Dos Rangers Fueron Consignados al Gran Jurado en Brownsville," *La Prensa,* June 6, 1918. The *Brownsville Herald* inaccurately identified Miguel as Florencio's brother. Articles in *La Prensa* list him as his parent. *La Prensa* made mention of the charges in a longer article about the demand for Mexican labor in Texas.

10. Dancy, testimony, "Proceedings," 543–544; David Montejano, *Anglos and Mexicans in the Making of Texas, 1836–1986* (Austin: University of Texas Press, 1987), 110–112. Examining the lives of people who lived in the borderlands, on the fringes of national powers, shows that they lived with relative autonomy from national governments and without giving much care to the societal and racial norms that governed the rest of the United States or Mexico. In his study of the annexation and incorporation of half of Mexico's territory through the Treaty of Guadalupe Hidalgo (1848), Montejano describes the nineteenth century as a period when the Anglo elite learned Spanish, adopted Mexican ideals of land use, intermarried with Mexican women, and became close family friends with landowning Mexican families.

11. Stevens, testimony, "Proceedings," 1432.

12. Historians William D. Carrigan and Clive Webb caution readers not to assume that the numbers tallied by historians equal the actual number of Mexicans killed by mobs in the United States. Instead, they hope their index will inspire new research while providing concrete evidence of the widespread horrors of lynching cultures in the United States. Carrigan and Webb, *Forgotten Dead: Mob Violence against Mexicans in the United States, 1848–1928* (Oxford: Oxford University Press, 2013), 5. For more about what numbers reveal or obscure, see Chapter 2 of this book.

13. Linda Gordon, *The Great Arizona Orphan Abduction* (Cambridge, MA: Harvard University Press, 1999), 256–259.

14. In his book *Lynching in the West,* art historian Ken Gonzalez-Day shows what he calls the "transracial" nature of lynchings in California. He demonstrates that mobs were guided by public anti-miscegenation and anti-immigrant sentiments as well as larger frustrations with the state judicial system. In California, African Americans, Native Americans, Chinese laborers, and Latinos of Mexican and Latin American descent were lynched. Gonzalez-Day, *Lynching in the West: 1850–1935* (Durham, NC: Duke University Press, 2006), 3.

15. See Monica Muñoz Martinez, "Recuperating Histories of Violence in the Americas: Vernacular History-Making on the US–Mexico Border," *American Quarterly* 66, no. 3 (2014): 661–689, and Chapter 2 of this book for further discussion of the practices of terror and intimidation.

16. "Trouble Zone along the Rio Grande Is Almost Deserted," *San Antonio Express,* September 11, 1915. See also James Sandos, *Rebellion in the Borderlands: Anarchism and the Plan de San Diego* (Norman: University of Oklahoma Press, 1992); Benjamin Heber Johnson, *Revolution in Texas: How a Forgotten Rebellion and Its Bloody Suppression Turned Mexicans into Americans* (New Haven, CT: Yale University Press, 2003), 2–3.

17. Michel-Rolph Trouillot rightfully reminds historians that universities and university presses are not the only loci of the production of historical narrative. He built on Marco Ferro's arguments that academics are not the sole teachers of history. For more, see Trouillot, *Silencing the Past: Power and the Production of History* (Boston: Beacon Press, 1995), 20, and Marc Ferro, *L'histoire sous surveillance: Science et conscience de l'histoire* (Paris: Calmann Levy, 1985).

18. These methods are inspired partly by ongoing struggles of mothers in the Americas who publicly mourn the murder and disappearance of their children. Public memorials and performances challenge state violence and judicial neglect while also serving as reminders of the pain carried by those living in the wake of state violence. For more, see Susana Rotker, *Captive Women: Oblivion and Memory in Argentina* (Minneapolis: University of Minnesota Press, 2002); Diana Taylor, *The Archive and the Repertoire: Performing Cultural Memory in the Americas* (Durham, NC: Duke University Press, 2003); Rosa-Linda Fregoso, *MeXicana Encounters: The Making of Social Identities on the Borderlands* (Berkeley: University of California Press, 2003); María Josefina Saldaña-Portillo, *The Revolutionary Imagination in the Americas and the Age of Development* (Durham, NC: Duke University Press, 2003). This work is also informed by scholars advancing research and methods for narrating histories of violence. See Karl Jacoby, *Shadows at Dawn: An Apache Massacre and the Violence of History* (New York: Penguin, 2008); Ned Blackhawk, *Violence over the Land: Indians and Empires in the Early American West* (Cambridge, MA: Harvard University Press, 2008); Alicia Schmidt Camacho, *Migrant Imaginaries: Latino Cultural Politics in the US–Mexico Borderlands* (New York: New York University Press, 2008); Lisa Yoneyama, *Hiroshima Traces: Time, Space and the Dialectics of Memory* (Berkeley: University of California Press, 1999), Marisa Fuentes, *Dispossessed Lives: Enslaved Women, Violence, and the Archive* (Philadelphia: University of Pennsylvania Press, 2016).

19. María Josefina Saldaña-Portillo gracefully shows that both Spanish and British colonialism in North America were space-making endeavors that carefully placed (and displaced) Indigenous subjects in landscape. See *Indian Given: Racial Geographies across Mexico and the United States* (Durham, NC: Duke University

Press, 2016) 7. Walter Prescott Webb, *The Texas Rangers: A Century of Frontier Defense* (Austin: University of Texas Press, 1995), 3, 11. Despite popular assumptions about Rangers as uniformly white, Indigenous and Tejanos also served as Rangers in the nineteenth century. Gary Anderson, *Conquest of Texas: Ethnic Cleansing in the Promised Land, 1820–1875* (Oklahoma City: University of Oklahoma Press, 2005) 10, 176–180; Robert Perkinson, *Texas Tough: The Rise of America's Prison Empire* (New York: Picador, 2010), 52–55.

20. As quoted in Perkinson, *Texas Tough,* 55, 97; Johnson, *Revolution in Texas,* 12; Webb, *The Texas Rangers,* 279; Karl Jacoby, *The Strange Career of William Ellis: The Texas Slave Who Became a Mexican Millionaire* (New York: Norton, 2016), 10–13.

21. Linda Gordon, *The Great Arizona Orphan Abduction* (Cambridge, MA: Harvard University Press, 1999), 262, 266; Kelly Lytle Hernández, *Migra! A History of the US Border Patrol* (Berkeley: University of California Press, 2010).

22. Some historians credit the Mexican rural police under the administration of President Porfirio Díaz with developing *la ley de fuga.* According to these accounts, the Rangers imported these brutal methods from Mexico. These suggestions displace the blame from Texas Rangers for their actions and frame Mexican officers as the root of this violent practice in the border region. To the contrary, prior to the Díaz regime, Texas residents complained that state agents did not hesitate to kill prisoners. Charles H. Harris and Louis R. Saddler, *The Texas Rangers and the Mexican Revolution: The Bloodiest Decade, 1910–1920* (Albuquerque: University of New Mexico Press, 2007), 27.

23. As quoted in Webb, *The Texas Rangers,* 227; editorial in the *Victoria Advocate* reprinted in the *Austin Daily Republican,* October 10, 1870.

24. Elliott Young, *Catarino Garza's Revolution on the Texas–Mexico Border* (Durham, NC: Duke University Press, 2004), 7.

25. Cortina's men would maintain control until December of that year when the US Army arrived in force to retake the region. The mid-1870s would again prove to be violent in west Texas when residents in El Paso, Ysleta, and San Elizario led a mob against new merchants who aimed to make a profit from salt deposits in the region. For generations residents had considered salt deposits located approximately 100 miles east of El Paso free for public use. Conflicts came to a head in 1877 and the US Army came to disperse the revolt. Miguel Levario writes that the El Paso Salt War defined the social context for Anglos living in west Texas. For more, see Levario, *Militarizing the Border: When Mexicans Became the Enemy* (College Station: Texas A&M University Press, 2012) 36; Montejano, *Anglos and Mexicans,* 6, 32–36, 73; Mario T. García, *Desert Immigrants: The Mexicans of El Paso, 1880–1920* (New Haven, CT: Yale University Press, 1982), 156–157.

26. Américo Paredes, *"With His Pistol in His Hand": A Border Ballad and Its Hero* (Austin: University of Texas Press, 1958), 138–141.

27. Olivier Razac, *Barbed Wire: A Political History* (New York: New Press, 2002), x, 5; Reviel Netz, *Barbed Wire: An Ecology of Modernity* (Middletown, CT: Wesleyan University Press, 2004). Razac explains, "This was prison by fragmentation, in which even the fragments were imprisoned. Barbed wire made the Indians' geographical and social environment hostile to them, so that it became a foreign territory where the tribal way of life was unimaginable and where nomadic wandering and hunting were impossible."

28. By 1875, barbed-wire fences effectively ended cattle drives of thousands of cattle transported from Texas to northern locations like Kansas City and forced cattlemen to patronize the railroads to move their herds north. Smaller ranchers without large properties could not sustain their herds and Mexican ranchers in particular suffered disproportionately high losses. Richard R. Flores, *Remembering the Alamo: Memory, Modernity, and the Master Symbol* (Austin: University of Texas Press, 2002), 46.

29. For more on the American property laws and the denial of property rights of Mexicans throughout the southwestern United States, see Richard White, *"It's Your Misfortune and None of My Own": A New History of the American West* (New York: Norton, 1993); Patricia Nelson Limerick, *Legacy of Conquest: The Unbroken Past of the American West* (New York: Norton, 1987); Montejano, *Anglos and Mexicans*; David Weber, ed., *Foreigners in Their Native Land: Historical Roots of Mexican Americans* (Albuquerque: University of New Mexico Press, 1973); Maria Montoya, *Translating Property: The Maxwell Land Grant and Conflict over Land in the American West, 1840 to 1920* (Berkeley: University of California Press, 2002); Audrey Smedley, *Race in North America: Origin and Evolution of a Worldview* (Boulder, CO: Westview Press, 2007).

30. Walter Prescott Webb wrote that Mexicans became "victimized by the law" in their person and property. Webb, *The Texas Rangers: A Century of Frontier Defense* (Austin: University of Texas Press, 1995), 175–176; Montejano, *Anglos and Mexicans,* 51–53. Some of the nineteenth-century residents of the Southwest who benefited from Spanish colonization in the Americas now found themselves being displaced by new forms of colonization.

31. Young, *Catarino Garza's Revolution*, 1, 7, 189–190.

32. The US military needed basic geographical mappings of the region to suppress its residents. For more on these efforts to map and represent this region to the broader US public, see Young, *Catarino Garza's Revolution,* especially chapter 7.

33. Quoted in ibid., 226.

34. For a fuller analysis of the social significance of the publications in *El Bien Público* and the brutality of Captain Bourke, see ibid., 246–251.

35. Gerarldo Cadava argues convincingly that the border continued to remain permeable through the mid-twentieth century. Cadava, *Standing on Common Ground: The Making of a Sunbelt Borderland* (Cambridge, MA: Harvard University Press, 2013).

36. Young, *Catarino Garza's Revolution*, 7, 40, 201–211, 215.

37. Ibid., 210–211.

38. Ibid., 209.

39. Montejano includes Webb, Duval, Nueces, Cameron, Hidalgo, Starr, and Zapata Counties in his calculations for deep south Texas. Montejano, *Anglos and Mexicans*, 106–109.

40. As quoted in ibid., 113.

41. *Carizzo Springs Javelin*, August 5, 1911, quoted in Montejano, *Anglos and Mexicans*, 131.

42. "Los Mexicanos de San Angelo Demandan a Los Sindicos de las Escuelas Públicas," *La Cronica*, June 25, 1910.

43. See Mario T. García, *Desert Immigrants: The Mexicans of El Paso, 1880–1920* (New Haven, CT: Yale University Press, 1981); Johnson, *Revolution in Texas*, 59.

44. Timothy J. Dunn, *The Militarization of the US–Mexico Border, 1978–1992* (Austin: University of Texas Press, 1996), 6–8; Montejano, *Anglos and Mexicans*, 106–117.

45. John Mckiernan-González reminds us that a mounted medical guard preceded the Border Patrol by forty years. In 1882 the US Marine Hospital Service drew a 146 mile-long line from Laredo to Corpus Christi and quarantined residents south of that line. Mckiernan-González, *Fevered Measures: Public Health and Race at the Texas-Mexico Border, 1848–1942* (Durham, NC: Duke University Press, 2012) 10; "Prison Camp Is a Real Showground," *El Paso Herald*, March 18, 1914; "Mexican Refugees Won't Be Sent Back," *New York Times*, January 13, 1914; Soldiers Shoot Mexican at Marfa," *El Paso Herald,* January 12, 1914; "Vaccinations Are Blamed for Deaths," *El Paso Herald,* February 14, 1914; Lona Whittington, "Road of Sorrow: Mexican Refugees Who Fled Pancho Villa through Presidio, Texas, 1913–1914" (master's thesis, Sul Ross State University, Alpine, Texas, 1976), 3, 21, 57, 72–73.

46. Nelson Greene, artist, *Uncle Sam Picking Up Mexican Revolutionists with Shovel for the International Rubbish Can,* Mexico, 1915 (photograph retrieved from the Library of Congress, https://www.loc.gov/item/2016681636/).

47. Dunn, *The Militarization of the US–Mexico Border,* 9; Evan Anders, *Boss Rule in South Texas: The Progressive Era* (Austin: University of Texas Press, 1982), 215–218; Arnoldo De León, *War along the Border: The Mexican Revolution and Tejano Communities* (College Station: Texas A&M University Press, 2012).

48. Harris and Saddler, *Texas Rangers and the Mexican Revolution,* 427; "Texas Ranger History," http://www.texasRanger.org/history/Timechaos.htm; José T.

Canales, testimony, "Proceedings," 678; E. M. Sorrenson, testimony, "Proceedings," 1034.

49. James A. Sandos convincingly argues that the leaders of the rebellion Aniceto Pizaña and Luis de La Rosa were inspired by the anarchist writings of Ricardo Flores Magón. See Sandos, *Rebellion in the Borderlands: Anarchism and the Plan de San Diego, 1904–1923* (Oklahoma City: University of Oklahoma Press, 1992). For more on the Magón brothers inspiring revolt, see Kelly Lytle Herández, *City of Inmates: Conquest, Rebellion, and the Rise of Human Caging in Los Angeles, 1771–1965* (Berkeley: University of California Press, 2017).

50. Thomas H. Kreneck and Bruce S. Cheeseman, "Map of the Santa Gertrudis Estate, 1871: A Foundation Document of King Ranch," *Southwestern Historical Quarterly* 108, no. 2 (2004): 232–244.

51. Montejano, *Anglos and Mexicans,* 110–112; Johnson, *Revolution in Texas,* 18.

52. Frank N. Samponaro and Paul Vanderwood, *War Scare on the Rio Grande: Robert Runyon's Photographs of the Border Conflict, 1913–1916* (Austin: University of Texas Press, 1992), 75–76; James L. Allhands, *Gringo Builders* (Iowa City: n.p., 1931), 265–266.

53. Frank Pierce, *A Brief History of the Lower Rio Grande Valley* (Menasha, WI: George Banta, 1917), 114, 91.

54. Trinidad Gonzales, "The Mexican Revolution, *Revolución de Texas,* and *Matanza de 1915,*" in *War along the Border: The Mexican Revolution and Tejano Communities,* ed. Arnoldo De León (College Station: Texas A&M University Press, 2012) 107–133; Pierce, *A Brief History,* 103; Judge James B. Wells, testimony, "Proceedings," 676.

55. Paredes, *"With His Pistol in His Hand,"* 31. For more on Texas Rangers acting under the authority of the state governor and being financed by Anglo ranchers, see Julian Samora, Joe Bernal, and Alberta Pena, *Gunpowder Justice: A Reassessment of the Texas Rangers* (Notre Dame, IN: University of Notre Dame Press, 1979); Harris and Saddler, *Texas Rangers and the Mexican Revolution.*

56. Montejano, *Anglos and Mexicans,* 33. Regarding *El Plan de San Diego,* historians continue to debate whether insurrectionists actually authored the manifesto or if it was planted to justify brutal repression.

57. C. L. Jessup, testimony, "Proceedings," 1102–1103.

58. Ibid., 1119–1120.

59. Saidiya Hartman asks, "What are the protocols and limits that shape the narratives written as counter-history, an aspiration that isn't a prophylactic against the risks posed by reiterating violent speech and depicting again rituals of torture?" Hartman, "Venus in Two Acts," *Small Axe,* June 2008, 1–14.

60. Paredes, *"With His Pistol in His Hand"*; Acuña, *Occupied America*; Robert Rosenbaum, *Mexicano Resistance in the Southwest: "The Sacred Right of Self-Preservation"* (Austin: University of Texas Press, 1981); Johnson, *Revolution in*

Texas; Robert Utley, *Lone Star Justice: The First Century of the Texas Rangers* (New York: Oxford University Press, 2002); De León, *War along the Border.*

61. Walter Prescott Webb, *The Texas Rangers: A Century of Frontier Defense* (Boston: Houghton Mifflin, 1935).

62. Ramón Saldívar noted that Américo Paredes's efforts to preserve vernacular cultures of Texas-Mexicans were particularly urgent because "even the dead are not safe from cultural eradication." Saldívar, *The Borderlands of Culture: Américo Paredes and the Transnational Imaginary* (Durham, NC: Duke University Press, 2006), 8, 12–13. See also John Morán González, *Border Renaissance: The Texas Centennial and the Emergence of Mexican America* (Austin: University of Texas Press, 2009); José Limón, *Américo Paredes: Culture and Critique* (Austin: University of Texas Press, 2012).

63. Chapter 5 of this book examines this history. For more, see González, *Border Renaissance.*

64. Elliot Young, for example, writes that if not for the corrido tradition, then the revolt of Catarino Garza in the late nineteenth century would have been all but forgotten. Growing studies of rebellion on the US–Mexico border focus on armed conflict. Young, *Catarino Garza's Revolution,* 2–8. For more on the history of rebellions in this region, see Johnson, *Revolution in Texas;* Sandos, *Rebellion in the Borderlands;* Juan Gomez-Quiñones, *Sembradores: Ricardo Flores Magon y El Partido Liberal Mexicano: A Eulogy and Critique* (San Francisco: Aztlan Productions, 1973); W. Dirk Raat, *Mexico: From Independence to Revolution, 1810–1910* (Lincoln: University of Nebraska Press, 1982); Linda B. Hall and Don M. Coerver, *Revolution on the Border: The United States and Mexico, 1910–1920* (Albuquerque: University of New Mexico Press, 1990).

65. For important insights into researching the aftermath of violence, see Hartman, "Venus in Two Acts," and Kidada E. Williams, "Regarding the Aftermath of Lynchings," *Journal of American History* 101, no. 3 (2014): 857–858.

66. Williams, "Regarding the Aftermath of Lynchings," 856.

67. Williams, *They Left Great Marks on Me,* 13.

68. In her first book, Vicki Ruíz refers to the "shadowing" of Mexican women's experiences by scholarly publications that relegate women to "landscape roles. . . . The reader has a vague awareness of the presence of women, but only as scenery, not as actors" (Ruíz, *Cannery Women, Cannery Lives: Mexican Women, Unionization, and the California Food Processing Industry, 1930–1950* [Albuquerque: University of New Mexico Press, 1987], xiv). This book expands the metaphor to examine how popular cultural memories similarly relegate some victims of racial violence to the margins. For more, see Vicki Ruíz, *From Out of the Shadows: A History of Mexican Women in the United States, 1900–1995* (New York: Oxford University Press, 1998).

69. Trouillot, *Silencing the Past,* 29, 162.

70. For debates about oral histories and testimony as archival sources, see Shoshana Felman and Dori Laub, *Testimony: Crises of Witnessing in Literature, Psychoanalysis and History* (New York: Routledge, 1992); Alessandro Portelli, *The Death of Luigi Trastulli and Other Stories: Form and Meaning in Oral History* (Albany: State University of New York Press, 1991); Robert Perks and Alistair Thomson, eds., *The Oral History Reader* (London: Routledge, 1998). For more on the relationship between history and memory, see Matthew Garcia, *A World of Its Own: Race, Labor, and Citrus in the Making of Greater Los Angeles, 1900–1970* (Chapel Hill, University of North Carolina Press, 2002), 9, 150–153.

71. By the late 1950s, both the University of California at Berkley and UCLA had launched oral history research centers modeled after one started at Columbia University. See Donald A. Ritchie, *Doing Oral History: A Practical Guide* (New York: Oxford University Press, 2003), 12, 22.

72. T. Fujitani, Geoffrey M. White, and Lisa Yoneyama, eds., *Perilous Memories: The Asia-Pacific War(s)* (Durham, NC: Duke University Press, 2001), 4–6, 21.

73. See Leigh Raiford, *Imprisoned in a Luminous Glare: Photography and the African American Freedom Struggle* (Chapel Hill: University of North Carolina Press, 2013), 16; Schmidt Camacho, *Migrant Imaginaries,* 30, 46–48.

74. Macarena Gómez-Barris describes representations of state terror by witnesses and people generations removed as evidence of the afterlife of violence. See Gómez-Barris, *Where Memory Dwells;* and Herman Gray and Macarena Gómez-Barris, *Toward a Sociology of Trace* (Minneapolis: University of Minnesota Press, 2010). For more leading examples, see Schmidt Camacho, *Migrant Imaginaries;* Nicole M. Guidotti-Hernández, *Unspeakable Violence: Remapping US and Mexican National Imaginaries* (Durham, NC: Duke University Press, 2011); Antonia Castañeda, "'*Que Se Pudieran Defender'* (So You Could Defend Yourselves): Chicanas, Regional History, and National Discourses," *Frontiers* 22, no. 3 (2001): 116–142; Emma Pérez, *The Decolonial Imaginary: Writing Chicanas into History* (Bloomington: Indiana University Press, 1999); Stephanie Camp, *Closer to Freedom: Enslaved Women and Everyday Resistance in the Plantation South* (Chapel Hill: University of North Carolina Press, 2003); Sarah Haley, *No Mercy Here: Gender, Punishment, and the Making of Jim Crown Modernity* (Chapel Hill: University of North Carolina Press, 2016).

75. Norma Longoria Rodriguez, interview by author, September 22, 2010, San Antonio, TX, digital recording.

76. Mireya Loza writes that in the case of oral history, "the practice of producing a record (an audio / video recording or transcript) turns the ephemeral repertoire of embodied practice / knowledge into an enduring unchanging material record. The interpretation of that material can change, but the material itself is frozen." Loza, *Defiant Braceros: How Migrant Workers Fought for Racial, Sexual, and Political Freedom* (Chapel Hill: University of North Carolina Press,

2016), 13–14. For another example of history that explores loss, see Allyson Hobbs, *A Chosen Exile: A History of Racial Passing in American Life* (Cambridge, MA: Harvard University Press, 2014).

77. Saidiya Hartman, "Venus in Two Acts," *Small Axe,* June 2008, 4–5.

78. For more on efforts of institutions such as universities seeking retrospective justice for their links to slavery, see the "Report of the Brown University Steering Committee on Slavery and Justice," published by Brown University in 2006. For an early charge that racial violence in the United States be seen as a violation of human rights, see William L. Patterson, *We Charge Genocide: The Crimes of the Government against Negro People* (New York: International Publishers, 1951).

79. As quoted in Alexa Mills, "A Lynching Kept Out of Sight," *Washington Post,* September 2, 2016.

80. Michael Rothberg convincingly shows that multidirectional memory, remembering that embraces an intercultural dynamic, has potential to create new forms of solidarity and new visions of justice. For more on this and on relational methods for writing history, see Rothberg, *Multidirectional Memory: Remembering the Holocaust in the Age of Decolonization* (Stanford, CA: Stanford University Press, 2009); and Natalia Molina, "Examining Chicana / o History through a Relational Lens," *Pacific Historical Review* 82, no. 4 (2013): 520–541.

1. DIVINE RETRIBUTION

1. At approximately 1,300 feet in elevation, the town sits on top of the Edwards Plateau on just over one square mile of land. This region is bound by the Balcones Fault to the south and east, the Llano Uplift and the Llano Estacado to the north, and the Pecos River and Chihuahua Desert to the west.

2. "Armed Mexicans Marching on Town of Rocksprings," *El Paso Times,* November 14, 1910.

3. "Quemado Vivo," *El Regidor,* November 10, 1910. Local reports noted that the mob apprehended Rodríguez on a ranch owned by Jim Hunter. *San Antonio Daily Express,* November 14, 1910, and *El Paso Times,* November 4, 1910; Arnoldo De León, *Mexican Americans in Texas: A Brief History* (New York: Harlan Davidson, 1999), 50; Charles H. Harris and Louis R. Saddler, *The Texas Rangers and the Mexican Revolution: The Bloodiest Decade, 1910–1920* (Albuquerque: University of New Mexico Press, 2007), 51–52; William D. Carrigan and Clive Webb, *Forgotten Dead: Mob Violence against Mexicans in the United States, 1848–1928* (Oxford: Oxford University Press, 2013), 81–82.

4. Carrigan and Webb, *Forgotten Dead,* 81–82, 141–143; De León, *Mexican Americans in Texas,* 50; Harris and Saddler, *The Texas Rangers and the Mexican Revolution,* 51–52.

5. The origins of this tombstone, the financing of the marker, and why the name is spelled "Rodriques" remain unknown. "Rodriques" is known as an alternative spelling for "Rodríguez." An inscription on the tombstone of Effie Henderson reads, "Lord she was Thine and not mine own. Though hast not done me wrong. I thank Thee for the precious loan, Afforded me so long."

6. For more on how spaces are saturated with memories, see Jan Gross, *Neighbors: The Destruction of the Jewish Community in Jedwabne, Poland* (Princeton, NJ: Princeton University Press, 2001).

7. J. B. McCrain, "Rocksprings, Texas," in *Handbook of Texas Online,* http://www.tsha.utexas.edu/handbook/online/articles/RR/hjr11.html.

8. "Necktie Party," *Lyford Courant,* August 6, 1915. The article responded to the vigilante lynching near San Benito, Texas, of a man they identified as Adolfo Muñoz. Quoted in Benjamin Heber Johnson, *Revolution in Texas: How a Forgotten Rebellion and Its Bloody Suppression Turned Mexicans into Americans* (New Haven, CT: Yale University Press, 2003), 86–87.

9. For more on how these justifications inscribed African American men and women as well as Southern white women in violence, see the following studies that examine the intersections of race, gender, and the history of lynchings: Crystal N. Feimster, *Southern Horrors: Women and the Politics of Rape and Lynching* (Cambridge, MA: Harvard University Press, 2009); Hazel Carby, "'On the Threshold of Woman's Era': Lynching, Empire, and Sexuality in Black Feminist Theory," in *"Race," Writing, and Difference,* ed. Henry Louis Gates Jr. (Chicago: University of Chicago Press, 1986), 301–316; Glenda Elizabeth Gilmore, *Gender and Jim Crow: Women and the Politics of White Supremacy in North Carolina, 1896–1920* (Chapel Hill: University of North Carolina Press, 1996); Jacquelyn Dowd Hall, *Revolt against Chivalry: Jessie Daniel Ames and the Campaign against Lynching,* rev. ed. (New York: Columbia University Press, 1993); Grace Hale, *Making Whiteness: The Culture of Segregation in the South* (New York: Pantheon Books, 1998); Diane Miller Sommerville, *Rape and Race in the Nineteenth-Century South* (Chapel Hill: University of North Carolina Press, 2004); Susanne Lebsock, *A Murder in Virginia: Southern Justice on Trial* (New York: Norton, 2004).

10. Quoted in William Carrigan and Clive Webb, "The Lynching of Persons of Mexican Origin or Descent in the United States 1848–1928," *Journal of Social History* 37, no. 2 (2003): 428.

11. *El Debate,* November 5, 1910, as quoted in Gerald Raun, "Seventeen Days in November: The Lynching of Antonio Rodríguez and American-Mexican Relations, November 3-19, 1910," *Journal of Big Bend Studies* 7 (1995): 159.

12. *El Diario De Hogar,* November 9, 1910, quoted in Raun, "Seventeen Days in November," 159–160.

13. Ibid.

14. Quoted in Harvey Rice, "The Lynching of Antonio Rodriguez" (master's thesis, University of Texas at Austin, 1990), 29.

15. Quoted in ibid., 11.

16. Ibid., 29, 35. One newspaper report alleged that when protestors encountered several African Americans, they showed their support of the demonstration by waving and saluting the students. Later protesters carried an African American man on their shoulders as the crowd moved toward the Municipal Palace. The student's reference to James Jackson Jeffries recalls the racial hostilities surrounding the rise of Jack Johnson as the first black heavyweight boxing champion in the world. For more on the historic fight and Jack Johnson, see Theresa Runstedtler, *Jack Johnson, Rebel Sojourner: Boxing in the Shadow of the Global Color Line* (Berkeley: University of California Press, 2012); and Gail Bederman, *Manliness and Civilization: A Cultural History of Gender and Race in the United States, 1880–1917* (Chicago: University of Chicago Press, 1996).

17. Práxedis G Guerrero, "Blancos, Blancos," *El Regeneración,* November 19, 1910.

18. Ibid.

19. The Treaty of Guadalupe Hidalgo, signed on February 2, 1848, ended the Mexican War, recognized the annexation of Texas to the United States, and ceded the modern states of California, Arizona, and New Mexico to the United States.

20. Ramón Eduardo Ruiz, *The Great Rebellion: Mexico, 1905–1924* (New York: Norton, 1980), 102–104, 107, 113, 115. Ruiz explains that Mexicans who embraced this nationalistic fervor included intellectuals, artists, middle-class politicians, entrepreneurs, and industrial workers demanding labor equality. For Ruiz, the strong reaction to the lynching of a Mexican citizen depicts the depth of the anti-American sentiment in the Mexican republic. Carrigan and Webb, *Forgotten Dead,* 142.

21. "Situation in Mexico Serious," *Newark Advocate,* November 11, 1910; "May Turn Tables in Mexico Disturbance," *Waterloo Reporter,* November 12, 1910; "Demonstración Anti-Americanista: Los Mexicanos Indignados Por el Linchamiento de Antonio Rodríguez," *El Regidor,* November 10, 1910. In 1922 another lynching of a Mexican man identified as Mr. Villareal Zarate in Weslaco, Texas, triggered the involvement of the Mexican government to protect its citizen from vigilante violence and to demand an investigation of the murder. See "Mexican Lynched: His Government Complains," *Reno Evening,* November 15, 1922. Like Rodríguez, Mr. Villareal Zarate was in legal custody and forcibly removed from prison by a mob.

22. Quoted in Rice, "The Lynching of Antonio Rodriguez," 29.

23. Raun, "Seventeen Days in November," 62.

24. "American Kills Rioting Mexican," *Dallas Morning News,* November 13, 1910.

25. "Armed Mexicans Marching on Town of Rock Springs," *El Paso Times,* November 14, 1910. Articles circulating similar ideas about fear include the following: "Mexicans on Warpath," *Advocate,* November 19, 1910; "Fear Fight at Rock Springs," *Laredo Times,* November 20, 1910; "Americans Are Warned," *Dallas Morning News,* November 12, 1910.

26. "Trouble at Guadalajara," *Dallas Morning News,* November 12, 1910; Raun, "Seventeen Days in November," 62. "Armed Mexicans Marching on Town of Rock Springs," *El Paso Times,* November 14, 1910.

27. Quoted in Raun, "Seventeen Days in November," 157.

28. "Messages Are Exchanged," *Dallas Morning News,* November 13, 1910, 1.

29. "Governor Campbell Probes Lynching," *Fort Worth Star Telegram,* November 11, 1910.

30. "Texas Governor Hears from Knox," *Dallas Morning News,* November 12, 1910; "Grand Jury to Probe Rock Springs Lynching," *Fort Worth Star-Telegram,* December 15, 1910. Inquest records for Edwards County prior to the late 1920s do not exist. Unfortunately, records from the late nineteenth and early twentieth century were lost in a fire.

31. "Atwell Discusses Trouble," *Dallas Morning News,* November 12, 1910.

32. Ibid.

33. Ibid.

34. For more, see Carby, "'On the Threshold of Woman's Era,'" 301–316; María Eugenia Cotera, *Native Speakers: Ella Deloria, Zora Neale Hurston, Jovita González, and the Poetics of Culture* (Austin: University of Texas Press, 2008); Leigh Raiford, *Imprisoned in a Luminous Glare: Photography and the African American Freedom Struggle* (Chapel Hill: University of North Carolina Press, 2013).

35. "Antonio Rodríguez Era Mexicano: Una Subscripcion Para Socorrer a Los Duedos," *La Crónica,* November 19, 1910. While *La Crónica* found no reason to doubt claims by Genoveva Rangel, the west Texas historian Gerald Raun described the alleged widow as playing "on the sympathies of the citizens of Guadalajara" and found that no further records or evidence proved her relation to Antonio Rodríguez. Raun, "Seventeen Days in November," 172.

36. "Rodríguez's Mother Is Found," *Advocate,* November 19, 1910.

37. Efforts to undermine sympathy for Antonio Rodríguez or diplomatic pressures from Mexico soon took on a form of theatrics. In Salt Lake City, Utah, the *Evening Telegram* reported that Mexican consulate Villasana returned to Eagle Pass, Texas, from Rocksprings, and had found "the most perfect friendship and good feeling existing between the Americans and their Mexican employees in Rock Springs." His investigation into the lynching allegedly concluded that Rodríguez was "either insane, or under an assumed name, was a fugitive of justice." "Consul Believes Rodriguez Insane," *Evening Telegram,* November 18, 1910. This report seemed mild compared with accounts by the *Charlotte Daily*

Observer that Rodríguez came back from the dead and walked around "alive and hearty" in Guadalajara. If not a divine act, then, the article reported, Rodríguez was an agent of the revolutionary leader Francisco Madero and Mexican authorities arrested him for questioning. The article continued with a tone of mystery and described efforts being made in Rocksprings to establish the identity of the man lynched and buried. "Dead Man Comes Back," *Charlotte Daily Observer,* December 30, 1910.

38. "Rodriguez May Be American," *Dallas Morning News,* November 13, 1910. The *El Paso Times* published the same quote received from Washington on November 13 as well.

39. Ibid.

40. Hadie Henderson Seale, "Lemuel Kenneth Henderson, Sr.," in *Edwards County History* (San Angelo, TX: Anchor, 1983), 581. Together Henderson and Dodson bought and raised cattle. They marked their herd with the brand W I L. The name of Henderson's first wife is written in this family biography as Virginia Dodson. Census records from 1880 recorded her name as Eugenie E. Henderson. This source documents Henderson's wife as twenty-two years old, established that she was born in Texas, and noted that her father was born in Virginia and her mother in Mississippi. Because the accuracy of census records is varied due to multiple conditions (including the capabilities of census workers and their ability to record answers legibly), I chose to privilege the accuracy of the family biography as written by Henderson's daughter Hadie Seal and record Henderson's first wife as Virginia Dodson. Tenth Census of the United States, 1880, Justice Precinct 3, Kimble, Texas, 284A, Records of the Bureau of the Census, Record Group 29, National Archives, Washington, DC (hereafter RBC, RG29, NAWD).

41. Seale, "Lemuel Kenneth Henderson, Sr.," 581. Causes of Virginia Dodson Henderson's death are not recorded in the family history, and as of yet I have not located sources that give insight.

42. "L. K. Henderson," Muster roll of Company F (July 2, 1885), Ranger Military Rolls, Military rolls, Texas Adjutant General's Department, Archives and Information Services Division, Texas State Library and Archives Commission. On July 2, 1885, L. K. Henderson received $59 for his duty. Seale, "Lemuel Kenneth Henderson, Sr.," 581. According to the family history, Texas Rangers in Henderson's company (under Captain Scott) "drew lots" to see who would remain in the force. Henderson drew a number that required him to voluntarily leave the force. For information about his property holdings in Texas, see Lem Henderson and Lillian Henderson, Val Verde, County, Texas Land Title Abstracts, Texas General Land Office, Austin, Texas.

43. Seale, "Lemuel Kenneth Henderson, Sr.," 581; Thirteenth Census of the United States, 1910, Justice Precinct 1, Edwards, Texas, 5B, RBC, RG29, NAWD. Census records for Edwards County 1910 note the children's ages as

follows: Brownie, 16 (recorded as Bunnie on the census); Gus, 11; Thomas, 9; Hadie, 5; and Lemuel Kenneth Jr., 7 months. In addition to the parents and children, the household included Wheat L. Bradford, who worked as a laborer on the Henderson stock farm, and Alice Loe, who worked as a private schoolteacher. It appears that by 1910 Mary and Laura from Henderson's first marriage no longer lived with their father.

44. Seale, "Lemuel Kenneth Henderson, Sr.," 581–582. In 1920 the Henderson household included parents L. K. and Mollie Henderson, Thomas, Hadie, Lem K. Jr., Ouida, and Onie. The couple continued to live on the ranch until March 15, 1937, when L. K. Henderson passed away, survived by his wife and ten children. After his death, Mollie Henderson moved from the family ranch to Rocksprings, where she lived until her death on June 22, 1951. Fourteenth Census of the United States, 1920, Justice Precinct 4, Edwards, Texas, 1A, RBC, RG29, NAWD. The census records the children's ages as follows: Thomas, 19; Hadie, 16; Lem K. Jr., 10; Ouida, 6; and Onie, 4. In the records the names of the two youngest children are spelled Onida and Ona, but for consistency I chose to privilege the names as provided by Hadie Seale in her family history. The census records Mollie Henderson's estimated date of birth as 1888, but her tombstone located in the Edwards County Cemetery notes her birthday as November 6, 1885.

45. Seale, "Lemuel Kenneth Henderson, Sr.," 582.

46. Raun, "Seventeen Days in November," 174–175.

47. For example, the newspaper *El Regeneración* in Los Angeles, California, continued to publish articles that referenced the lynching of Antonio Rodríguez years after the lynching. In "A La Huelga," the newspaper recalled Rodríguez as a Mexican laborer, a fellow proletariat, and questioned how many other innocent men from the working class had been beaten or killed in Texas. The article called on men and women to mobilize around the plight of the Mexican Revolution. See "A La Huelga," *El Regeneración*, December 9, 1916; "Regeneración Por Rangel, Cline, y Compañeros," *El Regeneración*, May 23, 1914.

48. "Texas Deplores It," *Brownsville Herald*, November 12, 1910.

49. Ibid.

50. "Quemado Vivo," *El Regidor*, November 10, 1910.

51. Carrigan and Webb, *Forgotten Dead*, 144–145; "Cobarde Infame e Inhumano Lynchamiento de Un Jovencito Mexicano en Thorndale," *La Crónica*, June 29, 1911; "Lo Mismo de Siempre," *La Crónica*, November 16, 1911; "Mob Law," *Laredo Times*, July 2, 1911. Despite protests from participants in El Primer Congreso Mexicanista in Laredo in 1911 and the family's appeals to a Mexican ambassador in Washington, Martínez was executed on May 11, 1914. For the father's correspondence with Mexican ambassadors, see León Cárdenas Martínez Sr. to Mexican ambassador, August 3, 1911, as reprinted in Francisco Arturo

Rosales, *Testimonio: A Documentary History of the Mexican American Struggle for Civil Rights* (Houston: Arte Publico Press, 2000), 111–112; "Al Beneficio de León Cárdenas Martínez," *La Crónica,* September 21, 1911. For more on the place of the lynching of Antonio Gómez and Antonio Rodríguez in the history of the Chicana/o civil rights movement, see Francisco Arturo Rosales, *Pobre Raza! Violence, Justice, and Mobilization among México Lindo Immigrants, 1900–1936* (Austin: University of Texas Press, 1999), 119; Francisco Arturo Rosales, *Chicano! The History of the Mexican American Civil Rights Movement* (Houston: Arte Publico Press, 1997), 61–62.

52. The newspapers can be translated as "The Infamous Coward and Inhumane Lynching of a Young Mexican Boy in Thorndale" and "The Same as Always."

53. "Consul Is Asked to Investigate Lynching: Mexican Government Orders Mr. Diebold to Look into Matter in Thorndale," *San Antonio Light,* June 21, 1911. The lynching of Antonio Gómez and the investigation of his murder are documented in articles in the *San Antonio Daily Light* in June and July of 1911.

54. In a similar fashion, *El Regidor* of San Antonio, Texas, situated the lynching of Rocksprings within widespread violence in the United States against ethnic Mexicans. In particular, it cited the growing fear that a Mexican man would be lynched for being accused of murdering the Andarke, Oklahoma, chief of police W. C. Temple that same month. "El Asunto se Complica," *El Regidor,* November 17, 1910.

55. Examples of these editorials in *La Crónica* include "El Antagonismo de Razas Es Fatal: Dignifiquese a la Raza Mexicana," November 19, 1910; "A La Raza Mexicana Del Estado de Texas," October 1, 1910; "Los Mexicanos En Texas," April 30, 1910. For more on the conference, see José Limón, "El Primer Congreso Mexicanísta de 1911: A Precursor to Contemporary Chicanismo," *Aztlán* 5 (1974): 88–89.

56. Carrigan and Webb, "The Lynching of Persons of Mexican Origin," 426; "Mexican Protective Society," *Laredo Times,* July 2, 1911. The paper reported that former Laredo residents Donanciano R. Davila and Emilio Flores started and led the organization as president and secretary, respectively.

57. Limón, "El Primer Congreso," 88–89. For more on the migration of Juan Crow laws in Texas, see David Montejano, *Anglos and Mexicans in the Making of Texas, 1836–1986* (Austin: University of Texas Press, 1987).

58. Limón, "El Primer Congreso," 93–94.

59. Quoted in ibid., 95. Historian Crystal N. Feimster notes that studies of lynching in the South tend to ignore how women responded to mob violence in the name of protecting white women and how the politics of lynching informed women's politics and anti-rape campaigns. She writes, "Whether they promoted or denounced lynching, participated in lynchings, or fell victim to mob violence

and rape, southern women, both black and white, forced their entry into the racial and sexual politics of the New South." Feimster, *Southern Horrors,* 5.

60. Sonia Hernández, "Women's Labor and Activism in the Greater Mexican Borderlands, 1910–1930," in *War along the Border: The Mexican Revolution and Tejano Communities,* ed. Arnoldo De León (College Station: Texas A&M University Press, 2012), 182–183; Sonia Hernandez, *Working Women into the Borderlands* (College Station: Texas A&M University Press, 2014); Clara Lomas, "Transborder Discourse: The Articulation of Gender in the Borderlands in the Early Twentieth Century," *Frontiers* 24, no. 2 (2003): 64–65; Teresa Palomo Acosta and Ruthe Winegarten, *Las Tejanas: 300 Years of History* (Austin: University of Texas Press, 2003), 51, 84–87. Women, like men, actively participated in the period of revolutionary conflict as nurses and soldiers but also served as guiding intellectuals who took action as journalists and editors to support groups like the Partido Liberal Mexicano.

61. Limón, "El Primer Congreso," 98–101.

62. Hernandez, *Working Women into the Borderlands,* 92–94; Johnson, *Revolution in Texas,* 145–146.

63. Carrigan and Webb, "The Lynching of Persons of Mexican Origin," 426.

64. For unlettered communities, Ramón Saldívar writes that vernacular oral traditions were an essential source of news and information in the early twentieth century. See Saldívar, *The Borderlands of Culture: Américo Paredes and the Transnational Imaginary* (Durham, NC: Duke University Press, 2006). Additionally, these traditions continued throughout the twentieth century as a source of community knowledge passed to future generations.

65. This research takes a cue from Carrigan and Webb, who make the case that "The story of Mexican lynching is not a footnote in history but rather a critical chapter in the history of Anglo western expansion and conquest." Carrigan and Webb, "The Lynching of Persons of Mexican Origin," 414.

66. Montejano, *Anglos and Mexicans,* 283–285.

67. Jim Crow laws are most popularly associated with the racial segregation of white and African American societies in Southern states. During the civil rights movement, Chicano / a activists raised public awareness of a long history of Juan Crow throughout the American Southwest. For more on the Chicano / a Movement in Texas, see David Montejano, *Quixote's Soldiers: A Local History of the Chicano Movement, 1966–1981* (Austin: University of Texas Press, 2010); Cynthia E. Orozco, *No Mexicans, Women, or Dogs Allowed: The Rise of the Mexican American Civil Rights Movement* (Austin: University of Texas Press, 2009); Emilio Zamora, *Claiming Rights and Righting Wrongs in Texas: Mexican Workers and Job Politics during World War II* (College Station: Texas A&M University Press, 2009).

68. Mature male Angora goats can weigh as much as 125 pounds while female goats weigh as much as 100 pounds. Sheep shearers regularly suffer from back and

shoulder injuries due to the strenuous work. Rogelio Muñoz, interview by author, August 30, 2005, Uvalde, TX, digital recording.

69. Americo Paredes, *"With His Pistol in His Hand": A Border Ballad and Its Hero* (Austin: University of Texas Press, 1958), 138–141.

70. For Saldívar-Hull and the cultural producers she analyzes, there are multiple sites where vernacular histories and generational memory are shared. Women have a central place in preserving alternative histories. See Saldívar-Hull, *Feminism on the Border: Chicana Gender Politics and Literature* (Berkeley: University of California Press, 2000), 25.

71. Muñoz, interview by author.

72. Rogelio Muñoz, "Mexican-Anglo Relations in Texas" (student essay, Fall 1970, Rogelio Muñoz private archive). His professor, George I. Sánchez, gave Muñoz an A and commented that he wrote an excellent essay.

73. Muñoz, interview by author.

74. The Texas Rangers were also a repressive force during agricultural strikes in the 1930s and again during the 1960s and 1970s, see Julian Samora, Joe Bernal, and Albert Peña, *Gunpowder Justice: A Reassessment of the Texas Rangers* (Notre Dame, IN: University of Notre Dame Press, 1979).

75. Juan Gómez-Quiñones, "Towards a Perspective on Chicano History," *Aztlán* 2, no. 2 (1971): 39; Limón, "El Primer Congreso," 102. Inspired by historian Juan Gómez-Quiñones's 1971 call for a "union of history as discipline and history as action on behalf of a community in its struggle for survival," Limón wrote, "If this new knowledge of historical ideological precedents lends moral and intellectual support to the contemporary struggle, this work has responded adequately to this call."

76. Raun, "Seventeen Days in November," 157; Limón, "El Primer Congreso," 88; Carrigan and Webb, *Forgotten Dead;* McCrain, "Rocksprings, Texas."

77. This assessment of the different uses and accounts of the lynching is by no means exhaustive. Although I was unable to interview relatives of Effie Henderson or Antonio Rodríguez, the Henderson family did participate in interviews that informed articles published in the 1960s and 1970s. The Henderson family also published their own family biographies that include accounts of the murder of Effie Henderson. My examination of primary sources, coupled with interviews, reveals the multiple uses of the memory of the lynching. Indeed, no one official account of the lynching exists, and this chapter aims to show the complexities of these memories rather than provide a singular interpretation of the events.

78. Sibyl Epperson et al., *Edwards County History* (San Angelo, TX: Anchor, 1983). The book committee consisted of Sibyl Epperson (chair), Alma Smart (president of the Woman's Club), Alta Dutton (treasurer), Lillie Shanklin (memorial pages), and Helen Fred (Edwards County historical chair). More than 700

families submitted histories for the publication, and according to the book's preface, "all were accepted and none refused."

79. Seale, "Lemuel Kenneth Henderson, Sr.," 582.

80. Ibid.

81. Herbert Oehler, "Murder Avenged by Burning at the Stake," *Real West* 20, no. 149 (1977): 46.

82. "Mob Metes Swift Justice to Murderer," *Kerville Mountain Sun,* November 5, 1910, as quoted in Oehler, "Murder Avenged by Burning at the Stake," 56.

83. Oehler, "Murder Avenged by Burning at the Stake," 47.

84. Vincent Vega, interview by author, August 8, 2009, Rocksprings, TX, digital recording.

85. Ibid.

86. Ibid.

87. Ibid. In another interview, Romana Bienek shared that relatives passed down a story that Antonio Rodríguez had cursed the town. Romana Bienek, interview by author, September 1, 2010, Rocksprings, TX, digital recording.

88. Muñoz, interview by author.

89. Anita Mata Torres, *Historias de Mi Gente: Nineteenth and Twentieth Century Uvalde County Texas* (Corpus Christi, TX: American Binding and Publishing Company, 2006), 146–148. Physical injuries range from being kicked by the animal, being cut by cactus or mesquite thorns hiding in the wool, or having a vein sliced open by the sharp clippers. The labor of sheep shearing ranged from the *trasquilador,* who simultaneously held down and sheared the sheep or goat; to the *lanero,* a young aspiring crew member who gathered the wool, medicated cuts inflicted on the animals, and also grabbed the next animal to be sheared; the *volteador,* who powered the clippers with his arms by cranking the machine; the *empacadores,* who packed the wool into long sacks; the *amolador,* who sharpened the clipper blades; and the *cocineros,* who cooked the meals.

90. Jose Canales Jr., interview by author, September 3, 2010, San Antonio, TX, digital recording.

91. Ibid.

92. Nicholas Gallegos, interview by author, July 31, 2009, Rocksprings, TX, digital recording.

93. Ibid.

94. Ibid. The author is currently developing a database of episodes of racial violence that includes multiple forms of violence that targeted multiple racial and ethnic groups. For more, see www.mappingviolence.com.

95. For more on cemeteries, see Marie Theresa Hernandez, *Cemeteries of Ambivalent Desire: Unearthing Deep South Narratives from a Texas Graveyard* (College

Station: Texas A&M University Press, 2008) 5. Hernandez builds on postcolonial theorist Ato Quayson's premise that violence and social traumas produce nations.

96. The residents and city officials that I spoke with do not know the exact date the fence dividing the cemetery was removed.

97. Helen Fred served as the Edwards County Historical Chair and led the historical book committee that compiled the entries for the *Edwards County History* referred to earlier in this chapter. See Epperson et al., *Edwards County History*.

98. Bienek, interview by author.

99. Ibid.

100. Ibid.

101. Ibid.

102. Local memories also speculate about what remains of Antonio Rodríguez are buried. From some accounts Bienek heard that only the head and the heart remained after Rodríguez was burned alive, so only those remains are buried. When she was growing up, she heard from her grandparents and parents that only his bones had been saved from the ashes of the fire and that those were buried without any remaining tissue.

103. Augustine González, interview by Nira González and author, October 31, 2010, Rocksprings, TX, digital recording.

104. Muñoz, interview by author.

105. Epperson et al., *Edwards County History;* Texas historical marker "Edwards County," located in Rocksprings, Texas.

106. Epperson et al., *Edwards County History,* 36–37. The next morning revealed a day as "tragic and pathetic as the night had been. Bodies were mutilated almost beyond recognition. Some rescuers washed the faces of the dead to find they were loved ones." Across Texas, newspapers reported the overwhelming need and asked for neighboring communities to offer assistance to help residents heal from the natural disaster as they mourned their losses. Aside from public assistance from the Red Cross and Blue Cross and the help of the Fifth US Cavalry from Ft. Clark, residents organized a citizens' committee for relief work who appealed to readers in Texas through the newspaper, the *San Antonio Light,* for support during the trying recovery.

107. Vega, interview by author.

108. William D. Carrigan, *The Making of a Lynching Culture: Violence and Vigilantism in Central Texas, 1836–1916* (Urbana: University of Illinois Press, 2004), 202–206.

109. "50 Years Later They Still Remember: The Night Rocksprings Blew Away," *San Antonio Express News,* April 9, 1977; "Rocksprings Destroyed by Tornado, April 12, 1927," *Texas Mohair Weekly,* April 8, 1977.

110. In 1967 the State Historical Survey Committee gave Edwards County a historical marker to recognize the founding and history of the county. The same

committee certified the Edwards County Courthouse as a Texas Historic Landmark in 1973. The Edwards County historical marker located on the town square is dedicated to the founding of the county and explains that the courthouse and county jail are two buildings that escaped destruction in the 1927 tornado. The plaque for the Edwards County Courthouse describes the late Victorian structure as being built with limestone quarried in south Texas in 1891. The plaque notes that after the deadly tornado in 1927 that killed seventy people, remarkably the courthouse needed only minor roof repair. In the Edwards County Cemetery, a tombstone lists the names of those who died in the tornado, honoring their lives and mourning their departure.

111. Muñoz, interview by author.

112. Romana Rendon Bienek, "Candle Light Vigil for Antonio Rodriguez 11/03/1910–11/03/2010, 100 Years," typed flyer, author's private collection.

113. Bienek, interview by author. No relatives of the Henderson family attended the memorial, but Bienek told the group that they gave their permission to have the Catholic priest bless Henderson's grave.

114. Bienek, interview by author.

115. Vega, interview by author.

116. "The Pioneer Coalsons," https://atlas.thc.state.tx.us/Details/5507014128.

117. "Texas Historical Commission: Undertold Markers," http://www.thc.texas.gov/preserve/projects-and-programs/state-historical-markers/undertold-markers.

2. FROM SILENCE

1. Frank Pierce, *A Brief History of the Lower Rio Grande Valley* (Menasha, WI: George Banta Publishing Co., 1917), 89–91; Benjamin Heber Johnson, *Revolution in Texas: How a Forgotten Rebellion and Its Bloody Suppression Turned Mexicans into Americans* (New Haven, CT: Yale University Press, 2003), 76–78. Frank Pierce describes the Austins as being killed by a chance encounter with the band. Benjamin Johnson interprets the killings as evidence of assailants targeting Anglo residents who embodied the new Anglo farming ascendancy.

2. For estimates, see James Sandos, *Rebellion in the Borderlands: Anarchism and the* Plan de San Diego, *1904–1923* (Oklahoma City: University of Oklahoma Press, 1992); Trinidad Gonzales, "The Mexican Revolution, *Revolución de Texas,* and *Matanza de 1915,*" in *War along the Border: The Mexican Revolution and Tejano Communities,* ed. Arnoldo De León (College Station: Texas A&M University Press, 2012), 107–133; Pierce, *A Brief History*, 103; Judge James B. Wells, testimony, "Proceedings of the Joint Committee of the Senate and the House in the Investigation of the Texas State Ranger Force," Adjutant General Records, Texas State Archives, Austin, 676.

3. Other references to this period include *la rinchada*. The word *rinchada* was derived from the derogatory term for Texas Rangers, *rinches,* commonly used in south Texas. See Richard Ribb, "*La Rinchada:* Revolution, Revenge, and the Rangers, 1910–1920," and Gonzales, "The Mexican Revolution, *Revolución de Texas,* and *Matanza de 1915,*" in De León, *War along the Border,* 56–106, 107–133.

4. Lon C. Hill, testimony, "Proceedings," 1145–1146.

5. In his study, Benjamin Johnson notes that to bury the bodies of loved ones in this period was to court death. *Revolution in Texas,* 118.

6. Kirby Warnock, "Trouble on the Border," http://www.borderbanditsmovie.com/story.htm.

7. Henry Lee Ransom, Scout Reports Company D 1915, Ranger Force Records 1901–1962, Texas Adjutant General's Department, Archives and Information Services Division, Texas State Library and Archives Commission.

8. Federal census records show the Longorias living with six children. All four sons are listed as working on the family ranch. Thirteenth Census of the United States, 1910, Justice Precinct 7, Hidalgo, Texas, 7B, Records of the Bureau of the Census, Record Group 29, National Archives, Washington, DC (hereafter RBC, RG29, NAWD). Norma Longoria Rodriguez points out that the Longorias had only five children, and at the time the census was conducted, two of their children would have been about eleven and five years old, too young to work on the ranch. The Bazáns, on the other hand, had five sons who would have been about eleven, seventeen, twenty-one, twenty-seven, and twenty-nine years old, and most likely the sons listed on the census worked on the ranch. Federal census records from 1910 list Antonio Longoria living with his wife, Antonia, since their marriage in 1897. Twelfth Census of the United States, 1900, Justice Precinct 6, Hidalgo, Texas, 4B, RBC, RG29, NAWD; Norma L. Rodriguez, "Antonia Bazán Longoria (1877–1966)," Los Tejanos, http://los-tejanos.com/essays.htm; Antonio L. Longoria, Hidalgo County Teaching Certificate, June 25, 1908, Norma Longoria Rodriguez private collection; Hidalgo County Treasurer John Closner to Antonio Longoria, "Estimado Amigo," June 6, 1914, Norma Longoria Rodriguez private collection.

9. James C. Scott, *Weapons of the Weak: Everyday Forms of Peasant Resistance* (New Haven, CT: Yale University Press, 1985), xvii, 36.

10. James Scott wrote of the clandestine movements of peasant workers: "Their safety may depend on silence and anonymity; the kind of resistance itself may depend for its effectiveness on the appearance of conformity; their intentions may be so embedded in the peasant subculture and in their routine, taken for granted struggle to provide for the substance and survival of the households as to remain inarticulate. The fish do not talk about the water." Scott, *Weapons of the Weak,* 301.

11. For cases where residents filed charges against the state through international courts, see Monica Muñoz Martinez, "Indemnities for State Murder: The US–Mexico General Claims Commission of 1923," *Social Text* (September 2011), http://www.socialtextjournal.org/periscope/going-into-debt/, and Chapter 3 of this book.

12. See Jean Franco, *Plotting Women: Gender and Representation in Mexico* (New York: Columbia University Press, 1989), 2.

13. For more on competing memories and their lasting influence on racial formation in Texas, see Richard Flores, *Remembering the Alamo: Memory, Modernity, and the Master Symbol* (Austin: University of Texas Press, 2002) and Chapters 5 and 6 of this book.

14. Quoted in Frank N. Samponaro and Paul J. Vanderwood, *War Scare on the Rio Grande: Robert Runyon's Photographs of the Border Conflict, 1913–1916* (Austin: Barker Texas History Center, 1992), 44; Evan Anders, *Boss Rule in South Texas: The Progressive Era* (Austin: University of Texas Press, 1982), 215–218.

15. Anders, *Boss Rule,* 219.

16. Chester Christopher, South Texas Oral History and Folklore Collection, James C. Jernigan Library, Texas A&M University, Kingsville, Texas (hereafter STOHFC, JJL, TAMUK).

17. "Keep Eye on Border Mexican," *Laredo Times,* April 23, 1916.

18. William G. B. Morrison, testimony, "Proceedings," 24, 32.

19. Charles H. Harris III and Louis R. Sadler, *The Texas Rangers and the Mexican Revolution: The Bloodiest Decade, 1910–1920* (Albuquerque: University of New Mexico Press, 2004), 105, 190.

20. Walter Prescott Webb, *The Texas Rangers: A Century of Frontier Defense* (Austin: University of Texas Press, 1995), 513; Robert M. Utley, *Lone Star Lawmen: The Second Century of the Texas Rangers* (Oxford: Oxford University Press, 2007), 26–29.

21. Harris and Sadler, *The Texas Rangers and the Mexican Revolution,* 10; Utley, *Lone Star Lawmen,* 10–13.

22. Harris and Sadler, *The Texas Rangers and the Mexican Revolution,* 427.

23. Moses, testimony, "Proceedings," 102.

24. Webb, *The Texas Rangers,* 513; Utley, *Lone Star Lawmen,* 11.

25. Mike Cox, "A Brief History of the Texas Rangers," http://www.texasranger.org/texas-ranger-museum/history/brief-history/.

26. Utley, *Lone Star Lawmen,* 27, 28, 260.

27. Pierce, *A Brief History,* 115.

28. For more on the practice of ethnic cleansing, see Johnson's chapter "Repression," in *Revolution in Texas,* 108–143; Elliott Young, *Catarino Garza's Revolution on the Texas–Mexico Border* (Durham, NC: Duke University Press, 2004), 311; Webb, *The Texas Rangers,* 478; David Montejano, *Anglos and Mexicans*

in the Making of Texas, 1836–1986 (Austin: University of Texas Press, 1987); Arnoldo De León, ed., *War along the Border: The Mexican Revolution and Tejano Communities* (College Station: Texas A&M University Press, 2012); Sandos, *Rebellion in the Borderlands;* Juan Gomez-Quiñones, *Sembradores: Ricardo Flores Magon y El Partido Liberal Mexicano: A Eulogy and Critique* (San Francisco: Aztlan Productions, 1973).

29. Pierce, *A Brief History,* 89–91; Gonzales, "The Mexican Revolution," 121–123. Frank Pierce's book records Gregorio's name as Gorgonio. Records from the Adjutant General Service Records show a John D. White that served in the Texas Volunteer Guard during the Spanish–American War. On November 18, 1901, John D. White received $11.44 for his service in Company F of the Fourth Texas Volunteer Infantry.

30. Quoted in Gonzales, "The Mexican Revolution"; "2 Men Wanted by Officers Were Killed," *Brownsville Herald,* July 24, 1915.

31. "Deputy Sheriff and Customs Inspector Forced to Kill Men," *Brownsville Daily Herald,* July 24, 1915. Also quoted in Samponaro and Vanderwood, *War Scare,* 75.

32. "Deputy Sheriff and Customs Inspector Forced to Kill Men."

33. B. F. Johnson, testimony, "Proceedings," 50–59.

34. W. T. Vann, testimony, "Proceedings," 547.

35. Sheriff Emilio Forto quoted in David Montejano, *Anglos and Mexicans in the Making of Texas, 1836–1986* (Austin: University of Texas Press, 1987), 116.

36. Quoted in Johnson, *Revolution in Texas,* 115.

37. Vann, testimony, "Proceedings," 574–575.

38. Johnson, *Revolution in Texas,* 116.

39. William Sterling, *Trails and Trials of a Texas Ranger* (Norman: University of Oklahoma Press, 1979), 259.

40. Vann, testimony, "Proceedings"; "Sheriff Vann Explains to Ranger Committee How to 'Ransomize,'" *Austin American Statesman,* February 8, 1919.

41. Quoted in Johnson, *Revolution in Texas,* 123.

42. Alba Haywood, testimony, "Proceedings," 79, 87, 90.

43. José T. Canales, testimony, "Proceedings," 945; "Masked Men Hold Up Officer, Take Prisoner, Lynch Him," *Brownsville Herald,* July 29, 1915. In the state investigation, Representative José T. Canales refers to the lynched victim as "Rodolpho Muñoz." See Chapter 4 for more sources that refer to Muñoz as "Adolfo Muñoz" and "Adolfo Muniz."

44. Morrison, testimony, "Proceedings," 28; Johnson, testimony, "Proceedings," 59. Pierce referred to the victim as "Adolfo Muniz." Pierce, *A Brief History,* 89–91; Gonzales, "The Mexican Revolution," 122–124.

45. Hinojosa served as a regular Ranger in 1910. Daniel Hinojosa enlistment and resignation papers, Texas Adjutant General Service Records, 1836–1935,

Archives and Information Services Division, Texas State Library and Archives
Commission. For more on Hinojosa, see Chapter 4.

46. Hill, testimony, "Proceedings," 1157–1159.

47. Ibid.

48. Anders, *Boss Rule,* 229.

49. Wells, testimony, "Proceedings," 670.

50. Ibid.

51. Ibid., 678.

52. Ibid. Wells acted as the defense attorney in 1903 for A. Y. Baker, a Texas
Ranger charged with the murder of Mexican rancher Ramón de la Cerda. Baker
later became a political boss of Hidalgo County and the sheriff who decided not
to conduct an investigation into the deaths of Bazán and Longoria. For more on
political machines, see Anders, *Boss Rule.*

53. Sterling, *Trails and Trials.*

54. Jesse Sterling Campbell, STOHFC, JJL, TAMUK.

55. Ibid.

56. Reynolds Rossington, STOHFC, JJL, TAMUK.

57. Henry Lee Ransom, Scout Reports Company D 1915, Texas Adjutant
General Service Records, 1836–1935, Archives and Information Services Division, Texas State Library and Archives Commission.

58. Mary Margaret McAllen Amberson, James A. McAllen, and Margaret H.
McAllen, *I Would Rather Sleep in Texas: A History of the Rio Grande Valley & the
People of the Santa Anita Land Grant* (Austin: Texas State Historical Association,
2003).

59. Wells, testimony, "Proceedings," 678.

60. Kirby Warnock, *Texas Cowboy: The Oral Memoir of Roland A. Warnock and
His Life on the Texas Frontier* (Dallas: Trans Pecos Productions, 1992), 43–50.

61. Warnock, "Trouble on the Border."

62. Ibid.

63. Ibid.

64. Ibid., 53–54.

65. Ibid., 75–82, 109, 159–161.

66. Warnock, *Texas Cowboy,* 53.

67. Ibid., 55–56.

68. Ibid., 56.

69. Ibid.; "Frank Warnock Shot to Death on Mission St.," *Brownsville Herald,*
October 25, 1915.

70. Roland Warnock explains in the book that the Sterling brothers spoke with
his boss and threatened his young ranch hand. Warnock later regretted not
reporting these threats to his father. Warnock, *Texas Cowboy,* 57.

71. Ibid., 57–58.

72. Ibid., 58.

73. In addition to the murders previously described, Roland Warnock also described Bill Sterling's murder of an innocent Mexican boy who lived in Monte Cristo. Warnock knew the boy and attested that the boy could not have harmed anybody much less the little girl he frequently played with. He alleged that when Sterling's sister accused the unnamed boy of attempting to rape her, "Sterling went out there and shot him just like a dog. It all happened down there when a man's life wasn't worth much because it wasn't nothing." Warnock, *Texas Cowboy,* 61, 63.

74. "Sterling Brothers Are Acquitted at Edinburg," *Brownsville Herald,* March 30, 1916; "Frank Warnock Shot to Death on Mission St."; "Edinburg Ranchers Acquitted: Men Charged with Killing Farmer Year Ago Get Favorable Verdict," *Galveston Daily News,* March 31, 1916; "Trial Attracts Wide Interest: Sterling Brothers Charged in Hidalgo County with Killing Frank Warnock," *Brownsville Herald,* March 16, 1916; Justice Court Precinct, No. 8, Hidalgo County #147, *State of Texas v. W. W. Sterling and E. A. Sterling.*

75. Paul Schuster Taylor, *An American-Mexican Frontier: Nueces County Texas* (Chapel Hill: University of North Carolina Press, 1934).

76. Norma Longoria Rodriguez, interview by author, September 22, 2010, San Antonio, TX, digital recording; Rodriguez, "Antonia Bazán Longoria."

77. Rodriguez, "Antonia Bazán Longoria."

78. Census records indicate that all the Bazán children were born in Texas and all could read and write in Spanish. Fourteenth Census of the United States, 1920, Justice Precinct 6, Hidalgo, Texas, 4A, RBC, RG29, NAWD.

79. Rodriguez, interview by author; Fourteenth Census of the United States, 1920, Justice Precinct 7, Edinburg, Hidalgo, Texas, 2B, RBC, RG29, NAWD; Letter of correspondence, Norma Longoria Rodriguez to Monica Muñoz Martinez, October 21, 2017, author's private archive.

80. Rodriguez, "Antonia Bazán Longoria"; Rodriguez to Martinez, October 31, 2017.

81. The Longoria grandchildren all inherited portions of the family ranch and maintain the property today. Epigmenia's daughter, Luisa Bazán Cavasos, bought a piece of land from her mother and donated land for a church.

82. Rodriguez, interview by author.

83. Warnock, "Trouble on the Border."

84. Ibid.

85. Marita Sturken encourages researchers to ask what memories reveal about how the past affects the present. Oren Baruch Stier suggests that examining cultural representations of the past offers opportunities to consider how past events maintain a presence in current day. See Sturken, *Tangled Memories: The Vietnam War, the AIDS Epidemic, and the Politics of Remembering* (Berkeley:

University of California Press, 1997); and Baruch Stier, *Committed to Memory: Cultural Meditations of the Holocaust* (Amherst: University of Massachusetts Press, 2003).

86. *Border Bandits,* directed by Kirby Warnock (Dallas: Trans Pecos Productions, 2004).

87. Warnock, *Texas Cowboy,* 59–60.

88. Jessica Belasco, "Film Puts the Spotlight on Ranger Slayings," *San Antonio Express News,* November 16, 2004.

89. Ibid.

90. Ibid.

91. Ibid.

92. Ibid.

93. Jesse Bogan, "The Story of S. Texas," *San Antonio Express News,* May 7, 2006.

94. Ibid.

95. *Border Bandits.*

96. The Texas Ranger History Museum and Hall of Fame in Waco, Texas, is the leading institution for celebrating Texas Ranger history. For more, see Chapter 5 of this book.

97. Rodriguez, interview by author. Norma Longoria Rodriguez explained that the discrepancy of the dates came when Heriberto Longoria bought a new tombstone for Antonio Longoria, but the wrong date was inscribed. Rodriguez to Martinez, October 31, 2017.

98. Rodriguez, interview by author.

99. Ibid.; Rodriguez to Martinez, October 31, 2017.

100. Ernestina Longoria Martinez and Armando R. Longoria, interview with Norma L. Rodriguez, July 26, 1992, Los Tejanos, http://los-tejanos.com/rangers .htm.

101. Rodriguez, interview by author.

102. Ibid.

103. Ernestina Longoria Martinez and Armando R. Longoria, interview with Norma L. Rodriguez. I believe this quote by Norma Longoria Rodriguez's uncle inspired her writing in the poem published in the *San Antonio Express News.* Norma L. Rodriguez, "The Old Windmills / Los Papalotes," *San Antonio Express News,* November 2, 2008.

104. Rodriguez, interview by author.

105. Rodriguez, "A Silence of the Heart," Somos Primos, June 2010, 126th online issue, http://www.somosprimos.com/sp2010/spjun10/spjun10.htm.

106. Ibid.

107. Rodriguez, interview by author.

108. Ibid.

109. Hernán Contreras dedicated a page on his website to challenging common misconceptions about the Texas Rangers. He writes: "This reign of terror resulted in a 'code of silence' by survivors who felt threatened and uncomfortable in even speaking about Texas Ranger atrocities. Many of the killings were never reported. Here we are collecting documented cases that were never reported." This site includes a digital archive with family photographs, documents, and narrative accounts of relatives' impact on society in south Texas. Contreras, "Texas Rangers: Reign of Terror," Los Tejanos, http://los-tejanos.com/rangers.htm.

110. Rodriguez, "The Old Windmills / Los Papalotes."

111. Ibid. Rodriguez worked as a Spanish and English teacher in Texas public schools in south, east, and central Texas. Her poem harkens back to the Spanish literary tails of Don Quixote she presumably taught as a Spanish teacher,but also to the words of her uncle Armando Longoria, who described in his oral history the San Guadalupe del Torero Ranch that remained after the family moved to Donna, Texas.

112. Norma Rodriguez, "La Escuelita: Antonio's Legacy," *La Voz de Esperanza* 27, no. 9 (November 2014): 18.

113. Ibid.

114. Rodriguez, interview by author.

115. Here the "politics of mourning" as described by David L. Eng and David Kazanjian as the creative process mediating a hopeful or hopeless relation to the past and between loss and history is particularly salient. See Eng and Kazanjian, "Introduction: Mourning Remains," in *Loss: The Politics of Mourning,* ed. David L. Eng and David Kazanjian (Berkeley: University of California Press, 2003), 2.

116. Rodriguez, interview by author.

117. Ibid.

118. Ralph Blumenthal, "New Charges Tarnish Texas Rangers' Image and Reopen Old Wounds," *New York Times,* October 31, 2004.

119. Lesley Tellez, "Documentary Spurs Valley Lawmaker into Action," *San Antonio Express News,* December 30, 2004.

3. DENIAL OF JUSTICE

1. Ronnie C. Tyler, *The Big Bend: A History of the Last Texas Frontier* (College Station: Texas A&M University Press, 1996), 8–10, 121, 137.

2. Miguel Levario, *Militarizing the Border: When Mexicans Became the Enemy* (College Station: Texas A&M University Press, 2012), 4, 8–11.

3. Tyler, *The Big Bend,* 158.

4. Robert Keil, *Bosque Bonito: Violent Times along the Borderlands during the Mexican Revolution* (College Station: Texas A&M University Press, 2004), 30–32.

5. Ibid., 27–29. Keil writes about his conversation with Captain Anderson during which he voiced his concerns and also notes that he smelled whiskey on the Rangers the night of the massacre.

6. Ibid., 30.

7. Ibid., 30–32.

8. Deposition by Eulalia González Hernández, April 5, 1918, evidence, "Proceedings of the Joint Committee of the Senate and the House in the Investigation of the Texas State Ranger Force," Adjutant General Records, Texas State Archives, Austin, TX, 848.

9. Keil, *Bosque Bonito*, 30–32.

10. Ibid., 31.

11. Tyler, *The Big Bend,* 162. The killing of Joe Sitters continued to motivate calls for the militarization of the border throughout the decade. In the 1919 legislative investigation into the Texas Rangers, several witnesses mentioned the killing in their testimonies. For an example, see the transcript of Senator C. B. Hudspeth, testimony, "Proceedings," 969–970. In the transcript the name "Chico Cano" is transcribed as "Chito Canna." See also Miguel Antonio Levario, "Cuando Vino La Mexicanada: Authority, Race, and Conflict in West Texas, 1895–1924" (PhD diss., University of Texas at Austin, August 2007), 60–62.

12. Keil, *Bosque Bonito,* 32.

13. The traumatic events induced Francisca Morales into premature labor. She gave birth just two days after the massacre. "The Porvenir Massacre in Presidio County, Texas on January 28, 1918," Harry Warren Collection, Archives of the Big Bend, Bryan Wildenthal Memorial Library, Sul Ross State University, Alpine, TX (hereafter HWC, ABB-BWML-SRSU).

14. "Porvenir Massacre—Harry Warren," Clifford Casey Collection, Archives of the Big Bend, Bryan Wildenthal Memorial Library, Sul Ross State University, Alpine, TX (hereafter CCC, ABB-BWML-SRSU).

15. Benita and Evaristo Albarado, interview by author, August 7, 2009, Uvalde, TX, digital recording.

16. "Porvenir Massacre," Harry Warren Journal, HWC, ABB-BWML-SRSU.

17. The *El Paso Morning Times* described the residents of Porvenir as "Mexican peons" implicated in the Brite raid. "State Department Probes Execution of Mexican Peons," *El Paso Morning Times,* February 8, 1918.

18. Naomi A. Paik, *Rightlessness: Testimony and Redress in US Prison Camps since World War II* (Chapel Hill: University of North Carolina Press, 2016), 15. Paik quotes Paul Gilroy, who argued, "their testimony calls out to us and we must answer it." Gilroy, *Against Race: Imagining Political Culture beyond the Color Line* (Cambridge, MA: Belknap Press, of Harvard University Press, 2000), 87.

19. Thirteenth Census of the United States, 1910, Presidio County District 8, 6A, Records of the Bureau of the Census, National Archives and Records

Administration, Washington, DC (hereafter NARA). Although Manuel Morales is not listed in the census records as being an owner of his home, on November 30, 1914, he traveled to Van Horn, Texas, to notarize the purchase of a portion of his property by Ramon Nieves.

20. "Quit Claim Deed Manuel Morales," Historical Collection of Maps, Texas State Archives, Austin (hereafter TSA); "East Part Presidio County Map: Land Office," Historical Collection of Maps, TSA; Benita Albarado, interview by author, August 7, 2009, Uvalde, TX, digital recording.

21. Harry Warren Financial Records, 1914, HWC, ABB-BWML-SRSU.

22. Inspector A. Ruiz Sandoval to Major General Candido Aguilar, February 9, 1918, Docket 561, Case Files for Mexican Claims against the United States 1925–1936 (Mexican Claims), Records of Boundary and Claims Commission and Arbitrations, 1716–1994, Record Group 76, National Archives at College Park, College Park, MD (hereafter RG 76, NACP).

23. Harry Warren Financial Records, 1914, HWC, ABB-BWML-SRSU.

24. Ibid.

25. "School Land Proof of Occupancy and Improvements," Presidio County 1910, Harry Warren Financial Records, HWC, ABB-BWML-SRSU.

26. Harry Warren School Attendance Records, HWC, ABB-BWML-SRSU.

27. Thirteenth Census of the United States, 1910, Presidio County District 8, 6A, NARA.

28. Keil, *Bosque Bonito,* 29.

29. Army Captain Harry Anderson to Governor William P. Hobby, undated, evidence, "Proceedings" 849-851; Benita Albarado, interview by author. The three brothers were Serapio, Juan, and Pedro Jiménez. One survivor of the massacre, Juan Bonilla Flores, recalled later that Morales successfully grew crops of cotton using water from the Rio Grande for irrigation, an enormous accomplishment for the arid climate of west Texas.

30. Cecilia Thompson, *History of Marfa and Presidio County 1535–1946,* vol. 2 (Austin, TX: Norex Press, 1985), 91, 98.

31. Surviving witnesses of the Porvenir massacre speculated that the Texas Rangers murdered the Mexican men to evacuate the families, leaving the irrigated land open to Anglo settlement.

32. Keil, *Bosque Bonito,* 28; Linda Davis, interview by author, June 7, 2010, Uvalde, TX, phone interview.

33. Flores, interview by Gode Davis, 2002, Uvalde, TX.

34. Keil, *Bosque Bonito,* 28–29; Linda Davis, interview by author. During my interview with Linda Davis, daughter of Robert Keil, she remembered that her father described the residents of Porvenir as family. Throughout the memoir Keil refers to the Porvenir residents as friends and described instances where residents

aided the cavalry by riding to their camp to alert them to large groups of mounted men gathering in Chihuahua.

35. For more on the early conflict between residents, agents, and the military in the Big Bend, see Ronnie C. Tyler, "The Little Punitive Expedition in the Big Bend," *Southwestern Historical Quarterly* 78, no. 3 (1975): 271–291.

36. Historians disagree about Pancho Villa's role in the raid on Columbus. For more on the debate about his role, see Haldeen Brady, *Pancho Villa at Columbus: The Raid of 1916 Restudied* (El Paso: Texas Western College Press, 1965); Levario, *Militarizing the Border.* For more on Pancho Villa himself, see Friedrich Katz, *The Life and Times of Pancho Villa* (Palo Alto, CA: Stanford University Press, 1998).

37. For more, see Tyler, "The Little Punitive Expedition," 271–291. As investigations of these raids on west Texas continued, reports suggested that the bands were not associated with Pancho Villa but instead possibly had ties to Carrancista soldiers.

38. "How It Looked: Glenn Springs Texas 1916–1920," map from W. D. Smithers Collection, ABB-BWML-SRSU.

39. The fire badly burned three other soldiers while two escaped with only minor injuries. Tyler, "The Little Punitive Expedition," 277–281, 290–291.

40. Cosme Bengochea, Vice Consul, to General Candido Aguilar, Mexican Secretary of Foreign Relations, February 6, 1918, Docket 561, Mexican Claims, RG 76, NACP. In the correspondence Bengoechea quoted Langhorne's telegram of February 5, 1918, in full.

41. Tyler, *The Big Bend,* 158–159.

42. Ibid., 178; English- and Spanish-language newspapers reported on the Brite raid. "Mexican Bandits Raid the Brite Ranch Again," *Philadelphia Inquirer,* January 4, 1918; "Cien Mexicanos que Asaltaron el Rancho de Brite Estan a Punto de Ser Capturados Las Fuerzas," *La Prensa,* December 27, 1917; "Las Tropas Americanas se Internaron en Mexico Para Perseguir a los Bandidos," *El Paso Morning Times,* December 27, 1917; "Los Bandoleros Hacen Otro Raid al Rancho Brite," *El Paso Morning Times,* January 4, 1918.

43. Captain James Monroe Fox to Adjutant General James Harley, December 17, 1918, Roy W. Aldrich papers, ABB-BWML-SRSU.

44. Thompson, *History of Marfa and Presidio County,* 90–98, 110, 121.

45. Ibid., 146–149.

46. Captain James Monroe Fox to Adjutant General James Harley, January 30, 1918, Roy W. Aldrich papers, ABB-BWML-SRSU.

47. Captain James Monroe Fox to Adjutant General James Harley, February 18, 1918, submitted as evidence, "Proceedings," 834–835.

48. Affidavits of Bud Weaver, John Poole, and Raymond Fitzgerald, April 22, 1918, Docket 561, Mexican Claims, RG 76, NACP; Affidavit of T. W. Snyder, April 23, 1918, Docket 561, Mexican Claims, RG 76, NACP; Mexican Reply Brief, Docket 561, Mexican Claims, RG 76, NACP.

49. Untitled Adjutant General Report on Porvenir massacre, submitted as evidence, "Proceedings," 838–839.

50. Chick Davis and Al Ritter, "Captain Monroe Fox and the Incident at Porvenir," *Oklahoma State Trooper* (Winter 1996): 35–42. The article published in *Oklahoma State Trooper* celebrates Captain Fox and explains that the Porvenir massacre only slightly tarnished his reputation and that in the end his actions were justified. The article includes a lengthy description of his Colt .44 revolver and explains that a collector exhibits the gun as a prized possession. Photographed in the article, the author guesses that Fox most likely used the gun at Porvenir. For more on this photograph, see Chapter 5.

51. Quoted in Glenn Justice, *Little Known History of the Texas Big Bend: Documented Chronicles from Cabeza de Vaca to the Era of Pancho Villa* (Millersview, TX: Rimrock Press, 2001), 157.

52. Testimonies of Juan Méndez, Luis Jiménez, Pablo Jiménez, Rosenda Mesa, Seberiano Morales, Gregorio Hernández, and Cesario Huerta, evidence, "Proceedings," 1586–1604.

53. Ibid., 1586–1605. An investigation by US Cavalry special investigator Colonel W. J. Glasgow on June 3, 1918, explained that some soldiers did accompany the Rangers on the night of January 25–26, but they did not participate in the searches or arrest of the Porvenir residents. They also accompanied the Rangers on the night of January 28–29 but again did not participate in the searches or the assassination of the residents. "September 13, 1926, Supplement to Information 126 Docket No 1018, dated Sept 9, 1925," and "Report of Result of Search for Evidence," May 11, 1932, by C. M. Bishop, Docket 561, Mexican Claims, RG 76, NACP.

54. Testimony of Juan Méndez, evidence, "Proceedings," 1586–1588.

55. "The Porvenir Massacre in Presidio County, Texas on January 28, 1918," HWC, ABB-BWML-SRSU.

56. Statement of Juan Méndez, "Proceedings," 1586–1588; Brief, February 15, 1935, Docket 561, Mexican Claims, RG 76, NACP.

57. Ignacio Bonillas, Mexican Ambassador, to Robert Lansing, Secretary of State, March 6, 1918 and March 23, 1918, Annex 91 and 94, Docket 561, Mexican Claims, RG 76, NACP; Testimonies of Felipa Castañeda, Juana Bonilla Flores, Eulalia Hernández, Rita Jácquez, Librada Jácquez, Estefana Morales, Francisca Morales, Alejandra Nieves, and Harry Warren, evidence, "Proceedings," 841–849. The widow testimonies are riddled with errors. For example, the testimony of Rita Jácquez, widow of Macedonio Huerta, is recorded as being given by

Macedonio Huerta, and Francisca Morales, widow of Manuel Morales, is named as Francisco. Harry Warren gave a deposition in Candelara on March 26, 1918.

58. Army Captain Harry Anderson to Governor William P. Hobby, undated, evidence, "Proceedings," 849–851; emphasis in original.

59. Ibid.; emphasis in original.

60. General Order No. 5, June 4, 1918, evidence, "Proceedings," 836–837.

61. James M. Fox to Governor William P. Hobby, June 11, 1918, evidence, "Proceedings," 839–840.

62. Jas A. Harley to James M. Fox, July 3, 1918; letter published in the *El Paso Herald,* July 3, 1918, and in the *Brownsville Herald,* July 12, 1918.

63. Ignacio Bonillas, Mexican Ambassador, to Robert Lansing, Secretary of State, July 19, 1918, Annex 97-A, Docket 561, Mexican Claims, RG 76, NACP.

64. For more on the proceedings and the ideologies that informed the committee's decision, see Chapter 4.

65. "Enlistment Oath of Service and Description Ranger Force, Bud Weaver, August 18, 1922," Bud Weaver, Texas Ranger Vertical Files, Archives, Texas Ranger History Museum, Waco, TX.

66. "Oath of Members Ranger Force, James M. Fox, June 6, 1925," and "Oath of Members Ranger Force, James M. Fox, February 19, 1934," James M. Fox, Ranger File, Texas Adjutant General's Department service records, Archives and Information Services Division, Texas State Library and Archives Commission, Austin, TX.

67. For more on the role of the Mexican consulate in challenging the culture of lynching in the United States, see William D. Carrigan and Clive Webb, *Forgotten Dead: Mob Violence against Mexicans in the United States, 1848–1928* (Oxford: Oxford University Press, 2013), especially chapters 2 and 3. For the authors' discussion of the Moreno case, see 134–137.

68. G. H. Knaggs to Consulate Donnelly, September 1, 1897, United States Congress, House of Representatives, *Lynching of Florentino Suaste,* 56th Cong., 2nd sess., Doc. No. 142 (Washington, DC: Government Printing Office, 1900), 31.

69. Linda Gordon, *The Great Arizona Orphan Abduction* (Cambridge, MA: Harvard University Press, 1999), 256–259. Jacqueline Goldsby convincingly shows that vigilante culture must be seen as state-sanctioned violence. For more, see Goldsby, *A Spectacular Secret: Lynching in American Life and Literature* (Chicago: University of Chicago Press, 2006).

70. Members of the grand jury in Lasalle County in November 1895 included J. A. Landrum, foreman; P. Philipe, J. F. Hillard, B. Wildenthall, J. M. Ramsey, E. Lesterjett, R. E. Chew, W. M. McCarthy, Tim Conlin, T. J. Buckley, and J. W. Baylor. The clerk for the District Court supplied the names to Consul Donnelly and testified that all twelve had great integrity of character and that he knew them

to be truthful, honorable, and law-abiding citizens. G. H. Knaggs to Consulate Donnelly, September 1, 1897, 29.

71. Ibid., 42.

72. *Nicolasa Batista de Suaste et al., v. Andre Armstrong et al.,* No. 603, United States Congress, House of Representatives, *Lynching of Florentino Suaste,* 27–28; *Cadimira Reyes de Montelongo v. N. A. Swink,* No. 604, United States Congress, House of Representatives, *Lynching of Florentino Suaste,* 25–26.

73. United States Congress, House of Representatives, *Lynching of Florentino Suaste,* 12.

74. Ibid.

75. Verbal statement of J. G. Smith to Consulate Donnelly, September 1, 1897, "Lynching of Florentino Suaste: Message from the President of the United States," December 6, 1900, United States Congress, House of Representatives, *Lynching of Florentino Suaste,* 30.

76. Mr. Romero Mexican Legislation to Secretary Sherman, July 30, 1897, *Lynching of Florentino Suaste,* 4–6. In the court case of Nicolasa Suaste, she did not charge Deputy Sheriff Swink with the murder of her son Pedro Suaste.

77. "Statement of Miss Suaste," Consulate General, Nuevo Laredo, Mexico, Joseph G. Donnelly, *Lynching of Florentino Suaste,* 33–34.

78. On October 9, 1895, both Martina and Concepción Suaste testified to Justice of the Peace M. T. Dunham of Lasalle County. He inquired about the shootings of Florentino Suaste, Nicolasa Suaste, Pedro Suaste, Juan Montelongo, and Mr. Saul that led to the death of the last three. Any of the daughters could have been questioned by Mrs. Suaste's lawyer, but it is unclear which daughter testified here. These two daughters Martina and Concepción and their brother Mauricio, approximately three at the time of the incident, are the only ones named of the four remaining siblings. Ibid., 20, 33–34.

79. Ibid., 20, 33–34.

80. Antonio Magnon, an American citizen living in Webb County, later testified in a deposition that he knew Nicolasa Suaste. He explained that in 1897 she had been indicted and tried for selling liquor in the United States without a license. The case was later dismissed. He reported that she lived in Devine, Texas, and alleged that she had the nicknames Anna, La Mescalena, and Mescal Anna, as she was supposedly making a living by selling mescal in the small rural town southwest of San Antonio, Texas. Antonio Magnon, deposition, September 3, 1897, "Lynching of Florentino Suaste: Message from the President of the United States," 26–27.

81. Ibid., 22–23.

82. Ibid., 27–28.

83. Ibid., 12.

84. Juliana again signed a contract for separation on August 1, 1922, leaving the children to her former husband. "Collection Summary of Harry Warren Papers 1835–1932," HWC, ABB-BWML-SRSU.

85. Quoted in Justice, *Little Known History,* 155.

86. Quoted in Harris and Sadler, *The Texas Rangers and the Mexican Revolution,* 353. Warren's reliability continued to be questioned by Harris and Sadler in their brief account of the Porvenir massacre. In their writing they refer to Warren as a troublemaker who had "gone native" twice. For a short while, Warren worked harvesting crops in Arizona before finding a teaching position.

87. Harry Warren to Colonel George T. Langhorne on July 21, 1919, HWC, ABB-BWML-SRSU.

88. The general found the matter outside his domain and agreed to speak with proper authorities only as an individual, not an official. Attorney General B. F. Looney to J. J. Kilpatrick on September 20, 1918, HWC, ABB-BWML-SRSU.

89. B. J. Pridgen to Whom It May Concern, undated, HWC, ABB-BWML-SRSU. Both Looney and Pridgen knew Warren from their days as students at the University of Mississippi. Looney considered him one of the best students and a bright acquaintance.

90. Justice, *Little Known History,* 155.

91. James Judson Kilpatrick Journal, James Judson Kilpatrick Collection, ABB-BWML-SRSU.

92. J. G. de Beus, "International Delinquency General: Standards to be Applied," in *The Jurisprudence of the General Claims Commission United States and Mexico: Under the Convention of September 8, 1923* (The Hague: Martinus Nijhoff, 1938), 1–10. The commissioner representing the Mexican government was Fernandez McGregor; Edwin Parker, succeeded by Fred K. Nielsen, represented the United States; and the presiding commissioners were C. von Vollenhoven of the Netherlands, succeeded by Kristen Sinballe of Denmark, followed by H. F. Aljaro of Panama.

93. Harry Warren to Juana Bonilla Flores, June 11, 1926, HWC, ABB-BWML-SRSU. Warren's collection contains copies of the contracts for Juana Bonilla Flores, Concepción González, Rita Chaveria, Alejandra Nieves, Francisca Morales, and Librada Jácquez. At the time they signed the contracts, all the women lived in Reeves County, Texas, except for Juana Flores, who lived in Colorado, Texas, and Concepción González, who lived in Presidio County. Alejandra Nieves and Francisca Morales signed their names with an "X," leading me to assume that the other women possessed at least minimal literacy skills.

94. Beus, "International Delinquency General," 1.

95. González included the ages of her children: seventeen, fourteen, eleven, nine, seven, five, three, one and a half, and four months of age, respectively.

Concepción Carrasco de Gonzalez, "Memorandum," Annex No. 1, Docket 561, Mexican Claims, RG 76, NACP.

96. United States Reply Brief, Docket 561, Mexican Claims, RG 76, NACP.

97. Memorial, February 15, 1935, Docket 561, Mexican Claims, RG 76, NACP.

98. Memorial, February 15, 1935, Docket 561, Mexican Claims, RG 76, NACP; *L. F. H. Neer and Pauline Neer (USA) v. United Mexican States (1926), Reports of International Arbitral Awards*, 60–66.

99. *L. F. H. Neer and Pauline Neer (USA) v. United Mexican States (1926), Reports of International Arbitral Awards*, 60–66.

100. Answer, April 26, 1935, Docket 561, Mexican Claims, RG 76, NACP.

101. Brief, July 5, 1935, Docket 561, Mexican Claims, RG 76, NACP.

102. United States Reply Brief, September 13, 1935, Docket 561, Mexican Claims, RG 76, NACP.

103. Ibid.

104. Ibid.; emphasis in original.

105. Fred W. Llewellyn, Major Judge Advocate General, to Bert L. Hunt, US Agent General Claims Arbitration, March 18, 1935, Docket 561, Mexican Claims, RG 76, NACP; Report of Special Agent J. L. Geraghty, El Paso, March 11, 1935, US Bureau of Investigation, Docket 561, Mexican Claims, RG 76, NACP. Claims records show that Filomeno Huerta continued his effort. The US attorneys received his affidavit on February 1, 1937. "Following Received from the Department of Justice," Docket 561, Mexican Claims, RG 76, NACP.

106. Supplement to Information 126, September 13, 1926, Docket 561, Mexican Claims, RG 76, NACP.

107. Ibid.

108. Testimonies of Martin Medrano, Anastacio Romero, and Julio Aranda, December 9, 1936, Further Evidence Submitted by Mexico, Docket 561, Mexican Claims, RG 76, NACP.

109. In its introduction to the General Claims Commission, a United Nations publication points out by way of contrast that the British Claims Commission found it possible to dispose of only twenty-one claims out of 110 within the two-year term provided by its compromise. *Reports of International Arbitral Awards*, vol. 4 (New York: United Nations Publications, 2006), http://legal.un.org/riaa/cases/vol_IV/7-320.pdf.

110. Ibid., 1.

111. Herbert W. Briggs, "The Settlement of Mexican Claims Act of 1942," *American Journal of International Law* 37, no. 2 (1943): 224.

112. The Senate passed a bill called the Settlement of Mexican Claims Act of 1942, filed by the Committee on Foreign Relations, to stipulate how American claimants would receive payment of their awards. Settlement of Mexican Claims

Act of 1942, Author Elbert Duncan Thomas, Democratic Party Senator from Utah, Committee on Foreign Relations, September 25, 1942, Congressional Session 77-2.

113. Briggs, "The Settlement of Mexican Claims Act of 1942," 232. For more on the international negotiations and their consequences on claimants, see Monica Martinez, "Indemnities for State Murder: The US–Mexico General Claims Commission of 1923," *Social Text* (September 2011), http://www.socialtextjournal .org/periscope/going-into-debt/.

114. Between 1942 and 1964, hundreds of thousands of Mexican laborers entered the United States for work through the Bracero Program. For more, see Mireya Loza, *Defiant Braceros: How Migrant Workers Fought for Racial, Social, and Political Freedom* (Chapel Hill: University of North Carolina Press, 2016); and Lori Flores, *Grounds for Dreaming: Mexican Americans, Mexican Immigrants, and the California Farmworker Movement* (New Haven, CT: Yale University Press, 2016).

115. L. H. Woolsey, "The United States–Mexican Settlement," *American Journal of International Law* 36, no. 1 (January 1942): 117–118.

116. See Martinez, "Indemnities for State Murder"; *Teodoro García and M. A. Garza (United Mexican States) v. United States of America* (1926), in *Reports of International Arbitral Awards,* 119–134.

117. *Teodoro García and M. A. Garza (United Mexican States) v. United States of America* (1926).

118. Ibid.

119. Ibid., 122–124.

120. *D. Guerrero vda. De Falcón (United Mexican States) v. United States of America* (1926), in *Reports of International Arbitral Awards,* 104–106. In this claim even the case name is gendered and heteronormative as it identifies the claimant "Vda. De Falcon." "Vda." is the abbreviation for *viuda,* or "widow" in Spanish. This ostensibly objective and neutral legal inscription here makes Dolores Guerra visible to the court as the widow of Gregorio Falcon. Relying on these gendered categories helps expose how women were required to use their gendered category strategically to navigate the judicial apparatuses. On racial violence in the policing of smuggling on the border, see George Díaz, *Border Contraband: A History of Smuggling across the Rio Grande* (Austin: University of Texas Press, 2015).

121. *D. Guerrero vda. De Falcón (United Mexican States) v. United States of America* (1926).

122. *Francisco Quintanilla (United Mexican States) v. United States of America* (1926), in *Reports of International Arbitral Awards,* 101–104.

123. Ibid. The family claimed that Quintanilla's death caused his parents losses and damages amounting to approximately 50,000 Mexican gold pesos. The tribunal found the United States liable for these losses.

124. Ibid. Available court records show that not all claims filed by Mexican nationals for deceased family members received an indemnity. For example, in the

case of *Linda Balderas de Diaz (United Mexican States) v. United States of America* (1926), the General Claims Commission found that the judicial system in Bexar County adequately investigated the murder of Mauricio Diaz, killed on February 8, 1920, in San Antonio, Texas. Although the legal process did not identify or punish the guilty party, officers did conduct an investigation. The commission found that their inability to identify the assailants in this case did not prove negligence on the part of American authorities. The commission did not sustain the charge for the denial of justice claim, and Linda Balderas de Diaz, mother of Mauricio Diaz, did not receive an indemnity.

125. *Salome Lerma de Galvan (United Mexican States) v. United States of America* (1927), in *Reports of International Arbitral Awards,* 273–275.

126. Ibid.

127. Briggs, "The Settlement of Mexican Claims Act of 1942," 232.

128. *Teodoro García and M. A. Garza (United Mexican States) v. United States of America* (1926).

129. For a larger discussion about this commission, see Martinez, "Indemnities for State Murder."

130. Although Chakravarti here is speaking specifically about war crimes, this is applicable to the Mexican cases when state police, US soldiers, and vigilantes waged war on local residents. Chakravarti, "'More than Cheap Sentimentality': Victim Testimony at Nuremberg, the Eichmann Trial, and Truth Commissions," *Constellations* 1, no. 2 (2008): 233.

131. For more examples of communities that mourn as a political act, see Alicia Schmidt Camacho, *Migrant Imaginaries: Latino Cultural Politics in the US–Mexico Borderlands* (New York: New York University Press, 2008); Nguyên-Vo Thu-Huong, "Forking Paths: How Shall We Mourn the Dead?," *Amerasia Journal* 31, no. 2 (2005): 157–175.

132. The West Texas Historical and Scientific Society donated the Harry Warren Papers to the Archives of the Big Bend at Sul Ross State University in 1968. Inventory of Donations, HWC, ABB-BWML-SRSU.

133. Elaine Carney to Clifford Casey, December 6, 1938, CCC, ABB-BWML-SRSU.

134. Clifford Casey to W. H. Fryer, November 14, 1946, CCC, ABB-BWML-SRSU.

135. Unfortunately, the letters from Carney to Casey did not include the names of the two residents interviewed who revealed the stories of their own encounters with violence. The story of the resident who found his father's dead body, for example, speaks to the dangerous climate, but without names this case is hard to investigate further.

136. Elizabeth McBride, "Editor's Introduction," in *Bosque Bonito,* xiii.

137. Robert Keil to James Day, Director, Texas State Archives, June 22, 1963, CCC, ABB-BWML-SRSU.

138. McBride, "Editor's Introduction," xiii.

139. Linda Davis, interview by author.

140. Ibid.

141. Ibid.

142. Ibid.

143. Benita and Evaristo Albarado, interview by author; Benita and Evaristo Albarado and author, interview by Reynaldo Leanos Jr., January 22, 2016, Austin, TX, digital recording.

144. Benita and Evaristo Albarado, interview by author; Benita and Evaristo Albarado and author, interview by Reynaldo Leanos Jr.

145. Benita and Evaristo Albarado, interview by author.

146. Ibid.

147. "Memorial for Marine Gararez," video recording, Evaristo Albarado, November 18, 2006, Reagan Wells, TX, Albarado private collection.

148. Flores, interview by Gode Davis.

149. Ibid.

150. Gode Davis, "In Memoriam: Juan Bonilla Flores," http://www.american lynching.com/main.html.

151. Linda Davis, interview by author.

4. CULTURES OF VIOLENCE

1. President Woodrow Wilson, Proclamation, July 26, 1918 (Washington, DC: Government Printing Office, 1918), Rare Books and Special Collections Division, Library of Congress, Washington, DC. The NAACP quoted the proclamation at length in its efforts to convince state governors to pass anti-lynching legislation. *Report of the National Association for the Advancement of Colored People for the Years 1917 and 1918: Eighth and Ninth Annual Reports* (New York: NAACP, January 1919), 25. For more, see Philip Dray, *At the Hands of Persons Unknown: The Lynching of Black America* (New York: Modern Library, 2003), 215–275; David F. Krugler, *1919, the Year of Racial Violence: How African Americans Fought Back* (New York: Cambridge University Press, 2014), 273–278.

2. Wilson, Proclamation, July 26, 1918. Historian Adriane Lentz-Smith writes that during Wilson's presidency, "as white southerners perfected a system of segregation and oppression and sought to export it beyond regional and national boundaries, many African Americans looked to use World War I to forestall white supremacy's ascent and to fulfill their quest for racial justice." Lentz-Smith, *Freedom Struggles: African Americans and World War I* (Cambridge, MA: Harvard University Press, 2009), 4.

3. For more on the Red Scare and labor organizing, see David Montgomery, *The Fall of the House of Labor: The Workplace, the State, and American Labor Activism,*

1865–1925 (Cambridge: Cambridge University Press, 1989); Dana Frank, *Purchasing Power: Consumer Organizing, Gender, and the Seattle Labor Movement, 1919–1929* (Cambridge: Cambridge University Press, 1994); Zaragoza Vargas, *Labor Rights Are Civil Rights: Mexican American Workers in Twentieth-Century America* (Princeton, NJ: Princeton University Press, 2007).

4. "A Letter to President Woodrow Wilson on Federal Race Discrimination," August 15, 1913, National Association for the Advancement of Colored People, NAACP Records, Manuscript Division, Library of Congress.

5. Wilson, Proclamation, July 26, 1918.

6. For foundational work on the history of white, black, and ethnic Mexican relations in Texas, see Neil Foley, *The White Scourge: Mexicans, Blacks, and Poor Whites in Texas Cotton Culture* (Berkeley: University of California Press, 1999).

7. Ibid., 17.

8. Martha Sandweiss describes the use of photography to beckon Americans westward in the nineteenth century; see, *Print the Legend: Photography and the American West* (New Haven, CT: Yale University Press, 2002). For more on the use of postcards and photographs to create an image of Mexico and foreign places, see Jason Ruiz, *Americans in the Treasure House: Travel to Porfirian Mexico and the Cultural Politics of Empire* (Austin: University of Texas Press, 2014).

9. Reformers had to confront the efforts of sociologists who issued research that linked blackness with criminality. The criminalization of African Americans took hold in the public imagination and was supported by racist academics. Historian Khalil Gibran Muhammad shows that conceptions of black criminality were pervasive and mobilized to inspire both policy and violence. He explains that at best black criminality was used to justify segregation and at worst was used to call for mob violence. For more, see Khalil Gibran Muhammad, *The Condemnation of Blackness: Race, Crime, and the Making of Modern Urban America* (Cambridge, MA: Harvard University Press, 2010); Leigh Raiford, *Imprisoned in a Luminous Glare: Photography and the African American Freedom Struggle* (Chapel Hill: University of North Carolina Press, 2013).

10. Ida B. Wells-Barnett, *The Red Record: Tabulated Statistics and Alleged Causes of Lynching in the United States* (1895; repr., Middletown, DE: Cavalier Classics, 2015); Mark Robert Schneider, *We Return Fighting: The Civil Rights Movement in the Age of Jazz* (Boston: Northeastern University Press, 2002), 4. Wells-Barnett refuted three primary justifications for mob violence: that lynchings were necessary to repress race riots, that lynchnigs would deter African Americans from voting, and that lynchings were they only adequate means for avenging the rape of white women. For more on the legacy of Wells and a look at women and gender in this period, see Crystal N. Feimster, *Southern Horrors: Women and the Politics of Rape and Lynching* (Cambridge, MA: Harvard University Press; 2009); Mia Bay, *To Tell the Truth Freely: The Life of Ida B. Wells* (New York: Hill and Wang, 2010).

11. *Tenth Annual Report of the National Association for the Advancement of Colored People for the Year 1919* (New York: NAACP, 1920), 15. These deaths underscored the contradictions of American patriotism. American citizens who risked their lives returned home and were systematically denied the full rights and privileges guaranteed to them by the American Constitution they fought to defend. For more on the contradictions of American patriotism and the long history of discrimination in the military, see Yemisi Jimoh and Francoise Hamlin, *These Truly Are the Brave: An Anthology of African American Writings on War and Citizenship* (Gainesville: University Press of Florida, 2015).

12. *Tenth Annual Report of the National Association for the Advancement of Colored People for the Year 1919*, 18–22.

13. *Report of the National Association for the Advancement of Colored People for the Years 1917 and 1918*, 29. For more on the debates on defining lynchings, see Christopher Waldrep, "War of Words: The Controversy over the Definition of Lynching, 1899–1940," *Journal of Southern History* 66, no. 1 (2000): 75–100.

14. *Tenth Annual Report of the National Association for the Advancement of Colored People for the Year 1919*, 15. The NAACP recorded Georgians claiming the lives of 385 victims and Mississippi claiming 373.

15. *Report of the National Association for the Advancement of Colored People for the Years 1917 and 1918*, 87; Schneider, *We Return Fighting*, 32. The *San Antonio Express* article gives insight into how even early anti-lynching activists eclipsed the lynching practices used against other racial and ethnic minorities in the state.

16. "Make the Lyncher a Political and Social Pariah," *San Antonio Evening News*, January 13, 1919, 4.

17. In response to escalating violence in Texas, representatives from Texas chapters, including George M. Bailey, editor of the *Houston Post,* and William S. Sutton, dean of the Department of Education at the University of Texas at Austin, joined the NAACP's call to sign for the first national conference on lynchings. *Report of the National Association for the Advancement of Colored People for the Years 1917 and 1918*, 33–36; *Tenth Annual Report of the National Association for the Advancement of Colored People for the Year 1919*, 20, 100.

18. NAACP, *Thirty Years of Lynching in the United States, 1889–1918* (New York: Arno Press, 1969), 99.

19. Had the organization recognized that state officials orchestrated some of the murders they reported, they may not have included them in their records on mob violence, as these records tended to exclude victims of murder by local police.

20. Richard Ribb, "*La Rinchada:* Revolution, Revenge, and the Rangers, 1910–1920," in *War along the Border: The Mexican Revolution and Tejano Communities*, ed. Arnoldo De León (College Station: Texas A&M University Press, 2012), 56–106.

21. *Thirteenth Annual Report of the National Association for the Advancement of Colored People for the Year 1922* (New York: NAACP, 1923), 30. Still, the contradictions here are immense for newspapers such as the *San Antonio Express*. Years earlier the newspaper treated the violence on the border as mundane. Rather than expressing outrage at the extralegal killings of Mexican residents, the newspaper claimed that the incidents were so common that it would no longer cover reports of unidentified Mexican corpses being found in the Texas landscape. The newspaper wrote, "The finding of dead Mexican bodies, suspected for various reasons of being connected with the troubles, has reached a point where it creates little or no interest. It is only when a raid is reported, or an American is killed that the ire of the people is aroused." "Trouble Zone along the Rio Grande Almost Is Deserted," *San Antonio Express,* September 11, 1915.

22. "Negro Pays Penalty of Fearful Crime on Flaming Pyre," *Austin American,* January 20, 1919; "Says Rangers Did Duty," *Houston Post,* January 21, 1919.

23. "Negro Pays Penalty of Fearful Crime on Flaming Pyre," *Austin American,* January 20, 1919. The NAACP first published the *Burning at the Stake* pamphlet on June 1919. It was republished by the Black Classic Press in 1986 (*Burning at the Stake in the United States: A Record of the Public Burning by Mobs of Five Men during the First Five Months of 1919* [Baltimore, MD: Black Classic Press, 1986], 11).

24. Letter from John R. Shillady to Governor W. P. Hobby, January 21, 1919, reprinted in *Burning at the Stake,* 12.

25. "Hill County Grand Jury Fails to Return 'Lynching' Bills," *Galveston News,* February 21, 1919; *Tenth Annual Report of the National Association for the Advancement of Colored People for the Year 1919,* 20.

26. On January 23, 1918, Governor Hobby wrote a series of letters in response to the lynching of Bragg Williams in Hillsboro. He wrote to E. A. Berry, assistant attorney general, to request his presence in Hillsboro to assist the court on the Bragg Williams case; to C. M. Cureton, the attorney general, also requesting his presence in Hillsboro; and to Judge Horton Porter, district judge in Hillsboro, to affirm that he received the judge's letter asking for assistants and to reassure him that Berry and Cureton would come to his aid. Records, Texas Governor William Pettus Hobby, Archives and Information Services Division (AISD), Texas State Library and Archives Commission, Austin, TX (TSLAC).

27. "Says Rangers Did Duty"; *Burning at the Stake in the United States.*

28. Letter of Correspondence from W. M. Hanson to Adjutant General James A. Harley, April 27, 1918, "Proceedings of the Joint Committee of the Senate and House in the Investigation of the Texas State Ranger Force," Adjutant General Records, Texas State Archives, Austin, 794–798.

29. At the end of the hearing, Moses continued to shape the outcome of the investigation by helping Chairman Bledsoe write a new bill for legislative vote. See Mike Cox, *Time of Rangers,* vol. 2, *Texas Rangers from 1900 to the Present*

(New York: Tom Doherty Associates, 2009), 91; Charles H. Harris and Louis R. Sadler, *The Texas Rangers and the Mexican Revolution: The Bloodiest Decade, 1910–1920* (Albuquerque: University of New Mexico Press, 2007), 459.

30. Canales, introduction of charges, "Proceedings," 149.

31. Ibid.

32. Ibid., 152.

33. Ibid., 153.

34. Ibid., 151.

35. William D. Carrigan and Clive Webb, *Forgotten Dead: Mob Violence against Mexicans in the United States, 1848–1928* (Oxford: Oxford University Press, 2013), 121–122.

36. H. L. Roberson, "Enlistment, Oath of Service, and Description Ranger Force," April 1914, Texas Adjutant General's Department service records (TAGDSR), Archives and Information Services Division (AISD), Texas State Library and Archives Commission (TSLAC), Austin, TX (hereafter TAGDSR, AISD, TSLAC); H. L. Roberson, "Enlistment, Oath of Service, and Description Ranger Force," May 1916, TAGDSR, AISD, TSLAC.

37. W. B. Sands, "Enlistment, Oath of Service, and Description Ranger Force," December 1915, TAGDSR, AISD, TSLAC; "Proceedings," 164–165, 980, 989. In the investigation, Roberson's initials are incorrectly listed as H. E. Roberson.

38. "Proceedings," 949–951.

39. Ibid., 946–948.

40. Ibid.

41. Ibid.

42. Benjamin Heber Johnson, *Revolution in Texas: How a Forgotten Rebellion and Its Bloody Suppression Turned Mexicans into Americans* (New Haven, CT: Yale University Press, 2003), 174.

43. William S. Sterling, testimony, "Proceedings," 1503–1504.

44. J. T. Canales, testimony, "Proceedings," 886–891.

45. Quoted in Johnson, *Revolution in Texas,* 174. Representative Canales claimed he refused to perform such an act because he was a Christian. This statement showed the audience that he was a man who respected the state and federal laws while also being a God-fearing Christian.

46. Telegram from Adjutant General Harley to Ranger Frank Hamer, December 23, 1918, submitted to evidence for "Proceedings."

47. Judge Dayton Moses, testimony, "Proceedings," 101–106.

48. W. W. Sterling, testimony, "Proceedings," 1412–1413, 1506.

49. Johnson, *Revolution in Texas,* 174.

50. J. C. Machuca, interview by Oscar Martinez, May 21, 1970, "Interview no. 152," Institute for Oral History, University of Texas at El Paso.

51. "Canales Testifies in Ranger Inquiry," *Dallas Morning News,* February 11, 1919.

52. Canales, testimony, "Proceedings," 855–856.

53. Ibid., 857.

54. Canales, introduction of charges, "Proceedings," 3.

55. In other words, Canales did not publicly question Rangers of the past who violently targeted Native Americans and rebellious ethnic Mexicans but was troubled by the violence facing elite ethnic Mexicans in the region. Canales, testimony, "Proceedings," 855–856.

56. The representative did not take issue with the ruthless violence agents used to target Native Americans. To the contrary, Tejanos and some local tribes profited from these genocidal killings in the nineteenth century. The Rangers' fall from grace, according to Canales, came when the state police turned their guns on landowning Tejanos like himself. Tejanos throughout the nineteenth century called for violence against Native Americans and participated in brutality to gain control of the region and to displace Native nations. For more on the Canales Scouts, see Ribb, *"La Rinchada."* On multiracial and ethnic coalitions targeting Native nations, see Karl Jacoby, *Shadows at Dawn: An Apache Massacre and the Violence of History* (New York: Penguin, 2008).

57. Canales, testimony, "Proceedings," 904.

58. Ibid., 1010–1013.

59. Ibid.

60. Ibid.

61. Ibid.

62. Ibid., 902–904.

63. Ibid., 903.

64. For more on the role of eugenics in immigration policy and border policing, see John Mckiernan-González, *Fevered Measures: Public Health and Race at the Texas-Mexico Border, 1848–1942* (Durham, NC: Duke University Press, 2012); Alexandra Minna Stern, *Eugenic Nation: Faults and Frontiers of Better Breeding in Modern America* (Berkeley: University of California Press, 2005).

65. By claiming to be a Texas-Mexican, Canales conceded to having ethnic markers of difference, but he also aligned himself with Texas traditions of revolution against the Mexican state. Canales, testimony, "Proceedings," 1010. For more, see John Morán González, *Border Renaissance: The Texas Centennial and the Emergence of Mexican American Literature* (Austin: University of Texas Press, 2009); Ramón Saldívar, *The Borderlands of Culture: Américo Paredes and the Transnational Imaginary* (Durham, NC: Duke University Press, 2006).

66. Canales, testimony, "Proceedings," 1011.

67. Ibid., 1010–1020.

68. Ibid., 870–880, 1416–1419; Evan Anders, *Boss Rule in South Texas: The Progressive Era* (Austin: University of Texas Press, 1982), 266. In the proceedings Canales's relative is listed as "Santavo Tijerino."

69. Canales, testimony, "Proceedings," 925–928.

70. Ibid.

71. Ibid., 857.

72. Ibid., 857–858.

73. Ibid. The court proceedings transcribed the victim's name as "Rodolpho Munoz." Historians have now noted that his name could have been Rodolfo Muñiz and that he was lynched on July 29, 1915. This is the same event that the NAACP referred to as the lynching of "Adolfo Muñoz" discussed earlier in this chapter and in chapter 2. See Trinidad Gonzales, "The Mexican Revolution, Revolución de Texas, and Matanza de 1915," in *War along the Border: The Mexican Revolution and Tejano Communities,* ed. Arnoldo De León (College Station: Texas A&M University Press, 2012), 118; Johnson, *Revolution in Texas,* 86.

74. Canales, testimony, "Proceedings," 857–859.

75. Ibid.

76. Ibid., 859.

77. Ignacio Bonillas, from Mexican Embassy to Robert Lansing, Secretary of State, Washington, August 31, 1918, "Proceedings," 821–823.

78. Canales, testimony, "Proceedings," 941–942.

79. Affidavit by Thomas I. Hester, in Donna, Texas, October 13, 1918, "Proceedings," 829–831.

80. Canales, testimony, "Proceedings," 942–944. Canales named Rangers Hinojosa, Hamer, Carr, Veale, Cunningham, and Johnson as only a few of those with the reputation of being killers. During the investigation, Knight explained to the committee that Ranger Johnson had been discharged days before the investigation, but Canales argued that not enough "killers" had been discharged.

81. Captain William Wright, testimony, "Proceedings," 1517–1519, 1522–1523.

82. John J. Edds, "Enlistment, Oath of Service, and Description Ranger Force," September 1915, TAGDSR, AISD, TSLAC.

83. John J. Edds, testimony, "Proceedings," 499–503.

84. Ibid., 502.

85. Frederico Lopez, testimony, "Proceedings," 1298–1302; Eduardo Izaguirre, testimony, "Proceedings,"1308, 1317–1318; Statement of Sabas Ozuna, September 2, 1918, evidence, "Proceedings," 766–767; Statement of John J. Edds, undated, evidence, "Proceedings," 763–766.

86. Adjutant General Jas A. Harley to Captain W. L. Wright, September 12, 1918, evidence, "Proceedings," 772.

87. Letter from J. J. Edds to Paul Perkins or Mr. Oscar Thompson, Hebbronville, Texas, September 3, 1918, "Proceedings," 770.

88. Captain Hanson to General James A. Harley, September 16, 1918, "Proceedings," 761–772.

89. Edds, testimony, "Proceedings," 763–766.

90. Ibid.

91. In the initial charges brought forward by Canales, he listed the date of Muñoz's murder as October 5. During the questioning of John Edds, he corrected the date.

92. Edds, testimony, "Proceedings," 487–490.

93. Ibid., 490.

94. Muñoz's parents and three brothers all lived in another house also located on the Los Saenz Ranch. Jesus Sanchez testimony in evidence, "Proceedings," 785–787.

95. Edds, testimony, "Proceedings," 504–505.

96. Ibid., 499–500. Edds noted during his testimony that the two local officials who conducted the investigation were "Mexicans themselves."

97. Ibid.

98. James B. Wells, testimony, "Proceedings," 715–717.

99. Hanson to Harley, October 23, 1918, "Proceedings," 780–781.

100. Edds, testimony, "Proceedings," 480–483; "Special Order No. 10," February 6, 1919, Adjutant General James Harley, TAGDSR, AISD, TSLAC.

101. Thomas A. Johnson, testimony, "Proceedings," 665–675; A. B. Hodges, enlistment papers for Company C and Graham Myers, enlistment papers for Company C, TAGDSR, AISD, TSLAC.

102. Johnson, testimony, "Proceedings," 671.

103. W. A. Anderson, testimony, "Proceedings," 664–666.

104. Johnson, testimony, "Proceedings," 672; Anderson, testimony, "Proceedings," 664–666.

105. Johnson, testimony, "Proceedings," 675; emphasis in original.

106. Anderson, testimony, "Proceedings," 665–666.

107. Claude Benton Hudspeth, testimony, "Proceedings," 993.

108. Ibid., 992, 993. Hudspeth spoke specifically about violence against African Americans but only generally about violence against Mexican residents. Here it can be assumed that he is referencing the Porvenir massacre that killed fifteen unarmed residents in west Texas.

109. Ibid., 994.

110. Ibid., 977.

111. For more on the racial and sexual dynamics of tropes of white feminine virtue and vulnerability used to incite mob violence, see Feimster, *Southern Horrors*.

112. Hudspeth, testimony, "Proceedings," 991.

113. Ibid., 970–972.

114. Ibid., 906–908.

115. Ibid., 909.

116. Moses comments in C. L. Jessup, testimony, "Proceedings," 1120.

117. Ibid.

118. *Slavery and Justice: Report of the Brown University Steering Committee on Slavery and Justice* (Providence, RI: Brown University, 2006), 39–47.

119. Report from *House Journal,* 36th Leg., Reg. Sess., 536–539. See Ribb, *"La Rinchada,"* 87, 90.

120. Report from *House Journal,* 36th Leg., Reg. Sess., 536–539.

121. As quoted in Ribb, *"La Rinchada,"* 87–90.

122. Ibid. Ribb writes that after the investigation William Hanson experienced a political resurgence and received wide support for his reappointment as the investigating officer for the adjutant general's office.

123. "Oath of Members Ranger Force, James M. Fox, June 6, 1925," and "Oath of Members Ranger Force, James M. Fox, February 19, 1934," TAGDSR, AISD, TSLAC. In 1996 the Texas Department of Public Safety Officers Association magazine published an article praising the law enforcement record of James M. Fox and noted that he also served as an officer in Corpus Christi, Brownwood, and Wichita Falls. That same article interpreted Fox's return to the state police as vindication for his role in the Porvenir massacre and recriminalized the residents as bandits. Al Ritter, "Death on the Rio Grande," *Department of Public Safety Officers Association Magazine,* March / April 1996, 53–55.

124. Harris and Sadler, *The Texas Rangers and the Mexican Revolution,* 452, 456–457.

125. *Tenth Annual Report of the National Association for the Advancement of Colored People for the Year 1919,* 34.

126. Kenneth R. Durham, "The Longview Race Riot of 1919," *East Texas Historical Journal* 18 (1980): 13–24; "More Troops Ordered Sent to Longview," *Dallas Morning News,* July 13, 1919; "Gregg County Now under Martial Law," *Dallas Morning News,* July 14, 1919; "16 White Men under Arrest at Longview," *Dallas Morning News,* July 15, 1919; "Longview Blacks Held in County Jail in Austin," *Austin American,* July 17, 1919; "More Race Riots Break Out Now at Longview," *Austin American,* July 13, 1919.

127. Durham, "The Longview Race Riot of 1919"; *Tenth Annual Report of the National Association for the Advancement of Colored People for the Year 1919,* 34–35.

128. Alain Locke, *The New Negro: Voices of the Harlem Renaissance,* ed. Arnold Rampersad (New York: Touchstone, 1997), xxvii, xv.

129. *Tenth Annual Report of the National Association for the Advancement of Colored People for the Year 1919,* 34.

130. Ibid.

131. Lewis L. Gould, *Progressives and Prohibitionists: Texas Democrats in the Wilson Era* (Austin: Texas State Historical Association, 1992); James Anthony Clark and Weldon Hart, *The Tactful Texan: A Biography of Governor Will Hobby* (Austin: University of Texas Press, 1973).

132. "Governor Recommends Sweeping Changes," *San Antonio Express News,* January 22, 1919. The problem remained; not one of the lynchings reported in Texas in 1918 resulted in a convicted perpetrator.

133. Quoted in Schneider, *We Return Fighting,* 30–31.

134. "Texas Judge Whips John R. Shillady," *New York Times,* August 23, 1919.

135. Schneider, *We Return Fighting,* 30.

136. "Texas Judge Whips John R. Shillady."

137. Ibid.; Schneider, *We Return Fighting,* 31–32.

138. *Tenth Annual Report of the National Association for the Advancement of Colored People for the Year 1919,* 33.

139. "Mob Attack on the Association's Secretary," in *Tenth Annual Report of the National Association for the Advancement of Colored People for the Year 1919,* 58. The NAACP published only 1,129 copies of President Wilson's address on lynching in the United States. Leigh Raiford eloquently argued that anti-lynching activists used photographs alongside statistics, dominant press accounts, and investigative reports in the effort to develop anti-lynching legislation. For more on activists' uses of lynching photos, see Leigh Raiford, "Lynching, Visuality, and the Un / Making of Blackness," *NKA: Journal of Contemporary African Art* 20 (Fall 2006): 22–31.

140. Schneider, *We Return Fighting,* 32; Steven Reich, "Soldiers of Democracy: Black Texans and the Fight for Citizenship, 1917–1921," *Journal of American History* 82, no. 4 (1996): 1478–1502.

141. "Investigation into Mexican Affairs," Sen. Doc. No. 285, 2 vols., 66th Cong., 2nd Sess. (Washington, DC: Government Printing Office, 1920), 3224–3226, 3247, 3315.

142. Ribb, *"La Rinchada,"* 88–90; "Investigation into Mexican Affairs," 3373.

143. The monument was erected on the capital grounds in 1907. "Terry's Texas Rangers Monument," State Preservation Board, http://www.tspb.state.tx.us/prop /tcg/tcg-monuments/04_terrys_texas_rangers/index.html; Thomas W. Cutrer, "Eighth Texas Cavalry [Terry's Texas Rangers]," in *Handbook of Texas Online,* http://www.tshaonline.org/handbook/online/articles/qke02.

144. Miguel Levario writes that Hudspeth owned a large sheep ranch near Del Rio, Texas. See Levario, *Militarizing the Border: When Mexicans Became the Enemy* (College Station: Texas A&M University Press, 2012), 98. For more on the Immigration Act of 1924, see Mae Ngai, *Impossible Subjects: Illegal Aliens and the Making of Modern America* (Princeton, NJ: Princeton University Press, 2004).

145. Kelly Lytle Hernández, *Migra! A History of the US Border Patrol* (Berkeley: University of California Press, 2010), 20–23.

146. For more on Hobby's career, see Clark and Hart, *The Tactful Texan.*

5. IDOLS

1. David Blight, *Beyond the Battlefield: Race, Memory and the American Civil War* (Amherst: University of Massachusetts Press, 2002), 191; Gregg Cantrell and Elizabeth Hayes Turner, "Introduction," in *Lone Star Past: Memory and History in Texas,* ed. Gregg Cantrell and Elizabeth Hayes Turner (College Station: Texas A&M University Press, 2007), 3, 10.

2. Andrés Tijerina, "Constructing Tejano Memory," in Cantrell and Turner, *Lone Star Past,* 184.

3. Ibid., 25.

4. Ibid.

5. W. Fitzhugh Brundage, foreword to Cantrell and Turner, *Lone Star Past,* xvi.

6. Ibid.

7. In their introduction, editors Cantrell and Turner call for historical projects that participate in "debunking the popularly held 'myths' about the Rangers" while also exploring the actual sources of modern memories about the legendary agency. Cantrell and Turner, "Introduction," 6.

8. These images often provided evidence that mob participants tortured victims with mutilation and sexual violence before they were hanged or burned alive. See Susan Sontag, *At the Same Time: Essays and Speeches* (New York: Farrar, Straus, and Giroux, 2008), 132; Amy Louise Wood, *Lynching and Spectacle: Witnessing Racial Violence in America, 1890–1940* (Chapel Hill: University of North Carolina Press, 2009), 76–77; James Allen, ed., *Without Sanctuary: Lynching Photography in America* (Santa Fe, NM: Twin Palms Publishers, 2000). For more on the circulation of these photographs, see Jacqueline Goldsby, *A Spectacular Secret: Lynching in American Life and Literature* (Chicago: University of Chicago Press, 2006).

9. For a discussion on how anti-lynching activists and civil rights organizations used these photographs to seek justice, see Leigh Raiford, *Imprisoned in a Luminous Glare: Photography and the African American Freedom Struggle* (Chapel Hill: University of North Carolina Press, 2013).

10. Frank N. Samponaro, Paul Vanderwood, and Robert Runyon, *War Scare on the Rio Grande: Robert Runyon's Photographs of Border Conflicts, 1913–1916* (Austin: Texas State Historical Association, 1992), xiii–1.

11. David Dorado Romo, *Ringside Seat to a Revolution: An Underground Cultural History of El Paso and Juárez, 1893–1923* (El Paso, TX: Cinco Puntos Press, 2005), 160–161.

12. Ibid. Horne also documented the Punitive Expedition in 1916 and its impact on west Texas; see Ronnie C. Tyler, "The Little Punitive Expedition in the Big Bend," *Southwestern Historical Quarterly* 78, no. 3 (1975): 271–291.

13. In return for a small fee, Horne made arrangements with Carrancista officers so that he could place his camera as close as possible to executions by firing squads. Romo, *Ringside Seat to a Revolution,* 160–161.

14. In her book *Regarding the Pain of Others,* Susan Sontag analyzes photographs of war. She states: "pictures taken by photographers out in the field at the moment of (or just before) death are among the most celebrated and often reproduced of war photographs." See Sontag, *Regarding the Pain of Others* (New York: Farrar, Straus, and Giroux, 2003), 59. This insight sheds light on one of Horne's most popular series of photographs titled "Triple Execution in Juárez." The first three photographs of the series captured three men standing before a firing squad anticipating their execution, and a fourth photograph shows the three lifeless corpses on the ground. "Triple Execution in Juárez," Walter H. Horne Collection, Photograph Collection, James C. Jernigan Library, South Texas Archives, Texas A&M University, Kingsville (hereafter WHHC, PC, JJL, TAMUK). In her assessment of the atrocities of war, Sontag notes that these photographs tend to show victims so mangled that they remain unnamed, anonymous victims. To this end, "the scale of war's murderousness destroys what identifies people as individuals, even as human beings." Sontag, *Regarding the Pain of Others,* 61.

15. "Walter Horne 1883–1921," Postcard Photographs Related to United States Military Involvement in Mexican Revolution, Yale Collection of Western Americana, Beinecke Rare Book and Manuscript Library, Yale University, New Haven, CT.

16. Romo, *Ringside Seat to a Revolution,* 161–163.

17. "The Body of a Mexican Bandit Leader," WHHC, PC, JJL, TAMUK.

18. Frank Pierce, *A Brief History of the Lower Rio Grande Valley* (Menasha, WI: George Banta Publishing Co., 1917), 114, 91.

19. Frank N. Samponaro and Paul Vanderwood, *War Scare on the Rio Grande: Robert Runyon's Photographs of the Border Conflict, 1913–1916* (Austin: University of Texas Press, 1992), 75–76; James L. Allhands, *Gringo Builders* (Iowa City: n.p., 1931), 265–266.

20. Hill alleged that Robert Runyon arrived by train the morning after to take photos of the bodies being removed. "They wanted to bury these Mexicans, so they got on the horses and put a rope on and dragged them, and this fellow took these pictures; he took about a dozen different views of Norias and the people around there and they were on sale at Brownsville. . . . I know these men were drug up there on horseback; I saw them drug." Lon C. Hill, testimony, "Proceedings of the Joint Committee of the Senate and House in the Investigation of the Texas State Ranger Force," Adjutant General Records, Texas State Archives, Austin, 1225.

21. Quoted in William Warren Sterling, *Trials and Trails of a Texas Ranger* (Norman: University of Oklahoma Press, 1968). Sterling made an insensitive quip

about the events captured in the photos by calling them the "Norias hearse." In the testimony Hill does not use that exact phrasing, although he may have in other contexts. Instead, he described the photographs being taken by chance. Hill, testimony, "Proceedings," 1225.

22. Hill, testimony, "Proceedings," 1220–1225.

23. Joe Taylor, testimony, "Proceedings," 1450–1452.

24. Frank Pierce recorded Jesus García, Mauricio García, Amado Muñoz, and the unnamed Muñoz brother as dying during the Norias raid. News that Jesus Garcia was killed also spread in the media. "El Combate Registrado en Las Norias Duró Más de Dos Horas," *La Prensa*, August 12, 1915.

25. Larry and Roy Todd, oral interview by Sonia Hernández, 2016, for the exhibition "Life and Death on the Border 1910–1920," Bullock Museum, Austin, Texas. Historian Martha Sandweiss describes the movement of a photograph from a store, to a scrapbook, to an attic, to a gas station as the "shifting fate of the image." Sandweiss, *Print the Legend*, 9.

26. "Scouts Reports for Company D in 1915 and Company B in 1918," Adjutant General Records, Texas State Archives, Austin, Texas.

27. Walter Prescott Webb, *The Texas Rangers: A Century of Frontier Defense* (Austin: University of Texas Press, 1995), 79–80.

28. Ibid., 14.

29. Ibid., 513.

30. Joe B. Frantz, "Remembering Walter Prescott Webb," *Southwestern Historical Quarterly* 92 (July 1988): 53–57; Necah Stewart Furman, *Walter Prescott Webb: His Life and Impact* (Albuquerque: University of New Mexico Press, 1976).

31. Controversy erupted when Webb did not complete the guide as previously agreed. See John R. Jameson, "Studies in Public History: Walter Prescott Webb, Public Historian," *Public Historian* 7, no. 2 (Spring 1985): 48–52; Walter Prescott Webb, "The Big Bend of Texas," *Public Historian* 7, no. 2 (Spring 1985): 59–60. In 1985 the *Public Historian* published the 1937 National Park Service press release authored by Webb. He described the "human-interest value" in creating a national park in a region with "two contrasting civilizations . . . How fitting it would be if the Big Bend of Texas, and the wild region opposite in Mexico, could be converted into an international park devoted to the pleasure and enlightenment of man, and to the promotion of peace and understanding between neighboring nations."

32. Willis Winters, "The Ford Motor Company at the Texas Centennial Exposition," *Legacies: A History Journal for Dallas and North Central Texas* 23, no. 1 (Spring 2011): 4–17.

33. "Texas Centennial," in *Handbook of Texas Online,* http://www.tshaonline .org/handbook/online/articles/lkt01; "1936 Texas Centennial Markers," Texas

Historical Commission, http://www.thc.state.tx.us/preserve/projects-and-pro
grams/state-historical-markers/1936-texas-centennial-markers.

34. Cantrell and Turner, "Introduction," 5.

35. Reenactment groups like the Frontier Battalion Texas Rangers profiled
Rangers who were soldiers and officers in the Texas cavalry who fought for the
Confederacy during the Civil War. One example is an online memorial to
Leander H. McNelly (1844–1877), http://www.fbtre.org/texas-ranger-memorial/.

36. Cantrell and Turner, "Introduction," 5–6.

37. Ibid., 6.

38. John Morán González, *Border Renaissance: The Texas Centennial and the
Emergence of Mexican American Literature* (Austin: University of Texas Press, 2009),
22–23.

39. Kevin E. Mooney, "Texas Centennial Music," in *Handbook of Texas Online,*
http://www.tshaonline.org/handbook/online/articles/xbt02.

40. Quoted in Edward Linenthal, *Sacred Ground: Americans and Their Battlefields*
(Urbana: University of Illinois Press, 1993), 61.

41. Texas State Historical Survey Commission, "Chalk Bluff Indian Massacre,"
1970, https://atlas.thc.state.tx.us/. The unveiling of this marker in 1970 coincided
with heightened racial tensions in the nearby town of Uvalde. Members of the
Mexican American Youth Organization publicly protested racial discrimination in
the town. A long-standing history of racial segregation in the public school system
encouraged students to walk out of their schools in protest in April 1970. A list of
student demands critiqued a public school curriculum that marginalized their
history.

42. See Jodi Byrd, *The Transit of Empire: Indigenous Critiques of Colonialism*
(Minneapolis: University of Minnesota Press, 2011); Juliana Barr, *Peace Came in the
Form of a Woman* (Chapel Hill: University of North Carolina Press, 2007); Ned
Blackhawk, *Violence over the Land: Indians and Empires in the Early American West*
(Cambridge, MA: Harvard University Press, 2008). Soldiers at Fort Clark
identified Comanches, Kickapoos, and Lipan Apaches as threats in the area. The
markers also do not make note of the Seminole scouts that helped the US and
Mexican armies protect settlers from "hostile Indians."

43. Don Graham, "Fallen Heroes," *Texas Monthly,* February 2005, https://www
.texasmonthly.com/articles/fallen-heroes/.

44. Julian Samora, Joe Bernal, and Albert Peña, *Gunpowder Justice: A Reassessment of the Texas Rangers* (Notre Dame, IN: University of Notre Dame Press,
1979), 10–11, 15.

45. J. B. Smith, "Remains Left behind when Waco Relocated Cemetery,"
Houston Chronicle, May 4, 2008; J. B. Smith, "Meetings on First Street Graves
Unearths Strong Feelings," *Waco Tribune-Herald,* July 9, 2014; Tommy Wither-
spoon, "City Seeks Descendants of Those Unearthed from First Street Cemetery,"

Waco Tribune-Herald, March 27, 2015; Laurel Chesky, "Over Their Dead Bodies: Rangers Desecrate Waco Cemetery," *Austin Chronicle,* January 30, 2009; Alwyn Barr, "Mullens, Shepherd," in *Handbook of Texas Online,* http://www.tshaonline .org/handbook/online/articles/fmu23.

46. Texas Ranger Hall of Fame and Museum, "Welcome to the Texas Ranger Hall of Fame and Museum," http://www.texasranger.org/texas-ranger-museum /visit/. At the time this book went to press, the website was undergoing revisions. A history of these revisions is on display on the new website, "Website Development 1997–2018," http://www.texasranger.org/texas-ranger-museum/visit/web site-development/.

47. The accompanying plaque describes Erath as the "father of Waco, champion of Texas surveyor, statesman, Ranger," and explains that the cenotaph holds a Texas Ranger Time Capsule to be opened by the people of Texas on June 6, 2098. The sons of the Republic of Texas George B. Erath Chapter No. 13, as well as the Dietz Memorial Company, sponsored the statue.

48. Texas Ranger Hall of Fame and Museum, "Texas Ranger Hall of Fame," http://www.texasranger.org/texas-ranger-museum/hall-of-fame/.

49. M. L. Rymsza-Pawlowska describes the 1970s as a period when Americans desired to engage and enact the past on a more emotional level. She studies museums that used affective exhibits to draw in visitors. See Rymsza-Pawlowska, *History Comes Alive: Public History and Popular Culture in the 1970s* (Chapel Hill: University of North Carolina Press, 2017).

50. Tony Bennett, *The Birth of the Museum: History, Theory, Politics* (London: Routledge, 1995).

51. Mike Cox, "A Brief History of the Texas Rangers," http://www.texas ranger.org/texas-ranger-museum/history/brief-history/.

52. This goal of inspiring pride in the Texas Rangers is in tension with the second portion of the museum's mission to serve as a repository of artifacts and records for the state agents and to facilitate study through its research center.

53. Texas Ranger Hall of Fame and Museum, "Junior Texas Rangers Program," http://www.texasranger.org/texas-ranger-museum/junior-rangers/. The museum also offers a special program for homeschoolers as well as Boy Scout and Girl Scout troops. Topics for groups include mapmaking, surveying, orienteering, crime scene investigation, crime prevention, public service, and history.

54. Texas Ranger Hall of Fame and Museum, "Crime Scene in a Box," http://www.texasranger.org/texas-ranger-museum/education/traveling-trunks/.

55. Texas Ranger Hall of Fame and Museum, "Suggested Reading for Teachers," http://www.texasranger.org/education/teacherreading.html. These readings were recommended for teachers as late as the summer of 2017. At the time this book went to press, this article was no longer on the website.

56. Linenthal, *Sacred Ground,* 61.

57. Christine Rothenbush in "History of the Texas Rangers," https://www
.c-span.org/video/?322695–1/history-texas-rangers.

58. Texas Ranger Hall of Fame and Museum, "Major Benefactors,"
http://www.texasranger.org/benefactors/Major_benefactors.htm. At the time this
book went to press, this article was no longer on the website.

59. Tammy Gordon, "Heritage, Commerce, and Museal Display: Toward a
New Typology of Historical Exhibition in the United States," *Public Historian* 30,
no. 3 (2008): 34–38, 48.

60. Vicki Ruíz, "Citizen Restaurant: American Imaginaries, American
Communities," *American Quarterly* 60, no. 1 (2008): 3, 5.

61. This is one of the most widely circulated group photographs of a Texas
Ranger company from this era. Jim Ryan, interview by author, July 31, 2009,
Sabinal, TX, digital recording. Captain William M. Ryan is also honored for his
role leading companies I, C, and D from 1917 to 1927. In his portrait Captain
Ryan is mounted on horseback with reins in hand, sporting a cowboy hat and
boots, a bow tie, and his pistol and rifle in their holsters. Some of the photographs
from this period are taken indoors, but more than half show the Rangers outdoors
near a campsite or with a scenic backdrop.

62. Amy Louise Wood describes the imagery of hunting photography in
lynching photos. See Wood, *Lynching and Spectacle: Witnessing Racial Violence in
America, 1890–1940* (Chapel Hill: University of North Carolina Press, 2009), 94.

63. Sontag, *Regarding the Pain of Others,* 87.

64. Author's unrecorded conversation with employees at Dairy Queen, Sabinal,
TX, June 24, 2009. The other young woman agreed with her coworker and
explained that she heard stories of a lynched black resident accused of raping a
white woman in Sabinal.

65. In December 1995, the Library of Congress had to close the exhibit "Back
of the Big House: The Cultural Landscape of the Plantation" just days after
installation due to some forty staff members who took offense and claimed the
exhibit lacked historical context and critical examination of slavery. Karen De
Witt, "After Protests, Library of Congress Closes Exhibition on Slavery," *New
York Times,* December 21, 1995; Gail Fineberg, "Plantation Exhibit Opens at
MLK Library," January 22, 1996, Information Bulletin, Library of Congress,
http://www.loc.gov/loc/lcib/9601/mlk.html.

66. For more on these contradictions, see Philip J. Deloria, *Playing Indian* (New
Haven, CT: Yale University Press, 1999).

67. For more on reenactments, see Lesley Martin, ed., *An-My Le: Small Wars*
(New York: Aperture Foundation, 2005); Tony Horwitz, *Confederates in the Attic:
Dispatches from the Unfinished Civil War* (New York: Pantheon Books, 1999).

68. Ryan, interview by author. Ryan actually started his career years ago when
he played an extra during the filming of *Lonesome Dove.* The film was shot in

Uvalde County. During the filming he befriended both Robert Duval and Tommy Lee Jones. Visitors to the Texas Ranger Hall of Fame and Museum website also received guidance on how to accurately dress like a Texas Ranger from different eras. The site provides historical photographs and dress guidelines. Texas Ranger Hall of Fame and Museum, "Texas Ranger Dress Regulations," http://www.texasranger.org/texas-ranger-museum/texas-rangers/dress-regula tions/.

69. Ryan, interview by author. As important, for Ryan, is the need to clear up common misconceptions that the Rangers no longer serve the public. To the contrary the Ranger force today is active with nearly 150 agents patrolling the state. Despite his efforts to memorialize the long history of the Rangers, Ryan also realizes that the myth and iconic figures have in some ways overshadowed the role of current Texas Rangers.

70. Ryan, interview by author. Scott Magelssen describes living history museums as cultural institutions that merge historical exhibits with live costume performance. These often compromise historical accuracy for the sake of increasing entertainment to encourage tourism. Scott Magelssen, *Living History Museums: Untold History through Performance* (Lanham, MD: Scarecrow Press, 2007).

71. Elaine Padgett Carnegie, "Badlands Texas Rangers: Part II," *Home of the Hill Country Herald,* http://hillcountryherald.net/history.html.

72. Ryan, interview by author.

6. RECKONING WITH VIOLENCE

1. Américo Paredes to Frank H. Wardlaw, February 21, 1957, Américo Paredes Folder: With His Pistol in His Hand—Correspondence on Research and Publications 1955–1959, 1973, Américo Paredes Papers, Benson Latin American Collection, University of Texas Libraries, University of Texas at Austin.

2. Frank H. Wardlaw to Américo Paredes, February 25, 1957, Américo Paredes Folder: With His Pistol in His Hand—Correspondence on Research and Publications 1955–1959, 1973, Américo Paredes Papers, Benson Latin American Collection, University of Texas Libraries, University of Texas at Austin.

3. Fregoso described what she learned from her father as "oppositional discourse." Rosa Linda Fregoso, "Reproduction and Miscegenation on the Borderlands: Mapping the Maternal Body of Tejanas," in *Chicana Feminisms: A Critical Reader,* ed. Gabriela F. Arredondo, Aida Hurtado, Norma Klahn, Olga Nájera-Ramírez, and Patricia Zavella (Durham, NC: Duke University Press, 2003), 326–329. Jonathan Scott Holloway keenly describes the alternative histories learned in African American homes in his book *Jim Crow Wisdom: Memory and*

Identity in Black America since 1940 (Chapel Hill: University of North Carolina Press, 2013).

4. The site includes tabs that organize the digitized archival collection by source type. Los Tejanos, http://los-tejanos.com/index.html.

5. For example, descendants of Pedro Longoria (born in 1732) have utilized message boards on the website Ancestry.com to develop a conversation over the past twelve years with distant relatives who are collectively creating a Longoria family tree. "Longoria," Ancestry.com, http://boards.ancestry.com/surnames .longoria/11.15.86.87.90/mb.ashx.

6. Hernán Contreras, "Hispanic Women of the Mexican American Frontier," Los Tejanos, Fall 2001, http://los-tejanos.com/essays.htm.

7. Hernán Contreras, "Reign of Terror," Los Tejanos, http://los-tejanos.com /essays.htm.

8. For more, see Chapter 2 of this book.

9. "Justice out of a Job" by Frederick Barr Opper, 1883, Prints and Photographs Online Catalog, Library of Congress Prints and Photographs Division, Washington, DC, http://hdl.loc.gov/loc.pnp/pp.print.

10. Glenn Justice, *Welcome to Glenn's Texas History Blog,* Rimrock Press, http://www.rimrockpress.com/blog/index.php?entry=entry070202–111903.

11. Not everyone who responded expressed enthusiastic support of the post. On April 18, 2008, José Dominguez questioned Justice's account because he was not an eyewitness to the massacre. He wrote, "let's not replace one whitewashed story with another." Alexa Nieves Saucedo, March 21, 2007, Manuel Casas, April 1, 2007, and Jose Dominguez, April 18, 2008, Rimrock Press, http://www .rimrockpress.com/blog/comments.php?y=07&m=02&entry=entry070202 –111903.

12. Domingo Garcia Cano, August 24, 2008, Rimrock Press, http://www .rimrockpress.com/blog/comments.php?y=07&m=02&entry=entry070202 –111903.

13. See Refusingtoforget.org. Trinidad O. Gonzales of South Texas College, John Morán González of the University of Texas at Austin, Sonia Hernández of Texas A&M at College Station, Benjamin Johnson of Loyola University in Chicago, and I were in attendance to coordinate the initiative. Curtis Smith, the chief of staff for Texas state representative Terry Canales of Edinburg, Texas, joined the meeting and participated in the brainstorming.

14. Stuart Hall wisely wrote, "Hegemonizing is hard work," and George Lipsitz accurately reflected that oppositional movements, too, must be multifaceted. See George Lipsitz, "The Struggle for Hegemony," *Journal of American History* 75, no. 1 (June 1988): 146–150.

15. The staff also receive ideas from visitors and colleagues across the country. The museum is named in honor of Robert "Bob" Douglas Bullock Sr., whose

political career in Texas spanned forty years. As the vice chairman of the State Preservation Board, he helped coordinate efforts for a state history museum. In an uncanny coincidence, Bullock was born in Hillsboro ten years after the lynching of Bragg Williams. Bullock graduated from the public schools and launched his political career in Hillsboro.

16. Walter L. Buenger, "'The Story of Texas'? The Texas State History Museum and Forgetting and Remembering the Past," *Southwestern Historical Quarterly* 105, no. 3 (January 2002): 485.

17. Ibid., 491.

18. Bullock Texas State History Museum, "2016 Annual Report," https://www .thestoryoftexas.com/upload/files/about/Bullock-Museum-Annual_Report_2016 -1.pdf.

19. Without knowing the activities that this grand dragon oversaw, it is difficult to place this object within a broader history of racial violence in the state. How did he fulfill the vows to white supremacy in his daily life when he took off the robe? This important object requires more research for a full understanding.

20. As this book went to press, the Southern Poverty Law Center identified nine chapters of the Ku Klux Klan, four chapters of neo-Confederate groups, seven neo-Nazi groups, five white nationalist groups, and one chapter of a group identified as racist skinheads among other hate groups in Texas. Southern Poverty Law Center, "Hate Map," https://www.splcenter.org/hate-map.

21. The saddle was on display courtesy of Enrique Guerra, San Vicente Ranch, Linn, Texas. Bullock Museum, "Life and Death on the Border, 1910–1920," https://www.thestoryoftexas.com/visit/exhibits/life-and-death-on-the-border -1910-1920.

22. This pattern of dispossession also impacts the material culture of these communities. The economic instability made keeping and preserving objects challenging.

23. Ken Gonzales-Day, *Lynching in the West: 1850–1935* (Durham, NC: Duke University Press, 2006).

24. Leigh Raiford, *Imprisoned in a Luminous Glare: Photography and the African American Freedom Struggle* (Chapel Hill: University of North Carolina Press, 2013), 88–89.

25. Edward Linenthal, "Violence and the American Landscape: The Challenge of Public History," *OAH Magazine of History* 16, no. 2 (2002): 13.

26. "Blood and Betrayal in the Southwest" [*Latino USA* podcast], Maria Hinojosa and Reynaldo Leanos Jr., NPR, March 11, 2016, http://latinousa.org /episode/blood-betrayal-southwest/.

27. Ibid.

28. Cindy Casares, "Texas Finally Acknowledges Rangers Killed Hundreds of Latinos," *Latina Magazine,* February 3, 2016.

29. Joe Holley, "Exhibit to Shed Light on Mexican-American Murders," *Houston Chronicle,* February 5, 2016.

30. Linda K. Pritchard, "Exhibition Review: 'Life and Death on the Border, 1910–1920, Bullock Texas State History Museum, Austin, Texas,'" *Journal of American History* 103, no. 3 (2016): 711–715.

31. Tom Dart, "Life and Death on the Border: Effects of Century-Old Murders Still Felt in Texas," *Guardian,* January 22, 2016.

32. Margaret Koch, *"Life and Death on the Border 1910–1920* Exhibit Summary," April 11, 2016.

33. Holley, "Exhibit to Shed Light."

34. Loza also cautions that other visitors left anti-immigrant sentiments that said very little about their reaction to the exhibit, "communicating instead the present-day debate about the role of Mexican laborers in American society." Mireya Loza, *Defiant Braceros: How Migrant Workers Fought for Racial, Sexual, and Political Freedom* (Chapel Hill: University of North Carolina Press, 2016), 179–181.

35. Lonnie Bunch, "The Definitive Story of How the National Museum of African American History and Culture Came to Be," *Smithsonian Magazine,* September 2016.

36. Lisa Yoneyama, *Hiroshima Traces: Time, Space, and the Dialectics of Memory* (Berkeley: University of California Press, 1995), 16.

37. Luis Jiménez, *Border Crossing (Cruzando el Rio Bravo),* Gift of Frank Ribelin, Museum of Fine Arts, Houston, TX, https://www.mfah.org/art/detail/14287?returnUrl=%2Fart%2Fsearch%3Fclassification%3DSculpture%257CPainting%26display%3Dlist%26artist%3DLuis%2BJim%25C3%25A9nez.

38. Dart, "Life and Death on the Border."

39. Rebecca Onion, "America's Lost History of Border Violence," *Slate,* May 5, 2016.

EPILOGUE

1. Anonymous no. 237, South Texas Oral History and Folklore Collection, James C. Jernigan Library, Texas A&M University–Kingsville. Translation mine.

2. To be sure, historians do not take oral histories at face value. One must place oral histories within the entire historical record available. Historians triangulate—checking memories against historical records, cross-checking them against other interviews, and tracking down leads.

3. For more, see the author's digital research project, www.MappingViolence.com.

4. Vicki Ruiz, "Citizen Restaurant: American Imaginaries, American Communities," *American Quarterly* 60, no. 1 (2008): 18.

5. "Fact Sheet: Summary of Executive Order 'Border Security and Immigration Enforcement Improvements,'" American Immigration Council, https://www

.americanimmigrationcouncil.org/research/border-security-and-immigration
-enforcement-improvements-executive-order; Jennifer Chan, "Immigration
Detention Bed Quota Timeline," National Immigrant Justice Center, January 13,
2017, http://www.immigrantjustice.org/immigration-detention-bed-quota
-timeline; Peter Wagner and Bernadette Rabuy, "Mass Incarceration: The Whole
Pie 2017," Prison Policy Initiative, March 14, 2017, https://www.prisonpolicy.org
/reports/pie2017.html. See updated information from the Federal Bureau of
Prisons reports "Inmate Race: Statistics Based on Prior Month's Data," https://
www.bop.gov/about/statistics/statistics_inmate_race.jsp, and "Inmate Ethnicity:
Statistics Based on Prior Month's Data," https://www.bop.gov/about/statistics
/statistics_inmate_ethnicity.jsp.

6. Bryan Stevenson, *Just Mercy: A Story of Justice and Redemption* (New York:
Spiegel & Grau, 2015), 313.

7. In a 2015 special issue in the *Journal of American History* on policing and the
carceral state, guest editors called for more research that confronts the intertwined
histories of policing. See Kelly Lytle Hernández, Khalil Gibran Muhammad, and
Heather Ann Thompson, "Introduction: Constructing the Carceral State," *Journal
of American History* 102, no. 1 (June 2015): 19.

8. Josiah McC. Heyman, "Special Report: Why Caution Is Needed before
Hiring Additional Border Patrol Agents and ICE Officers," American Immigration Council, April 24, 2017, https://www.americanimmigrationcouncil.org
/research/why-caution-needed-hiring-additional-border-patrol-agents-and-ice
-officers.

9. "Children on the Run: Unaccompanied Children Leaving Central America
and Mexico and the Need for International Protection," United Nations High
Commissioner for Refugees, Regional Office for the United States and the
Caribbean Washington, DC, 57, http://www.unhcr.org/en-us/about-us/back
ground/56fc266f4/children-on-the-run-full-report.html.

10. "90-Day Progress Report to the President on Executive Order 13767:
Border Security and Immigration Enforcement Improvements," April 25, 2017,
internal Department of Homeland Security document made available by the
Washington Post, https://www.washingtonpost.com/apps/g/page/politics/planning
-for-trumps-deportation-force/2194/.

11. United States Border Patrol Southwest Border Sectors, "Southwest Border
Deaths by Fiscal Year (Oct 1st through Sept 30th)," https://www.cbp.gov/sites
/default/files/assets/documents/2016-Oct/BP%20Southwest%20Border%20
Sector%20Deaths%20FY1998%20-%20FY2016.pdf.

12. Jason De León, *The Land of Open Graves: Living and Dying on the Migrant
Trail* (Berkeley: University of California Press, 2015), 3–5.

13. "Texas' Brooks County Is 'Death Valley' for Migrants," *NBC News,* July 9,
2014, www.nbcnews.com/storyline/immigration-border-crisis/texas-brooks

-county-death-valley-migrants-n152121; Manny Fernandez, "A Path to America, Marked by More and More Bodies," *New York Times,* May 4, 2017, https://www .nytimes.com/interactive/2017/05/04/us/texas-border-migrants-dead-bodies .html.

14. Lindsey Bever, "Dozens of Bodies Found in Mass Grave Near South Texas Border Crossing," *Washington Post,* June 23, 2014; Molly Hennessy-Fiske and Mya Srikrishnan, "Mass Graves of Unidentified Migrants Found in South Texas," *Los Angeles Times,* June 21, 2014.

15. "Operation Identification: Forensic Anthropology Center," http://www .txstate.edu/anthropology/facts/outreach/opid.html.

Acknowledgments

This book would not have been possible without the families that preserved their histories and shared them with me. Their memories and private collections provided access to disavowed histories. Over the years I have had countless meetings with descendants and residents who entrusted me with their stories. Benita and Evaristo Albarado, Romana Rendon Bienek, José Canales Jr., Linda Davis, Nicholas Gallegos, Augustine González, Nira González, Norma Longoria Rodriguez, and Vicente Vega all spent hours answering my questions. The Albarados met with me over a dozen times. Norma Longoria Rodriguez shared her collection of documents and photographs preserved by her cousins and extended family. Later in the development of this book I continued to meet descendants, like Arlinda Valencia, who preserved their family histories and were leading commemorative efforts. I am inspired by the strength and generosity of these descendants.

I am forever grateful to my parents, Maria Elena and Joe, who passed on the principles they learned from their parents, Armandina, Fructuoso, Genoveva, and José. I admire my father, who never restricted his daughters. He has an exceptional ability to strike up a conversation and listen to the life stories of strangers. Listening alongside him undoubtedly prepared me to be an oral historian. My audacious mother taught me to challenge social injustice and to be a transformative educator. She continues to share with me the wisdom she earned as a public educator for over forty years, fighting for social change. My parents taught me to think critically and deeply about the world around me. They have been my greatest advocates, and completing this book would not have been possible without them.

I cherish my relationship with my sister, Andrea. In a world of obstacles, her strength and formidable spirit inspire me to continue, even on my worst days. I am eternally thankful for the perspective and encouragement she regularly provides me. She traveled with me to the far reaches of Texas for research, helped me process the information, and knows this work better than anyone. I would be lucky to have one ounce of the passion and creativity she possesses. Alexis is deserving of an Olympic medal for his patience during my stress and worry. He helped me escape the pressures of work and the tragedies of history, and came home with my favorite foods when I needed them most. I am ever grateful for his complete confidence in me and for filling my days with love and laughter. I offer deep thanks to family in the northeast, who provided love and encouragement, especially Ida, a tower of strength, Keith, Regina, Crystal, and DJ.

The hospitality of family and friends throughout the state of Texas sustained me as I commuted back and forth from the East Coast. My *tías* Veronica and Alicia are uplifting supporters. Each of *las tías* Muñoz hosted me and offered transportation to and from the San Antonio airport. Their unwavering support humbled me; their insightful conversations about living in the borderlands proved invaluable, and their home-cooked meals using Mama Grande's recipes nourished my spirit. I offer endless thanks to my *tías*: Dora, Gracie, Irma, and Olga. I am especially grateful to my *tío* Rogelio, who in 2005 initiated this long journey and who continues to teach me about history and politics.

My *primas* in Texas also provided healthy respite from isolating stints of archival research. I thank Diana, Letty, Lisa, Melissa, Nilda, Nori, Patty, Rachel, and Yvonne and their beautiful children for hours of laughter and unending encouragement. Sandra always knew when I needed motivation. From Hawai'i to southern California, no distance could keep my loving *primos,* Roy and Steve, from teaching and supporting me. I am also grateful for my motivating *primo* Armando, who inspires me. During summers and holiday breaks in Uvalde, as I shuttled from archive to archive, my cousins Patty, Osman, Lalo, Hiram, and Roy and *tío* Oscar provided essential moral support. I am grateful to have two inspiring *primas* on the East Coast. Elena provided inspiration and encouragement all along the way. Since I left Texas, my cousins Masiel and Ray and their kids Benjamin, Sebastian, Mia, and Jack have been my biggest supporters. Their New Jersey home became a haven. Masiel has been an older sister to

Andrea and me since we were young. Without her guidance, love, and support this book could not have come to fruition.

Writing can be a lonely process. In this case, the content often became overwhelming. Without my friends and family this work would easily have consumed me. The remnants of my sanity are thanks to weekend escapes for good food and laughs with Kristin Bartholomew, Margaret Danielson, Sonia Gupta, Elizabeth Henthorne, Marisa Hernandez-Stern, Jennifer McMillan, Alice Sorenson, and Jennifer Esparza Vickers. I couldn't have finished this book without my friends Sally Vaughn Reinhardt, Mimi Velasquez, and James O' Rourke.

I am forever grateful to my editor, Kathleen McDermott, who shepherded this project from proposal to book, found the peer reviewers who helped shape the book, and read the project closely and with care. Thanks to David Lobenstine, who helped me untangle my thoughts, and John Donohue, my production editor. This project also has received wise feedback during conferences and at invited presentations. I thank my hosts at the University of California, San Diego; Yale University; the University of Michigan; Bullock Texas State History Museum; the University of Texas at Austin; the Benson Latin American Studies and Collections Library; the University of Texas at Rio Grande Valley; Florida International University; Columbia University; Queens University; Northwestern University; the University of Santa Cruz; Texas A&M University Corpus Christi; and Rutgers University. Thank you also to the participants in the Newberry Seminar in Borderlands and Latino Studies, the Bancroft Seminar at the University of California, Berkeley, the Ethnic Race and Migration Working Group at Yale, the Center for Mexican American Studies (CMAS) Writing Group at the University of Texas at Austin, and the faculty and students who inspired my research and writing. The astounding CMAS staff—Alberto González, Luis Guevara, and Natasha Saldaña—helped me stay the course.

A number of scholars have selflessly contributed to my professional development. Rachel Ida Buff, Ernesto Chávez, Raúl Coronado, Licia Ficol-Matta, Macarena Gómez-Barris, Frank Guridy, Laura Gutiérrez, Ramón Gutiérrez, Mike Innis-Jimenez, Karl Jacoby, Lisa Lowe, Kristin Navarro McElhaney, Chris Zepeda Millan, Natalia Molina, David Montejano, Lorena Oropreza, Cynthia Orozco, Deborah Paredes, Monica Perales, Robert Self, Kidada Williams, Elliot Young, Deborah Vargas, and Emilio Zamora read drafts and offered crucial and timely advice. Geraldo Cadava, Brian Delay, Nicole Guidotti-Hernández, and Evelyn Hu-Dehart read the manuscript in its entirety. Vicki Ruíz is a force who influenced my research and writing all along the way. She also offered invaluable mentorship. Her contributions to the field, in research and leadership, provide endless inspiration.

To my impassioned conspirators John Morán González, Trinidad O. Gonzales, Sonia Hernández, and Benjamin Johnson, moving into public history with Refusing to Forget has given me new faith in the possibilities for restorative justice. I owe Sonia Hernández special thanks for giving me strength and sharing her Tejana wisdom. Antonia Castañeda generously advises my public efforts. Our work is a part of her legacy, inspired by her impassioned vision. I must also thank the staff at the Bullock Texas State History Museum, especially Margaret Koch and Kate Betz, who have elevated the museum with innovative projects and welcomed new visitors to the museum. Jenny Cobb brought the exhibit to life, and Mike Juen treated the descendants and their artifacts with care and respect. I also thank Alfredo Santos and Juan Sanchez.

The questions explored in this book germinated from countless conversations with mentors, colleagues, friends, and family. I benefited from an astonishing depth of faculty expertise. At Yale University I had the privilege of working with exceptional scholars who expected analytical diligence and brought out my best work. Alicia Schmidt Camacho's insightful questions facilitated my best writing. Joanne Meyerowitz's probing questions led me to archival treasures, and she offered insightful advice for constructing and analyzing disparate archives. They both believed in this project from its inception. Michael Denning and Stephen Pitti provided invaluable feedback on multiple drafts of papers, chapters, and articles. Their intellectual generosity enriched this project. Both also facilitated intellectual communities that became safe, supporting venues. In particular, the Working Group on Globalization and Culture at Yale provided a collaborative environment that enriched my own research and provided an alternative model to academic research. The following offered perceptive advice: Ned Blackhawk, John Butler, Hazel Carby, George Chauncey, Kathryn Dudley, Jonathan Holloway, Mary Ting Yi Lui, Michelle Nearon, Birgit Brander Rasmussen, James Scott, K. Sivaramakrishnan, and Laura Wexler. Matthew Frye Jacobson seriously considered a bold request to develop a public humanities initiative at Yale. Collaboration on this effort reinvigorated my commitment to a more dynamic career in academia and profoundly shaped my work.

I can easily trace my initial interest in the relationship among historical narratives, public memory, and social relations of power to conversations with the faculty at Brown University. María Josephina Saldaña-Portillo and Evelyn Hu-Dehart first encouraged me to pursue a career in academia, and both continue to be invaluable advocates. Matthew Garcia advised my first attempts at archival research outside of the library and inside homes. Since then he has provided ongoing and vital mentorship. I continue to be energized by my colleagues in American studies, ethnic studies, and the public humanities. Matthew Pratt

Guterl generously read my entire manuscript (some chapters multiple times) and advises my progress forward; Robert Lee is a transformative colleague and guiding presence; Susan Smulyan opened doors for collaboration and innovative public humanities; and Ralph Rodriguez, Kevin Escudero, Sandy Zipp, and Daniel Kim are crucial interlocutors. Steve Lubar's generative questions push the boundaries of my projects. I am also grateful to be surrounded by the excellence of my fierce feminist colleagues Leticia Alvarado, Elizabeth Hoover, Adrienne Keene, Elena Shih, and Deborah Weinstein. They create a working environment built on mutual respect and committed research. At the Center for Public Humanities, the fellows, especially Jim Egan, Holly Ewald, Elizabeth Francis, Marta Martinez, and Dietrich Neumann, provide endless inspiration. James McGrath has been an important friend and interlocutor as I finished the book and managed a second project in the digital humanities. I am grateful for my impassioned mentors on campus, including Liza Cariaga-Lo, Gail Cohee, Françoise Hamlin, Nancy Khalek, Besenia Rodriguez, Patricia Rose, Felicia Salinas, Naoko Shibusawa, and Patricia Ybarra. Besenia, whom I first met when I was a student at the Institute for Recruitment of Teachers, inspired confidence in my abilities and blazed a path for me to follow.

One of the joys of teaching at Brown is the opportunity to work with students. I am especially thankful to members of the Mapping Violence research team: Felicia Bevel, Jonathan Cortez, Emily Esten, Maggie Unverzagt Goddard, Danielle Gomez, Amelia Grabowski, Cole Hansen, Ricardo Jaramillo, Edward Jiao, Nnamdi Jogwe, Jonatan Perez, Liliana Sampedro, Nicole Sintetos, Jeremy Wolin, and Phoebe Young. They participated in valuable conversations and inspired new research questions. Lilian Mengesha and Claritza Maldonado helped in the final stages of writing. Thank you, Maggie Unverzagt Goddard, mapmaker extraordinaire, for the map included in this book.

As a Mellon Mays undergraduate fellow (MMUF), I also benefited from advice from Mellon fellows. In particular, Maurice Stevens and Shanna Benjamin helped me find my writing stride, and Cally Waite sustained the MMUF network. My colleagues at the Institute for Recruitment of Teachers provided essential camaraderie. Founder Kelly Wise is a true visionary. Under fearless directors Alexandra Cornelius-Diallo, Chera Reid, and Asabe Paloma, I found models of excellence in administration, teaching, and writing. I had the privilege of teaching alongside Kelechi Ajunwa, Karina Fernandez, Maly Fung, Shivohn Garcia, Ernest L. Gibson III, and Mike McGee. Trusted conversations with Denise Galarza Sepúlveda and Reginald A. Wilburn gave me strength and determination. In particular, I am humbled by the generosity of Clemente White, whose commitment stirs enthusiasm in all those around him.

I am also indebted to a vast network of generous colleagues and friends who guided me through the trials and pitfalls of academic life: Megan Asaka, Ryan Brasseaux, Kimberly Brown, Simone Browne, Geraldo Cadava, Aaron Carico, Marcia Chatelain, Amanda Ciafone, Kaysha Corinealdi, Karilyn Crockett, Matthew Delmont, Larissa Brewer Garcia, Melissa Garcia, Dan Gilbert, Julia Guarneri, Sarah Haley, Tisha Hooks, Nicole Ivy, Eli Jelly-Shapiro, Tiffany Joseph, Hong Liang, Uri McMillan, Christina Moon, Madison Moore, Dara Orenstein, Emmanuel Raymundo, Elizabeth Son, David Stein, Lauren Tilton, Quan Tran, Sam Vong, Sarah Wald, and Susie Woo. Mireya Loza, April Merleaux, and Naomi Paik were invaluable supporters who coached me through trying times, read innumerable drafts, and gave me crucial advice for completing projects while maintaining a hint of composure. I am a better friend, teacher, and writer because of Van Truong and Simeon Man. Conversations with Van always provided clarity and hope. While I was living with Simeon, he became my partner in the library, in the kitchen, and on the dance floor. Even 3,000 miles away, he continues to be my most insightful sounding board and generous friend. The Histories of Violence Collective has remained an invaluable source of support. Kathleen Belew and Jessie Kindig are my great collaborators and read my work with a committed and careful eye. They helped me find solidarity in research and writing. In Latinx studies I have found uplifting colleagues. In Mike Amezcua, Nick Bravo, Geraldo Cadava, Lori Flores, Albert Laguna, Priscilla Leiva, Rosina Lozano, Dixa Ramirez, Elda Maria Roman, and Mario Sifuentez I am fortunate to have generous and inspiring collaborators. My formidable friend Ana Minian helped me all along the way. I am deeply grateful I started this journey with colleagues like Armando Garcia and Sasha-Mae Eccleston.

Completing this book required intellectual support but also financial and institutional support. The following institutions provided fellowships and funding: the Andrew W. Mellon Foundation, the Woodrow Wilson Foundation, the Social Science Research Council, the Mellon Mays Graduate Initiatives Program, the Recovering the U.S. Hispanic Literary Heritage Project, the Yale University Program in Agrarian Studies, the Howard Lamar Center for the Study of Frontiers and Borders, the Center for Mexican American Studies at the University of Texas at Austin, the Center for Public Humanities at Brown University, the Texas State Historical Association, the Humanities Texas National Endowment for the Humanities, the Center for the Study of Race and Ethnicity in America at Brown University, the Department of American Studies at Brown University, and the Office of the Vice President for Research at Brown University. This book was made possible in part by a grant from the Carnegie

Corporation of New York. The statements made and views expressed are solely the responsibility of the author. Any errors are my own.

Chapter 2 revises and expands on preliminary discussion in "Recuperating Histories of Violence in the Americas: Vernacular History-Making on the US–Mexico Border," *American Quarterly*, Volume 66, Number 3, September 2014, pp. 661–689, and I thank the journal for the opportunity to publish there.

Index

honoring, 227–229, *228, 229;* "dark history" of, 104; demythologizing of, 230; deployed to stop lynch mobs, 48; establishment of, 11; García (Florencio) and, 1–2; headquarters at King Ranch, 21; heroic mythology created around, 240–246; Hillsboro lynching (1919) and, 180, 181–182; as idols of Texas state history, 104, 289; *la ley de fuga* used by, 90; loyalty Rangers, 88; memorialization of, 231; as mythical heroes, 24; NAACP investigated by, 220; Native American nations fought by, 74; as outlaws of racist terror, 23–24; pacification of the border and, 21–22; Porvenir massacre and, 121–126, 134–136, 139, 148, 150–151, 169; public memorials celebrating, 108; revenge-by-proxy technique, 89, 131, 212; slavery and, 11; Special Rangers, 87, 88, 94; stationed on ranches, 84, 87, 88; Terry's Texas Rangers monument, 224, *225;* valorizing accounts of, 23

Texas Rangers, investigation of (1919), 182–195, 222–226; continuing racial violence following, 216–218; crimes of Ranger Edds, 198–205; failure to change culture of impunity, 213–216; *Life and Death on the Border* exhibit and, 282; mentioned in Texas Ranger Hall of Fame and Museum, 252; public display of extralegal violence and, 195–208; public image remediation measures following, 229–230, 240; Runyon photographs as evidence, 237–239; white supremacy and mob violence, 208–213

Texas Rangers, The: A Century of Frontier Defense (Webb), 240–241, 242, 246, 254, 262

Texas Rangers, The (film, 1936), 243

Texas State Historical Association, 33, 75

Texas State History Museum, 275

Thirty Years of Lynching (NAACP), 179

Thompson, Oscar, 200

Thorndale lynching (1911), 48, 75

Tidwell, State Rep. William Madison, 183, 211

Tijerina, Andrés, 230

Tijerino, Santiago, 194–195

Tilson, State Rep. Thomas J., 183

Todd, Larry and Roy, 239–240

Todd, William Aaron, 239

Tonkawa nation, 10

T. O. Ranch, 215

Torres, Guadalupe, 136

Torres, Jose, 150

Torture, 7, 92, 166, 175, 196–197

Trails and Trials of a Texas Ranger (Sterling), 107

Travis, William, 244

Travis County, 139, 215

Trouillot, Michel-Rolph, 25

Tulsa race riot (1921), 214

Turner, Elizabeth Hayes, 242

Tyler, Ronnie, 130

Undertold Markers, 74, 273, 274

Underwood, Louis, 140, 143

United Farm Workers, 51

United States, 38, 42; charged with wrongful deaths, 125, 155; incarceration in, 296–297; territorial expansion of, 14

United States Holocaust Memorial Museum, 283

University of Texas at Austin: Center for Mexican American Studies (CMAS), 264; Institute of Oral History, 291

US–Mexico border, 2, 4, 22, 23, 219; American fears of vengeance at, 45; "bandit wars" along, 77, 210–211; creation of, 10; free movement across, 3; idyllic image in promotional literature, 176–177, *177;* immigration policing and, 292; mapping and